ROUTLEDGE LIBRA
DEVELOPM

G000090149

CIRCULATION IN 1
COUNTRIES

CIRCULATION IN THIRD WORLD COUNTRIES

Edited by
R. MANSELL PROTHERO

and

MURRAY CHAPMAN

Volume 73

Routledge
Taylor & Francis Group

LONDON AND NEW YORK

First published in 1985

This edition first published in 2011
by Routledge
2 Park Square, Milton Park, Abingdon, Oxon, OX14 4RN

Simultaneously published in the USA and Canada
by Routledge
711 Third Avenue, New York, NY 10017

Routledge is an imprint of the Taylor & Francis Group, an informa business

First issued in paperback 2013

© 1985 Routledge & Kegan Paul

British Library Cataloguing in Publication Data
A catalogue record for this book is available from the British Library

ISBN 13: 978-0-415-58414-2 (Set)
eISBN 13: 978-0-203-84035-1 (Set)

ISBN 13: 978-0-415-59496-7 (hardback)
ISBN 13: 978-0-415-84654-7(paperback)

eISBN 13: 978-0-203-83678-1 (Volume 73)

Publisher's Note
The publisher has gone to great lengths to ensure the quality of this reprint but
points out that some imperfections in the original copies may be apparent.

Disclaimer
The publisher has made every effort to trace copyright holders and welcomes
correspondence from those they have been unable to contact.

Circulation in Third World countries

edited by
R. Mansell Prothero
and
Murray Chapman

cartography by
Alan G. Hodgkiss

Routledge & Kegan Paul
London, Boston, Melbourne and Henley

First published in 1985
by Routledge & Kegan Paul plc

14 Leicester Square, London WC2H 7PH, England

9 Park Street, Boston, Mass. 02108, USA

464 St Kilda Road, Melbourne,
Victoria 3004, Australia and

Broadway House, Newtown Road,
Henley-on-Thames, Oxon RG9 1EN, England

Set in Times, 10 on 11 pt
by Columns of Reading
and printed in Great Britain
by Robert Hartnoll Ltd, Bodmin, Cornwall

© Routledge & Kegan Paul 1985

Library of Congress Cataloging in Publication Data

Circulation in Third World countries.
Includes bibliographies and index.
1. Migration, Internal–Developing countries–
Addresses, essays, lectures. I. Prothero, R. Mansell.
II. Chapman, Murray.
HB1952.C57 1985   304.8'09172'4   84-8323

British Library CIP data also available

ISBN 0-7102-0343-8

For Peggy and Lin, who respectively maintain
the homes from which we periodically circulate.

Contents

Illustrations

(Note: data are from field surveys unless stated otherwise)

Contributors

Guy T. Ashton, Social Anthropologist at the Inter-American University of Puerto Rico, San Germán

Jim Belote and **Linda Belote**, Social Anthropologists at the Michigan Technical University, Houghton, MI, USA

Surinder M. Bhardwaj, Geographer at Kent State University, Kent, OH, USA

J. Stace Birks, Geographer/Manpower Adviser to the Government of the Sultanate of Oman

Ray Bromley, Geographer at the Centre for Development Studies, University College, Swansea, UK

Lynne Brydon, Social Anthropologist at the University of Liverpool, UK

Murray Chapman, Geographer at the East-West Population Institute and the University of Hawaii, Honolulu, HI, USA

Edward M.K. Douglas, Demographer at the University of Waikato, Hamilton, New Zealand

Walter Elkan, Economist at Brunel University, Uxbridge, UK

Sidney and **Alice Goldstein**, Demographers at Brown University, Providence, RI, USA

William T.S. Gould, Geographer at the University of Liverpool, UK

Graeme J. Hugo, Geographer at Flinders University, Adelaide, South Australia

Dawn I. Marshall, Geographer at the Institute of Social and Economic Research, University of the West Indies, Bridgetown, Barbados

J. Clyde Mitchell, Social Anthropologist at Nuffield College, Oxford, UK

Shekhar Mukherji, Geographer at Visva Bharati University, Santini Ketan, West Bengal, India

Harold Olofson, Cultural Anthropologist at the Forest Research Institute, Laguna, Philippines

Jean Treloggon Peterson, Social Anthropologist at the University of Illinois at Urbana-Champaign, IL, USA

R. Mansell Prothero, Geographer at the University of Liverpool, UK

Ronald Skeldon, Geographer at the University of Hong Kong

Kenneth Swindell, Geographer at the University of Birmingham, UK

Adrian P. Wood, Geographer at the University of Zambia, Lusaka

Preface

These essays are about circulatory movements, in which people move from their places of residence for varying periods of time but ultimately return to them. It is a collaborative effort which arises from a long association. In the 1950s, one of us examined seasonal movements of population from North West Nigeria, which at the time were termed 'labour migration' (Prothero 1957, 1959). The other worked in the second half of the 1960s with a much broader perspective on circulatory movements on south Guadalcanal in the Solomon Islands (Chapman 1969, 1970). Our contact with one another extends from the time of Chapman's fieldwork and until the mid-1970s was maintained by correspondence and with two brief meetings in Canada (1972) and New Zealand (1974).

In 1975/76 Chapman was able to 'circulate' from Hawaii to spend a sabbatical year with Prothero in Britain, supported in part by a grant from the Social Science Research Council, U.K. (Grant HR3731/2). During this time, we explored some of the cross-cultural comparisons to be made between circulation in tropical Africa and the island Pacific. This work heightened our fascination with circulation and reinforced our belief in the critical importance of its comparative study. We decided to assemble a multi-disciplinary collection of essays, drawn from various parts of the Third World, and this volume is the result.

The other outcome of our 1975/76 collaboration was an International Seminar on the Cross-Cultural Study of Circulation, sponsored jointly by the Population Institute of the East-West Center in Hawaii and the Institute for Applied Social and Economic Research in Papua New Guinea, with financial assistance from the National Science Foundation, U.S.A. (Grant SOC77-26793). It was held at the East-West Center in April 1978 and brought together people from a range of social science disciplines. This seminar was concerned particularly with circulation in Melanesia, but it incorporated commentaries from Africa south of the Sahara, India, and South East Asia (Chapman 1978, 1979, East-West Population Institute 1978). The main content of this seminar is being published by Routledge and Kegal Paul as a companion to the more general volume on circulation in Third World countries. The volumes complement one another.

In choosing contributions for this Third World volume, we have been deliberately eclectic in respect of kinds of circulation discussed, areas dealt with, and disciplines involved. Circulation is a grossly neglected aspect of population mobility, but in the past decade there has been an increasing amount of research on it within the multi-disciplinary field of population studies: from demography, economics, geography, political economy, social anthropology, and sociology. Geographers have made many important contributions and half the essays in this volume are from them, with the rest mainly from social anthropologists and sociologists. More than half of the contributing geographers have participated in inter-disciplinary projects, especially applied to census, manpower, health and educational planning.

Contributions have come from three directions: work of long standing and of seminal importance, from which we and others have drawn guidance and inspiration; more recent research involving fieldwork which has attracted our attention; and field studies in which we have played an initiating role. Apart from the contribution from Elkan, all the essays are published for the first time. The fact that they exemplify different disciplinary perspectives on circulation we see as of major importance. It is remarkable that so much of common concern about human mobility emerges and which reflects to a considerable extent many of the views set out in our first essay. All contributors were aware of our views, but they were in no way constrained by them in making their contributions. By no means is there consensus, but differences of opinion relate less to the nature of circulation and far more to its role in the changing and evolving patterns of human mobility over time. The nature of these divergencies and their significance for present ideas and future work are discussed.

The Third World is the exclusive focus of this volume, in part because our own research has been conducted there. It is also because the contemporary processes of change in population mobility are operating at a faster pace in Third World societies than elsewhere, thus furnishing great scope to study a variety of forms and to examine the reasons for both constant fluidity and broad patterns over longer periods. By comparison, there is only fragmentary evidence of past circulatory movements in the now more developed parts of the world. Despite the pitfalls of cross-cultural comparison in time as well as in space, detailed and first-hand inquiry of contemporary circulation in Third World societies may throw some light on the previous experience of more developed countries.

The papers present evidence of the widespread presence of circulation. There are examples from all the major regions, as defined by the United Nations: Latin America (4) and the Caribbean (1), Africa (7) and the Middle East (1), South (2) and Southeast Asia (3), and the Pacific (1). Areal coverage, however, was a secondary consideration compared with the context in which circulation had been studied. We sought several contributions from indigenous scholars, while all the 'expatriate authors' have a great depth of experience of the areas about which they write. That more essays refer to Africa is symptomatic of the long-standing concern with circulation in that continent, where some of the most influential work was done from the 1940s to the 1970s. Papers on themes we had hoped to include, on commuting to agricultural work in Nigeria and on relationships between language and circulation in Mexico, unfortunately did not materialize.

The papers have been grouped on the basis of four major perspectives: holistic, ecological, social, and economic. Inevitably there is overlap in approach, methodology, and substance. Virtually all papers refer, for example, to the indirect if not the direct effect of ecological or political factors on circulation and no essay is without substantial comment upon the role of social and economic influences.

Acceptable terminology is a particular difficulty in the study of population movement and, as our introductory chapter makes clear, this is not surprising given the range of disciplinary and theoretical goals evident in its research. 'Population mobility' or 'population movement' is the general term used for the territorial flow of people. The critical distinction between 'migration' and 'circulation', the two major types of population mobility, denotes whether or not a return to place of origin is involved. Hybrid terms such as 'circular migration' are especially confusing. These have been retained, and placed within single quotes, only when they refer to a particular literature (as in economics) or are critical to the intellectual history of circulation. When first used, terms signifying particular kinds of circulation also are placed within single quotes: thus 'commuting', 'labour migration', and 'pendular migration'. The fact that standardization has been possible underlines the great forbearance of authors, to whom we extend our considerable thanks. Since essays range widely in time and region, pounds sterling and dollars U.S. have been adopted as baseline currencies.

We are grateful to those who agreed to contribute, made their papers available, and then were prepared to revise them according to editorial suggestions. Bringing together work of authors who are geographically so widely spaced, by editors separated by 150 degrees of longitude, has inevitably involved much longer delays than we would have wished. We apologize to those contributors who responded most quickly to our invitation and whose work therefore had to await the arrival of others.

Besides our contributors there are many others who have helped to make this volume and whom we wish to thank. Alan Hodgkiss and his colleagues in the Drawing Office, Department of Geography, University of Liverpool, have prepared all the illustrative material. Joan Rourke of the same Department typed final drafts of a number of the papers. The work on the index has been undertaken by R. Mansell Prothero. We are most grateful to Norman Franklin of Routledge & Kegan Paul for agreeing to publish this book, for his great patience in extending the time for completion of the manuscript, and to him and his colleagues for the production.

Like people written about in this volume, we have maintained contacts between Hawaii and Liverpool through a constant stream of letters in both directions, cables, and the occasional telephone call. But our collaboration has been much assisted by being able to meet on three occasions since 1976: in Hawaii in 1978, and in Liverpool in 1978 and again in 1979. We thank the National Science Foundation (Grant SOC77-26793), the East-West Population Institute in Hawaii, and the Universities of Hawaii and Liverpool for in various ways making these face-to-face contacts possible.

R. Mansell Prothero
Murray Chapman

1 Themes on circulation in the Third World

Murray Chapman and R. Mansell Prothero

> To study and define fully settled groups is nothing else than to
> formulate an abstraction; to grasp and describe groups in
> movement, in so far as possible, means to describe life itself
> (Brunhes and Vallaux 1921: 201).

People are in constant movement. Defined in space and time,
these movements involve both displacement and reciprocal flows
of human beings. Scholarly effort has focused more upon displacement, commonly referred to as migration and defined as
any permanent or quasipermanent change of residence from one
location to another (e.g. Lee 1966: 49). Less well understood are
the reciprocal flows, called circulation, which involve the
interchange of individuals and small groups between places
(origins and destinations) that frequently are of differing size and
function, such as villages and towns or regional centres and
primate cities. Such movement ultimately concludes in the place
or community in which it began (Figure 1.1).

Zelinsky (1971: 255-6) defines circulation as 'a great variety of
movements, usually short-term, repetitive, or cyclic in nature,
but all having in common the lack of any declared intention of a
permanent or long-lasting change in residence'. Having been
studied within many disciplines, circulation is designated by a
confusing variety of terms: 'return migration', 'circular migration', 'wage-labour migration', 'seasonal mobility', 'sojourner
movements', 'transhumance', 'commuting'.

For the people who circulate, the basic principle involved is a
territorial separation of obligations, activities, and goods.
Throughout the Third World, this separateness manifests two
major influences. On the one hand is the security associated with
the home or natal place through access to land and other local

1

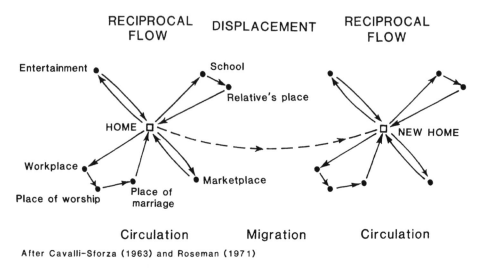

After Cavalli-Sforza (1963) and Roseman (1971)

FIGURE 1.1 Reciprocal flows and displacement of people

resources for food, housing materials, and trading items; through kinship affiliation; through the presence of children and the elderly; and through common values and beliefs. There are, on the other hand, the locationally more widely spread opportunities and associated risks involving local political and religious leaders; kinsfolk; marriageable partners; items for exchange or trade, ceremonials and feasts; and the introduced goods and services of wage employment, commerce, medicine, education, religion, politics, and entertainment. The great variety of circulation resulting from such territorial disjunction (Figure 1.1) has attracted the attention of many social and behavioural scientists, who have adopted in their research a range of philosophical positions, theoretical constructs, and analytic methods.

Historical antecedents

During this century, three major viewpoints on circulation recur: it permits the integration of distinct places and circumstances; it results from socioeconomic disequilibrium; and it involves the interchange of labour between one mode of production and another. All three perspectives overlap, rather than being discrete or mutually exclusive, since they reflect varying levels of enquiry and changing socioeconomic contexts. At different periods, their complementary nature has been much obscured by the vigour with which scholars have favoured one interpretation over another.

The concept of circulation as the beneficial integration of distinct places or communities dates from the 1920s, mainly characterizes the work of human geographers, and originated with the French led by Vidal de la Blache (1845-1918). Among French geographers, *circulation* refers to the reciprocal flow not only of people but also of ideas, goods, services, and socio-cultural influences (de la Blache 1926: 349-445; Sorre 1961: Part IV). It is the underlying dynamic of population distribution and the connecting mechanisms of varying lifeways. As such, the focus in circulation study may be upon patterns of flow, as of the international movement of passengers and commodities (Capot-Rey 1946), or even more importantly upon the intrinsic nature and meaning of places: their evolution, persistence, and integration (cf. Bhardwaj, in this volume).

This approach is found in studies undertaken within several disciplines. Skinner, an anthropologist, argues that the spatial and economic integration of late Imperial China was achieved by the 'sojourner strategies' adopted in many localities, by which men with training and skills in management, business, crafts, services, or soldiering worked during their adult lives in higher-order towns and cities.

> Whereas an ambitious man was likely to leave his local community to work or study elsewhere, his family's residence normally remained unchanged . . . Residence was maintained in one's native place, . . . [which] . . . was in the short run of generations virtually an ascribed characteristic; abode, by contrast, was impermanent. Although a man's abode could vary in the course of his career, his residence perdured. Moreover, membership in . . . the community of one's residence, and hence in the higher-order local and regional systems of which that community formed a part, persisted even when a sojourner was upwardly mobile. It was precisely because those who left could be counted on to return that a man with aspirations to get ahead could expect support from members of his local system beyond the limits of family and lineage (Skinner 1976: 335).

Such persistent circulation gradually endows places and regions of origin with heightened meaning both for the locally born and for outsiders. To analyse the identity of Tamil country (Tamilakam), southeast India, from the second to the nineteenth centuries, the historian Stein invokes the concept of circulation to test 'that evidence of movements provides for some of the conceptions of space − the cognitive maps − of the Tamils at various times in their past' (Stein 1977: 9). After examining stone

3

and copper inscriptions, temple records, hymns, poems, and other literary sources, he concludes:

> The congruence of actual movement and the spatial conceptions of Tamils beyond the ancient *nadu* [locality] was gradual; for most peoples, the process occupied almost a millennium. Rarely was the relationship between the cognitive conception of Tamilakam and the movement of any Tamils isomorphic . . . However, actual circulation of Tamil folk did over time approximate that conception (Stein 1977: 24-5).

A similar interpretation is implicit in the research of social anthropologists who record that movers, when at their destination, continue to be linked with their natal communities by a cross-flow of remittances, investments, food, and visiting kin (e.g. Ross and Weisner 1977). At least as a first point of reference, most geographers and social demographers favour a less comprehensive view of circulation and consider it to involve the interchange only of people between complementary places or situations, studied either as individuals or at various levels of aggregation (e.g. Goldstein 1978).

The idea of circulation emerging in response to socioeconomic disequilibrium derives from anthropological research on wage labour within the plural societies and dual economies of southern Africa. Generally associated with the British functionalist school, this perspective originated in the 1920s and 1930s but was crystallized in Wilson's classic study of migrant workers in Broken Hill, Northern Rhodesia (now Kabwe, Zambia).

> The social structure of Broken Hill today is characterized by the presence of a disproportionate number of young men and by a constant circulation of population between itself and the rural areas, between itself and other towns of Northern Rhodesia, and between itself and other territories. The disproportion and the circulation are intimately connected . . . ; they are phenomena of disequilibrium (G. Wilson 1941-2: 3).

This process was investigated further by Mitchell, who called it 'labour circulation' and who documented within the context of Rhodesia its close link with urbanization and structural pluralism (Mitchell 1961b, 1969b).

In general, Africans moved to earn cash with which to pay head taxes, buy trade goods, and meet school fees or, more ambitiously, to accumulate bride price and invest in agricultural land. This fact led Elkan (1960) and other neoclassical economists to use the term 'target worker', to express what they considered the key factor in this alternating flow of wage labour between village homes and places of employment on plantations, in the mines, and at urban centres. Briefly, the neoclassical position was that the circulation of labour between poorer and better-endowed areas constituted an adjustment of the indigenous population to regional disparities in economic development. Thus Berg (1965: 161) argued that, for west Africa, this flow 'continues to benefit both the labor-exporting villages and the recipient areas', most particularly because of a seasonal fit between the slack period for agriculture throughout the densely-settled savannah and the peak demand for cocoa and coffee workers in the forest belt immediately to the south. But whereas labour circulation throughout much of tropical Africa was relatively spontaneous, the political context within South Africa meant that as early as the 1870s it was strictly controlled and highly regulated. Francis Wilson (1972b: 3) labelled it 'oscillating migration'.

Since the 1970s many economists and sociologists, notably in African and Latin American studies, are associated with the view of circulation as the interchange of labour between different modes of production both within and between countries. Their approach, more macroscopic than those previously noted, is especially concerned with the great transnational flows of labour; it derives inspiration from dependency theory and is dominantly Marxian in its analyses of society and polity. To satisfy basic socioeconomic needs, the migrant worker is seen as locked into the world capitalist system and must move cyclically, and mostly involuntarily, between domestic (precapitalist) and introduced (capitalist) modes of production (e.g. Burawoy 1976; Gregory and Piché 1978). A most forthright exponent of this position is Amin, a political economist who argues that throughout west Africa the uneven penetration of capitalism, as distinct from the autonomous and well-integrated development of rural areas, has created such sectoral, class, and spatial inequalities that 'economic (so-called "rational") choice and notably the decision of the migrant to leave his region of origin, is then completely predetermined . . .' (Amin 1974: 88-9).

Despite recent intellectual fashion, these politicoeconomic analyses of labour circulation are not new and have parallels in the economic and social histories of continental Europe, North America, and various parts of the colonial world. In 1916 Ranneft, a Dutch scholar, examined the 'movement of people in Java', and recognized three phases in the development of the Indonesian economy. During the last, a period of 'capitalistic production' beginning about 1860, reciprocal flows of villagers were far more evident than migration (reflecting the differential impact throughout Java of investment from Europe) and impeded the emergence of a local proletariat based in the towns and/or the countryside. Instead, the Javanese involved themselves in both capitalist and peasant modes of production; they were 'traditional men' with a strong stake in their villages of origin (Ranneft 1916, cited by Hugo 1982: 72).

Another historical parallel lies in the concept of 'sojourner', especially as applied from the 1930s by historians and sociologists to the movement of Asian labourers to North America. Based on a study of Chinese laundrymen in Chicago, Siu (1952) delineated the sojourner as constituting a new personality type:

> one who clings to the cultural heritage of his own ethnic group and tends to live in isolation, hindering his assimilation to the society in which he resides, often for many years. The sojourn is conceived . . . as a 'job' which is to be finished in the shortest possible time. As an alternative to that end he travels back to his homeland every few years (Siu 1952: 34).

But, as Hune (1977: 39) notes, if migrant workers from the Pacific rim were placed by definition beyond the American experience, then 'they are treated extraneously, not because they are outsiders, but because they contradict the majority society's conception of what the immigrant experience is believed to be'.

Until the late 1970s, these three perspectives of circulation tended to remain specific to different disciplines, with little reference to one another. Yet common to most research was an emphasis upon Third World situations, especially upon peasant and tribal peoples resident mainly in villages, rural market centres, and small towns, which constituted the loci of their circulatory flows.

Typologies and data bases

The many forms of circulation, and the resultant profusion of terms in the literature, have stimulated a concern with typologies of population movement. These efforts, basically descriptive and initially related to the coordinates of time and space, have been amplified to include the purposes served by reciprocal flows and the perspectives of those involved.

For Gould and Prothero (1975), the fact that circulation does not alter the long-term distribution of people distinguishes it from migration (cf. Figure 1.1). Taking tropical Africa as an example, they differentiated the spatial dimension of recurrent flows into rural and urban environments and the temporal into daily, periodic, seasonal, and long-term (Table 1.1). In this way sixteen categories of circulation are identified, which can, for example, be related to various health hazards to reveal 'different effects in the exposure of population to disease, in the transmission of disease, and in the development of programmes for the improvement of public health' (Prothero 1977: 264-5). Similarly, de Gonzales (1961) was concerned with the effects of wage-labour mobility upon the family and takes period of absence from the home village as the basis for distinguishing between moves that are seasonal, temporary nonseasonal, recurrent, continuous, and permanent (cf. Ashton, in this volume).

Although such typologies are basically descriptive devices, presented originally to focus attention upon circulation and distinguish it from migration, gradually the categories of

TABLE 1.1 *Typology of circulation in tropical Africa, with examples of associated activities and health hazards*

Space	Time			
	Daily	*Periodic (24 hours-12 months)*	*Seasonal (one or more)*	*Long-term (12 months-several years)*
Rural-rural	Cultivating* Collecting (firewood, water) (1)	Hunting (1)	Pastoralism (1) (3)	Labouring (1) (3)
Rural-urban	Commuting (1)	Pilgrimage (1) (2) (3) (4)	Labouring (1)	Labouring (1) (2) (3) (4)
Urban-rural	Cultivating (1)	Trading (2)	Labouring (1)	Trading (2) (3)
Urban-urban	Intra-urban commuting (3)	Pilgrimage (2) (4)	Trading (2)	Official/ commercial transfer (4)

Some examples of health hazards

   (1) Exposure to diseases from movements through different ecological zones (e.g. malaria, trypanosomiasis, schistosomiasis, onchocerciasis)

   (2) Exposure to diseases from movements involving contacts between different groups of people (e.g. smallpox, poliomyelitis)

   (3) Physical stress (e.g. fatigue, undernutrition/malnutrition)

   (4) Psychological stress–problems of adjustment

   * Examples of activities/groups associated with different categories of circulation.

Source: Prothero 1977: 265

TABLE 1.2 Time and forms of mobility in Third World research

Place and date of field research	Circulation 'Commuting'	'Oscillation'	'Circular migration'	Migration	Range of time
Indonesia 1973 Villages: west Java (Hugo 1978)	Regular travel to and from work or education (not necessarily each day)		Continuous absence for up to 6 months	Continuous absence for at least 6 months	Daily journey to at least 6 months
Indonesia 1975-6 Hamlets, central Java (Mantra 1981)	Absent for 6-24 hours		Movement for at least 1 day but return within 1 year	Intentional shift of residence for at least 1 year	6 hours to at least 1 year
Malaysia 1977 Villages, north Kelantan (Maude 1981)	Regularly absent, but return at least once each week		Continuous absence for up to 12 months while retaining household membership	Continuous absence for at least 12 months but might return later	Weekly journey to at least 1 year
Vanuatu 1969-70 Tongoa island (Bedford 1973a)		Routine absence for 1 day to less than 1 month	Absence for at least 1 month, with intent to return	'Permanent' move with no intent to return, but may visit	Routine daily to 'permanent' migration
Peru 1971-2 Communities, Cuzco department (Skeldon 1977)		('Pendular migration') Absent for up to 3 months	('Semipermanent migration with return') Absent for several years	Definitive change of residence; no return except visiting	Less than 3 months to definitive residential change

Source					
Liberia 1976 Village, Nimba county (Smith 1977)		('Regular circulation') Absences up to 24 hours: for work, trade, subsistence	Absent for at least 24 hours and no more than 1 year. Short-term: 24 hours to up to 1 month; Long-term: 1 month to 1 year	'Permanent' change of residence	Daily journeys to 'permanent' change of residence
Hawaii, 1971 Village, Puna district (Mukherji 1975)	Daily absence for 5-6 hours for work or education		Absent for at least 24 hours with intent to return Short-term: 24 hours to 1 year; Long-term: at least 1 year	Shift of 'permanent' residence: maximum, 40 years	5-6 hours to 40 years
Papua New Guinea 1974-6 Simbu, New Ireland provinces (Young 1977)		Routine daily movements to brief casual visits	Returned after period away from village	Resident outside village during survey	No specific range
Thailand 1976-7 Village, Chiang Mai province (Singhanetra-Renard 1981)	6 hours to 5 months: daily/weekly travel to work, school, trade; seasonal/periodic travel to wagework, kin business		Absent 1 week to 14 years, but maintain household registration and may visit periodically	Definitive shift of residence, from at least 1 week to 'total displacement', through marriage, adoption, flight	No specific range during data collection. Continuum of time, 6 hours to 'total displacement', established from field record
Range of time	5-6 hours to 5 months	Daily to less than 3 months	1 day to 14 years	1 week to 'permanent' migration	5-6 hours to 'total displacement'

movement defined in them have become imbued with analytical significance and theoretical meaning. While different kinds of circulation may be complementary, they have tended to be viewed as generally exclusive of each other − an impression that has been reinforced by the need of research workers to determine minimal criteria for the collection of field data in Third World societies. Thus time, for instance, is divided into discrete segments in seven out of nine local or regional studies undertaken during the 1970s (Table 1.2, columns 2-5). On the other hand, the composite record (row ten) reveals a less tidy framework, since 'commuting' ranges from five or six hours to five months and 'circular migration' from one day to fourteen years. Singhanetra-Renard (1981) obtained a parallel result in northwest Thailand (row nine), when abandoning the assumption that forms of mobility are discrete in time, and thereby highlighted the great flexibility in and complementary nature of people's movement on the ground.

Another classificatory approach is to conceive of mobility as a continuum and relate it to the social, economic, and political contexts within which it is enmeshed. According to Conaway (1977), more than forty different studies suggest that the nature of circulation reflects the degree to which communities of origin are integrated with 'national political or sociocultural systems'

TABLE 1.3 *National systems and circulation*

Regional characteristics in a national system	*Categories of circular movement*	
Least amount of economic security, least amount role/status flexibility. Frontier, economically depressed, non-modern, non-industrialized regions. Access to national rights and privileges curtailed by limited communications and socio-geographical marginality.	I.	Seasonal, non-seasonal, planned and sporadic movement
	II.	Extended moves: weeks to several months
	III.	Once a life-time or several moves lasting one or more years
Greatest economic security and role/status flexibility. High degree of regional-national integration and communication entailing modernization, industrialization. Nationally recognized rights and privileges widely enjoyed.	IV.	Weekends spent at home base, weekdays at place of employment
	V.	Daily commuting

Source: Conaway 1977: 3

10

(Table 1.3). From this perspective, daily commuting exhibits the accessibility of education, health services, franchisement, minimum legal wages, and social justice, whereas seasonal wage-earners from frontier regions enjoy far fewer of the rights and privileges available in the national system.

In the specific case of rural-urban mobility in Indonesia, Hugo (in this volume) argues that to array the most ephemeral to the most permanent of voluntary transfers along a continuum greatly clarifies the varying degrees of commitment which individuals have to their villages of origin and to their city destinations (Table 1.4). For west Java, indices of such commitment would be the primary domicile of the family of procreation as distinct from those of its mobile members; the different locations of land, dwellings, or other property owned; the ratio of income or goods remitted between households of destination and origin; the frequency of return visits; the primary orientation of social or political roles performed by movers within village and city; and whether their official registration had been transferred from place of origin to place of destination (cf. Chapman 1978: 564-5). Hugo's emphasis upon the degree and content of commitment that persons have to differing locales thus removes the classification of movement from dualistic frames of reference. It also begins to capture the inherent ambiguity and fluidity that is so much a feature of Third World societies (cf. Marshall and Wood, both in this volume). Moreover, in determining whether or not a move is circular, the emphasis is shifted to the actions of those involved rather than their declared intent to return at or before moment of departure, which several commentators have rejected as opaque or impractical (e.g. Goldstein 1978: 13; Ward 1980: 129; cf. Zelinsky 1971: 225-6; Gould and Prothero 1975: 42).

As with the detailed analysis of reciprocal flows, it is difficult to test and refine such typologies because of lack of pertinent information. Data from national census and large-scale surveys yield only cross-sectional snapshots of forms of behaviour that are both complex and exceedingly sensitive to time. Intercensal comparisons based upon questions about places of birth and of residence identify long-term displacements of people (cf. Figure 1.1), but provide limited insights into the ongoing relationships within and between movement processes, population redistribution, and socioeconomic change. Most evidence about Third World circulation consequently derives from micro studies. Prospective mobility registers have been used in village-based research in the Solomon Islands, Liberia, central Java, and northwest Thailand (Chapman 1975; Smith 1977; Mantra 1981; Singhanetra-Renard 1981), but more widespread has been the

TABLE 1.4 *Rural to urban population mobility in a Third World context*

Type of spontaneous mover	Characteristics of move	Commitment to city	Commitment to village
Commuter	Work in city but return to village each evening. Can occur regularly (each weekday) or spasmodically (to market produce etc.)	Very little financial or social investment in city. Mixes with urban dwellers but on a limited basis.	High. Family remains in the village. Retain all political and social roles in village. May have village based income source. Bulk of income earned in city spent in village.
Seasonal or shuttle migrant	Search for work to augment meagre agricultural incomes.	Very little financial or social investment in city. Sleep in open, group-rented room or employer-provided barracks. Social interaction almost entirely with other migrants from village. Employment in traditional or day-laboring sectors.	Family of procreation remains in the village. Retain all political and social roles in village. Remit bulk of income (after living expenses) to village. Retain village citizenship. Almost total orientation to village. Usually retain work source in the village.
Target migrant } Short term sojourner	Come to city for limited period (though longer than a season) to accomplish a specific purpose (e.g. reach a particular education level).	Moderate. May bring family of procreation. Seek more permanent accommodation, e.g. individually rented room. Have more interaction with settled urban population but retain close contact with fellow villagers in city. Usually employed in traditional sector.	Strong links maintained with family in village through visits and letters, although some roles may be temporarily given up. Remittances remain regular and high. Usually retain village citizenship. Usually retain a source of income in the village.
Life cycle stage migrant }	Migrants who move to the city at one or more specific stages of their life cycle.		

Working life migrant	Migrants who spend their entire working lives in the city but intend, and eventually do, retire to their home village.	High. Family of procreation always accompanies. Purchases or builds individual housing, occupies employer (e.g. government) supplied housing or rents housing on long-term basis. Often in formal sector occupations. High level of interaction with settled urban population but retain contact with fellow migrants through associations etc. Always transfers citizenship to city. Assists new arrivals to city from home village.	Sufficient links maintained with village to ensure acceptance on eventual return. Investments in housing and land although unable to maintain most social and political roles. Periodic remittances to family. Return visits made at end of fasting months and for important life cycle ceremonies.
Permanent migrant	Migrants committed totally to exchanging a rural for an urban way of life.	Total.	Very little.
Undecided migrant	Migrants who have no clear intentions to either stay in the city or return to the village.	Unknown.	Unknown.

Source: Hugo 1981: Table 1

13

retrospective collection of movement histories (see Goldstein and Goldstein 1981).

The common complaint, that details about individuals, small groups, and communities are not susceptible to wider comparative analysis, reflects both conceptual and technical misunderstanding expressed most often in 'the myth of uniqueness and typicality' (Chapman 1981: 86). At the technical level, a codified means of synthesizing biographical data has been evolved by French scholars, based upon their experience in north and west Africa (Haeringer 1972). Conceptually, cases studied at the microscale are neither unique, in the sense of being idiosyncratic, nor typical, in the sense of representing some statistical norm. Rather, their selection according to criteria indicative of specified research goals means that findings may be generalized to other cases for which the same contextual conditions hold. Such generalizations, however, do not derive from statistical extrapolation but from an astute mix of logic and intuition proceeding from a detailed understanding of a piece of social reality (cf. Mitchell, in this volume).

The difficulties of recall, always present in the retrospective collection of mobility as with other data, can be alleviated by the use of the life-history matrix. First constructed by Balán and his associates (1969) during research in Monterrey, Mexico, this permits unstructured discussion about a person's lifecourse according to changes in critical events (birth, marriage, education, occupation, land ownership), which may be related to moves between various places at different times. Urban and rural research in Mexico (Balán, Browning, and Jelin 1973), Brazil (Perlman 1976), Colombia (Corno 1979), and Thailand (Lauro 1979a; Singhanetra-Renard 1981) has demonstrated that this technique requires a sensitive understanding of the people under study if it is to capture the details of mobility intertwined with other life events. Otherwise, a standard retrospective record will result: that is, a chronology of more permanent and long-distant movements without reference to their varied contexts. Considerable problems remain in the processing of such longitudinal data but Lauro (1979b), in a promising development, has identified lateral and vertical relationships within a field record to ensure that links and contingencies in mobility behaviour were not frozen − as usually occurs − into cross-sectional snapshots (cf. Balán et al. 1969).

Evidence of circulation can be gleaned from the demographic record of some countries of francophone Africa, where multiround surveys have constituted a basic instrument of data collection, with identical questionnaires being administered at regular intervals to the same population or in the same region (e.g. Lacombe 1969, 1972). Further information may be derived from a sequence of national censuses, but few demographers have plumbed this source. In a notable exception, Goldstein and Goldstein (1979) have investigated rural-urban flows for Thailand by comparing place of birth with places of residence for 1965 and 1970. Despite the inevitable coarseness of this matrix, they show that repeat and return migration accounted for more than a tenth of all recorded movements and that about one in four adults who returned to small towns and rural areas originated from cities (cf. Goldstein and Goldstein, in this volume).

Recent explanatory models

Since the early 1960s, considerable effort has been expended in attempts to explain reciprocal flows, despite the major problems in documenting their nature, magnitude, and persistence. Four emphases have dominated: changes in circulation as response to modernization; circulation in the context of social field and social network; circulation as a means to maximize family welfare and avert risk; and circulation as a result of the penetration of peasant and tribal societies by capitalism.

Circulation and modernization

In a most ambitious statement, the 'hypothesis of the mobility transition', the geographer Zelinsky argues that 'there are definite, patterned regularities in the growth of personal mobility through space-time during recent history, and these regularities comprise an essential component of the modernization process' (Zelinsky 1971: 221-2). A society will pass through four unilineal 'phases' of mobility experience – premodern traditional, early transitional, late transitional, and advanced – during its transformation from a traditional-subsistence to an urban-industrial state, in the course of which there is 'vigorous acceleration of circulation'.

This evolution in mobility assumes a repetition of the Western experience, whose applicability to the Third World has been challenged in several studies. Throughout Indonesia, for instance, changes in mobility patterns after about 1500 did not conform to this sequence and the most influential forces have been those of colonization rather than of modernization (Hugo, in this volume). Even after the independence of Indonesia, movement behaviour reflected for many years much of the social and economic structure of the colonial era. Likewise Bedford (1973b), in documenting a

15

transition for wage-labour circulation in Vanuatu from 1850, concluded that it represents dual participation in two socio-economic systems: one traditional and the other introduced. Bedford (1973a: 140-1) commented in similar fashion to Hugo:

> There is no transitional sequence applicable to all societies, even though there is inter-dependence between mobility and socioeconomic changes associated with modernization. The manner in which these relationships are manifested in move-ment behaviour . . . is very much dependent on the society in which change occurs . . . It is thus more realistic to conceive of a number of transitional sequences with different explanatory frameworks providing the necessary links between pattern and process (cf. Peterson, Skeldon, Wood, in this volume).

In response to this and other conclusions from research in the Third World, Zelinsky has declared that circulation is 'sympto-matic of the problems of underdevelopment' and consequently 'promises to endure, with further variations and complexities, as long as underdevelopment persists' (Zelinsky 1979: 185, 187). Despite the difficulties of assembling data to counter the ahistoricism of this position, there is increasing evidence that circulatory flows were a fundamental fact of precontact societies and that their basic dimensions often persist to the present day.

First reported by Prothero (1957, 1959), the *masu abucin rani* of northern Nigeria − 'men who eat away in the dry season' − are villagers who customarily moved from their home areas and thus conserved food supplies. Despite some element of pressure implied in the English translation, the practice was voluntary: families travelled to other places, usually over quite short distances, to work at crafts or labouring, to maintain social contacts, and to meet various kinds of obligations. Workers were paid in kind and in cowrie shells, the currency of the time. Apparently, by the 1930s, population growth and pressure upon land resources meant, at least in some marginal areas, that the need to move became more of a necessity and extended over longer distances. These involved young adult males: *yan tuma da gora* ('sons who jump with a gourd'), so named because of the limited equipment which they carried.

Apart from such environmental impediments, Swindell (1984) suggests that changes in precolonial circulation after 1900 reflect mainly the abolition of domestic slavery and only secondarily the imposition of head taxes and the introduction of a new currency. Abolition released vast numbers of agricultural workers, traders, and labourers, who subsequently engaged in dry-season circula-tion and sought wage employment in areas of both urban expansion and cash-crop development (cocoa, coffee, cotton). On the other hand, improvements in the colonial apparatus and the greater stability of the new currency reduced the comparative advantage of regularly travelling considerable distance. Yet the practice of *cin rani* persisted and, despite marked changes between 1900 and 1930 in the nature of moves made, the major destinations, and the types of employment secured, there was considerable overlap in systems of circulation before and during the colonial period.

Circulation, social field and social network

The concept of social field and social network underpins several decades of research in south-central Africa by the sociologist Mitchell, who views labour circulation as a continuing dialectic in specified political and economic settings between the centrifugal attraction of wage employment and the centripetal power of village obligations, social relationships, and kinship ties (cf. Mitchell 1959, 1969). During the 1960s, this formulation was expanded in Melanesia to include all reciprocal flows, irrespective of purpose or duration (Chapman 1976). Critical to Mitchell's approach is his distinction between 'necessary' and 'sufficient' conditions: between the more aggregate and mainly economic factors as opposed to the personal needs and dispositions that surround the decision to circulate. Even so, 'we can only appreciate the causal factors in labour migration by trying to see town and country or reserve and labour centre as one social field and to analyse the forces operating within it. I doubt whether social science is yet in a position to be able to do this' (Mitchell 1959: 279).

About the same time, when studying wage labourers in East London, South Africa, the anthropologist Mayer (1961) reported that one group (Red Xhosa) maintained intense links with their natal communities, and another (School Xhosa) did not and readily accepted urbanizing influences. Whereas the social networks of the former spanned village and town, those of the latter were divided into disjoint sets (village *or* town) with little connection between the two. On this basis, Garbett and Kapferer (1970: 195) argued that rural-urban mobility should be viewed as a total field of 'social and economic relationships involving both town and country', within which the decisions of potential movers are constrained through time by the structure of social connections of which they are part. This notion was formalized in a decision model specifying 'the individual set in a network of social relationships' (Garbett 1975: 124). The analysis of labour circula-

17

tion thus involves different levels of abstraction, which Mitchell in this volume has crystallized in the distinction between the 'setting' and 'situation' of social action – the macroscopic economic, political, and administrative context as against the particular circumstances within which movers are enmeshed – and between 'social field' and 'social network': the diverse social forces that connect places of origin and destination, some aspects of which affect the kinds of mobility decisions taken by the individual.

Numerous studies have documented the varied links between communities of origin and destination, which may be so intense that social structures are bi- or multi-local and the varied locations of village movers become a socio-spatial extension of the natal place (Ryan 1970). Less well understood are the processes that underpin such connections. Based upon complementary research in Nairobi, Kenya, Ross and Weisner (1977: 362-3) suggest six possibilities: continuing availability, to those away, of land, livestock, and other rural resources; the social acceptability of these resources being owned and controlled by patrilineal, patrilocal groups of frequently absent males; presence within the village of family members to work local holdings; a level of simple agricultural technology that reduces the need for on-the-spot farm management; norms of reciprocity that derive from common kinship, language, and culture; and reasonable accessibility and travel cost between village and town (cf. van Amersfoort 1978: 21-2).

One of the few cross-national tests of such propositions is provided by Strauch (1980, 1984), from the standpoint of Chinese communities in Malaysia and Hong Kong. While kinship ties are equally strong in both places, so that people shuttle back and forth between rural domiciles and urban workplaces, the Hong Kong community is less cohesive in that it contains recent immigrants from China, who gradually transfer their allegiance from rural valley to urban metropolis. Strauch's (1980: 19) conclusion is strongly reminiscent of Mitchell and Garbett:

> Patterns of population mobility are determined by a dialectic comprising individual needs and calculated choices on the one hand and overarching frameworks of political and economic systems on the other. Such systems present some options but preclude others, thereby structuring the range of [mobility] choices open to the individual.

As with most of the functionalist literature, Mitchell's explanatory framework is time free. It assumes that labour circulation will cease whenever a balance is struck between the counterposed sets of centripetal and centrifugal influences and implies that it is a transitory phase in the transformation from a basically rural to a dominantly urban society. By contrast, a study of Nairobi over two generations by the economist Elkan (in this volume) has established that longer and longer periods of city residence need not be accompanied by the emergence of a permanent and urban-based proletariat, who depend entirely upon wage incomes and whose ties with rural areas of origin become increasingly tenuous.

Circulation, family welfare and risk aversion

The view that labour circulation reflects the attempt of rural households to maximize family welfare and/or avert risk also arises from field research in tropical Africa, notably of factory workers in Kampala, Uganda (Elkan 1959, 1960) and of migrant cocoa farmers in southern Ghana (Hill 1963). After stressing the 'tenacity with which people cling to their land', Elkan (1959: 195) notes:

> [If] a man were to withdraw permanently from the countryside, he would be giving up both a part of his income and also a form of insurance against unemployment or ill-health. If there were provisions against these risks, . . . the value to a man of his farm would be correspondingly diminished, but the farm would still yield him an income, and this is so irrespective of whether the wage he earns in town is high or low and whether or not family houses are available in town.

Such thinking was overshadowed by the Todaro (1969) model, based upon unemployment research in Kenya and deeply rooted in neoclassical economics. Rural-urban movement was posited as a response to expected earnings, defined as the combination of rural-urban wage differentials and the likelihood of securing a job in town, as manifest in levels of urban unemployment. Yet the original model, as well as its many revisions (Todaro 1976: 36-46), is silent about the vast circulation of labour that occurs within rural areas, where wage differentials are assumed not to exist, and about why workers persistently return to their villages even when wage differentials and levels of unemployment remain constant.

For decades, social scientists have pointed to the kinds of economic calculus that underpin the dynamics of rural lifestyles and the reciprocal flow of wage labourers. Brookfield (1970: 14-15) observed, when reviewing the work of geographers in the south Pacific during the 1960s:

> Peasants have greater opportunity to minimize risk, especially when they continue to produce a large part of their own food, and sustain an institutionalized system of reciprocity in full operation. Cash-cropping as a partial activity as distinct from

19

full cash-crop specialization, and migrant labour as distinct from full commitment to wage employment, become choices competing for inputs. Other choices include subsistence, entrepreneurship, and sundry forms of investment. In the game against an uncertain external world, peasant strategy is to keep the range of choices open and to widen the range wherever possible. Within this range they can then select according to inclination, or according to a wholly rational process which seems to operate as though they had a series of indifference curves, calibrated by perceived net return. Freedom to shift inputs also facilitates the meeting of reciprocal obligations, by means of which individuals in turn sustain their own access to reciprocal aid, and hence maximize the range of choices. The system is thus self-sustaining, and adaptive.

Such principles were rediscovered by economists in the late 1970s and formalized in several parallel, but largely independent statements (Stark 1978; Fan and Stretton 1980; Roberts with Elizondo 1980). Thus Fan and Stretton generalize from circulation research in southeast Asia and propose two complementary models, one of which considers the spatial allocation of a family's labour resources and the other the mobility options available to a particular member. The recurrent but temporary employment of villagers as *samlor* drivers in Bangkok (Meinkoth 1962), ice cream vendors in Jakarta (Jellinek 1978), textile workers in Bandung (Hugo 1978a: chapter 6), and carpenters and masons in Manila (Stretton 1981) may each and all be explained by the simultaneous effort of the household to maximize the income available from the rural and urban sectors, with expenditure allocated between urban and rural goods so as to enhance its utility to the family. There is little risk in such a strategy, especially within communities at the knife-edge of subsistence, since family members capitalize upon the absorptive capacity of the informal sector, depend upon kinship networks to identify longer-term jobs, depart during slack periods of the agricultural cycle, leave behind dependents and travel alone to the worksite, spend little in town on overnight shelter, and return to the rural household whenever their labour is needed for planting and harvesting subsistence and cash crops.

Integral to this process are transportation links between places of origin and destination, and the flow of remittances between them. Since the early 1970s, throughout southeast Asia for example, the connection of many villages by laterite and metalled roads to highways and hence to potential workplaces has enabled residents to commute up to forty kilometres each day by bicycle, motor cycle, and other small vehicles, as well as to take public transport over far greater distances (e.g. Leinbach 1981). The socioeconomic links between absent worker and natal family are manifest in what Caldwell (1976: 337) has termed 'wealth flows': money, goods, services, and guarantees that are transferred in both directions. While the money remitted from urban incomes undoubtedly confers a net benefit on recipient households, often ensuring their basic needs and very survival, evidence about its broad effect on rural development and social change is inconclusive and academic opinion sharply divided (cf. Rempel and Lobdell 1978; Byres 1979; Lipton 1980; Stark 1980).

Very few studies consider the precise relationship of forms of mobility to regional agricultural structure, household characteristics, disposition of family labour, and the mix of rural incomes derived locally and from other regions (Goddard 1974). In a more recent study, Roberts with Elizondo (1980) examined the undocumented movement of farm workers to the United States from four quite distinct areas of rural Mexico. In Bajio, the most commercially oriented of the four, mechanization of cereal and vegetable production is well advanced, farm revenues derive from several sources, and household incomes are high and stable even though families are large. Here, regular circulation to the United States not only helps defray the cost of farm machinery and supplies, including imported foodstuffs, but also has no adverse impact upon the family labour force. In Oaxaca, at the opposite end of the socioeconomic spectrum, the subsistence cultivation of corn dominates, few opportunities exist for off-farm employment, and household incomes are both low and unstable. Consequently most movement is to quite distant urban centres within Mexico, since circulation across national boundaries is far too risky an alternative. Viewed from the standpoint of how rural households deploy family labour off the farm, circulation is an inherent part of a complex response to agricultural change, rather than simply a residual outcome of the disparity between the local supply of and demand for farm workers (see also Roberts 1982).

Circulation and capitalist penetration

Labour circulation is similarly the focus of more structural explanations, partly in reaction to models of social field, social network, risk aversion, and utility maximization, partly out of concern that too little attention has been paid to the political and economic processes within which individual acts of movement occur (cf. Mukherji, in this volume). The penetration of peasant and tribal societies by capitalism is claimed deliberately to increase local demands for cash, commonly by such mechanisms as new currencies, head taxes, and trade stores, so that adult males have little option other than to participate in a system of migrant labour to satisfy minimal needs. Overall, as a result, regional differences are intensified, village economies are impoverished through residents having to subsidize absent members, and the stratification of rural society is either initiated or enhanced.

Common elements in this politico-economic transformation of Third World societies are the needs of the capitalist world system, the character of preexisting social formations, and the historical context, couched most often in abstract terms and in Marxist frames of reference. Although the particular, yet contrasting structures of the capitalist and the domestic, rural sector each control their means of production and reproduction, the encroachment of the former expropriates the surpluses of the latter for its own perpetuation ('reproduction'). For Meillassoux (1972, 1975), the availability and movement of labour to workplaces during the slack season in agriculture depends entirely upon societies peripheral to the capitalist sector. Adult males, unaccompanied by families, receive low and basically subsistence rates of pay during seasonal employment, while the entire cost and effort of sustaining potential wage labourers at other times during the agricultural cycle is borne by the rural community, as is also expenditure on rearing children, caring for the sick, and providing for the elderly.

Rey (1973), on the other hand, takes a less cosmic view of this unequal relationship. He attaches far greater importance to the internal differences and class conflicts found within local communities themselves, especially of how these permit the capitalist sector to strike alliances with groups or leaders who have authority over indigenous (domestic) sources of labour. In a lineage-based society, where elders control the availability of women for marriage, young men can be encouraged to go away to work and earn money for bride price. In such a situation, some of the proceeds from capitalist exploitation accrue to those groups or leaders dominating the domestic mode of production. If, however, internal conflicts or distinct social groupings do not exist or are less manipulable by outside capitalist interests, then the circulation of wage labourers may be less evident or even absent.

Very little field research supports the details of this process and Gerold-Scheepers and van Binsbergen (1978: 30) complain of the failure of Marxist scholars to 'translate eloquent and illuminating abstractions into ordinary, prosaic case studies'. This contrasts with the description that the geographer Townsend (1980: 286) provides for the Hube of Morobe Province, Papua New Guinea, where about half the able-bodied men and a quarter of the women usually are away.

> At home, many nubile women grow anxious about their prospects in life, many old people regret the passing of the vitality of the village, and many young people keenly anticipate the day of departure. One-third or more of potential coffee production is neglected each year. Probably twenty per cent of the migrant men each morning confront the humiliating search for wagework; many migrant women are frustrated by the lack of [food] gardens and the consequent loss of their role as providers and domestic managers. A kind of modern diaspora, but without a sense of destiny. How did this situation come about?

Proceeding beyond broad notions of peripheral capitalism and the articulation of contrary modes of production, Townsend (1980) presents a framework that gives far greater attention to the agents involved, their role in shaping new values, and the people's perceptions of and responses to unfamiliar ideologies. He traces how, between 1884 and 1932, the Lutheran mission both initiated and sustained an 'ideological, cultural and material revolution' with such success that gradually 'development came to be seen as a state to be attained, by correct practice and accommodating association with Europeans' (ibid: 290). The positive response to the wage-labour opportunities resulting from the expansion of the world capitalist system, in the form of coconut plantations and gold mining, was shattered during the Second World War, as the Hube saw destroyed the myth of European omnipotence. There followed a resurgence of local autonomy, notably through the establishment of trade stores and cooperatives to grow coffee, but improvements in transport links and marketing facilities slowly reduced rural isolation. By the 1970s, wage-earners were staying in town longer and more and more families were leaving their villages to join husbands and sons. This emergent pattern coincided, however, with a reduced demand for untrained or semi-skilled labour so that households became far more dependent on the urban environment at the very time they were forgoing revenue from local coffee groves and the subsistence productivity of wives and daughters. Concludes Townsend (1980: 293): 'The Hube case is just one example of how societies have been changed detrimentally . . . by their articulation with the world capitalist system. One can understand Hube's present condition only by analysing the successive demands of the world system (converts, labour, raw materials, markets) and the means by which these demands were implemented and transmitted'.

As with Zelinsky's hypothesis of the mobility transition, most structural models emphasize discontinuities rather than continuities in the process of circulation over time, while the socioeconomic changes portrayed have the same remorseless and preordained character as do Zelinsky's 'phases of mobility'. Structuralist explanations assume, far too often, that peasant and tribal societies before colonial contact were socially and economically undifferentiated, indulged in no trade or in no exchange of labour, and did not subsequently filter the impact of capitalist forces according to the principles of indigenous, domestic production (see Swindell 1979, but cf. Murray 1978, 1980). As two neo-Marxists have cautioned: 'We should not be too sure that under all conditions modern migrations constitute a negative phenomenon' (Gerold-Scheepers and van Binsbergen 1978: 31).

Conditions do exist that relate plausibly to the politico-economic transformation of Third World societies, yet may be found upon closer inspection to reflect factors like the cumulative inertia of persistent isolation. From 1960 until 1972, and mainly in response to population pressure, one third of all able-bodied men from the Islamic Riff of Morocco circulated to the Netherlands as unskilled workers. Socioeconomic pressures upon the Riff homeland have intensified since the mid 1970s, as husbands found it more and more difficult to hold their jobs during regular visits to north Africa, a consequence of European-wide recession and stricter regulation of migrant labour. 'The problematic situation in which [Riff society] finds itself today is not a consequence of colonial or neocolonial capitalistic penetration. The very tragedy of the Riff is its isolation that has protected the area from effective penetration by the outside world in the past, and now also insulates it from effective government-sponsored change' (van Amersfoort 1978: 25).

The need for integrated explanation

Although circulation in the Third World occurs between a great diversity of regions, places, and communities, the dominantØb empirical focus is upon rural-urban flows, notably of wage-labourers. Does this mean that most circulation in the country-side is transitory, one day to be redirected towards towns or cities and perhaps replaced by permanent relocation? Rural community studies, on the contrary, reveal the coming and going of people for reasons of kinship, marriage, ceremony, local trade, subsistence agriculture, social welfare, and political asylum to be just as important as those reciprocal flows that postdate the incursion of western-style money (e.g. Chapman 1975: Tables 9.4-9.6; Mantra 1981: Table 4.15; Mukherji 1981: Table 8.9; Singhanetra-Renard 1981: Table 6.7). 'Circulation, rather than being transitional or ephemeral, is a time-honored and enduring mode of behavior, deeply rooted in a great variety of cultures and found at all stages of socio-economic change' (Chapman and Prothero 1977: 5).

The choice of explanatory models displays similar partiality. The explanation that wage-labour circulation results from the uneven and differential spread of capitalism into peasant and tribal societies is as tautologous as the neoclassical models that Amin so resolutely condemns (Amin 1974: 90-3; cf. Chapman 1975: 143). For, as Hugo (1982: 72) observes, economic explanations are as complementary as they are exclusive. Maximization of welfare and aversion to risk point to processes operating at the level of the small community, the household, and the individual, whereas structural perspectives emphasize more aggregate realities (the region, the country, the continent) and broader forces more apparent at that scale. The prospect for more integrated theory is recognized by Gerold-Scheepers and van Binsbergen (1978) who, in a refreshingly balanced presentation, argue that structural analysis is common to both Marxist and functionalist perspectives of circulation.

> As marxists may be expected to turn to concrete empirical research in order to substantiate and enrich their theories, and as structural-functionalists will discover the riches of marxist theory in terms of synchronic scope and particularly historical depth, it can be hoped that these two approaches . . . will grow towards one another, producing . . . a viable social theory of African migration (1978: 32).

A painstaking study of how families in Lesotho are affected by the persistent labour circulation of village males leads Murray (1981: 175) to a similar conclusion: 'The anthropological method of prolonged participant observation offers an invaluable opportunity of revising or elaborating, with appropriate empirical evidence, some of the rather abstract formulations proposed by the radical theorists of underdevelopment'.

Such commentaries underline the need for conceptual synthesis. Today, as from time immemorial, Third World peoples have circulated between places and circumstances of complementary attributes and character. Connections of kin, as well as comparable resources, parallel social practices, and common world views, tie together locationally-spread communities which, given the consequent cross-flows of people, social scientists have come to designate as places of origin and of destination. With the differential penetration of capitalism into the territory or state of which these communities form part, there is a perceptible increase in the number of such places. In addition, they are more diverse, more unlike, and become progressively linked by a greater variety and intensity of cross flows: food, money, gifts, information, ideas, technologies. These reciprocal connections define social fields, within which the choices of small groups and individuals gradually become both more intricate and more contingent, as households seek collectively through the act of circulation to maximize family welfare and their members to avert risk. The continuing dialectic between local households and communities on the one hand, and their cultural, socioeconomic, and political environments on the other, may be conceived as one of changing sets of relationships. Such relationships, as well as the transformations experienced by both whole communities and the wider society, denote processes of far greater subtlety and complexity than can be reduced to a remorseless sequence of lineally-arranged stages from things 'rural' to things 'urban'.

The essays which follow are concerned with these relationships and with the transformations experienced, at scales ranging from individuals through communities to national and international societies. They illustrate the subtle and complex processes which are involved. The problems associated with attempts at integrated explanation and prognosis for the future, from both conceptual and technical points of view, are discussed in the light of the evidence from these essays in the editorial essay which concludes the volume.

Part I
Holistic perspectives

The papers presented under this heading have certain broadly based and wide-ranging things to say about circulation. At the same time each of them is firmly grounded in the field area and the research experience of the author. This is particularly true of the reflections on circulation associated with wage labour by Clyde Mitchell. He has been for us and for many others in various disciplines a mentor and an inspiration.

Mitchell's work in south-central Africa in the 1950s and 1960s established major principles relating to circulation, particularly with reference to the influence of aggregate and individual factors on who moves and why decisions to move are taken. These principles were based on his own research and that of others, particularly colleagues at the Rhodes-Livingstone Institute (now the Institute for Social Research in the University of Zambia). They have been extended and developed through further work in south-central Africa.

The essay here not only illuminates the past, it is also looking forward. It underlines both conceptual and technical issues involved in the study of circulation, and links earlier work on the process of labour circulation with more recent concerns with social fields and social networks. That the actions of individuals can be understood only by being placed within their diverse contexts is the crux of the distinction that Mitchell makes between the macro 'setting' and the micro 'situation' in which actual and potential movers find themselves. Setting and situation and social field and social network refer to different scales and levels of enquiry which must be recognized.

Mitchell's seminal work must be seen in the setting of a racially and economically plural society in south-central Africa. Harold Olofson has been concerned with the traditionally highly mobile

Hausa-speaking people of northern Nigeria, who through travelling and trading have been involved in a diaspora throughout West Africa and which has extended into Central and North Africa. In 1976 he published a paper on *Yawon Dandi* ('the walk of Dandi') a form of movement associated with deviance from the norms of Hausa society. Here he examines *Yawon Dandi* in the wider context of the many forms of Hausa mobility and then relates this to Hausa ideas on conformity and noncomformity. Two contradictory aspects of Hausa society seem to inform spatial mobility: the stable interdependence of the domestic group and the individual search for independence and freedom. Consequently once individuals make their way beyond the entrance of the compound of the domestic group no cognitive distinction is made between a brief stroll or a long-distance journey.

While himself inevitably an alien in Hausa society Olofson, taking a lexical approach, examines Hausa terms for different forms of mobility (the emic view) and relates them to categories used by western researchers (the etic view). In this way he is able to provide a view of mobility from the 'inside', from the standpoints of those who are involved in movement. To further emphasize the 'inside' perspective Olofson classifies each movement as open or closed and as circular or linear, rather than in terms of permanence or impermanence which is one of the most common distinctions made in the literature on population movements. In these various ways the paper is pointing important directions in which future work on mobility should be undertaken.

The paper by Graeme Hugo on rural-urban mobility in western Java takes more of an outside view, though it notes that there are indigenous terms which differentiate temporary and permanent movements. It is important for its integrated use of various data and for what is said on the classification of mobility. Both past and recent census data are related with village-level data collected in the field, the former cross-sectional and the latter a mix of cross-sectional and longitudinal. From the analysis of these data a classification of mobility in western Java emerges — 'commuting', 'circular migration', 'migration' — which expresses various forms of village/city relationships. Official censuses in the past were more sensitive than those of recent time to movements between villages and city which did not involve permanent change of residence. From his own investigation Hugo demonstrates the great volume of temporary movements which is likely to continue. While the populations of major Indonesian cities will increase, significant proportions of these populations will circulate between countryside and town.

Without exception contributors to the volume are conscious of changes over time in forms and patterns of mobility. Many of them comment on the limited perspectives that can be achieved with studies that are cross-sectional, and where for lack of evidence comparisons cannot be made with the past. Ronald Skeldon sets out to examine changes which have occurred in the mobility of rural communities in southern Peru in the more distant and the recent past and relates these changes to what is happening at the present. He blends documentary evidence for the distant past with the products of his own field research for the more recent past and the present. This evidence is used to outline the transition which has occurred in forms and patterns of mobility and to speculate for the future. Two basic processes are discernible. The first and earlier was a gradual enlargement of orbits of circulation which gave villagers access to different kinds of resources. Thus for Peru as a whole within the last three decades there has been a progressive shift in the pivot of circulation from urban to rural places. Skeldon contextually acknowledges and tests the concept of mobility transition, getting at the processes through which mobility changes over time. His conclusions have some measure of agreement but also some challenging variance with some of our conclusions and those of others.

2 Towards a situational sociology of wage-labour circulation

J. Clyde Mitchell

Labour circulation in Southern Africa

Labour circulation is the process in which people periodically leave their permanent residence in search of wage employment at places too far away to enable them to commute daily, stay at these labour centres for extensive periods and then return to their homes.[1] This type of labour mobility has manifested itself in many different parts of the world at different times in history. It is manifested in one of its most clear-cut forms in the present day Republic of South Africa particularly in respect of the Black labour force in the gold mining industry (see, for example, van der Horst 1942, chap. 12; F. Wilson 1972; First 1979). The practice of employing Black workers for limited periods without allowing them to establish permanent residence, has existed since the diamond mines were established in the Cape in the 1860s, and probably developed out of the earlier employment of Hottentots in agriculture for over a century previously.

Certainly the industrial growth of South Africa after the discovery of gold in 1881 has been based on the unskilled labour of temporary in-migrants to the mining and commercial towns from both neighbouring and more distant tribal areas in Southern Africa. This form of labour supply became a keystone of the social, economic and political structure of South Africa. The policy of the present government of South Africa involving the notion of the 'homelands' in which the temporary Black workers are deemed to have the full political and personal rights which are withheld from them in the White-created and White-controlled towns or White farms and plantations, is merely a formalization of a practice which has been the basis of South

African industrial and commercial development for a very long time.

The British territories to the north of South Africa – the Crown Colony of Southern Rhodesia, and the Protectorate of Bechuanaland, Northern Rhodesia and Nyasaland – presumably because they were established on the basis of economic expansion from South Africa, had adopted similar patterns of social and economic organization and in them unskilled manual labour was sought from temporary migrants from tribal areas. In these territories, as in South Africa, it was not easy initially to entice Africans into wage employment. They were able apparently to meet all their essential needs within traditional life. An important goad to increasing the labour supply was a tax imposed on all males who were deemed fit enough to work. Once migrants had been prised out of their traditional subsistence-based social systems then the blandishments of trade goods were sufficient to start the circulation between labour centres and the rural homes.

It is not surprising that some attention, both official and academic has been devoted to an examination of the phenomenon of 'migrant labour' in both South Africa and the surrounding territories. Official enquiries like the *Native Economic Commission* (1932) in South Africa, the *Report of the Commission Appointed to Enquire into the Disturbances in the Copperbelt, Northern Rhodesia* (1935) in Zambia and the *Report of the Committee appointed by His Excellency the Governor to Enquire into Migrant Labour* (1935) in Malawi were examples of enquiries instigated at almost exactly the time when the deleterious consequences of the migrant labour system had begun to attract the attention of governments. Labour circulation was one of the existential social facts of the life of Africans at the time when scholars from various disciplines were beginning to make studies of conditions in Southern Africa after the 1914-18 War.

In the inter-war years the characteristics and consequences of labour circulation in Southern Africa were commented on by historians (Macmillan 1930), by political scientists (Buell 1928), by administrators (Hailey 1938, Browne 1933), by anthropologists both in the rural areas (Hunter 1936, Schapera 1938) and in the towns (Hellman 1948, Wilson 1941-2), and by scholars motivated by Christian sentiments (Merle Davis 1933). Schapera's study of labour migration from Botswana though it was conducted during the 1939-45 war was only published in 1947.

Except for Wilson's (1941-2) classic study of urbanization in Northern Rhodesia (now Zambia), labour circulation appears in these studies as an elemental phenomenon, existing in its own right, having consequences for rural production, for housing in towns, for family life and for health in both rural and urban locations. Its existence was taken as given and the attention was directed rather to its social effects: there seemed little interest in going beyond a commonsense understanding of labour circulation, locating it within a theoretical framework through which it could be understood in general terms independent of both time and place of occurrence.

Migration as an epiphenomenon

Since scholarly interest was first directed to the topic of labour circulation in Southern Africa some fifty years ago it has remained remarkably intractable to thoroughgoing analysis. Observations here relate in particular to sociological (and social anthropological) analyses but they may be equally true for other disciplines. Part of this analytical recalcitrance derives from the great difficulties in collecting suitable data to carry adequate theoretical formulations.

Rather more important, however, has been the difficulty of establishing a set of conceptual categories through which a sound theoretical analysis may be conducted. The most obvious difficulty seems to be the fallacy of assuming that the most obvious feature of labour circulation is also its most important theoretical characteristic. A person's move from one location to another, however great or small the distance, is an immediately observable phenomenon. Not surprisingly it has been the starting point of a number of different types of study. Yet this apparently simple phenomenon, perhaps precisely because of its superficial simplicity, seems to have yielded little of its rationale to a diverse set of scholars. From Ravenstein's formulations of his laws of migration (1885, 1889) to the present day the topic has been continually studied.

The analytical obduracy of the phenomenon lies in the disjunction between the act of movement and the range of widely diverse circumstances which lead to it. The simple fact that an individual on some specific occasion moves from place A to place B may arise from many different circumstances. It is a complex phenomenon and to explain it adequately in respect of some specific person requires appropriately complex analysis. As a commonsense or real phenomenon movement it is not directly amenable to theoretical analysis. Analysis involves the initial epistemological operation of typifying the phenomenon in terms of certain of its aspects to make it intelligible within some conceptual framework. Which framework provides the basis of conceptualization of course depends upon the interests of the analyst. This implies that the same elemental event of migration may be subsumed into as many different conceptual schemata as there are analytical disciplines interested in it. From this argument it follows that a particular empirical act of migration must be a somewhat different phenomenon in each subject discipline.

Establishing the frequency or rate of movement, its direction and its pattern is an essential but only the *first* step in its analysis. The real analysis takes place when the observer seeks to show why the frequency of rate of movement is what it is, why people move in some directions and not in others, and why particular regularities crop up in what at first sight appear to be acts of individual decision-taking.

The implication of this is that superficially similar phenomena such as a particular type of movement pattern, for example, may turn out to be dissimilar when classified not by the pattern itself but by underlying features of which the pattern is merely an epiphenomenon. There are clear implications for comparative analysis: is labour circulation in modern Melanesia comparable with labour circulation in Africa? There will of course be differences in the geographical separation of place of wage-earning from the place of origin which may lead to different durations of stay at either end. The relative cost of travel in relation to wages may make it difficult for a work-seeking migrant to take his family with him − a contingency which is likely to have immediate consequences for the pattern of circulation of men. But these variations which are understandable almost in commonsense terms − which does not mean that they are not worth pointing out − leave what seems to be the central problem untouched. It is the *circulation* we need to explain not the movement. To do this we need to go beyond the descriptive facts of the phenomenon to its underlying dispositions − for which much more must be taken into account than merely the fact of movement.

Like death, migration exists only after it has happened, restricting us therefore essentially to *post facto* analysis. It should be possible from an analysis of relevant information to estimate the probabilities that a person with a given set of social and economic characteristics located in some defined setting is likely to move within some given time.[2] This is obviously not easy to do and possibly for this reason does not seem to have been accomplished. It would require long-term longitudinal studies at the places of origin of migrants in which details likely to induce a potential migrant to move are recorded and related to the fact of movement when it takes place. But which particular details should be noted out of the plethora that characterize a potential migrant turns upon our understanding of the circumstances which predispose a previously static person to move.

The same difficulty bedevils the study of movement at other phases of its process. A return migrant becomes so when he or she returns to the place of origin, but until the actual return takes place the movement has to all intents and purposes been permanent. In the same way a person is classified as being involved in circulation only after making several trips between place of origin and places of work. An expressed intention to return is not in itself sufficient so to classify a circulator since there is abundant evidence that people may hold an intention in perpetuity without ever putting it into effect. Circulatory movement is an abstract typification derived from an examination of a number of different instances in the past and as a typification would apply exactly in no one particular instance. These typifications while representing the observer's perception of some identifiable regularity in the past derive their *dynamic* quality from the way in which theoretic propositions deriving from some discipline or another may be related to the typification.

The essentially abstract nature of the concepts with which we are dealing, however real their superficial manifestations and particularly the connection of these concepts to yet higher order abstract statements of theoretical relationships, highlights the danger not unfamiliar to those conversant with the literature on movement of 'misplaced concreteness'. There is the tendency for analysts working from some limited perspective of some theoretical discipline to discuss movement as if their analyses of it constituted a total description of the phenomenon. The analyst's model, of course, is simply a capsule statement of the essential connections among aspects of movement which may be related to a wider general understanding of the nature of human behaviour.

Setting and situation in circulation

The complexity of phenomena in the real world may be reduced to dimensions that we are able to handle in our conceptual frameworks by distinguishing between two rather different perspectives in the analysis of phenomena. These two perspectives relate respectively to what the analyst may take for granted and what must be treated in greater detail. The underlying assumption here is that total social reality is so complex and may be taken at so many different levels of abstraction that unless some pragmatic procedure is adopted then the possibility of achieving any cogent understanding of any aspect of social behaviour, particularly in a comparative framework, is impossible.

We may designate the field of one perspective the *setting* and the other as the *situation* of the social action. This distinction is a matter of perspective not of substance, implying that the observer for purposes of analysis is treating some features of the complex set of relationships being examined as given while attention is directed to details of some other features which are deemed to be dependent upon the wider setting in which they are located. Labour circulation, as it has been described in Southern Africa, occurs within a particular type of setting, one in which industrial and commercial development based upon capitalist enterprise rooted in the metropolitan country has been established among societies based essentially upon modes of subsistence production and consumption. The legal, administrative and political structure in which African workers are recruited, employed, housed, paid and provided with medical and welfare services is part of this setting. Equally relevant are the modes of production, care and support in the rural homes of the workers. The sociologist seeks to examine the consequences of this overall setting for the behaviour of workers, in particular the extent to which the workers' appreciation of the need for money and appreciation of social obligations and rights in rural homes represent essentially opposed interests and lead to continual circulation between the two physical locations in which these opposed interests may be served.

The social setting is provided by the macroscopic economic, political and administrative structures of the regions in which the migrant is involved, while the social situation is represented by the particular set of circumstances in which migrants actual or potential find themselves. The sociologist can then examine the calculus of choice the migrants or potential migrants may employ given the constraints imposed upon them by the wider system of social, economic and political relationships in which they are involved.

Frequently sociological analyses of labour circulation are conducted either in terms of the setting or in terms of the situation: which of these may be used appears to be a matter of the particular orientation of the analyst. An increasing number of studies of labour migration, for example, are being made in a Marxist framework, starting with the 'political economy' analysis of the African labour supply by Arrighi (1967). A number of works have appeared since which develop the argument that capital accumulation in colonial Africa has been accelerated by the extension of the surplus product available to employers when workers are paid wages at labour locations insufficient to maintain them and their dependants without the additional support provided by the village economies from which they are temporary absentees (for example, Trapido, 1971, Magubane and O'Brien, 1972, Wolpe, 1972, Legassick, 1974, van Onselen, 1975, Burawoy, 1976, Perrings, 1979). These studies are more interested in the social system creating the conditions which give rise to the circulation of labour rather than the *process* of labour circulation itself.

Seldom does a study successfully describe both the setting of labour circulation and the situations in which it occurs. One of the most successful of these is one of the oldest − Godfrey Wilson's (1941-2) study of urbanization in Northern Rhodesia (now Zambia). The significance of his work is that at the time of writing the issue emerging out of labour circulation in the minds of the colonial administrators was the development of an urban proletariat and the problems which would flow from it. The problem was conceived in terms of 'detribalization' − the rejection by migrants of tribal ways of living and of tribal norms and practices. The same assumption underlies the 'Bantu Homelands' policy in South Africa: that the right and proper place for the permanent residence of an African is the rural village and trips to urban areas ought to be for short periods − to earn cash and to supply the need for cheap labour. Wilson's argument was that an urban proletariat was indeed developing, that this was a normal process of social development, but that it was being impeded by the uneven investment of capital in the mining industry in Northern Rhodesia as against in rural development. The veracity of this fact has recently been very sharply confirmed in modern Zambia. Labour circulation was a natural concomitant of uneven capital investment and in Wilson's near epigrammatic formulation: 'the circulation of population [was] the keystone in the unstable arch of the Northern Rhodesian economy' (Wilson 1941-2: 38). His work served to set labour circulation firmly in its social context and to trace its connections with wider aspects of the colonial social system.

Having done this Wilson set out to trace the impact of the wider colonial setting on the lives of the migrants involved. He provided detailed analyses of the relationship of the migrants with their kin left in the rural areas, of the changes in the relationships between men and women in these circumstances and the effect of these changes on marriage. In this way he was able to link the behaviour of people in specific situations to the wider setting in which they were placed.

The strategy of separating setting from situation is essentially expediential. It is consistent with and indeed draws from the argument of Devons and Gluckman (1964: 163ff) discussing the procedures social scientists must adopt to reduce their tasks to manageable proportions. In any study, they argue, an anthropologist 'cuts off a manageable field of reality from the total flow of events by putting boundaries around it both in terms of what is relevant and in terms of how and where he can apply his techniques and analysis.' But circumscribing the field of study in this way naturally implies that a certain amount of material which is directly relevant to the problem on hand is treated in considerably less detail than the rest. This is a price that must be paid. The acceptance of a description of a setting, for example, at a somewhat less sophisticated level of analysis than an examination of the social situation within that setting is what Devons and Gluckman refer to as the 'limits of naivety'. This procedure imposes the obligation upon the analyst of constant awareness that the formulation of the setting is indeed naive and is therefore subject to revision if it becomes apparent that the analysis of the social situation is being impeded by it. Research thus becomes a working out of the dialectic between settings and situations.

The analyst should also appreciate that it is perfectly justifiable to treat what is here called the setting − the overall economic and political structure of a social system − as an object of study in its own right. An analyst choosing to do so clearly could afford to be naive about the social situations generated by the system under study. The one kind of study by no means vitiates the other. If anything they are complementary.

Lastly, it is incumbent upon the analyst who is studying social situations to be explicit about the assumptions being made about social settings.[3] This provides essential material for a reader to appreciate the analysis and enables subsequent observers to sophisticate the analysis by elaborating the specification of the setting. It is particularly important to specify settings in an attempt to develop comparative studies since an essential precondition for comparative analysis is ensuring that the settings are indeed comparable before seeking similarities or differences in the social situations within them. Social situations cannot be compared if the settings in which they are located are radically dissimilar.

This distinction between settings and situations is not only a heuristic procedure through which the analyst is able to simplify the task at hand. The setting refers to aspects of the social system which are at a higher level of abstraction than those relating to social situations. The social setting refers to the overall general features of the social system within which the acts of movement of individuals are located. The sum total of actions of individuals whose economic and social and political relationships to one another constitute *in toto* the 'social system' are summarized and stated in succinct and adumbrated form in the specification of the social system. In this sense the setting must of necessity be more abstract than social situations.

Incidence and rate

Appreciation of this difference allows some clarification of obscurities in an earlier formulation about labour circulation in Southern Africa. In 1959 an attempt was made to counter the tendency at that time to present long lists of factors purporting to be 'causes' of labour migration without trying to differentiate the importance of these factors. Two related polarities were distinguished − necessary and sufficient conditions for migration on the one hand, and 'the rate and incidence of migration' on the other (Mitchell 1959). At that time general economic circumstances were postulated as providing the necessary conditions for migration to occur and accordingly they determined the *rate* of migration. These general economic conditions which were the same for everyone did not provide sufficient conditions for migration, since not everyone subject to the same general economic condition did in fact migrate. General economic conditions, it was argued, therefore could not determine the *incidence* of migration. In the terminology now proposed economic conditions − the price of foodstuffs, the wage levels pertaining at labour centres, the agricultural productivity potential of the area involved − provide part of the setting of labour migration. How many people will choose to migrate from the area from year to year will depend very largely on the features of the setting. The particular people who will respond to these general conditions cannot be specified by variables at this general level of abstraction. To do this the social situations of migrants and potential migrants in the area need to be examined, to find out for example the specific kinship and other obligations in which they are involved, the extent to which others are available to perform roles in maintaining rural production and the maintenance of buildings, the possibility of postponing imminent involvement in essential rituals and so on. These enquiries are at a lower level of abstraction and represent in a sense a rather different order of reality in relation to labour migration.

This distinction between necessary and sufficient conditions for labour migration elicited some criticism particularly from van Velsen (1963) and from Gugler (1969). Van Velsen complained that while postulating economic circumstances as constituting necessary conditions for the migration of people *out* of rural subsistence areas into wage earning centres, personal circumstances were relied upon to account for their *return* to these rural areas. The legal and administrative arrangements governing the residence of Africans in town or in White-owned plantations were not included as a general set of conditions appropriately a part of the setting and thus contributing towards creating the necessary conditions for return migration. The logic of the standpoint may be maintained by arguing that just which migrants returned and precisely when they returned would need to be explained by situational factors. Similarly Gugler argued that political and social, as well as economic circumstances could be construed as rate-influencing factors. This is undoubtedly true. In terms of the terminology now being used general political and social structural features should be included as part of the setting of labour circulation. The distinction is not in terms of the type of variable involved − whether we are referring to social, economic or political factors influencing movement − but rather in terms of the degree of generality of the variables and hence abstraction at which we handle these variables in relation to the problem being examined.

The same comment might be made about the criticisms of a sociologically sensitive economist Francis Wilson (1972) to the 1959 formulation of the model and his suggested modification to a subsequent elaboration of it (Mitchell 1969b). Wilson, like van Velsen and Gugler, objects to the equation of economic factors with providing necessary conditions and of social factors with providing sufficient conditions for both migration and circulation. Wilson modifies a diagram which had been produced to illustrate how labour circulation could be related to the life cycle of a typical migrant (Mitchell 1969b, fig. 3: 179) in order to include economic pressures on a migrant to move out of labour centres back to his area of origin. The point is well taken and is indeed one which is conceded in relation to the criticisms by van Velsen and Gugler. But the diagram which had been produced to illustrate the sorts of factors impinging upon migrants or potential migrants to or from labour centres was intended to refer to the sort of issues which a migrant at that stage of his life would have to take into account before making a move. The diagram relates not to the rate of circulation but to incidence. For a deeper understanding of labour circulation we need to isolate both the general large-scale factors influencing the rate of circulation and the small-scale factors influencing its incidence.

But the articulation of small-scale with large-scale phenomena presents particular problems largely because propositions relating to these two types of explanation are cast at entirely disparate levels of abstraction. In that sense we are dealing with different phenomena. The same elemental unit of behaviour − the movement of a person from one location to another − may be construed quite differently by one theorist who is subsuming the particular move into a general explanation of the flow of population out of an impoverished rural area into an area where there are employment opportunities, and another theorist who is looking at the set of pressures backed by a system of norms which impinge upon a person with specific kinship and family obligations. Both interpretations are valid, neither falsifies the other: they are explaining different phenomena.

Social fields and circulation

Recently Garbett and Kapferer (1970) have suggested that integrated large-scale and small-scale studies might be achieved effectively by adopting what they call a 'decision model'. This notion is most fully developed by Garbett (1975) where he sets out to explain different patterns of work-seeking circulation in a rural area of north-eastern Rhodesia.

There appeared to be two ideal-types of migrants moving out of the region in search of employment. The first sought work in the comparatively distant urban areas, and they usually took their wives with them. The removal of the wives from the fathers-in-law's villages involved migrants in heavy financial costs, for by local custom sons-in-law lived in their fathers-in-law's villages until most of the marriage payments had been made. If sons-in-law wanted to take their wives off to the towns the fathers-in-law demanded a substantial proportion of the marriage payments prior to their removal. The whole set of relationships between father-in-law and son-in-law was therefore changed. When the migrants reached town they found it difficult to remain in contact with their home villages and were relatively ignorant of what was happening there. Their contacts in the towns were presumably with co-workers, neighbours and co-religionists, rather than with people from their home areas unless these happened to be close kinsfolk.

The other group of migrants was in sharp contrast. In the main they had elected to seek wage employment close-at-hand on White-owned farms to which many others from their local area had gone in the past. These migrants were able to congregate during their leisure time to exchange news of what was happening at home. They were visited frequently by wives and kinsfolk and themselves were able to make relatively frequent trips back to their homes. They did not remove their wives from their fathers-in-law's villages and were able to provide some of the services to their wives' families during visits back. These migrants were able to remain locked into the rural social system in contrast to those who had gone to the towns who were consequently isolated from it.

Garbett fits these characteristics of movement into a scheme in which the need for cash for everyday existence had become general for the African population, but that ways of acquiring it were severely constrained by the control over economic opportunities which the White minority exercised. The majority of Africans had to earn money by working for White employers either on the farms or in the towns. Garbett noted that approximately 70 per cent of the males in working ages were away from their rural homes in wage-earning employment. Once the need to move had established itself, then the individual was faced with having to make some choice of how he could maximize benefits and minimize disadvantages. What are likely to be disadvantages and what benefits will differ for individuals. The migrant had to decide whether his position in the village as a whole, by reason of his recent marriage and the costs incurred with his father-in-law, the possibility of meeting these costs from kinsfolk, the probabilities of obtaining employment in the towns with the education and skills he possessed, would make it more advantageous for him to seek employment on one of the local farms or to go further afield to one of the towns.

These choices, severely constrained as they are by the wider political and economic setting, are based on individual decisions. To leave it at this, however, would entail particular explanations of every act of migration. What the sociologist (and the social anthropologist) hopes to do is to set the regularities in decision-making in a more general appreciation of the specifics of social structure and the culture in which the population is involved. Garbett argues that we may arrive at a *general* understanding of individual acts of migration by positing that events in the wider economic, political and social system will operate as biases on the choices open to potential migrants thus producing constancies in movement such as the general rate and the direction of flow of movement. But within these general circumstances each individual potential migrant is faced with choices of a different sort. Each potential migrant is embedded in a network of social relationships and these relationships in turn influence his strategies in accordance with his investment and commitment to particular relationships. Any choice a potential migrant makes in terms of his existing social relationships operates in turn as yet further constraints on future action. 'The individual is envisaged as moving through time in a career path which is full of fateful choices. Having committed himself to the line of action other alternatives become impossible or more difficult to pursue.' (Garbett 1975: 124)

Garbett thinks of the total set of an individual's relationships as a 'social field', a notion which has been used in the social sciences (Gluckman, 1947; Lewin 1952). The notion seems to have been taken over from physics in which a field is defined as the area or place under the influence of or within the range of some agent. Its value in sociological analysis is the imagery evoked of a dynamic system of forces surrounding the actor, subject to readjustment and realignment – possibly dramatic realignment – if changes occur in the system, even if they take place in parts of the system apparently not immediately impinging upon the actor under consideration. In conception it is inimical to such notions as 'structure' or 'institution' which carry connotations of regularity and stability. The features of social life normally described in the language of institutions such as kinship, local associations, membership of religious congregations and political alignments, become in the social field equivalent pressures conspiring with or counteracting one another to influence the behaviour of an actor. Ostensibly incommensurable aspects of social life such as the need for money on the one hand and adherence to a religious congregation on the other become comparable: for example, to allow the observer to assess whether a potential migrant is likely to forego his need for money in order to remain a member of the congregation or withdraw from the congregation and migrate.

The attraction of this way of examining labour circulation from the standpoint adopted in this paper is that setting and situation are both combined and retained in the notion of the decision field. At present, however, it seems that the notion of the social field is used as a metaphor rather than as an analytical procedure for explaining migratory behaviour. Until such times as we are able to assess the differential influence on an actor of both elements located in the setting and also of elements in the situation deemed to be operating in the field then it seems that we shall have to be satisfied with its heuristic role in our thinking.

Circulation and the social network

Garbett refers to the decision model as being constructed round the notion of an 'individual set in a network of social relationships'. The 'network of social relationships' is here synonymous with the social field and refers to a general set of unspecified relationships of many different kinds. The word 'network' connotes that while the different relationships in the set are considered to be connected with one another their precise interconnection is unknown. The 'social network' in a strict sense however, would refer to a set of relationships anchored on a potential or actual migrant in which the precise connections among the strands are specified through as many steps away from the individual as is apposite. The social network then, it may be argued, is an identified and specified segment of the social field and should not be equated with it.

This distinction was implied in discussing structural analyses of urban-social systems:

> often when we turn to empirical data the network ramifies
> back into the rural areas and decisions made by the people in
> the rural areas are seen to affect their kinsmen in the towns. In
> other words it is imperative that we should conceive our
> problems in terms of the interaction of parts of a total social
> field as Gluckman puts it and not in terms of 'societies' or
> 'cultures'. These social fields embrace both urban and rural
> areas and are empirical frames of reference for the analysis of
> social behaviour (Mitchell 1964: 39).

The notion of the social network in its more restricted sense has played an important part in the thinking of several who have been interested in the explanation of labour circulation. When the model of labour circulation in terms of the resultant of opposed economic and social ties was first formulated (Mitchell 1959) it postulated social ties and 'the social system operating particularly through the network of social relationships tend[ing] to act centripetally to hold a man within its hold and to resist the influence pulling him away' (1959: 40). There was not access to field material then in sufficient detail to enable the specification of the propositions set out. Neither was there any awareness at the time that Philip Mayer was working along similar lines and in 1961 published a book on East London which documented the existence of a special type of social network which spanned both rural and urban areas and effectively locked urban-based migrants into relationships with people in the rural areas (Mayer 1961). The town dwellers referred to seem, in retrospect, to have been almost unique. They were Xhosa tribesmen who had actively rejected assimilation to Western European life-styles and because of this were sealed off from the urban industrial society in which they lived except for the purely instrumental relationship of wage-earning. Mayer used the word 'incapsulated' to describe them. Other migrants who had accepted Western European life-styles had very different kinds of social networks.

Mayer modified and specified this formulation of labour circulation in two additional papers (1962, 1964). They cover much of the same ground but the more recent was published in a less easily accessible source and in this Mayer made a number of observations germane to an understanding of labour circulation from a sociological point of view and the rule of the social network in rural-urban relationships.

Mayer starts his analysis by distinguishing several different meanings of the notion of 'urbanization'. As far as labour circulation is concerned he reaches much the same sort of conclusion as that in Mitchell (1959) though he does not quote this. 'I mean by an urbanized African one who no longer feels the pull of the country home, because all his important personal ties are bounded by the town in which he lives' (Mayer 1964: 25). By contrast the temporary migrant will be one whose important personal ties are still located in his rural home. However Mayer draws attention to important differences between South African towns. In Cape Town and East London the migrants are nearly all drawn from one ethnic group — the Xhosa — whereas in Johannesburg there is considerable ethnic diversity. In East London the rural-based population *par excellence* are the incapsulated migrants referred to previously, but in Cape Town where the same ethnic group predominates this particular group does not seem to exist. They are even less evident in Johannesburg. Yet there are close-knit coteries of migrants in all these cities but they do not actively reject European ways-of-life as the so-called 'Red' migrants do in East London. These coteries are nearly always drawn from the same area of origin and Mayer points out that subdivisions occur among 'Red' migrants in East London on the basis of their common origin from relatively small areas in the rural hinterlands. In Cape Town and Johannesburg and indeed on the Copperbelt of Zambia the same phenomenon occurs. Wilson and Mafeje (1963) call these coteries 'home-boy cliques' and describe how migrants to Cape Town particularly from districts or 'village' locations in the Eastern Province, share rooms, mess together and care for one another in illness and unemployment.

The existence of similar grouping in the Copperbelt has been recorded by Harries-Jones (1969, 1975). His interest in what he has called 'home-mates' was not in relation to the extent to which the cliques reflected the rural-rootedness of their members but rather in the way in which these cliques provided the basis of political recruitment to early nationalist parties. Other evidence from the Copperbelt suggests that the ethnic composition of single-quarters on the mines was most clear-cut among those migrants who are known to be essentially circulatory – the Nyakusa and other migrants from Tanzania (Mitchell, Unpublished survey data). Similar groupings have been reported for Windhoek in Namibia (Pendleton 1975: 15).

'Home-mate' groupings in towns are symptomatic but not conclusively indicative of a state in which migrants are torn between opposed sets of interests in different geographical locations. Elsewhere (Mitchell 1970: 94ff) three ideal-type circumstances are distinguished in which the same superficial appearance of a home-mate grouping belies different circumstances. Elaborated in terms of network concepts there are:

(a)   The home-mate grouping is composed of people who knew one another in the rural area before moving and whose links in the town are reinforced through common and intense links with friends and kinsmen in the rural area. 'Intense links' are those in which 'individuals are prepared to honour obligations or feel free to exercise rights implied by [this link]' (Mitchell 1969a: 27).

(b)   The home-mate grouping is composed of people who knew one another in the rural area before migrating, who continue the association with one another in intense network relationships in town but whose friends and kinsmen are not likely to know one another in the rural area. These seem to be the home-boy groupings described by Wilson and Mafeje (1963: 47ff). The probability of circulation exists but it is lower than with the first type.

(c)   The home-mate grouping is composed of people who did not know one another in the rural area and whose friends and kinsmen in the rural area are unlikely to know one another. The groupings may be coterminous with a voluntary association based on ethnic identity. The relationships among the members are not likely to be very intense and among these people the probability of circulation is lower than in the other two types. The probability of circulating back and forth between rural home and wage-earning centres is directly related to the interconnectedness and intensity of social networks spanning both locations.

There appear to be only two studies in which this proposition in its unelaborated form set out in 1959 has been subject to test in

Africa,[4] one direct and one indirect. Parkin (1975: 145-155) used data from a study of Luo migrants in Nairobi to test the proposition and from his findings refutes it. The ethnic group that he describes have relatively well paid jobs, have been in Nairobi for long periods and have not spent more than the conventional annual vacation periods of several weeks in their rural areas of origin. Where possible they have bought their houses in Nairobi, they belong to urban associations and tend to send their children to schools in town. Yet at the same time they are constantly receiving visitors from their rural homes. Many have established businesses and have erected substantial houses in the rural areas. They therefore have economic links in the town and strong social links with the rural areas. In terms of the earlier formulation these migrants would have been expected to move regularly between the two foci of interest. In fact they do not.

Unemployment was high in Nairobi when Parkin was making his study. Labour turnover was low and people with secure jobs could not risk leaving them for longer than a normal annual vacation period. But on the other hand Parkin records that while the men may not have been circulating between town and country their wives and children were. The men may be considered circulators by proxy given the tight employment situation. Why then did they maintain a stake in their rural homes at all? Parkin suggests that with the increasing power of the Kikuyu over economic opportunities and political office in Nairobi the security of the minority Luo in the town was becoming more and more uncertain, and their only security was in their home area where their future status was ensured if they had maintained economic and social investments.

Here the point raised earlier about the post facto definition of migrancy behaviour becomes relevant. It is doubtful if dynamic conclusions can be drawn from synchronic studies such as Parkin's. The particular Luo in his urban sample are presumably the residue of several cohorts who had migrated to Nairobi earlier, others having either moved on to other parts of Kenya or returned to their districts of origin. By the same token some of those in Parkin's sample might have returned to their rural areas soon after he had completed his study. Admittedly the migrant who comes to town and spends a long time there with only short visits back to his rural area of origin is very different from those labour circulators in Southern Africa who make several trips to their rural homes during a stay at a labour centre, and these stays are sometimes of several years duration. This is reflected in the number of visits to rural homes by length of absence from their homes by African male town dwellers in 1951-4, shown in Table 2.1.

TABLE 2.1 *Number of visits home by period of absence from rural areas: Males all urban areas: Northern Rhodesia: 1950-5 population estimates*

No. of visits	Years since first left rural home								Totals
	0-4	5-9	10-14	15-19	20-24	25+	NK		
None	32,517	651	5,824	2,889	1,976	1,841	32		54,729
One	5,005	7,977	5,675	3,396	2,259	2,011	0		26,324
Two	282	1,664	2,482	1,753	1,075	1,295	0		8,551
Three	32	234	808	638	445	685	0		2,843
Four	10	23	240	253	188	280	0		993
Five	0	0	35	53	43	67	0		198
Six	0	0	0	22	10	53	0		85
Seven	0	10	0	0	0	32	0		42
Eight	0	0	0	0	0	10	0		10
Twelve	0	0	10	0	0	0	0		10
'Frequently'	63	133	88	54	97	126	0		562
Not known	970	807	1,074	651	578	666	722		5,469
Totals	38,879	11,499	16,236	9,709	6,671	7,066	754		99,816

(Based on 8,931 cases)

Source: J.C. Mitchell, Rhodes-Livingstone Institute, Northern Rhodesia Urban Surveys, Dec. 1950–May 1955

Nevertheless it is clear that the rationale underlying wage-labour circulation obviously needs to be more complex than has so far been postulated. The setting needs to be specified more completely to take account of such factors as employment opportunities and ethnic competition for both jobs and political power. But variations within the setting will still have to be explained by situational factors. Parkin presents material in general terms so there are no data on individual variations in migratory behaviour among the people in his sample.

Weisner (1976) presents material from Nairobi which provides an interesting contrast to Parkin. It refers to a different ethnic group (Luyia) which, from Weisner's description relating to approximately the same period, displays the typical circulatory wage-labour behaviour. He sets up a type of decision model relating to an urban-rural field.

> From the point of view of an individual man who is part of a homestead in a rural community, the decision to migrate to the city (or to return to the country from the city) is made according to complex judgements and sets of personal circumstances within both rural and urban contexts (Weisner 1976: 201).

He provides an instructive case-history of an individual of the ethnic group studied, a case-study which recounts very well the shuttling of an individual between rural home and urban work centre as his fortunes wax and wane.

Weisner sets out to examine the extent of interconnection in rural- and urban-based networks and for this purpose sought out twenty-four men in a suburb of Nairobi who were from a localised area in the part of Kenya from which this particular ethnic group came. He then asked each of these twenty-four respondents to name a patrilineal kinsman at present resident in the rural area who matched himself in both age and educational level. Each of the twenty-four urban respondents was then asked if he knew each of the other forty-seven persons on the list and how often they had visited during the last twelve months. Weisner then sought out each of the twenty-four nominated persons in the rural area and asked them the same questions. He was able thus to produce one of the rare published detailed examples of a social network with both rural and urban sectors, to demonstrate their inter-connectedness.

The interest as this paper is concerned, however, is that his findings confirm a point made by Parkin: the links among urban clansmen were in general as dense as − in fact denser than −

they were among rural, and as dense for rural-urban or urban-rural links as for rural-rural. This is reflected in a summary from a table of Weisner (1976: 214) (see Table 2.2). On the surface therefore the proposition advanced about the distribution of ties in rural as against urban areas is contradicted by this evidence as well.

TABLE 2.2 *Densities of links between rural and urban kinsmen: Kenya circa 1970*

		Urban	Rural	Total
	Links existing	252	236	488
C	Urban links possible	380	440	820
h	Density (%)	66.3	53.6	59.5
o	Links existing	217	230	447
o	Rural links possible	440	462	902
s	Density (%)	49.3	49.8	49.6
e	Links existing	469	466	935
r	Total links possible	820	902	1722
s	Density	57.2	51.7	54.3

Source: Abstracted from Weisner's Table 2 (1976: 214)

Weisner did not quote the Mitchell (1959) paper and was presumably not exercised to test the effect on circulation of network connections in towns as against those in rural areas. In fact to have tested the spirit of the proposition would have needed information which is rather more difficult to obtain. As pointed out earlier the centrifugal effect of network connections is not related to density *per se* but rather to intensity, although it is probable that the two are related. Intensity refers to the degree to which persons linked by a relationship will honour the obligations implied by that relationship. The data needed for migrants or potential migrants at different points of their migratory history therefore relate to the location of those people in whom the migrant has most binding personal investments. This is akin to Philip Mayer's notion of 'all the *important* personal ties' (my italics) being bonded by the town (see p. 43 above). Information of this sort makes onerous demands to which few fieldworkers can respond.

Operationalizing the model

Dichotomous concepts like 'necessary and sufficient conditions', 'rate and incidence', 'setting and situation' serve the purpose of highlighting contrasting distinctions, making us more sensitive to them in our analyses. But in the analysis of labour circulation in the real world the difficulty of grounding these logically clear-cut notions on empirical data becomes immediately apparent. This is particularly true if we try to understand labour circulation in terms sufficiently general to allow us to gain insight into its manifestations in different parts of the globe and at different points in time.

While still retaining the original intention of providing some basis of discriminating amongst the plethora of factors postulated as influencing labour circulation, it should be possible though not easy to assess the independent influences upon circulation of factors at different levels of abstraction. The phenomenon to be explained – the dependent variable – is the probability of a person's moving between labour centre and rural home within some specified period of time. The factors which the analyst construes as affecting this probability constitute the independent variables and which of these are included in the model depends on the scale of the study.

First of all the analyst will need an adequate description of the setting within which the movement is taking place. This will need to be in fairly general terms to specify the set of economic, political, legal and administrative circumstances bearing on potential migrants or potential return migrants in both sending and receiving areas. These include the level of real wages in both locations, the division of labour in the sending area by which rural production is maintained, transport facilities and costs, administrative control exercised over movement and how this may be coped with, housing conditions in the receiving area and the regulations governing access to housing, and other features which bear in a general way on all potential migrants in the sending or in the receiving area.

Secondly the analyst will need data on the institutional arrangements in both receiving and sending areas which operate within the wider setting to allow migrants to leave, and also to support them in receiving areas. The kinship system and local organization, the structure of voluntary associations, the operation of 'home-mate' groupings and similar sociological features are at this level of abstraction. Consideration of these arrangements allows the fieldworker to distinguish between *categories* of migrant such as younger sons in lineage from older sons, or men in their wives' villages in systems where virilocal marriage is practised in a patrilineal society as against men living in their own patrilineal villages. Institutional arrangements in receiving areas such as systems of stratification or land-holding in town operate at the same level of abstraction.

Finally the individual circumstances of each potential migrant or potential returnee will need to be specified. It is there that social network data need to be collected, but unfortunately experience with methods of collection is very limited. Formal survey procedures have been developed particularly by sociologists in America, which require respondents to name their 'best friends' − usually up to some practical limit − and either to estimate the extent to which these best friends interact, or to visit each named person (as Weisner did) and get them to answer questions about the remaining members of the set.

Some of the most detailed information about network relationships has been built up from general ethnographic records but this requires the fieldworker to be very systematic in recording interactions so that all possible links possibly at several steps removed from the anchor person may be considered and assessed. It seems that more formal procedures along the lines of Q-sort techniques might be experimented with. Since great emphasis is placed on 'intensity' a procedure might be adopted by which a respondent is asked to enumerate those people, whether they are physically present in the locale of study or not, whom he or she feels could be called upon to provide support or services when needed. The level of support or the type of service could be quite varied and several different types may be included. The procedure then would be to get the respondent to sort cards bearing the names of these people into four or five piles representing the certainty with which the respondent felt that support or services would be provided. Each person in the set would be asked to perform the task. From this network data could be produced which would enable determination of the extent to which important links are with people in the present locale of residence or not.

Tedious fieldwork is involved which would probable engender some resistance from respondents, but it seems to be the only way in which sufficient *systematic* information can be assembled to allow formal network analysis procedures to be used. The alternative of participant observation is hardly possible unless the fieldworker is going to be prepared to work intensively for long periods in both sending and receiving areas. Nevertheless observation must be combined with formal data collection procedures since the latter will be cognitive rather than interactional. For an adequate analysis both are needed. The difficulty with observation data is that they must of necessity be processual in the sense that the observer tries to gauge the actor's assessment of alternative strategies open to him or her in each situation given the constraints of the settings. From this the observer hopes to be able to appreciate in general terms the considerations which lead potential migrants to move or potential returnees to return.

When the appropriate data relating to many of the different levels of causative factors have been assembled the analyst appears to have two contrasting strategies of analysis available. If the data are particularly extensive in respect of settings, subsettings, and situations the relationship between the probability of moving or not moving within a specified time period may be related through some type of numerical analysis. Since both the dependent variable (the probability of moving or not) and many of the independent causative variables are likely to be discrete in character some form of discrete multivariate analysis might be used, as for example, log linear procedures. The hope would be that the relative strength of factors located in the setting, subsetting or situations on the probability of moving could be estimated while all other factors are held constant.

There is however a constraint on this type of procedure which arises specifically from the methodological distinction stressed in this paper − the distinction between settings and situations. Where variables in a multiple regression derive from the overall context in which other variables are located there may be difficulties in separating out one effect from another. This is similar to the problem of handling what are known as 'structural effects' (Blau 1960) or 'compositional effects' (Davis *et al.* 1961).

If the data are drawn from the same setting, as most national studies of labour circulation tend to be, the contextual effects are the same for all potential migrants or returnees so that no inference may be drawn about the effect of the setting on labour circulation. An examination of the effects of settings calls particularly for comparative studies.

If the data refer to material in only one setting − and a micro-setting at that − then it seems that the analyst must of necessity resort to the alternative strategy of analysis − that of the case study. There is widespread confusion about the role of the case study in systematic enquiry, which is rooted in a misunderstanding on the basis of generalization from a case study. The basis of inference from a single case is not that the particular case is deemed to be 'representative' or 'typical' of all cases, as is the basis of statistical inference, but that in a sense it is *atypical* in that the logical connection between its constituent parts makes relationships apparent which were formerly obscure. Generalization from the case study is premissed upon the universality of the theoretical propositions relating relevant aspects of the case to one another, not upon its 'representativeness' of some universe of 'cases'.

In the end the signal advances will come from a combination of analyses at different levels of abstraction, informed by a sense of justifiable naivety, oriented to systematically collected detailed but focused information. These may be combined with extensive life-histories, and above all longitudinal observations over sufficiently long periods so as to increase the likelihood that at least some of those under observation will make decisions and move, thus enabling the observer to assess the validity of alternative explanations of behaviour relating to labour circulation.

Acknowledgment and Notes

The author wishes to thank Margaret Grieco of Nuffield College for discussions on labour circulation which have rekindled an interest in and tightened up his thinking on this topic.

1 Graves and Graves distinguish between 'foraging' patterns involving 'temporary forays into neighbouring regions in order to supplement local resources', and 'circular migration' which involves 'the establishment of more or less permanent ties between two economic systems, one rural and one urban, and the periodic movement of labour between them'. 'Circular migration', they argue, 'shares with the foraging patterns the characteristic of supplementing limited resources in the rural community through temporary out-migration. But where the foraging migrant retains a primary identification with his rural community, circular migrants establish a dual identity' (Graves and Graves 1974: 119-120). I find it difficult to distinguish the two other than by degree since all 'foragers' presumably have some 'identity' in the shape of network contacts in the places to which they have migrated to secure the scarce resources they seek.

2 While it may be technically possible to do this I am not aware of any attempt to do so. Presumably it would require fairly long term longitudinal studies at the places of origin of migrants in which details deemed likely to dispose a potential migrant to migrate are monitored and related to the fact of migration when it takes place.

3 I have elsewhere referred to this in relation to the study of comparative urbanism as 'specifying the contextual parameters' (see Mitchell, in preparation). Failure to do so leads to invalid criticisms as for example those of Wirth's hypothesis about urbanism based on data from contexts which immediately define the data as irrelevant.

4 Chapman and Prothero (1977: 3) refer to an application of this notion by Chapman and Bedford to circulatory movements of a wider kind than wage labour circulation but I have not been able to consult these sources.

3 The Hausa wanderer and structural outsiderhood: an emic and etic analysis

Harold Olofson

This paper analyses a category of mobility which the Hausa of northern Nigeria view as improper or illegitimate (Olofson 1976). The 'walk to Dandi' (*yawon Dandi*) refers to the movement of Hausa to lands outside Hausaland in areas of the Hausa diaspora, or to cosmopolitan centres beyond the walls of the ancient Hausa cities.

It is also used as a metaphor for the state of mind of a migrant who might travel anywhere in the world with the thought of evading family responsibilities and leaving his kin in the dark as to where he has gone. This could come about as a result of involvement in home village or town in shameful circumstances, or in irreconcilable domestic conflict, or as a result simply of a desire to gain experience in the wider world and express individuality. Frequently it involves trading from town to town. This type of mobility became easier in Hausaland in the colonial period, when the end of slavery made it easier for children, husbands, or wives to run away from their families.

To understand such a phenomenon it is necessary to place it within the context of other Hausa concepts of spatial mobility; then to examine its emic content − how it is viewed from inside the culture − by pointing up its structural contrast with more socially acceptable modes of behaviour; and lastly to proceed to explore the sociocultural genesis for this type of movement in particular and for the amazing range of Hausa spatial mobility in general.

A classification of Hausa spatial mobility

Table 3.1 shows a combined *etic* and *emic* classification of Hausa mobility. *Emic* refers simply to Hausa-language terms for

54

movement, *etic* to an analytical typing of mobility used by the social scientist from outside Hausa culture to aid in cross-cultural comparison. Both etic and emic views are essential to facilitate an understanding of mobility within a society and its relevance to the wider anthropology and geography of movement.

Here the terms 'migration', 'spatial mobility', and 'movement' are used loosely since the Hausa do not seem to have easy one-to-one equivalences for them in the ways they are variously defined in English scientific jargon (e.g. Fortes 1971: 1-2). They are entered pragmatically in the left-hand column in the table. Nor do the Hausa seem particularly interested in devising complex hierarchies in classifying mobility. All of the terms on the right-hand side of the table are thus to be viewed as equivalent.

Where more than one emic term exists corresponding to one etic category, they have a similarity which the etic classification points up. This similarity is true not only from an analytical view, for most Hausa would also recognize and see as sensible the etic classifications on the left-hand, though often they have no corresponding inclusive categories for use in everyday language (e.g. a direct translation in Hausa of 'religious migration').

As being of key importance in Hausa categories of movement (Olofson 1976: 66), *k'aura* is placed at the top of the list, for almost all of the other kinds of mobility can lead, as intermediate stages, to a permanent change of residence. *Yawon Dandi* is quite the opposite of *k'aura* in that it is conceived as open-ended, an aimless, pointless wandering, but it is also true that movement in etic categories B, C, D, E, and G can easily lead to it rather than to *k'aura*. *K'aura* by definition cannot result in *yawon Dandi*, although *yawon Dandi* could conceivably lead to settlement in a new place after some years of wandering.

Frequently an emic category can be entered opposite more than one etic category. This is especially true for those emic categories corresponding to etic categories C, D, E, and G, which tend to be movements in the dry season between the harvest and the onset of the next rains when there is time for non-farming activities. They could all be combined with *cin rani*, except that they are not necessarily restricted to a particular season as it is. Similarly, *yawon k'wadago* often takes place at any time when the poor who practise it feel the need, and could be found under C or even possibly as part of *yawon Dandi*. *Yawo* or prostitution could be classified as an itinerant occupation, but its illegitimacy is more significant in the Hausa view of woman than the fact that it is also an occupation.

The etic categories are described as either *linear* or *circular*,

TABLE 3.1 *A classification of spatial mobility in Hausaland*

Etic classification	Type of mobility	Emic classification	Designation of migrant
I. Legitimate mobility			
A. Permanent shift in residence (linear, closed)	*k'aura* (permanent migration)		(In most cases, except where other entries are given, migrants can be designated by the addition of the prefixes *mai-* (pl. *masu-*), 'owner of' or *d'an* (m.), *'yar* (f.), *'yan* (pl.), 'child of'; but where *yawon*, 'walk of' is included in the emic category it is omitted before the addition of these prefixes.)
B. Seasonal migration (circular, closed)	*cin rani* (eating the dry-season) *yawon k'wadago* (the walk of paid labour, e.g. in wet-season)		as above, plus many others
C. Itinerant occupations (circular, closed)	*sha'anin yawo* (walking business) *yawon neman kud'i/abinci* (walk of looking for money/food) *fatauci* (long-distance trade) *yawon kasuwanci* (walk of marketing) *yawon rok'o* (walk of praise-singing) *yawon bara* (walk of begging) etc. etc.		*farke* (long-distance trader) *d'an kasuwa* (marketer); *dillali* (middleman) *marok'i* (praise-singer)
D. Religious migration (circular, closed)	*(yawon) almajiranci* (walk of) studenthood = *yawon (neoman) karatu* (walk of (looking for) reading) *(yawon) mallamanci* ((walk of) teacherhood) *hajji* (pilgrimage)		*almajiri* (student) *almajiri* (student) *mallami* (teacher) *alhaji* (pilgrim)

E. Visiting (circular, closed)	yawon gaisuwa (walk of greeting)	
F. Transfer (circular, open)	zuwa anguwa ((going out) to the ward)	
G. Recreational-educational movement (circular, closed)	canji (change)	
(a) casual	yawon sha iska (walk of drinking air)=	
	yawon (ganin) gari (walk of (seeing) the town)=	
	zagaya gari (strolling about town)	
(b) sight-seeing	yawon bud'in ido (walk of opening the eye)=	
	yawon gane-gane (walk of looking-looking)	
H. Marriage (both circular and linear, closed)	aure (marriage)	does not apply
	e.g. auren takalmi (marriage of sandals)	
I. In-migration of strangers		bak'o (pl. bak'i) (stranger)
		'yan kudu (children from the south)
II. Illegitimate mobility		
J. Liberational migration (circular, open)	yawon Dandi/duniya/barriki (walk to Dandi/in the world/to the barrack-towns)=	location word preceded by d'an/'yar/'yan
	'yawo' ('walk' – euphemism for prostitution) or	karuwa (prostitute)
	yawon karuwanci (walk of courtesanship)	
	shiga uwa-duniya (entering the mother-world) and many others (see text)	

and *open* or *closed*. *Linear* relates only to *k'aura*, in that this is a direct shift in residence of an individual or family from one place to another without the intention of return. *Circular* approximates to the term *circulation* as it is used currently by geographers studying mobility (Gould and Prothero 1975). In this sense all categories other than *k'aura*, including some marriage-based movements (see below) could be described as *circulation*. Where circulation results in return to point of departure, this is described as *closed*; but should the migrant decide to wander from one place to another, with or without the intention of returning home, breaking contact with his place of origin, yet not settling down elsewhere, this is *open* and is epitomized by *yawon Dandi*.

The broad etic categories of legitimate as opposed to illegitimate mobility are based on the extent to which the emic categories are viewed by Hausa as expressions of useful activity, leading especially to household and family cohesion. Much legitimate mobility has as its end 'useful work' (*aiki mai'amfani*), with the socio-economic purpose of keeping together the migrant's compound. As 'liberational migration', *yawon Dandi* is illegitimate. The individual expresses his own individualistic, selfish pleasures and ambitions by 'wandering' in the world, temporarily or in the long-term freeing himself or herself from family ties, living in rented quarters on the way, and engaging in activities considered useless or 'sham' (*banza*) if not indeed downright disreputable.

The distinction between 'illegitimate mobility' and 'liberational migration' should especially make sense to the Hausa who see *yawon Dandi* as radically different from other kinds of spatial mobility. One interesting point is that our thinking about *yawon Dandi* in these etic terms, in order to make comparisons with other types of movement within the same society and in other societies (for example, the mobility of 'hippies' in the United States), has helped us to understand the nature of *yawon Dandi* as it is viewed from within the culture. This is another good reason for accompanying emic with parallel etic classifications.

Legitimate mobility

Spatial mobility pervades Hausa society and legitimate movements and the maintenance of kin ties are closely related. *K'aura* emphasizes the permanent leaving of a place, but only in the special use of the word as a euphemism for death, when the migrant leaves the world (*duniya*) and enters the afterworld (*Lahira*), is there a suggestion that a boundary is crossed. A permanent settlement will have a core of *'yan k'aura* from other towns, or their descendants, who have evolved from the status of *bak'i* ('strangers') to that of known and trusted permanent residents or *'yan gari* ('children of the town'). Thus many Hausa settlements have a history, sometimes partly mythical, of particular individuals who first came and settled, occasionally as refugees from elsewhere. It is the permanently resident migrants and their descendants who give a settlement its socio-economic identity, not those who come and stay for a few years and then leave.

Very commonly, chain migration will occur as relatives come to join the *'yan gari*. A census of compounds in three neighbourhoods of Funtua in southern Katsina in 1970-1, showed that a notable number of migrant compound heads had moved to settle permanently near to, or at first with, relatives. When females were involved, the migrant usually had come to be near a daughter or brother after divorce from, the death of, or abandonment by the husband. Males frequently came to live near siblings or uncles who sometimes found wives for them. One migrant had come to live with an elder brother because all of his relatives in his former place had died or moved away. Another came to live near his mother's junior sister who had weaned him. The frequent activation of connections among close bilateral kin to help establish residence suggests that kin obligations in Hausaland are not as weak as some ethnographers have suggested (Cohen 1969: 41-2; Salamone 1973: 120; Bamisaiye 1974: 200).

Cin rani, legitimate dry-season mobility, can evolve into *k'aura* should the mover decide to stay in his dry-season locale; or he may extend his stay past the rains and into months and years of moving from town to town as a *d'an duniva*.

A dry-season migrant is frequently accompanied by relatives, or goes to reside with bilateral kin during his sojourn. Of a small sample of 48 dry-season migrants who made Funtua their destination, 15 had come with wives; 13 brought their own children, brothers, or sons of elder brothers in addition to wives; and six had brought such relatives but not wives. Only one came with the specific purpose of only visiting a relative, but six came to live with relatives. Interestingly some of these referred to the relative with whom they lived by a kin-term which brought the relative into a much closer relationship to the migrant than was actually the case. For example, one migrant claimed to be living with *'ya* ('elder sister') whereas upon closer questioning he was found to be living with *'yaruwa* ('female cousin'), the daughter of his father's elder brother. This same phenomenon has been noted for the Hausa in Ghana; as patrons *vis-à-vis* clients, and co-residents of the same compound even cross-ethnically, they establish fictive kin ties with all the terminology, rights and duties which these provide in the absence of real kin (Schildkrout 1973: 53-6). The same principle appears here to be at work even within kin circles: this may express respectfully a migrant's right to ask for aid from a relative in the form of dry-season accommodation.

Itinerant occupations is probably the most ubiquitous category of spatial mobility in Hausaland, and a large number of traditional activities are involved. Many of them, such as *yawon rok'o* ('the walk of praise-singing') require the holder to frequent heavily settled areas, or where there is community (*jama'a*) in order to gain adequate subsistence; but they are also a means whereby goods and services are circulated to rural areas.

A striking example of Hausa mobility is given by a *maibara* ('beggar') in Funtua. This man had once walked as a pilgrim to Mecca, where he stayed thirteen years before walking back. When he returned some unknown ailment struck his legs, and after a period of using a walking stick, he became completely immobile. Eventually a man gave him a four-wheeled push-cart (*amalanke*), formerly used by porters to move loads in the market, which was fitted with a metal frame and diagonal cross-bar in the rear for back support. For a while his younger brother pushed him around. Later he went away from his home town on *yawon bara*, placing himself and his cart on a lorry or train for free passage to all of the larger Hausa cities. He hired *masutura* ('pushers') from the ranks of Koranic students and former porters, to whom he paid four shillings a day out of an income of alms ranging from twelve to fourteen shillings. On the occasion of market-day in a nearby town, he was pushed there from Funtua and back on the same day, a round trip of fourteen miles.

Religious mobility includes those ubiquitous movements which function in sending out the faithful to bathe in the brotherhood of Islam and to effect the exchange of religious information between separated Moslem communities which are thus knit together. Thus religious kinship is strengthened by the circulation of scholars, teachers, students, and pilgrims who are not limited in their travel by the boundaries of Hausa society. This religious kinship sometimes comes to characterize the relation between students and teachers repeatedly across generations. For example, in one case in Funtua, a group of brothers living together had invited the son of their former teacher to come from another town and dwell permanently with them in his own *shiva* (portion of the compound) to instruct their several children and thus support himself.

Visiting, yawon gaisuwa ('the walk of greeting') occurs with short-term visiting beyond kin or friends, living in different compounds or towns, particularly on occasions such as marriage and naming ceremonies. It can involve an individual spending several months or even years moving from town to town to live with bilateral kin who, in a far-flung network, offer choices of residence and other support. A young man may do this in the course of learning a craft, acquiring more and more knowledge as he moves among fellow craftsmen in different urban settings. In the same way a Koranic student may call upon kin to support him while he pursues his learning.

A Funtua bicycle dealer, when a boy of about fifteen, learned the occupation of hiring out bicycles from his elder sister's husband. From there he went to Katsina to stay with his father's younger brother for three years as a student, then to Kano to live with his mother's brother for another three years, still studying the Koran, and then to his mother's sister in Zaria for fifteen months, to continue his studies. In a fourth move he went to his elder sister in Jos for three years. While in Jos he became the *yaro* ('boy') of a bicycle mechanic. For this man he did what he called *aikin bauta* ('work of "slavery" '), buying his master's groceries and washing his clothes without pay, in return for being taught repair work. When he returned to Funtua he had saved up enough to start his own hiring and repair business. This is an excellent example of how kin obligations may be called upon far beyond the original co-residential group.

Transfer, canji in contemporary Hausa, combines the attributes of circular and open, thus suggesting that where persons in political, administrative, educational, civil service, or business posts are transferred from one place to another, the movement involved is in many cases similar to *yawon Dandi* in form if not in function or meaning. For example, an agricultural extension agent had been transferred once or twice a year for several years. Only when he retired and had broken his relation with *canji* altogether could he move permanently to reside in Funtua.

Recreational-educational movement, whether this involves the casual stepping out of the house for fresh air, or a more committed journey some distance away to gain knowledge of the people and business in another town or country, is regarded favourably by the Hausa who value the insights provided into urban life, activity, and manners. Sight-seeing can influence an individual's penultimate decision to move permanently to a place he has thus seen (sometimes when this recreation is a by-product of some other type of spatial mobility) or to wander there if he does *yawon Dandi*.

Marriage (*aure*) does not appear to be considered a type of spatial mobility by the Hausa in the same sense that they do *k'aura* and others, particularly because it results in a restriction in the movement of women. But it should have a separate etic status. First of all, a marriage may set up a chain of movements. For example, there is the movement of the bride to the house or town of the groom, return to her parents for several months at the birth of children, the moving out of children for weaning and adoption, following the husband should he change residence, running away to her parents and retrieval by the husband. Secondly, in their classification of marriages the Hausa distinguish on the basis of the relative freedom of the wife from *auren kulle*, or almost complete seclusion, to *auren iahilai* ('the marriage of the ignorant') where the wife has almost complete freedom. Also involving a factor of mobility is *auren dauki-sandanka* ('marriage of take up your staff (and walk)') where old couples live in separate compounds and visit each other (Smith 1955: 52-3). There is also *auren takalmi* ('marriage of sandals') where a man may have wives in different towns, which is connected with age, and is suitable for a husband who visits the towns in question on regular circles of *yawon kasuwanci* ('the walk of marketing').

Illegitimate migration and structural outsiderhood

The Hausa look doubtfully on *yawon Dandi* in a way which highlights by contrast the value which they place on the maintenance of the domestic group. There are numerous lexical variations for this category. Bargery (1934) gives around forty of them, reflecting regional dialects and with varying nuances of meaning. This suggests that we are dealing with a social problem (in the Hausa view) which goes back at least to the first part of the century. The term *ragaita* is 'wandering or roving about aimlessly, an unsettled life, vagrancy with no settled means or place of earning a livelihood'. It is also 'gossiping', which the Hausa consider disruptive of social relations and see stereo-typically as given to old women who are free to move from compound to compound. It is related to the adverb *ragai*, 'aimlessly, contemptuously' and thus refers to an aimless existence which holds a contempt for proper modes of living. *Gilo* is like *ragaita* but involves also working as a casual labourer. *Shashanci* is 'going from place to place gossiping or for immorality', with the immoral dimension of this word appearing in the synonym (*yawon*) *filai*, 'itinerant prostitution', where *filai* comes most likely from the French *fille* via the Hausa of francophone Niger. *Shashanci* is derived from the noun *shashasha*, 'a person who leaves what is good and worthwhile for that which is bad and worthless, an unreliable person'. He thus ignores his role as a family member (see the quotation from an informant in Olofson 1976: 76). *Shashasha* in turn is a variant of *shiru*, 'a fool whose mind wanders off on tangents and who cannot stick to a point'. The use of this word could characterize the wanderer's mental capacities. *Galallawa* implies the treatment of something in a cheap manner, of 'giving up one's belongings to be appropriated by anyone'. The position of a husband whose wife must dissolve her marriage before a judge because of being abandoned comes to mind here. *Galudava* has also the meaning of 'partial impotence'. This reflects an evaluation of a man who does not choose to father children, acquire his own farms, trade, or craft, and increase his estate. *Katangala* refers to 'the wandering about of homeless vagrants; a person with no friends, relations, means, or influence; a thing left about carelessly as if unwanted; the wandering about of horses or cattle left untethered'. Thus one informant said quite naturally in English 'If a man is a good son, his parents will tie him at one stall like a horse'. Finally, *hazarniva* is also 'squandering money', and suggests again the wastefulness of wanderlust and the inability to apply it to a socially acceptable realm of human affairs.

The dual opposition of gida and Dandi

The presence of such terms as those above and the knowledge that there are numerous 'children of the world' certainly does not speak too well for the closeness of the Hausa family. However, the attitude of the Hausa toward this must also be taken into consideration. They see *Dandi* as the inferior opposite to *gida*, 'compound'. As they say, *zaman gida ya fi yawon Dandi*, 'living at home or in one's land and place is better than the walk of Dandi'. If an informant was asked to state the opposite of *gida*, he would most likely take it to mean 'compound' and say *waje* ('outside') or *daji* ('bush'). But if he was asked first to state what is the opposite of *(yawon) Dandi*, there is a great likelihood that he would answer *(zaman) gida*, where *gida* would mean 'home'. The opposition between the terms achieves clarity only in certain contexts of discussion.

The dual opposition *gida : Dandi* can be analysed in terms of suboppositions, intuitively derived by the researcher. These as a cluster tend to reveal liberational migrants as occupying a sociocultural position *structurally outside* the one which good

63

people strive for. The first of these is the opposition between sanity and madness. It is significant that in a culture where spatial mobility takes so many forms even madness (*hauka*) can be migratory. Some Hausa schizophrenics are in constant aimless movement from town to town. For acting as if they had no familial ties children taunt them by calling them bastards (*shegu*), and their accumulated dirt and ragged clothing suggest that they have lost all sense of shame (*kunya*). At the other extreme is the schizophrenic who remains motionless and has to be fed by hand, and is related to movement by being in such stark contrast to it. No one would ever refer to a normal person who is doing *yawon Dandi* as a madman, nor would anyone say that an insane person is a *d'an Dandi* when it is more obvious that he is a madman. But they share a similar outside position *vis-à-vis* kin statuses and roles. Both are said to have 'entered the mother-world' (*shiga uwa-duniya*), to act as if they were orphaned or illegitimate — but only the *d'an Dandi* does so with knowledge of what he is doing. With the schizophrenic it seems that his 'loss of sense' and inability to communicate occurs at the same time as when all parts of his social field attain an equally meaningless status to him, so that either he will move errantly in it, or consider no place worth moving to. He may lose the distinction between 'home' and 'the world'. Though the sane individual leaving home, due either to stress or relish for personal adventure, may not be looked upon as mad he may certainly be taken as foolish by many.

Secondly, Neil Skinner has suggested in a personal communication that the adventures of certain characters in recent Hausa novels could be considered as *yawon duniya*. These stories represent fantasies and adventures which frequently involve the widespread travels of their heroes (Skinner 1971). Certainly one of the attractions of the walk to Dandi is the element of the unknown, the gaining of worldly knowledge and experience, the seeing of far-away, wonderful places. Indeed, as Alhaji Mamman Shata sings in one of his recorded songs, *yawon duniya mafarki ne* ('the walk of the world is a dream').

The members of itinerant dance troupes, comprised of young males and prostitutes who have for a while forsaken setting up their own families, and considered by most citizens as children of the world whose form of entertainment is immoral, frequently abandon teams which stay too long in any one town and move to others. They have a great taste for seeing new towns and faces. It is true that the Hausa value 'sight-seeing' but not when it involves forgetting more important things, and to the extent that *yawon Dandi* can lead to such forgetfulness in the search for experience it is considered unrealistic, childish, and like the fanciful flights of imagination that characterize novels is not to be taken seriously. Thus there is the contrast between reality on the one hand, and fantasy and dream on the other.

A third contrast is between stability and substance on the one hand, and wind and air on the other. Another term frequently is used synonymously with *d'an duniya*, namely *d'an iska* ('child of the wind'). In one defintion of *d'an iska*, the Hausa do not usually have a migrant in mind, but a person who is evil, even if he is stationary and well-to-do. But it is frequently used for an unemployed child of the world, or one with a very low status such as porter, truck-pusher, procurer, or prostitute's servant, or a migrant to Dandi who has run into very hard times; someone who is forced to take up a life of crime, to become a devil (*iblis*). Thus there are those who believe that *d'an duniya* and *d'an iska* are the same, and because this is so the former term is strengthened in its pejorative connotation. To some the metaphor of the wind as referable to *yawon Dandi* becomes clear when they are asked why the word *iska* ('wind') is used to describe evil people. One informant stated,

'Air moves freely. No one has control over it. No one can say a wind has parents of any consequence. Perhaps *'yan iska* cannot trace their parents anymore and go about endlessly from town to town. Because of this they are spoken of as *shegu*, bastards.'

Another said,

'The wind cannot stay in one place; when it blows hard you feel it on your body, and someone six miles away can feel it, too. The *'yan iska* have no special place to live. They are nothing, like the air.'

Thus again we have a structural positioning similar to *yawon duniya*. However, whereas the true child of the wind may be a criminal, the child of Dandi is only a deviant in the type of his mobility. In many cases he may still endeavour to conform to Hausa norms of deference and to the tenets of Islam.

A fourth contrast is between 'shamefulness' (*kunya*) and 'shamelessness' (*rashin kunya*). This will be dealt with later, but we note here that *yawon Dandi* is connected with *rashin kunya* for two possible reasons. First, the migrant, no matter how good a Moslem he may profess to be, will still come in contact with and possibly learn shameful behaviour in the culturally hetero-geneous Dandi, such as spending much time with prostitutes, going to the cinema, drinking alcohol, and gambling. Secondly, the migrant may have left home to escape social pressure because of embarrassing circumstances. In the first Dandi is seen as a place of irreligious temptations; in the second, family quarrels, poverty and debt, adultery, gossip and false accusation, and suchlike may give the migrant cause to remove himself from having to deal with these matters. Furthermore, the domestic group as well as the entire network of kin and all social relations require the nicest manipulation of norms of behaviour to which shame is central. The household is the centre of propriety and can actually be termed a 'public' or 'community' (*jama'a*) in Hausa. The Hausa say of their family life, *Allah fisshemu kunyar zaman tare* ('may Allah see us through the shame of living together').

A final contrast is that between Islam and paganism. The one who enters the mother-world will usually go to a culturally heterogeneous place where there are many tempting sins. A prostitute has already committed the irreligious act of breaking familial bonds or escaping purdah, and a small minority of urban prostitutes are traditionally associated with the pre-Islamic *bori* spirit possession cult. Also, the land of Dandi or any urban centre given that name is subject to Western, modern, Christian influences. Dandi can be classed as belonging to the Land of War (*dar-ul-harb*), as against the Land of Faith (*dar-ul-Islam*). It is a place of *haramci*, unlawful behaviour which is religiously forbidden. An effort to counteract this may certainly account in part for the religious fervour of the Hausa in Yorubaland who find themselves strangers amidst what to them is a pagan culture, and also might account in part for the Hausa belief in the 'mystical dangers' of their taking Yoruba wives (Cohen 1969: 53-4).

The above discussion has given the following set of contrasts, positive on the left and negative on the right:

Gida (home)	*Dandi/duniya (the world)*
1 sanity	a structural similarity to madness
2 reality	fantasy, dream
3 stability, substance	wind, air
4 shamefulness	shamelessness
5 Islam	paganism, *haramci*

The terms in each column help to understand the Hausa attitude toward *yawon Dandi* and *zaman gida*. Those in each group tend to relate to one another. For example the terms on the right almost all share in common notions of shame, bastardy, and *banza* ('falseness, uselessness'). Following Turner (1964) this set defines a kind of structural outsiderhood and inferiority unique to the Hausa cultural experience.[1] It points up by contrast a Hausa cultural preference for familial interdependency and domestic status and roles on the one hand, and on the other a not unfrequently known search by some individuals for independence, floating extra-kin relations, and freedom − a search that flies in the face of normative attitudes.

The sociocultural background to Hausa spatial mobility and yawon Dandi

We are now in a position to speculate about the sociocultural elements which inform Hausa spatial mobility generally and the walk of the world in particular.

Yawo and the field of the world

The frequent use of the word *yawo* in Hausa terms for spatial mobility is interesting. At first, there seems to be no common characteristic, other than movement, which separates all of those emic categories beginning with the term *yawo* from those which do not. Both *yawon k'wadago* and *cin rani* are low status and imply poverty; both *k'aura* and *yawon kasuwanci* are equally serious in intent and related usually to livelihood, while *yawon bud'in ido* is more light-hearted. Movement designated by all of the terms, whether *yawo* is customarily mentioned or not, have historically involved walking more than transport by animal or vehicle, although today cheaper vehicular transport is usually involved. Also, whereas a term like *yawon bud'in ido* implies more mobility, *yawon duniya* is a more committed form of circulation.

At a deeper level, it is intriguing to speculate whether there *is* a kinship among all of the terms in which *yawo* is used, such that a stroll in the town immediately outside of the compound, and a wandering in the wide world, are equally a 'walk'. There is the impression that in the Hausa view there is not much cognitive distinction between stepping a few yards from the door of the compound and travelling a hundred miles away, and that movements of the order of the first can easily and naturally extend to the second. Thus we have the case of a man who abandoned his family almost on impulse by changing his day's 'walk of marketing' into a 'walk of the world' which lasted for many years (Olofson 1976: 73). This suggests a cognitive distinction, however, between the *gida*, centre of the family and the domain of women, and the town and the whole world made up of towns which become in Islamic societies the domain of men, largely forbidden to proper women of child-bearing age. Thus the entire world outside of the *zaure* ('entrance-parlour') becomes one vast, equally-charged behavioural field wherein men move near and far to pursue their business (*harka*, 'interaction'). For married women too, restricted by purdah to *cikin gida* (the interior of the compound) except for special occasions, a few yards beyond the compound might as well be much more. The centre of the field is the *gida* and its domestic group is the major reference point − except for the vagrant insane and other wanderers.

Spatial mobility of the young

Through Hausa child-rearing, independent and relatively far-ranging spatial mobility begins at a much younger age than in, for example, British and American cultures. Children of both sexes, once they have learned to walk well, will soon be given a free run even in a large town, and will learn their way around it in some detail. Even at the age of not much more than six small girls can be engaged in hawking the products of their restricted mothers, and boys may be selling from hand-trays small amounts of goods given to them by their fathers in return for a small commission or gift. Thus as early as possible they gain knowledge involving transactions. These activities for boys are likely to increase once they are circumcised, when they are believed to have gained 'sense'. Children of both sexes are pressed early into service to act as messengers between compounds for women in purdah. By the time he is eight or nine, circumcised, and possibly a Koranic student, a Hausa boy will have no trouble ranging a city in search of alms.

The structure of domestic space

Also related to socialization is the structural disposition of domestic space with respect to male-female relationships. The Hausa male has no place within a compound which he can truly consider his own − unless of course he is wealthy enough to have a very large compound. Much of his leisure time, rest, eating of meals, and work as a craftsman, takes place in the *zaure* or just outside the entrance to the compound. The interior of the compound belongs to the wives, where they cook, wash, and take care of children, and where they are so restricted that the husband is expected to go to market to do the day's food shopping. One elder pointed out a similarity between the *zaure* and the walls of a city: just as the city walls are neither inside nor outside a city, so is the *zaure* neither inside nor outside a compound. In other words, though wives are frequently shy of coming there, where they might too easily be seen from the street, and it is used mainly by men, the *zaure* is still seen as a passage-room built into the wall of the compound. The city and the world beyond it are the true domain of men, and from early age boys learn to make full use of spatial mobility in that domain. This is more true with the onset of puberty when they begin to be pulled away from their mothers and sisters to sleep in the *zaure* or some other room nearby. The outside, the town, is also the playground of girls, so that by contrast when they marry the consequent seclusion may become unbearable to many of them.

Norms of behaviour

One who goes into Dandi may leave home to escape social pressures arising from conflict within the compound, a problem which was referred to by Alice Dry, one of the early social researchers in Hausaland, in a passage on migrants of the *'yan Dandi* category, though she did not use that term herself:

> The very detached attitudes towards both infants and children help produce the low emotional tone of the society where strong emotional expression is deprecated and emotional attachments are rare. As a result of this lack of personal relationships the Hausa finds a large part of his security in his membership of the group . . . For the child the group is small, but for the adult it extends to all Hausas. From the center of the group, his own family, the adult can expect full physical support, while from the periphery he will get at least shelter and bare subsistence. With this widespread security it is easy for any member of the society faced with a difficult situation to solve his problems by simply going away from them. This running away from any situation of strains is the normal pattern, and the consequent easing of tension before they become internalised results in an extremely low incidence of neurosis . . . Authority is inevitable and therefore un-questioned, direct disobedience is inconceivable, but the art of non-compliance reaches a high level; and should authority become really importunate it is always possible to go away. (Dry 1956: 169-70).

Parts of this generally correct statement may be qualified. The point that 'running away from any situation of strains is the normal pattern' seems wrong in the sense that *yawon Dandi*, which occurs frequently (though *how* frequently is not known), is considered deviant. Dry's idea of a 'very low emotional tone' also needs careful thought. This may have come from observation of first-born avoidance, which is a societal norm. But how can this low tone be measured? Is it more or less than the lack of emotion said to be characteristic of the English? In any case, there is rarely a complete lack of personal relationships as is implied. Both sexes have relations of trust in bond-friends. Children, especially last-born children, have such relations with parents, and there is much affection between grandparents and grand-children. The structure of sentiment is different from that known in Dry's own culture (English), and, moreover, is much more *highly* structured, for among kin there are distinctive play or joking relations, fondness relations, and shame and respect relations. Dry states a case for explaining migration in *negative* terms; a lack of 'emotional tone' makes it easy for a person to leave. There is rather more likely a *positive* contributing factor, namely the elaborate system of behavioural norms which pressure some personalities in some instances to seek escape.

The Hausa have a complex of concepts relating to the presentation of self according to which individuals are scrutin-ized. This involves elaborate codes of deference and demeanour which if not followed will bring to the offender accusations of anti-sociability, evilness, or at least suspicions of not being well. Shame, *kunya*, is at the core of the system. It can be variously translated according to situations to which the word applies: modesty, embarrassment, shyness, or face. There is also respect or *girmamawa*, literally 'giving size' as in 'giving face'; cheer-fulness or *fara'a*; the presentation of one having self-respect or *mutumci*; patience or *hakuri*; kindness or *kirki*; and an admirable presence or *kwarjini*. A person has to achieve a proper balance of these to have good character. They form an interactive system, such that a person whose *fara'a* makes him overloud in public endangers his *kunya*. On the other hand a personality rarely given to smile may be said to not like people, or to have too much shame. *Kunya* and *girmamawa* reinforce each other. There is respect involved in treating others with shame, and shame in presenting proper rituals of respect to age and authority.

In any instance of social stress with 'loss of face', especially within the compound, all of these systematically interrelated dimensions seem to be brought into play and into the judgment of an individual, so that the strain in the social relations is magnified. Relations are also affected in a society which leaves little room for privacy. When this happens there is pressure against the assumptions – the hopes pervading all human relations – that a man or woman is what he or she claims to be, or is what others want; that what the actor says or does outwardly is also meant in the heart. When all of this becomes doubtful, and a definition of self and situation cannot be maintained, pressure could become so great that to leave becomes the only solution. It is interesting to note here that an ensuing migration is analogous to what the Hausa call *borin kunya*, where an individual who commits a very embarrassing *faux pas* in an interaction only loses more by attempting to regain face. When a family member runs away, the situation is possibly made worse by his doing so. Not only has he committed the original 'sin', whatever that may be, but he has gone to Dandi as well. The family is exposed to the shame of having one of its own, potentially at least, a prostitute or child of the wind.

Some personalities thus find, at some time in their lives, existence in a Hausa compound to be difficult. The allocation of the inside to females and the outside to adolescent and adult males demarcates boundaries. The pressure emanates from the social expectation at all levels of community that interaction take place according to narrow and rigid norms of generally acceptable behaviour. The newly married woman may find the social life in restricted quarters, with hostile, jealous or authoritarian co-wives and husband's female relations, uncomfortable perhaps intolerable. Once a wife steps a few feet out of the compound without permission of the husband, she is already in the 'world' and might as well be miles away. Thus it is that many who do run away do not simply go to the neighbours or home to a father who would only send them back, but flee to a prostitute's compound in a distant town and take up an independent life. Sons and husbands also may seek flight when they find that norms interfere with their individuality.

It cannot be said that all migration which the Hausa call *yawon duniya* is necessarily the result of shameful flight. However, connotations of shame do tinge, more or less, the kind of structural outsiderhood which being in Dandi implies, connotations that spill over from the situation described above to other kinds of reasons for moving and staying away from home.

Concluding perspective

The last section began by suggesting how the word *yawo* might have come to be used for movement in space relatively near the compound and to far-distant destinations. It has become apparent that the field into which men and women move themselves from their compounds, the 'world' which is properly masculine whether near or far, has become a symbol of selfish and self-seeking individualism.

However, it is a mistake to overstress the lack of kin obligations among the Hausa because of this, nor should their positive evaluation and maintenance be overstressed. The most realistic point of view, which requires further research to be demonstrated in detailed cases, is that there seems to be in Hausa society a tension, a countervailing set of pressures, between individualism and the apparent need for dependency on, and interdependency with, kin or kin substitutes.

Several clues as to the correctness of this perspective appear in the data. The relation of fathers and sons is instructive. This is a prime relation of trust. Sons may be the only ones to know the commercial and financial secrets of their fathers and they expect to inherit from them. Beneath the shame-respect there appears to lie a stratum of fondness. Unhappy is the man who has no son. Yet it seems that sons may also chafe under the authoritarian rule of their fathers while they remain at home. Thus, after the death of the father, a set of brothers even of the same mother may eventually acquire separate compounds and lands, becoming the masters in their own homes. To do this before his death is shameless, as it is to leave him or to look for an occupation different from his. Previous work has shown that even in the cases of *yawon Dandi* many will wait until the death of a father before setting out (Olofson 1976). But it is said that sons do run away while their fathers are still living, and when they do their fathers may curse them and because of this they run into bad luck in Dandi. But the temper of the fathers will cool and they will long for the return of their sons.

Despite the frequency with which brothers decide to dwell apart, due to what is known as *d'anuwanci*, 'brotherhood', (i.e. the rivalrous ill-feeling between brothers), a centripetal tendency may still develop under changed circumstances – so that brothers return to each other, or a man claims his brother's son for adoption, or patrilineal kin frequently set up domestic units together (Smith 1955: 32-3, 48).

Moreover, a son who leaves home to go to another town, or into the diaspora, may set himself up in a dependency relation of patron-clientship (*barantaka*) with an older, wealthier man who becomes again a sort of father to him. A patron may have several such clients for whom he may supply food, lodging, clothing, and occasionally even an arranged marriage.

Women who run away exhibit much the same need. In expressing their free will they go to a courtesans' compound where they come to some extent under the control of the head or 'mother' of the courtesans (*magajiya*). Many women leave one husband they do not like to pursue this life for the purpose of finding a man whom they *would* like as a husband – a notion which is quite foreign to the Western view of prostitution.

Yusuf (1975) in an article on Kano traders, writes of a modal Hausa commercial personality, where a man is

> highly individualistic when it comes to organizing his commercial enterprise. The desire to fare best in most situations and to 'save the face of one's home' even if it may involve the shaming of one's paternal siblings and friends, are among several of the prime factors which possibly enable the Hausa to be among the most indefatigable traders in all of Africa.

He goes on to suggest that clientship and long-distance entre-preneurship are means of 'proving one's worth in his natal home' though this is true only in terms of asserting personal worth, not in terms of undergoing a sort of socially expected *rite de passage* into manhood. Thus the Hausa strain toward individuality is emphasized. But a few lines later, Yusuf brings another tendency to the fore:

> as income grows, the trader will attempt to bring his kinsmen together and gradually expand his household. By enlarging his compound, he attracts more dependents and thus increases his social and economic obligations in the domestic or customary exchange sphere (Yusuf 1975: 179).

With this comes prestige. Commercial individualism eventually leads to a large compound of dependent kin and clients.

In a parallel manner for some, the combination of behavioural norms in a particular family situation restricts them too much and drives them out. Relatively few of these individuals probably remain 'out' forever, most eventually re-establish themselves in a domestic group, either their own or that of someone else.

In sum, we believe that the opposition *gida : Dandi*, and even the formation of the great Hausa diaspora, revolves much around these contradictory or at least countervailing tendencies. It is not entirely clear what is the ultimate origin of an individual's expressions of, on the one hand, a 'radical' assertion of individuality and mobile personality which makes *yawon Dandi* to a great extent a phenomenon of expressive culture, and on the other a 'conservative' dependency or interdependency within a domestic unit, where the patriarch needs his kinsmen and clients for purposes of his own prestige as much as they need him economically. It seems that the fulfilment of these two needs can

73

be met nicely, either simultaneously or successively. But it is hoped that future studies of how Hausa socialize their children, within the behavioural field involving both the domestic scene and the world beyond the *zaure*, will throw more light on this dynamic aspect of their society.

Acknowledgment

Research for this paper was carried out in Funtua, southern Katsina, northern Nigeria, in 1970-1 and was financed by the Centre of International Studies, University of Pittsburg.

Note

1 The application of Victor Turner's (1969) concept of 'structural outsiderhood' to *yawon Dandi* developed in this paper might seem to be more accurately devoted to the analysis of the world of Hausa scholars, students, and pilgrims. Admitting this, it is questionable whether the Hausa might see this world not as 'structurally outside' but rather much more 'inside' and to the point in terms of the most deeply held values of everyday life and culture. There is also a great difference in 'structural outsiderhood' as used here and by Turner in that his concept points up the holiness of the condition as in the case of religious orders while *yawon Dandi* is an emically quite profane kind of phenomenon. Turner's concept can be used to analyse more types of social phenomena than he originally intended.

4 Circulation in West Java, Indonesia

Graeme J. Hugo

The 1971 Census of the Republic of Indonesia classified 7.34 million persons, or 6.4 per cent of the national population, as migrants. Superficially these figures would appear to confirm the conventional stereotyping of most Indonesians (particularly the inhabitants of Java) as immobile peasants who are born, live and die in the same house, scarcely travelling beyond the confines of their village. The failure of any more than a trickle of Javans to move to the Outer Islands of Indonesia under resettlement schemes has reinforced this image.[1] However the moves made by the persons defined for census purposes as migrants represent only one highly selective sub-set of the complex totality of population mobility in Indonesia. The aim here is to demonstrate the nature and importance of temporary population movements, the bulk of which are not detected by conventional census and survey questions, by examining such mobility in one of the provinces of Indonesia.

The sub-set of population mobility detected by the migration questions included in the sample enumeration of the 1971 Indonesian census was of persons who had more-or-less permanently changed their place of usual residence and in doing so had crossed a provincial boundary (Figure 4.1). Since only inter-provincial movement was measured most short and medium distance movers were regarded as non-migrants. This problem was exacerbated not only by the fact that most provinces were large in both population and areal terms but also by wide variations in their size and shape.[2] Perhaps more importantly the census enumeration was conducted on the basis of a complex combined *de jure/de facto* principle which meant that most persons temporarily absent from their usual place of residence on census day were enumerated as non-migrants even if in moving

75

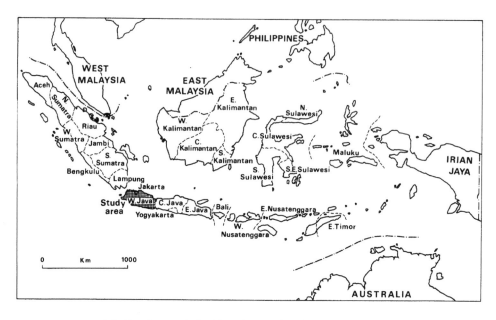

FIGURE 4.1 South-east Asia: Provinces of Indonesia and study area

they had crossed a provincial boundary (Hugo 1978a: 11).

Although the inter-provincial, more-or-less permanent, migration detected by the census is but one aspect of population mobility in Indonesia, in the absence of alternative statistics census migration data have been interpreted as representing total population movement trends in much of the contemporary literature. This has not always been the case. Several pre-Independence commentators, not blinkered by models of migration developed in Western contexts and who did not restrict their analysis to published census-type statistics presented a quite different picture of the mobility of Java's inhabitants. Haan (1912 I: 31-2) characterized the Sundanese of West Java in the pre-1800 era as 'wanderers'. Scheltema (1926) drew on his own long experience in the Netherlands East Indies as well as the writings of his colleague Ranneft (1916) to produce a classification of population movement in Java which, with minor modifications, the present writer found to have considerable relevance in contemporary West Java (Table 4.1). The most striking feature of Scheltema's classification, an interpretation of which is presented below, is its clear recognition of the importance of various types of non-permanent population movements in Java.

The colonial officials undertaking the only comprehensive and reliable, pre-Independence census of the Netherlands East Indies in 1930 made the following comment on Javan mobility (Volkstelling, VIII, 1936: 46). 'The population movements in Java and Madura have been numerous and the number of migrants is great. This is not a phenomenon of the more recent times only since reports from former years point to the great mobility of the population of Java.' This perception of Javan mobility is quite different to those of more recent students who have based their analysis on 1961 and 1971 census inter-provincial migration data (e.g. McNicoll 1968). However the 1930 census mobility data is still the most comprehensive collected for Indonesia and allowed a greater range of mobility types to be detected. This was possible first because the 1930 Volkstelling employed much smaller migration-defining regions and hence permitted movers covering only short distances to be identified, and secondly because it collected some data on non-permanent population movements.

TABLE 4.1 *An interpretation of Scheltema's classification of population mobility in Java (Scheltema 1926: 872-3)*

	Type of movement	Scheltema's example
(i)	Local movements	Movements to a neighbouring village (e.g. marriage migration).
(ii)	Temporary movements	Movements to an area to construct railway or irrigation works or to go on the *haj* (pilgrimage to Mecca).
(iii)	Periodic movements	Movements caused by seasonal demands for labour, especially in agriculture.
(iv)	Semi-permanent moves	People who earn their living in one place while their family stays at another e.g. clerks and servants working in the city while their family stays in their home village.
(v)	Permanent movement	(a) Within Java. (b) To other Indonesian islands. (c) To overseas destinations.

The significance of population movements *per se* in Indonesia may be demonstrated by focusing, in one region of that country, on a wider range of types of population mobility than can be detected in census sources. Accordingly some of the findings of a

1973 investigation into population mobility in the western third of the island of Java are examined here. The study area in 1976 supported 22 per cent of Indonesia's 130 million people on 2.5 per cent of the national land area of 2.03 million km². By any of the conventionally used criteria the region must be classified as economically underdeveloped. At the time of study annual average per capita income was estimated to be less than US$50 (Daroesman 1972: 50), some 80 per cent of the rural population earn incomes below the national poverty line of minimum subsistence standards (White 1979: 94) and the bulk of the labour force engage in semi-subsistence activities. The province has high fertility (Total Fertility Rate = 5.6) and high but falling mortality rates (Life Expectancy at Birth is estimated to be 44). The region was selected for study because it contained, and was the major source of migrants to, two of Indonesia's largest urban centres: the national capital of Jakarta (1976, 5.4 million) and Bandung (1971, 1.2 million). The material included is drawn from a larger study (Hugo, 1975 and 1978a) which is based on an analysis of available documentary sources of mobility information for the entire province, on extensive fieldwork in the region and especially on intensive surveys of 14 village communities which were selected on a purposive basis to be reasonably representative of the major source areas of movers from rural West Java to the cities of Jakarta and Bandung. The villages studied are in no way a random sample of all West Javan villages but they illustrate patterns of population movement between village and city which investigation indicated are significant over wide areas of the province.

Contemporary circulation in West Java

One of the earliest findings of reconnaissance fieldwork in the study area was that the rural West Javans have two distinctly different concepts of outmovement from their village which are generally referred to locally as *pindah* and *merantau*.[3] Although dictionaries (Echols and Shadily, 1963) define these terms similarly – the former as 'to move' and the latter 'to leave one's home area' – they have come to connote important differences in the mover's intended duration of absence. Although it was not possible to gain any consistent expression of this difference in absolute time terms a mover talking in terms of *pindah* will generally have no plans to return to his village to live but if he regards his move as *merantau* he has intentions of returning.[4] This distinction is institutionalized in that persons intending to move out of the village permanently are required to obtain a different type of permit than those leaving the village temporarily and that each type of move is recorded in separate registers maintained by village officials. As fieldwork proceeded it became increasingly apparent that non-permanent mobility strategies were dominant in most villages. This study focuses particularly on movements from village to city but similar patterns were also observed with respect to movements between rural areas.

To some extent an element of circularity may be detected in the interprovincial migration data of the 1971 Indonesian sample census. Persons were asked both their province of birth and the province in which they last resided before moving to their present province of residence. In any single province persons whom the birthplace information showed were born in that province, but the province of previous residence data indicated had at some time lived outside that province, had obviously engaged in circular migration which had terminated with them returning to their province of birth. These persons are referred to here as 'lifetime return migrants' and in 1971 they comprised 1.53 million persons, a fifth of all interprovincial migrants. The extent of lifetime circular mobility evident in census interprovincial migration statistics is perhaps surprising given that the time criterion adopted in the enumeration prevented the detection of most movers who were absent from their home province for less than six months, but it does point to the major significance of circularity in Indonesian population mobility.

One of the major origins of migrants returning to their province of birth was the metropolitan centre of Jakarta. Table 4.2 shows that 63.2 per cent (270,620 persons) of outmigrants from the capital were persons returning to their province of birth. Since many of these return migrants were accompanied by children born to them in Jakarta it can be safely inferred that the phenomenon of return movement accounts for substantially more than two thirds of the migration out of Jakarta. The study area of West Java is clearly the most significant recipient of lifetime-return migrants from Jakarta.

The figure obtained for lifetime return migration from Jakarta is equivalent to 15 per cent of the lifetime migrants residing in Jakarta at the time of the 1971 census. However since the census migration figures included only people who had fulfilled the requirement of living continuously in Jakarta for at least 6 months, the return migrants detected were only a subset of all movers who had circulated between Jakarta and their birthplaces.

The fact that census lifetime return migration represents only the 'tip of the iceberg' of a much larger and complex pattern of movement between village and city is indicated in the data

TABLE 4.2 *Lifetime return migration from Jakarta to other Indonesian provinces, 1971*

Province	Lifetime return migrants	% of all migrants from Jakarta
Aceh	4,371	77.7
North Sumatra	2,765	44.2
West Sumatra	12,702	88.5
Riau	1,973	35.2
Jambi	1,376	35.4
South Sumatra	6,282	33.1
Bengkulu	939	58.7
Lampung	2,144	9.9
West Java	115,350	69.4
Central Java	72,083	77.4
Yogyakarta	5,977	52.1
East Java	16,695	43.2
Bali	4,219	34.2
West Nusatenggara	4,360	94.9
East Nusatenggara	460	92.7
West Kalimantan	0	0
Central Kalimantan	0	0
South Kalimantan	34	6.9
East Kalimantan	570	33.2
North Sulawesi	14,249	84.2
Central Sulawesi	74	48.7
South Sulawesi	2,825	65.9
South East Sulawesi	65	100.0
Maluku	722	43.2
Irian Jaya	385	34.5
Total	270,620	63.2

Source: Indonesian Census of 1971, Series C Tabulations

collected in the fourteen survey villages. Figure 4.2 shows the relative incidence of three types of village-city population movement in the survey villages. Only movements to seek to engage in work or formal education were considered, so that a wide range of moves to visit relatives, seek entertainment, go shopping etc. are ignored. The unshaded portions of the circles indicate the proportion of moves to urban areas which fulfilled census migration time criteria. The unshaded sections thus include two types of rural-urban movers

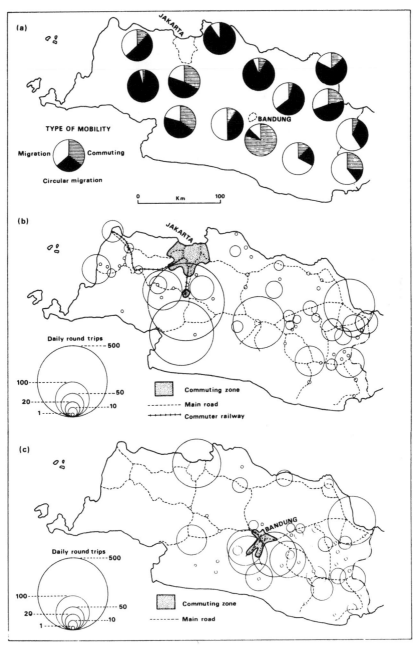

FIGURE 4.2 (a) West Java survey villages: mobility strategies of males
moving to urban centres, 1973
(b) Number of round trips made each day by buses from seven localities
in West Java to Jakarta, April 1973. (Source: Propinsi Java Barat,
Jabatan Lelis Lintas Dan Angkutan Jalan Raya)
(c) Number of round trips made each day from seven localities in West
Java to Bandung, April 1973 (Source: as in b)

(a)   Persons permanently changing their place of residence from the village to a city.

(b)   Persons temporarily moving to a city but who spent at least 6 continuous months in that city before returning to their village. The incidence of circulation between the survey villages and urban areas which does not fulfil the census time criteria is indicated in the shaded sections of the diagram. A distinction is made between *commuting* where the mover regularly (though not necessarily every day) goes to a city to work or attend an educational institution but returns most nights, and *circular migration* in which the mover's absence usually involves him sleeping at his destination for continuous periods of up to six months.

Commuting

Long distance commuting to urban areas from peripheral, essentially rural districts is a mobility phenomenon usually associated with so-called 'developed' Euro-American countries and the greatly enhanced individual mobility which advances in transportation technology have made possible. Yet in many peri-urban areas of Third World cities a distinctive commuter culture is emerging. The huge scale of this contemporary rural-urban commuting can best be appreciated by standing at the edge of the city of Yogyakarta in central Java (1971 population 342,267) during the early morning and observing the flow of tens of thousands of commuters from surrounding rural areas which cram the three major roads leading into the city aboard packed minibuses and buses and an unending stream of bicycles and pedestrians (Inst. of Rural and Regional Studies 1977; Mantra 1978; Mudjiman 1978). Daily commuting by foot to work in urban areas from villages up to 12 km away is not uncommon in Java (Castles, 1967: 53; Hugo 1978a: 105), but greatly increased ownership of bicycles and the availability of bus and mini-bus public transport services have resulted in considerable extensions of the commuter-sheds of Indonesian cities.

In the West Java study area the two major centres of Jakarta and Bandung have become very important destinations of commuters. A substantial daily flow of workers to and from Jakarta and the West Javan *kabupaten* adjoining the Jakarta metropolitan area (Tanggerang, Bogor and Bekasi) has been recognized since the early 1950s (Ormeling 1953). Since then massive economic expansion in Jakarta and major improvements in public transport have greatly increased the number of commuters from these three *kabupaten*, which were known by the Dutch as the capital's *Ommelanden*. Unfortunately a comprehensive set of data relating to the number of commuters travelling daily is not available. A 1975 estimate (Kompas, 16 January, 5) indicated that 60 per cent of the workforce in *Kecamatan* Depok (a sub-region of *Kabupaten* Bogor with a population of 170,000 inhabitants) worked in Jakarta, as well as some 100,000 other persons living elsewhere in *Kabupaten* Bogor. This does not include the inhabitants of Bogor City who commute to Jakarta and who are estimated conservatively by municipal officials to include 20 per cent of the city's total workforce (i.e. 11,000 persons). Express bus and rail services facilitate commuting of higher income groups who live in the comparatively cool and healthy 'hill station' climate of Bogor and work in Jakarta.

The increasing significance of commuting in the *Ommelanden* is reflected in the fact that at the 1971 census the percentages of workforce members living in the *rural* sections of Tanggerang, Bogor and Bekasi who were employed in agriculture were only 40.9 per cent, 46.4 per cent and 65.7 per cent respectively. It is further indicated indirectly in the huge number of public transport vehicles which enter Jakarta each day along the three main roads from Tanggerang, Bogor and Bekasi from destinations within those *kabupaten* (i.e. those designated 'local' in the table) (Table 4.3). The table takes no account of the substantial volume of commuting by railroad from Bogor and Tanggerang.

TABLE 4.3 *Daily public transport traffic flows into Jakarta and Bandung along main roads, August 1973*

	No. of vehicles entering city		
	Bus	*Mini-bus and automobile*	*Bemo*[a]
Jakarta (total)	2,096	11,992	92
Jakarta (local)	1,065	6,626	92
Change 1971-3 (%)	+112.4%	+106.9%	+338.1%
Bandung (total)	1,473	11,491	226
Bandung (local)	646	6,219	226
Change 1971-3 (%)	+39.0%	+40.1%	+927.3%

[a] Three-wheeled jitney

Source: Statistics supplied by Direktorat Jenderal Bina Marga Jawa Barat

Rural-urban commuting is also well established around the other urban centres of the survey area, especially the city of Bandung. Only 52.9 per cent of the rural work force in the *kabupaten* surrounding Bandung had agricultural occupations in 1971 while the daily flow of mini-buses and *bemos* into the city from its commuter-shed was almost as large as the traffic into Jakarta, despite the latter's greater size and attractive power.

It is useful to distinguish between autochthonous commuters (i.e. natives of an area who travel to urban work places) and allochthonous commuters (i.e. persons who have migrated to homes in the commuter zone). The latter, for example, are most important in the areas immediately adjacent to Jakarta and Bandung's urban boundaries and in Bogor. Commuting is often part of a suburbanization process involving migration from the central city to its periphery in search of better housing for limited money and perhaps more rural surroundings which are similar to those in the home village. Fieldwork indicated that the substantial movement from Jakarta to northern Depok and of Bandung people to nearby Cimahi is generally motivated by the availability of cheaper housing. In some cases commuting represented the only way in which people could stay in the city with their families because costs of inner city housing were beyond their means. The movement of Jakartans to Bogor however can not be primarily motivated by these factors since living costs are as high there as in Jakarta. Rather this is largely a continuation of the trend established when the Dutch Governor General shifted his palace to Bogor in the mid-eighteenth century − a search by upper income groups for a more congenial and comfortable living environment.

The autochthonous commuters are influenced in their decision to *stay* in their home village by many of the factors that motivate allochthonous commuters to migrate out of the central city. Urban residence means higher costs for housing, food and schooling as well as separation from relatives and friends and from a familiar and valued way of life. As with some of the allochthonous commuters there is no choice − some commuters earn so little that they simply cannot afford to live in the city. Thus *becak* (pedicab) drivers from the south of Bandung cannot earn a living from agriculture in their village and the meagre returns they obtain from hours of strenuous work in the city certainly is not sufficient to enable them to support their families in an urban residence. In fact their income is so near subsistence that if a special half-fare they have negotiated with local bus operators was withdrawn, they and their families would not have enough to eat. The choice in this case is thus between commuting and insufficient food intake. In the case of a government servant from southwest of Bandung working in the city however, the decision is between a *better* standard of housing, food etc. in the village than in the city and the social and cultural benefit of closeness to kin groups and rural surroundings.

Despite the impact of improved transport the time constraint of the definition of commuting used here considerably restricts the distance that commuters can traverse. Commuting was only of major significance in those survey villages located within 50 km of a significant urban centre (Figure 4.2). The heaviest rates of commuting were recorded in a village located some 18 km southeast of Bandung Municipality. In this village, as in many surrounding Bandung and Jakarta, a distinctive type of 'commuter culture' is emerging. At 5.00 a.m. each weekday morning one can see more than one hundred villagers waiting alongside the Bandung road for buses to the City which are crammed both inside and on their roofs with commuters. On arrival in the City they hire a pedi-cab from a middleman (often a Chinese merchant or an army officer) for the twelve hours (US$ 0.30) from 6 a.m. to 6 p.m. They then push it around the City in all types of weather in a search for fares to make up the heavy overheads of US$ 0.50 (including a minimal US$ 0.10 for food and drinks during the day). It is dark by the time they wearily return to the village with their meagre net takings rarely exceeding US$ 0.25. It is only in recent years that the improvement and relative cheapening of public transport have made commuting possible. Before 1970 the *becak* drivers could return only once a week and had to spend many cold, wet nights sleeping cramped in their pedicabs, the legacy of which is apparent in the poor health of many of the older *becak* drivers.

The strong frictional effect of time and travel cost severely limit the distance which commuters can travel. However in West Java as in many parts of the non-Western world there is growing evidence of people living beyond the commuting limit, yet gaining the benefits enjoyed by autochthonous commuters by engaging in circular movements between their home area and their place of work or schooling.

Circular movements

Non-permanency in outmovement from villages is a pattern which can be traced back several hundred years in West Java, perhaps even to the shifting agricultural systems which dominated the economy of the region up to the period of Javanese colonization from the east during the sixteenth century. In the colonial era a wide range of types of temporary mobility were in evidence (Table 4.1). To some degree these movements are discernible in the 1930 Census migration statistics since a separate category of persons 'temporarily present' at the place of enumeration was recognized. In West Java these amounted to 83,360 persons or 0.76 per cent of the total population of the Province. However there is evidence that these figures grossly understate both the extent and influence of temporary migration (a)   Because the bulk of the persons 'temporarily present' were breadwinners their movement will have had an effect not only on them but also on their families remaining in the villages of origin and thus impinge on a greater number of people than the above figure would suggest.

(b)   More importantly, a census is taken at one point in time. Because the rates of temporary migration vary considerably with different seasons and conditions in villages, census figures will not include large numbers of temporary migrants who are absent from the village at other times of the year, but happen to be in the village on census night.

(c)   Moreover the 1930 census takers reported that substantial numbers of people returned to their home village expressly to be enumerated. (Volkstelling I, 1933: 93).

> During census-taking from several sides was received the information that a number of persons − either on order of their village headman, or from their own will − returned to their villages in order to be enumerated there; very probably a large percentage of these persons would have belonged to the group of persons temporarily·present, if they had not returned home. It may be possible as well that they had two domiciles; it seems that for instance servants from Buitenzorg in Baravia or coolies from Bantam in Priok (sic) or workmen from Garoet (sic) in the service of tea-estates in Bandoeng, Tjianjoer and Soekabumi (sic) sometimes own small houses in their own birth district or elsewhere.

Clearly, circular mobility was well-established in West Java by the time of Indonesian independence in 1945; however it is possible to identify some developments which have favoured its recent expansion. Among the most significant of these is the recent rapid growth in the public transport sector (Table 4.4). Between 1968 and 1977 the number of persons per registered motorized vehicle fell from 571.4 in West Java. Clearly for mass short-term movements a reliable, cheap, efficient transportation system is necessary. For permanent movement costs of transport are generally a minor consideration. In temporary movements, transport constitutes a significant continuing cost. In West Java the vast majority of the population rely upon public transport for distances which cannot be reasonably covered by walking or bicycle. The complex public transport system is made up of a huge range of vehicles which vary greatly in their fare structures, speed, efficiency and labour intensity. These vary from pedicabs and three-wheeled jitneys over short, usually intra-urban distances, through mini-buses of varying size and vintage, to buses and trains. There is the well-established practice of 'hitching' rides on the back of passing trucks. Rail transport is important for some commuting near Jakarta and Bandung and for inter-city travel, but in general road vehicles are dominant. Buses are the most important form of transport used by temporary movers, particularly in circular mobility (Figures 4.2 and 4.3). Many of the bus terminals are foci of feeder services of small mini-buses, pedicabs and horses and carts. This is a pattern hardly characteristic of a 'static' society.

TABLE 4.4 *Ownership of motorized vehicles in West Java province*[a]

Type of vehicle[b]	No. in 1968	No. in 1977	Increase 1968-77	Annual increase
Cars, jeeps, mini-buses	27,322	85,941	214.5	11.36
Buses	1,838	4,701	155.7	8.19
Trucks and pickups	13,564	50,559	272.7	12.15
Motor cycles	47,577	214,131	350.1	11.82
Total (excluding motor cycles)	42,724	141,201	230.5	11.41
Total (including motor cycles)	90,301	355,322	293.5	11.59
Population	21,632,684[c]	23,911,478[d]	11.1[e]	1.98

Source: Indonesian Central Bureau of Statistics

Notes:
[a] Not including Jakarta where increases have been much greater
[b] Figures do not include armed forces motor vehicles
[c] Population figure relates to 1971 Census
[d] Population figure relates to 1976 Census
[e] Population increase 1971-6

In 1973 each day 1,027 buses made 2,526 round trips between West Java origins and Jakarta and 852 buses made 1,914 round trips to Bandung. At an average of 38 passengers per bus this would mean a daily influx of 95,000 persons to Jakarta and 72,500 to Bandung, by bus alone. Some impression of the total volume of movement into the two cities can be gained from traffic counts taken on some of the main roads leading into them (Table 4.3). Perhaps the most striking figures in the table are those showing the growth of traffic into Bandung and Jakarta between August 1971 and August 1973. The number of public road transport vehicles entering Jakarta doubled while the flow into Bandung increased by a third. These trends are indicative of the rapid increase in personal mobility in West Java since 1967.

Another local factor conducive to the development of circular mobility is the fact that seasonal variations in Java's rice growing areas create seasonal slacks in local labour demand. Rice makes intensive labour demands for very limited periods, namely at the time of land preparation, seeding and above all, harvest. There is a period of serious food shortage between planting and harvesting known as *Musim Paceklik* which means literally 'the empty season'. Single cropped areas which lack artificial irrigation systems (Sawah Tadah Hujan) such as those along the northern coastal plain also have a long dry season (*Musim Kemarau*) in which labour demand is also minimal. Due to these seasonal influences there is substantial underemployment in rural areas for much of the year.

Landowners may be able to produce enough to tide them over such periods but the landless and smaller landholders are usually forced to seek income elsewhere. In addition to limited agricultural work available there are local non-farm activities (Byerlee and Eicher 1972: 16). These include consumer goods manufacturing, trading and services; marketing and processing agricultural products; and manufacturing agricultural implements. Frequently however such local opportunities are insufficient to meet the demand, and movement outside the village occurs.

It would be wrong however to depict all circular movement as a push from the village in order to obtain subsistence. In the village studies, although this motive is a dominant one among many circular movers for others temporary movement is a chance to supplement income and *improve* their standard of living.

During the agricultural slack seasons there are substantial temporary movements between rural areas. The planting and harvesting peak labour demand seasons are offset from one region to another due to variations in the local environment and in the growing period of different varieties of rice. Traditionally Javanese and Sundanese rice farmers have been obliged to allow anyone who wishes, to participate in the harvest of their land for a share (fixed by custom) of what is harvested. The ecologically determined offsetting of harvesting thus traditionally allowed rural people to supplement their income by moving seasonally to adjoining agricultural districts. However large numbers of people, particularly the landless groups, are now travelling far beyond their immediate neighbourhood to seek harvesting work (Collier *et al.* 1973: 36-7; Franke 1972: 181). In West Java the largest movements of this kind are along the northern coastal plain from the regions of most severe population pressure in Central Java, Cirebon and Indramayu to the Krawang region.

However, in the area studied the main regions of non-agricultural employment especially in *Musim Paceklik*, are the urban centres of Jakarta and Bandung and these also are the main destinations of circular migrants from West Javan villages. Elsewhere a range of indirect measures has been employed to show the large scale of this circular movement between rural and urban areas (Hugo, 1975: 319-27). One of the major pieces of evidence is the scale of public transport flows into the cities from points outside of their commuter zones. A large number of very small centres in West Java have *direct* daily bus services to Bandung and Jakarta (Figure 4.2); which could only be maintained by the heavy interaction between city and village associated with circular movement.

In the survey villages the predominant destination of circular migrants were urban areas, especially Jakarta, with established precedents for circular movement between village and city dating back to colonial times. Its contemporary large scale and shorter periodicity is recent. In all but one of the survey villages more than half of the stock of circular migrants in 1973 had begun this pattern of mobility since 1970. This cannot be explained simply in terms of movers being predominantly new entrants to the workforce. Standardization for age indicated that many of the persons who had recently taken up circular movement were the established members of the workforce when they first adopted this mobility strategy.

To the majority who are male, circular movement involves separation not only from parents, siblings, friends, the family home and land but also from wife and children. The periodicity of departure and return thus has important implications for the village and its inhabitants.

There is a clear, but not completely consistent, negative

relationship between the distribution of usual durations of absence in Jakarta for movers from each village and accessibility to the Capital as it is indicated by shortest road distance, travel time and travel costs (Figure 4.3). The frequency of return to the village is obviously not a simple function of the friction of distance but rather the result of a trade-off between the constraints imposed by the transport costs incurred in returning and the ability of movers' incomes to meet these costs. Discussion with migrants during fieldwork supported detailed questionnaire evidence that circular migrants will tolerate spending up to 15 per cent of their total urban earnings on travel to and from the village. This figure appears to have become an important threshold in regulating the periodicity of circular movement between rural West Java and Jakarta.

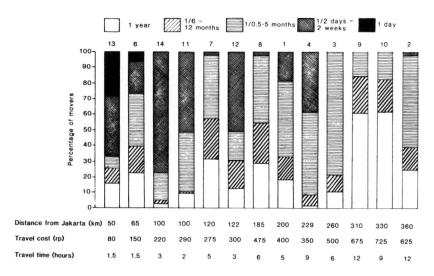

FIGURE 4.3 *West Java survey villages: duration of absence of movers to Jakarta 1973 (Note: only 13 villages are included; in one village sample there were only 6 moves to Jakarta)*

Motivations for moving

It is not possible here to present a comprehensive analysis of the causes of movement between the survey villages and the urban centres of Jakarta and Bandung. Growing population pressure on agricultural resources in the villages was the predominant (although not the only) factor in motivating many to circulate between village and city. Evidence from the survey villages suggested that circular movement and commuting have become

90

an entrenched pattern of behaviour and do not simply represent a passing phase in which movers 'test' the urban environment before settling permanently in the city. Only 1.6 per cent of temporary movers indicated that they had intentions of eventually settling in an urban area while 93.2 per cent definitely intended remaining in the village and 5.3 per cent were undecided.

Those engaging in rural-urban circular movement and commuting when asked to give reasons why they did not move permanently to the city in which they worked gave answers representing a blend of the strong social benefits of living in the village and the economic costs of settling a family permanently in the city. In all villages more than half of the movers mentioned that settlement in the city would involve separation from family, but many fewer saw the generally more pleasant life style of the village to be the main factor stopping them migrating definitively. Adopting a circular strategy is not an economically irrational response to the traditionally strong social attraction of the village. In most villages more than a half of the movers gave the high urban cost of living and the expense of housing as a reason for not settling in the city. Moreover in several villages respondents indicated that they could not support their family on their urban earnings alone and thus were forced to retain sources of income which required continued residence in the village. In fact in many cases circular movement and commuting are ingenious strategies which maximize the economic benefits which movers gain from the limited employment opportunities available in the involuted urban traditional sector. Rather than improve their economic position, permanent residence in the city with increased day-to-day living costs would involve a loss for the majority of temporary movers. The fact that the strategy allows highly valued social benefits of village residence to be maintained is thus often not the predominant cause of villagers adopting temporary rather than permanent movement but is an additional, though certainly appreciated benefit of it.

The migrant in the city

The romantic vision of the wide-eyed, solitary villager arriving 'Dick Whittington-like' to make his fortune in the alien city where he knows no-one is the exception rather than the rule among rural-urban movers in Third World situations. Certainly most of the circular movement and commuting observed in the survey villages occurs through well defined networks. The journey to the city quickly becomes routine after an initial introduction through a relative or friend from the village.

Kinsmen and friends from the village play a crucial role in assisting movers to find work and a place to stay. Jackson (1978) in his study of patron/client relationships among Sundanese (the dominant ethno-linguistic group in West Java) in Bandung, has shown how these traditional authority linkages have been modified in the urban context. Whereas the village *bapak* (patron) supplies access to land and agricultural employment to his *anak buah* (clients) Jackson and Oostingh (1970: 134-42) have described how access to income is provided within the national and government bureaucracies, nationalized enterprises and private business. Such activities operate not only between patrons and clients, but also within overlapping kinship and friendship networks. It is common knowledge for example that *koneksi* (connection) preferably of a family nature, is an all important requirement for access to many sought after lucrative jobs.

An example from one survey village will serve to illustrate the importance of connection for movers to obtain employment in the modern sector. The most casual visitor cannot but notice the ubiquitous presence of the advertising paraphernalia of international airlines. Inside walls of houses have posters depicting the luxuries of jet travel and world tourist resorts, village men invariably light *kretek* (cigarettes) from books of 'Garuda Airlines' matches, village records are kept in folders with 'Qantas travel' engraved on the spine and several substantial stone houses have airline symbols prominently on their facades. These are outward signs that over 100 villagers are employed by airlines at Jakarta's airport, ranging from administration to cargo and baggage coolies. This can be traced back to one villager gaining an administrative post in the 1950s and taking advantage of the boom in international air traffic since the mid '60s, to gain employment for young men from his village.

Informal links are important to gain access not only to employment in the modern and administrative sectors but also for non-wage employment in the traditional sector, whether a worker is completely self financed or relies on obtaining merchandise and equipment from a middleman. Thus traders from one village who sell groundnuts grown in their village in Jakarta give newcomers hints about how and where to sell. Many bazaar sector jobs however involve dealings with some form of middleman. Few *becak* drivers for example own their own pedicab but rent them on a 12 or 24 hour basis. Similarly, most hawkers and sidewalk vendors have to obtain their goods from merchants. A mover is thus unlikely to gain access to these occupations unless he has capital. If he is known to the merchant however, goods can be obtained on a credit basis. Migrants from particular villages and areas establish relationships with particular middlemen so that kinsmen and friends whom they recommend are able to gain access to them. The middleman in return gets a trusted, continuous supply of labour to sell his goods. Thus the bread sellers from one survey village have gained a virtual monopoly in Jakarta because they have special arrangements with bakeries. Clearly, *koneksi* has an important role in not only cushioning rural migrant adjustment to the requirements of bazaar sector occupations but also, and more fundamentally, in facilitating access to employment within that sector. It is not surprising that a substantial degree of occupational clustering was observed among movers from particular regions. In most of the survey villages for example more than half of the temporary migrants to cities worked in one or two occupational niches as Table 4.5 shows.

Similarly 'group adjustment' to urban conditions was observed in the housing arrangements made by circular migrants with one overwhelming consideration in mind − to keep costs to an absolute minimum so that remittances to the village are maximized. To this end most movers are willing to put up with uncomfortable sleeping conditions.

Nearly two thirds of circular migrants in urban areas slept in a *pondok* − a room shared with fellow migrant workers, usually from the same village, which is rented by the group or provided by the *tauke* (merchant or middleman who provides the trading equipment, pedicabs, goods for selling etc. used in urban occupations). A group of ten bread sellers from one of the survey villages rent a tiny room for US$ 0.24 per day, arranging their selling activities and return visits to the village so that they can sleep in shifts to maximize use of it. A *pondok* usually is no more than 6 metres square, devoid of furniture and houses 10-40 occupants who sleep shoulder to shoulder on floor matting (Critchfield 1970: 19; Jellinek 1978). In some cases larger groups of migrants rent small houses. In other cases employers in Jakarta and Bandung provide their workers with sleeping places. Some 8 per cent of movers however are forced to sleep in the open. These were mainly men who slept in their hired pedicabs and construction workers who slept in uncompleted buildings on which they were employed. A few others slept on the pavement or beneath bridges. Several movers from one survey village who sleep in the open in Jakarta reported that they suffered severe illness as a result of exposure to wind and rain, especially during the influenza season.

Housing conditions for most temporary dwellers in Jakarta and

TABLE 4.5 *West Java survey villages: occupational specialization in urban areas of movers who are in the work force*

Village	n	Main occupation	Proportion of all working movers			Percentage in two main occupations
			%	Second occupation	%	
1	74	Ground nut hawker	65	Government/army	15	80
2	55	Cooked food/cigarette hawker	35	Day labourer	22	57
3	91	Cooked food hawker	43	Jewellery hawker	21	64
4	70	Pedicab driver	57	Day labourer	16	73
5	82	Pedicab driver	41	Factory worker	34	75
6	100	Labourer	35	Hospital worker	13	48
7	87	Kerosene hawker	32	Household domestic	15	47
8	77	Airline/hotel workers	32	Household domestic	10	42
9	87	Kitchen utensils hawker	60	Government/army	12	72
10	88	Driver	27	Government/army	26	53
11	87	Pedicab driver	38	Construction worker	20	58
12	92	Carpenter	49	Government/army	28	77
13	99	Barber	31	Bamboo worker	20	51
14	104	Bread hawker	42	Driver	32	74

Source: Field Survey 1973

Bandung are thus poor and more uncomfortable and unhygienic than those in the village. Little wonder then that most movers take every possible chance to return to the village for periods of rest. However the varied and flexible pattern of housing arrangements is a crucial element in circular movement. Movers themselves and those who employ them adapt to the realities of the housing situation in urban West Java. More comfortable housing would consume most of the meagre incomes of the majority who move.

An important aspect of mobility between the survey villages and urban areas is that most circular migrants entered jobs in the labour intensive, low productivity, predominantly small scale, informal sector of the urban economy (Geertz 1963; Armstrong and McGee 1968; Missen 1972; McGee 1973). This is influenced by a number of considerations. First, formal sector employment demands a 6-day working week and regular working hours, while the time commitment of informal sector workers to their urban jobs is such that they have some freedom in selecting which days and which hours of those days they work. This flexibility is much more compatible with circular migration.

Secondly, entrance to the informal sector is much easier than to the formal sector because of its greater absorptive capacity. In the formal sector new employment opportunities usually arise when increased demand for goods or services creates a need for greater output. The informal sector on the other hand, like the traditional Javanese agricultural system, has a capacity to 'involute' (Geertz 1963: 32-7). Thus goods from rural areas as well as those manufactured within the urban sector itself

> are purchased on the basis of carefully managed credit
> relationships; they flow through the sector on a sliding price
> system, and are secured in fractional quantities, involving
> fractional risks and gaining fractional profits. Goods, risks,
> returns and employment are accordingly shared among a large
> number of individuals (Missen, 1972: 331).

Banana leaves of high quality are obtained from a particular species which thrives on the cool mountain slopes of the remote margins of one of the survey villages. Because the leaves must be fresh and pliable when used for wrapping cooked food (their main use in the city) they must be sold within a day or so of being cut. Despite this time constraint and the fact that the good is transported only 55 km it is sold and resold six times. Thus through intense fractionalization of the income opportunities that are available jobs are created independently of increases in production. Limited work and income is shared, but per capita

95

productivity is very low.

A third reason for taking work in the informal sector relates to differences in the incomes which movers working in formal and informal activities receive. The urban incomes of most temporary movers from the survey villages are not only low in absolute terms but also in relation to those earned by the Jakarta resident population (Hugo 1978: 236-9). Nevertheless they represent a considerable improvement on village wages for agricultural work. The fact that higher incomes can be earned in the city is tempered by the knowledge that more income is needed to meet the basic day to day subsistence needs in the city and that incomes from the urban informal sector are subject to considerable day to day fluctuations with market changes, increasing competition and the need to pay fines to city officials. Under such conditions circular movement has two advantages over permanent migration as a strategy to take maximum advantage of income opportunities in the urban informal sector.

By moving to the city alone and leaving wife and family in the village, the mover effectively reduces the cost of subsistence from what it would be if the whole family moved to the city. Not only is living cheaper in the village but the solitary mover can put up with cheaper, less comfortable conditions than could his family in the city at a bare minimum. Movers from the survey villages were able to save, on average, at least one third of their income. At the same time movers' options in the village are kept completely open so that the risk of not being able to earn subsistence is reduced by spreading it between income opportunities in both village and city.

Much circular migration of West Javans is thus a practical solution to the dilemma of insufficient accessible income to provide for families if they worked permanently in either the village or the city. Decisions to maximize income and the value gained from it by working in both rural and urban sectors and/or to 'earn in the city but spend in the village', represent a skilful and efficient use of scarce resources.

Conclusion

The study of population mobility in West Java reported here indicates the significance of repetitive population movement as an enduring and numerically important rural-urban mobility strategy of considerable social and economic significance to both rural and urban areas. Circular mobility has a long history and in recent years it has increased greatly. Movement of population out of Javan rural areas has been stepped up in response to increasing pressure on limited agricultural jobs in rural areas brought about by substantial population growth and probably also changes in agricultural practices involving a more commercial orientation among landowners and some replacement of labour inputs with machinery and other capital inputs (Collier 1978). Great improvements in public transport during the last decade have made non-permanent, circular movement from villages to large urban areas possible over a much wider area of rural Java than was the case previously. The simultaneous expansion of the so-called bazaar sector of the urban economy in cities like Jakarta and Bandung has been symbiotically related to the increase in circular migration.

Many important questions arise concerning the circular mobility described. Among them is whether or not it represents a transition stage in some evolutionary sequence of mobility change associated with economic and social development which will eventually lead to movers settling permanently in the city. Skeldon (1977) has recognized in Peru three general types of mobility on the basis of their duration, which he calls pendular migration, semi-permanent and permanent migration. With increasing modernization, migration from rural communities to urban areas passed through a definite transitional sequence from pendular to permanent migration. Nelson (1978) has suggested that this tendency toward permanency in migration is a general one. It is probably too early however to judge if such an evolutionary sequence will occur in West Java although current temporary movers appear to have a strong long term commitment to bilocality which combines activity in both rural and urban areas.

Another important issue relates to the extent to which the patterns of mobility discussed here are specific to the study area and how far they are of wider significance in the South-east Asian region. Circular mobility has in fact received scant research attention in South-east Asia, particularly when compared to Africa. Goldstein's (1978) recent survey of the existing literature on circulation in South-east Asia establishes this but also points to the growing significance of circulation in the region. Circular mobility with similarities to that in West Java has been recognized in Malaysia (Nagata, 1974), Thailand (Singhanetra-Renard 1981; Meinkoth 1962; Textor 1956) and the Philippines (Meijzenberg 1975; Stretton 1981). In Indonesia, several studies undertaken since the 1973 West Java survey have pointed to the growing importance of circular mobility. Jellinek (1978) has made an illuminating study at the 'urban end' of the process to demonstrate the nature and significance of circular migration to Jakarta. Temporary movement and commuting from village to city have also been shown to be major forms of mobility to the cities of Yogyakarta and Surakarta in central Java (Mantra 1978; Institute of Rural and Regional Studies 1977; Mudjiman 1978) and to Ujung Pandang in South Sulawesi (Forbes 1977). Papers presented at a recent workshop (Hugo and Mantra 1979) indicated the types and incidence of temporary forms of mobility in several regions of Indonesia including Aceh, West Sumatra, South Sumatra, South Kalimantan, Irian Jaya, Bali, Madura and several parts of Java.

It is significant that much literature on circular migration referred to above is based on local level studies. Macro studies which utilize census or large scale survey data rarely detect such mobility largely because they employ questions and definitions, mostly derived from censuses and surveys conducted in Western contexts, which were expressly designed to detect more or less permanent movements. Another reason for the scant attention paid to non-permanent migration between rural and urban areas is the fact that most studies of rural-urban movement in Southeast Asia have concentrated exclusively on the urban end of the migration process. This imbalance is demonstrated in a review of the literature concerned with the impact of migration in which seventeen pages are devoted to the impact in urban areas and three pages on that in rural areas (Findlay 1977, chap. 4). Temporary movers are very difficult to detect in random sample surveys of urban areas because they rarely become official urban residents and hence do not appear in registration statistics which are frequently used as sampling frames. Nor do these movers have permanent residences so that they will not be detected in surveys of urban households.

Even if it is accepted that non-permanent movement between village and city in Southeast Asian situations is occurring on a large scale and is of considerable numerical significance, some would still argue that it is not of importance to detect, measure and study such mobility. They would argue that because the permanent redistribution of population from rural to urban areas and complete replacement of a rural way of life with an urban way of life on the part of the movers which occurred in the West was associated with the continuing process of modernization, efforts should be concentrated on that form of mobility. However, there is clear evidence that non-permanent rural-urban mobility also has significant social and economic implications for both urban and rural areas. The proposition that urbanization and/or economic development in all Third World countries will necessarily blindly follow precisely the same path blazed by Euro-American societies is difficult to sustain.

Notes

1 Government and private schemes to resettle people from Inner Indonesia (Java, Madura, Bali and Lombok) to other less densely populated islands, especially Sumatra, Kalimantan and Sulawesi, date back to 1905. The net population redistribution achieved by these 'transmigration' schemes by 1971 amounted to only one year's current population growth in Java.
2 The migration-defining regions (provinces) varied in size from 576 km^2 (Jakarta) to 413,000 km^2 (Irian Jaya) and in population from 519,366 (Bengkulu) to 25,526,714 (East Java).
3 Subsequent investigation has indicated that similar *merantau* and *pindah* concepts are held by residents in several regions of Indonesia. See for example Hugo and Mantra (forthcoming).
4 Some regions of Indonesia have special words for commuting. In Yogyakarta (Mantra, 1978) for example commuting is denoted by the word *ngiaju* and differentiated from other circulation (*nginep* or *mondok*). In Bali the word *ngajag* is used to denote commuting, especially that involving small scale traders.

5 Circulation: a transition in mobility in Peru

Ronald Skeldon

Circulation is a form of population movement which involves no permanent shift in the place of residence of an individual. The time away from that place of residence, as defined in studies of circulation, can vary from as little as twenty-four hours (Chapman 1975, 1976) through one month (Bedford 1973a) to periods of up to several years (Mitchell 1959; Elkan 1967; Parkin 1975; May and Skeldon 1977). With such a broad definition circulation can cover much of the total spectrum of possible human mobility types. To argue that circulation is a type of non-permanent movement in a transition in mobility means that it must be an intermediate between two other forms and that it is in the process of changing from the one to the other (Zelinsky 1971; Bedford 1973b). This paper argues that there are transitional types of mobility, although whether these are to be called circulation will depend on definition. Some forms of circulation, mainly those that are short-term, appear to be persistent while those that involve longer absences from the usual place of residence can perhaps be regarded as transitional. This generalization is subject to qualification dependent on specific conditions.

Background to circulation in Latin America

Unlike the situations in Africa, Asia and the Pacific, where circulation seems to be the dominant pattern, population movement in Latin America has generally been assumed to be permanent (Nelson, 1976). The massive movement of population to the cities, especially to the squatter settlements around the largest urban centres, has been the major concern of the literature on migration in Latin America. Although other types

100

of movement have been recognized, for example movements to colonization zones in Amazonia and seasonal agricultural moves, these have been considered of minor importance compared to the rural exodus to the principal cities.

Compared to other parts of the developing world Latin America is more urban. It is estimated that in 1975 60 per cent of the population lived in urban areas compared with 24 per cent for Africa, 31 per cent for East Asia and 23 per cent for South Asia (United Nations, 1975). To a large extent the different colonial histories explain the contrast in levels of urbanization. Political independence came to Latin American countries from early in the nineteenth century while most of the rest of the developing world was subject to direct colonial rule until the mid-twentieth century. Colonial demands for labour gave rise to the systems of circulation that until recently have dominated the literature on population movements in Africa and the Pacific. The indigenous societies were tapped for short- or medium-term migrants to work on plantations or in mines. These migrants were generally housed in company compounds, were not encouraged to settle or participate in the town proper and they were commonly returned to their communities on completion of contract. Depopulation of the indigenous areas was feared in some areas, notably the Pacific, and repatriation would ensure the maintenance of the groups and also guarantee a future supply of labour for the colonial economy (Burawoy 1976). Hence it is generally when political independence has been attained that more permanent migration to the cities can develop, and urbanization then accelerates.

Although labour migration is not important for the most part in Latin America today compared to the volume of cityward movement, parts of the continent were once characterized by systems of circulation of labourers. Circular movements for tribute were known in Inca Peru but the most common circulation was seasonal between different ecological zones (Murra 1975; Gade 1975: 21-2). In colonial Peru where thousands of Indians were drafted to the mines at Huancavelica and Potosi, the *mita*, or tribute of labour, compelled one seventh of all males (later increased to one fifth as the indigenous population declined) to give service to the Spanish crown every year. Each year 14,000 adult males were to go to Potosi and many of these took their wives and families (Rowe 1957: 172). Others were sent to serve their *mita* in the cities. At certain times of year an estimated 100,000 men from all over Peru came to the city of Cuzco to construct buildings, sweep streets and generally maintain the city (Cieza de Leon 1945: 243-4).

101

The fact that much of this movement to fulfil *mita* was permanent, in that many never returned to their villages but were caught in perpetual debt at their destinations, or more likely died of abuse or exhaustion, does not invalidate the theoretically circulatory nature of the system. As in the other parts of the developing world the colonial society introduced new forms of mobility and these were mainly based upon the circulation of labour.

In contrast to the colonial period the nineteenth century, after the disruptions caused by Independence, appears to have been characterized by relative immobility. Economic stagnation led to the decline of the cities and rural communities were turned in on themselves with contact between towns and country effected mainly through the elite (Cotler, 1969; Dutt 1976: 126). The mode of the Latin American community studied by the anthropologist is the closed corporate peasant community which is isolated from both the city and neighbouring communities (Wolf 1957). The geographer Isaiah Bowman (1916: 63) who visited the southern Andes of Peru in the early twentieth century observed that 'the agricultural Indians of the Andean valleys and basins . . . are as fixed as the soil from which they draw life'.

The modern pattern of population movements in Peru

The permanent and pronounced migration to the cities would therefore appear to be a product of the twentieth century and most particularly of the last thirty years. To study the evolution of these movements during this century migration histories were collected in twenty-six village communities in the department of Cuzco in southern Peru in the early 1970s (Figure 5.1). In some of these communities it was possible to talk to those who considered themselves the earliest migrants to the cities of Arequipa and Lima in the modern period; they were the only people from their village at these destinations at that time. From them a picture could be built up of how migration from these villages had evolved up to the early 1970s.

Elsewhere the evolution of the general pattern of population movement from these Cuzco communities has been described (Skeldon, 1977) and only the bare outline is given here. Peruvian society has been transformed from one that was primarily rural (65 per cent in 1940) to one in which the urban sector has emerged dominant (60 per cent urban in 1972, projected to reach 72 per cent by the year 2000). Population mobility has evolved through a series of stages which are transitional. Movement from any particular community, be it a village or a group within a village, evolves from a state of relative simplicity based on local circular movements, through stages of great complexity when time away from the community and the destinations are highly variable, to another stage of relative simplicity based on permanent long-distance movements to the largest cities (primarily Lima). In this last stage the rural villages are declining in population. The rate of diffusion of this system throughout the country varies, but generally the greater the distance from the capital and the poorer the people the less advanced the stages in the transition. As the system tends to diffuse down a socio-economic hierarchy so too it follows the urban hierarchy, being more advanced in departmental and provincial capitals than in those small settlements at the lower end of the hierarchy. Hence in the most isolated Indian communities of the Andes patterns of local circulation are still dominant.

Here the changing pattern of circulation from two of the communities studied in Cuzco is examined more closely, and then the picture is broadened to reconsider, in the light of persistent forms of circulation today, the almost unanimous impression that mobility in Latin America is characterized by permanent moves.

Migration from communities in Cuzco

Pre-1950 patterns

Of the 108 heads of family interviewed in 1971 in four high mountain basin communities at over 3,500 metres in the province of Acomayo only one had never been outside the basin, even for a few days, and another had only been as far as the provincial capital, Acomayo. Rather than being 'fixed as the soil from which they draw life' these peasants have been highly mobile, almost all being return migrants, and the history of mobility goes back to the early years of the century. The destinations and the duration of movements, however, have varied over time and there have been differences from community to community.

In the first half of this century there was very little long-term movement from the villages in this area. Almost all the peasants were illiterate and they took part in short-term circulation only. In the 1920s and 1930s the peasants of the district capital of Sangarará, a nucleated village of about 1,800 in 1971, participated in trading and commerce, but this tradition goes back much further as the oldest inhabitants could remember fathers and uncles engaging in trade. They took the products of the basin, *ch'uno* (potatoes that have been preserved by a process of freeze-drying), potatoes and beans to the subtropical valleys of La Convención to the north (Figure 5.1) and returned with the narcotic leaf, *coca*, to sell or exchange in the Acomayo market. These trips occurred mainly between the harvest in May and the beginning of the planting season in October. The movement was dominated by males and they made their first trip when they were quite young, usually in their early teens, when they accompanied their fathers to help look after the animals and to carry and prepare food. One old man could remember making trips to the subtropical valleys every year for twenty-two years.

This seasonal movement need not necessarily have been a single out and return journey. One route from Sangarará to the subtropical valleys could take the traders through the city of Cuzco and many of them made several trips between the *coca* valleys and Cuzco to sell in the main market of the department before returning to the village. Just over half of those who had engaged in the trade in the 1920s and 1930s worked temporarily in the city of Cuzco during their trips to the *coca*-producing valleys. They worked as day labourers, either as porters, carrying heavy loads within the city, or on construction projects making adobe bricks. Other temporary employment at this time was in the construction of the main railway line to Cuzco from the south and the spur line from Cuzco into the *coca*-producing valleys of La Convención. Traders never spent more than two weeks to one month in any of these labouring jobs and commonly spent a few days only. Before the completion of the railway line into La Convención a round trip from Sangarará to the *coca* valleys with animals took between four and six weeks and few of the traders were away longer than three months, even assuming several trips between Cuzco and the valleys and some time spent labouring in the departmental capital.

To find any deviation from this pattern of circular mobility in Sangarará before 1950 we must look at families that were relatively well off in the community and could afford to send their children to school. These children too had participated in the *coca* trade but they also spent longer periods away from Sangarará. However, they were few and they too tended to move within the ambit of Sangarará-Cuzco and the subtropical valleys. One man had spent eight years in Cuzco attending school, although he never completed primary school and panned for gold in the valleys of Quince Mil during his holidays. Another worked for two years in Cuzco and earned enough money to move to La Convención where he rented his own land to grow *coca* and later coffee. He stayed twelve years before returning to Sangarará.

Two migrants were found who had broken out of this pattern

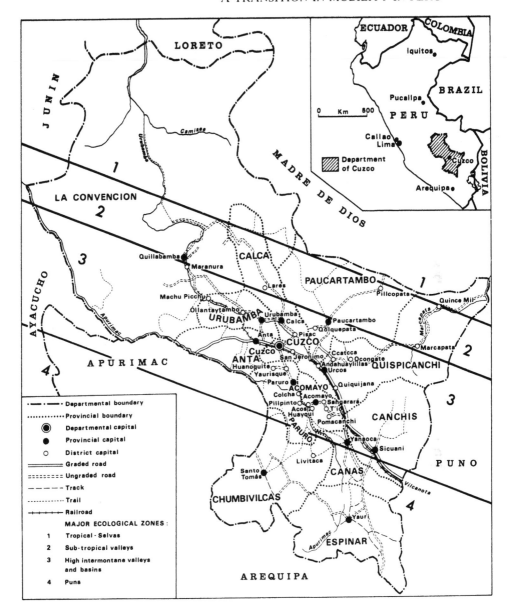

FIGURE 5.1 Department of Cuzco, Peru

105

of local movement. After schooling in Cuzco one joined the army and learned the trade of shoemaker. On leaving the army he moved to Arequipa, the second city of Peru, to practise the trade and after six months there he brought his cousin down to join him and the two of them remained in Arequipa another half year before returning to their village. At that time, the late 1940s, they were the only Sangarareños in Arequipa.

Four of the longer-term circular migrants were the most influential members of the community in 1972. Two had returned to set up the most prosperous store in the village, another was the president of the village community (*comunidad indígena*) and a fourth was running for mayor (*alcalde*). To conclude that their mobility had led to their positions would be deceptive as they did come from the 'big peasantry' or wealthier sector of Sangarará, but the education and experience gained while outside the village can only have reinforced their influence.

Before 1950 there was, as far as could be ascertained, no permanent migration from Sangarará, although almost every man had spent some time away from the village. In a neighbouring community, the district capital of Pomacanchi, a village of just over 3,000 inhabitants in 1972, there were interesting similarities and contrasts with Sangarará. In Pomacanchi there were a few families which could be considered part of the provincial and departmental elite, while in Sangarará there was none. The sons and daughters of this local elite group married into families in the provincial capital, Acomayo, and the departmental capital, Cuzco, and members of this group have always moved in regional, national and even international networks. One member of a Pomacanchi family had studied in Buenos Aires in the 1930s and two members of another family were more or less permanent residents in the United States in the 1970s.

However, it is at the level of the mass of the villagers that the comparisons with Sangarará can be most validly drawn. Unlike Sangarará, there was no tradition of trading to the subtropical valleys. Out of twenty-two heads of household interviewed who were over 40 years old only three had been to the valleys: two of these had been only once and the third had been often, but as a musician in a group not as a trader. However, like the Sangarareños, some of the peasants went to the city of Cuzco to work as casual labourers for short periods between May and October, although this pattern was more weakly developed; only nine of the twenty-two heads of household had done so, whereas almost all the Sangarareños had worked in the departmental capital. As many as six of the Pomacanchino heads of household had never worked outside the village but had only been away to visit friends, and another two had only been away very briefly to work in smaller towns nearby. None of these people had more than one year of schooling, none could speak Spanish but were monolingual Quechua. The five remaining heads of household had spent at least one year outside Pomacanchi, and of these three went to school in Cuzco and two were regularly employed there in trades. They all returned to look after their land and houses in Pomacanchi and two of them occupied posts in the local administrative structure in 1972.

The pattern then was similar to Sangarará in that there was relatively little permanent migration from the community, the more educated or trained villagers spent longer periods away and the mass of the peasantry engaged in local circulation to the departmental capital. The principal difference was the lack of a well defined cyclical movement to the subtropical valleys, which can perhaps be best explained in terms of access to land. The pre-Columbian communities, known as *ayllus*, were not contiguous settlements but consisted of a series of colonies dispersed across different altitudinal zones in the Andes. This allowed each group to control very different ecological zones with grazing, potato, maize and subtropical crop 'niches' that were possibly tens of kilometres away from each other. When the *ayllus* were reduced into nucleated villages (*reducciones*) by the Spaniards in the late sixteenth century, theoretically allowances were made so that each *ayllu* had access to land in at least grazing, potato and maize zones. However, during the inspection and delimitation of the *reducciones* in Acomayo in 1656 by Fray Domingo de Cabrera Lartaum the *ayllus* of Sangarará complained that they had not received enough land for maize. Ever since that time there has been litigation over land. The limited maize lands or *maizales* that Sangarará did possess in the valley of Acomayo were gradually taken over by the Spanish and mestizo landowners in the provincial capital. The last community *maizales* were taken in the 1930s and in the 1970s only a handful of Sangarareños possessed land they could plant for maize in the deep sheltered valleys of Acomayo.

On the other hand, a shortage of land does not seem to have plagued Pomacanchi and many of the villagers still had *maizales* in the Apurimac valley in the 1970s. No evidence could be found of land or boundary litigation for Pomacanchi and informants assured that they had enough land. They moved to their *maizales* at up to a day's walk away from Pomacanchi and stayed for short periods during the year to carry out necessary agricultural tasks. In this way the majority of Pomacanchinos participated in a local system of circulation.

107

The short-term circulation from Sangarará was not to seek a better world or an escape from the arduous way of life at high altitude. It was primarily to earn money to defray the costs of sponsoring a religious festival. Status in Andean villages, and in fact in peasant communities throughout the Indian areas of Spanish America, is gained through sponsoring a festival for a saint (Fuenzalida 1970). These festivals form a complex hierarchy of civil-religious offices known as cargos (Cancian 1965). The amount of money required to fulfil the social and religious obligations of the fiesta is substantial, especially for those high in the system, and each person tries to outdo the previous holder. In Pomacanchi, with its more extensive land resources, there was not the same need to go outside the community to accumulate the necessary wealth. As their *maizales* were eroded the Sangararenos incorporated the subtropical valleys and the city of Cuzco into their resource base as ecological niches, following the traditional Andean system of control over distinct ecological zones. Psychologically they were still moving within the confines of their community to gain or augment a value that was internal to the community – a religious cargo. They did not participate in the life of the city but kept together when there, sleeping in the open or in one of the beer shops (*chicherías*) that today still line the streets close to the central market where the porters find much of their business.

Today there are no *coca* traders in Sangarará and relatively few peasants go to take short-term labouring jobs in Cuzco from either Sangarará or Pomacanchi. The peasants who once did so are now too old. The religious cargo system still exists, although it is in decline and is being replaced by more modern fiestas such as *corte monte* or *yunsa* brought in by returning migrants (Guillet 1976: 299-300). This system of circular movement to exploit distinct ecological niches of the community resource base was profoundly modified after the late 1940s with an accelerating tempo of change in the second half of the century.

Post-1950 patterns

The eradication of malaria in the late 1940s and improved transportation into La Convención with the completion of the road engendered an economic boom in the subtropical valleys that saw a changeover from an economy based on sugar-cane and *coca* on the valley floors to a coffee-based economy on the valley slopes. Recruitment of contract labourers was not a recent phenomenon – recruiters were active in the early years of the century in the main towns of the region and in the communities of the Urubamba (Bowman 1916: 74) − but with the economic expansion of the 1940s and 1950s labour recruiters ranged further afield. The first Sangareños went to the valleys under contract in the mid-1940s and the movement became widespread from Pomacanchi and Sangarará in the 1950s. Out of thirty-four heads of household in the 20-40 age group interviewed in the two communities fifteen had been contracted to serve in La Convención. The contractors came to the villages and took groups of five or six peasants at a time; their contracts lasted for ninety days after which they were free to return to their villages. Fourteen of the fifteen returned to the valleys more than once, some ten times or more, and all but two also worked as short-term labourers in the city of Cuzco. Not one in this group had more than three years of schooling and several had never been to school.

Hence the earlier pattern of illiterate or semi-literate peasants engaged in local circulation to the valleys and the city of Cuzco continued into the 1950s and even 1960s much as before. The main difference, apart from the fact that Pomacanchinos were going to the valleys for the first time in large numbers, was that there was an element of force involved in the movement and several teenagers were taken unaccompanied by their parents or relatives. Secondly, the migrants were put in a situation where they could stay on in the valleys after their first contract if they wished. In the period before 1950 not one of the Sangareño traders stayed any length of time in the valleys but in the later period three of the heads of household did so. Two of them made enough money to be able to rent their own land, one staying for ten years and the other for five before returning to their village.

The number of villagers renting land in La Convención at this time was much larger as six of the remaining heads of household interviewed moved independently to the valleys to join friends and relatives who already held land there. Each of these migrants spent several years in the valley (one even still held land there in 1972) before returning to Sangarará or Pomacanchi. After returning to their village three moved again to Cuzco, Arequipa or Lima.

Of the remaining thirteen heads of household in the 20-40 age group two, both from Pomacanchi, had been outside the basin only on brief visits, three had been involved in short-term circulation to Cuzco to work in construction or as porters and another two had been cattle-traders circulating between Cuzco, their communities and centres in the department of Puno to the south. The remaining six in this group had all spent over three years away from Sangarará or Pomacanchi and had been to the cities of Arequipa and/or Lima. These six, plus the two who had gone on to Lima and Arequipa after their time in the valleys, make a total of eight heads of household out of thirty-four who could be considered as long-distance circular movers.

Only one of the eight moved directly to Lima; all the others moved in steps via La Convención or Cuzco to Lima or Arequipa. Some had led peripatetic lives. One had lived in Cuzco, Arequipa, Lima and Pasco before returning to Sangarará. Another worked in Quince Mil, Maldonado, Pucallpa, Iquitos and Arequipa before returning to resume life in the village. All had returned more or less permanently to their communities, although three hoped to leave again as soon as possible. Seven out of the eight had finished primary school and, with the exception of the two youngest, these migrants had moved to Arequipa and Lima in the 1950s.

Hence, although the earlier pattern of local circulation persisted among the less educated peasants into the second half of the twentieth century, the most notable feature was that the mobility field extended and became more complex. Young people broke away from the system of short-term circulation to settle in the valleys, and longer-term circulation to the larger cities by the better educated was under way by the early to mid-1950s. The better educated pioneer the more extensive migration field – they are the active migrants and are followed by the less educated as more passive migrants (Hagerstrand 1957).

This small sample of heads of household does not give an exact impression of the magnitude of population movement to Lima and Arequipa in the late 1950s and 1960s. Many of those who left in the recent past are still away. The total of thirty-five heads of household of all ages in Sangarará reported fifteen children in Lima, two in Arequipa and four in Cuzco. The total of forty heads of household in Pomacanchi reported ten children in Lima, seventeen in Arequipa and six in Cuzco. A difference in bias between the two communities is noticeable: Sangarará towards Lima and Pomacanchi towards Arequipa, although the most recent trend in Pomacanchi is towards Lima.

It is difficult to estimate accurately the number of migrants from a particular community who are living in the larger cities at any one time. The majority of the Sangarareños lived in crowded temporary conditions in *tugurios* in central Lima and a number were minors who were there illegally without having arranged the necessary travel documents. By contacting the clubs in the major urban centres that represented the villages or groups within the villages, and through observing the club functions and discussions with members and other migrants, rough estimates could be made. In mid-1972 there were around 120-40 **Sangarareños** in Lima, ten in Arequipa and fifty to sixty in Cuzco. From Pomacanchi there were about 150 in Lima, 300 in Arequipa and 120 in Cuzco. Therefore, for Sangarará there was approximately one migrant in these three cities for every ten Sangarareños in the village. The case of Pomacanchi is more pronounced with the equivalent ratio one for every five.

The long-distance migration to Lima and Arequipa from Pomacanchi and Sangarará is of fairly recent origin. For example, the first club of Pomacanchinos in Arequipa was founded in March 1956 with thirteen members out of a total of between twenty-five and thirty migrants from that village there at that time. The personal names of the members indicate the importance of the wealthier families in the village. In the 1960s another club was formed by the more 'Indian' Pomacanchinos as they were described by one of the founders of the original association. The names confirm this, showing the increasing participation of the humbler villagers as the migration process evolved.

Young male Sangarareños find part-time employment easily in Lima. One of the earliest migrants from the village who went to Lima in the early 1950s built up a small business around a newsagency and obtained the franchise for the distribution of newspapers in certain parts of the city. His nephew migrated to Cuzco via La Convención and Arequipa in the late 1950s and managed through his help to obtain a similar franchise for Cuzco. In both cities these two Sangarareños have a constant demand for paper-boys. Schoolboys from the village sell papers in Cuzco during their holidays and for some this is their first step in migrating to the capital. In Sangarará they know that once they arrive in either city they will be able to find a job. Working as a paper-boy is only a temporary measure while seeking a permanent job, or before returning to the village, so there is a constant turnover and a continuous demand for paper-boys.

As contacts are built up between origin and destination mobility increases. Once an awareness of opportunities in the capital exists in the villages, and once there are friends to help the migrants when they arrive there, then direct movement from village to large city develops. The period when these contacts are being built up has been called 'the migration transition' (Skeldon 1977: 406-7). It is during this time that there is a high probability of migrants returning from the various destinations of the extensive migration field and both step and stage migration are important. In the Cuzco communities groups of return migrants were found who had led itinerant lives, staying up to several years at several destinations. They seem to symbolize the

111

transitional period. The movement from both Sangarará and Pomacanchi in the 1970s was away from this phase with relatively few people engaged in local circulation to the valleys or to Cuzco to work − this was mostly restricted to the poorest peasants − and most of the young people moved straight to the largest cities, primarily Lima. The migration field becomes less extensive as the migrants concentrate on fewer destinations. In 1971 there were not even enough young Sangarareños in the city of Cuzco to enter a soccer team in city competitions. This was a very different situation from the early 1960s when the Sangarará club in Cuzco was an extremely dynamic association. Their members had since returned to the village, moved on or lost interest as they developed closer ties in the city with people from other parts of the department.

As the migrants move further away the time spent at the destinations becomes longer giving the impression of a more permanent movement. The earliest migrants to Lima and Arequipa returned to their villages within a few years at most; later migrants stayed longer. What appears to be happening is that the point around which circulation takes place changes gradually from village to city. In the early phases of the transition the centre of gravity of circulation is the village, although considerable time is spent away at various destinations, some of which may be urban and some of which may be rural. As the process evolves, the pivot of movement shifts to the city, although the migrants still participate in the life and economy of the village. Until 1969 it was obligatory for the leaders of the Pomacanchi club in Arequipa to travel back to the village for the annual festival. The regional associations in the cities can play an active role in lobbying and collecting funds for home-town development and the migrants, although living in the city, are still very much oriented towards the village (Doughty 1969, 1970; Jongkind 1974; Mangin 1959; Skeldon 1976).

As the transition evolves, the migrants gradually lose contact with their village, visits back home become irregular. Closely associated with this is the changing size and distribution of the migrant community from each village in the city. When this is small and concentrated in one particular neighbourhood of the city, as is usually the case early in movement to Lima when the majority of migrants reside in the city centre, communication and involvement with the home village are important. Once regular employment is secured and experience of the urban area is gained the migrants tend to move out of the crowded rented accommodation in the central city to establish their own homes in the barriadas at the edges of the urban areas (Dietz 1976: 26-37).

112

Secondly, as the volume of movement from any particular village to Lima increases, factions develop in the migrant community. For example, the more 'Indian' Pomacanchi club was founded in Arequipa in the 1960s causing a split in the original migrant community. A fourth club of Sangarareños was founded in Lima in 1972 (Mangin 1959: 27). The original solidarity of the migrant group breaks down and the members disperse throughout the city. It is at this stage, when the numbers of regional associations from a particular village are multiplying, that their functions become more purely recreational and geared to the urban social system rather than oriented towards migrant self-help or home-town development. The home village declines in the circulation pattern around the urban place of residence and the field of circulation becomes limited mainly to intra-city mobility and movement to other urban centres. When the majority of village communities reach this stage, and Peru has still a long way to go in this respect, the process of urbanization will have slowed down since the national society will be dominantly urban.

The general pattern of outmigration from Cuzco

Movement from Sangarará and Pomacanchi was quite poorly developed compared to that from the communities of Colcha or Ollantaytambo where longer-term circular movements to Cuzco and the valleys had been well developed by the late 1920s and movement to Lima under way by the 1940s. On the other hand, movement from Sangarará and Pomacanchi was well developed compared to that from communities in the province of Paucartambo, where even in the 1970s short-term circulation to the city of Cuzco and local haciendas was the dominant pattern (Figure 5.1).

In the census a migrant is defined as a person who is registered on census night in a province other than that of birth. From an examination of census data for the pattern of outmigration from provinces in the department of Cuzco, where of course village or even district variations cannot be distinguished, the general trend described for Sangarará and Pomacanchi may be found. Long-distance movement (movement to destinations outside the department) increased dramatically in the 1960s with Lima emerging as one of the principal destinations (Table 5.1). For example, from the province of Acomayo, in which Sangarará and Pomacanchi are located the total outmigration was 6,640 in 1961. By 1972 this had increased to 10,548. In 1961 only one quarter of the outmigration from Acomayo was to destinations outside the department of Cuzco. By 1972 this proportion had increased to

113

TABLE 5.1 Outmigration from Cuzco by province, 1961 and 1972 (in row percentages)

	Migration to departments other than Cuzco			% of migrants who leave the department of Cuzco	Migration to provinces in the department of Cuzco			% of migrants who move to other provinces within Cuzco	Total number of outmigrants
	Lima-Callao	Arequipa	Other departments		Cuzco	La Convención	Other provinces in Cuzco		
Cuzco 1961	44.2	17.3	17.2	78.7	—	7.0	14.3	21.3	41,758
1972	53.2	10.7	15.8	79.7	—	5.9	14.4	20.3	43,652
Acomayo	9.7	4.9	10.1	24.7	22.4	33.0	19.9	75.3	6,640
	25.3	9.4	9.3	44.0	20.5	22.4	12.6	55.5	10,548
Anta	11.8	1.0	5.4	18.2	32.9	29.4	19.5	81.8	11,087
	36.5	2.6	6.0	45.1	32.0	16.5	6.4	54.9	19,451
Calca	11.0	1.6	6.8	19.4	30.5	30.8	19.3	80.6	6,483
	30.8	3.0	7.7	41.5	25.4	23.2	9.9	58.5	9,967
Canas	6.1	5.8	4.6	16.5	22.0	9.0	53.5	84.5	4,495
	15.8	14.8	7.3	37.9	20.8	8.3	33.0	62.1	7,392
Canchis	12.5	17.6	16.7	46.8	16.8	10.5	25.9	53.2	17,241
	27.8	19.6	16.6	64.0	14.1	8.3	12.6	35.0	27,416
Chumbivilcas	4.3	35.5	6.7	46.5	16.8	8.6	28.1	53.5	7,148
	11.7	44.1	6.2	62.0	16.4	7.6	14.0	38.0	11,354
Espinar	3.8	36.8	6.7	47.3	10.1	3.5	39.1	52.7	5,874
	8.9	54.1	9.2	72.2	7.2	2.8	17.9	27.9	10,684
La Convención	10.6	1.2	17.8	29.6	38.8	—	31.6	70.4	4,364
	24.9	4.0	13.8	42.7	36.9	—	20.5	57.4	11,083
Paruro	7.9	2.0	4.0	13.9	34.6	38.2	13.3	86.1	6,386
	20.0	4.8	3.2	28.0	36.5	26.0	9.5	72.0	10,675
Paucartambo	15.0	1.7	10.5	27.2	35.0	9.6	28.2	72.8	2,898
	19.3	2.8	8.2	30.3	38.4	9.0	22.3	69.7	4,292
Quispicanchi	9.1	3.3	14.5	26.9	36.5	14.0	22.6	73.1	10,343
	27.1	6.9	12.3	46.3	30.9	10.3	12.5	53.7	17,224
Urubamba	10.3	1.6	5.9	17.8	32.8	35.3	14.1	82.2	10,648
	28.4	3.1	6.4	37.9	31.0	22.0	9.1	62.1	15,052

Source: República del Perú, *Censos Nacionales: Población, Vivienda y Agropecuario, 1961*, departmental volumes. Lima: Oficina Nacional e Estadística y Censos, 1970-4; República del Perú, *Censos Nacionales: VII de Población, II de Vivienda, 4 de Junio de 1972*, national summary and departmental volumes. Lima: Oficina de Estadística y Censos, 1974-6

44 per cent with over 25 per cent going to Lima-Callao. Although the absolute number of migrants to the local destinations increased, the swing away from the local destinations of La Convención (the valleys) and from the city of Cuzco towards the national capital and Arequipa was clear. In 1961 the outmigration from the province of Cuzco, in which the city of Cuzco is located, was the most advanced with 78.7 per cent leaving the department. This proportion had hardly increased by 1972, when it was 79.7 per cent, but there was a clear swing away from Arequipa towards Lima. Even the movement from other departments where there had been well developed outmigration in 1961 showed that the trend towards Lima had continued and intensified. For example, the movement to Lima-Callao accounted for 52.4 per cent and 60.9 per cent of the total outmigration from Apurimac and Ayacucho respectively in 1960.

TABLE 5.2 *Growth of provinces of Cuzco, 1961-72*

| | *Population* | | *% per annum* |
	1961	*1972*	*increase 1961-72*
Department of Cuzco	611,972	715,237	1.4
Province of Cuzco	95,088	143,343	3.8
Province of Acomayo	30,754	29,980	− 0.2
Province of Anta	45,090	46,330	0.2
Province of Calca	39,320	46,191	1.5
Province of Canas	28,604	31,546	0.9
Province of Canchis	70,488	75,616	0.7
Province of Chumbivilcas	51,030	58,312	1.2
Province of Espinar	36,982	41,461	1.0
Province of La Convención	61,901	84,161	2.8
Province of Paruro	31,728	31,536	0.0
Province of Paucartambo	26,455	29,983	1.1
Province of Quispicanchi	62,000	62,155	0.0
Province of Urubamba	32,532	34,623	0.6
Province of Lima	1,632,370	3,002,043	5.3
Peru	9,906,746	13,572,052	2.9

Source: República del Perú, *Censos Nacionales: Población, Vivienda y Agropecuario, 1961*, departmental volumes. Lima: Oficina Nacional de Estadística y Censos, 1970-4; República del Perú, *Censos Nacionales: VII de Población, II de Vivienda, 4 de Junio de 1972*, national summary and departmental volumes. Lima: Oficina de Estadística y Censos, 1974-6

By 1971 the Lima-Callao share of outmigration from these two important sources of movement to the capital had increased to 63.3 and 68.0 per cent. The corresponding increase in Lima-Callao's share for the department of Cuzco as a whole was from 20.2 per cent in 1960 to 31.7 per cent in 1972.

The rural population of Peru increased at about half of one per cent per annum between 1961 and 1972 compared to the annual growth of total population of 3.4 per cent over the same period, which even allowing for some reclassification of rural to urban areas is a very slow rate. The rural population of the department of Cuzco for the 1961-72 period grew at less than one tenth of one per cent per annum and the province of Acomayo appears to have lost rural population over this period (Table 5.2).

Just over one fifth of the total population of the department of Cuzco is 40 years of age or more (Table 5.3). The areas from which there is relatively little movement, apart from short-term local circulation (for example, rural[1] Qolquepata, and in fact the whole province of Paucartambo, and rural Ccatcca) reflect the age distribution of the department as a whole. However, where outmigration is fairly pronounced as in the urban sector of the districts of Acos, Pomacanchi and Sangarará the proportion over 40 years of age rises to about 30 per cent, and in the case of urban Colcha, where outmigration was the most pronounced of all the communities studied, the proportion was over 40 per cent. There are relatively few people left in the principal economically active age group of 15-39 years in Colcha. In Cuzco, as almost everywhere else, the migrants are young people and where outmigration of the population is developed, this cohort is reduced and where it is pronounced the community can decline. For example, urban Colcha declined from 714 in 1940 to 617 in 1961 to 532 in 1972.

There is generally a lag in the diffusion of the migration transition from provincial capitals through district capitals to the rural *anexos*. However, in the area around Colcha heavy outmigration affected the rural areas also with the 15-39 cohort depleted. Movement from the *anexo* of **Araypallpa** in the district of Colcha was pronounced and direct to Lima.

It is clear from these age data that women participate heavily in migration. This is in contrast to African or Melanesian movements which are dominated by young men, but it is typical of Latin America (Gilbert 1974: 113-14). The early circulation from Sangarará and Pomacanchi which has been described and the earliest long-distance movements were mainly of men. However, as can be seen from the age-sex data women from these communities do participate (Table 5.3). The earliest

TABLE 5.3 *Broad age categories in Cuzco, 1972*
(in row percentages)

			0-14	15-34	40
Department of Cuzco					
(total population)		M	41.6	34.5	21.5
		F	42.6	35.0	22.3
Sangarará	(urban)	M	41.7	30.3	28.0
		F	35.2	33.9	30.9
Pomacanchi	(urban)	M	43.2	28.5	28.4
		F	37.3	30.4	32.3
Acos	(urban)	M	43.2	26.6	30.3
		F	33.2	28.2	38.6
Colcha	(urban)	M	45.8	16.9	37.2
		F	38.0	16.2	45.8
	(rural)	M	40.8	27.8	31.5
		F	40.1	27.1	32.8
Qolquepata	(urban)	M	48.1	31.7	20.2
		F	39.1	34.8	26.2
	(rural)	M	44.6	33.6	21.8
		F	42.6	35.8	21.6

Source: República del Perú, *Censos Nacionales: VII de Población, II de Vivienda, 4 de Junio de 1972*, department of Cuzco, table 2. Lima: Oficina Nacional de Estadística y Censos, 1974.

Note: Unfortunately the published Peruvian census data do not give the breakdown of age by 5-year age cohorts at the district level; only the broad categories are given.

migrants from Pitumarca, a hamlet above Sangarará, to Lima were female and the pronounced migration from Colcha was due in great part to the early movement of girls to both Cuzco and Lima. Young girls easily find work as domestic servants in the cities and it has been estimated that two-thirds of the economically active female migrant population in Lima participated in the servant system (Smith 1971). Recruitment is primarily through friends and word of mouth and certain villages became noted for their domestics. This was the case of Colcha which was sending girls to Cuzco in the 1920s and to Lima by the 1940s. If a *patrona* is satisfied with her servant she will ask her if she knows of other girls who would like to work for a friend who may be looking for a servant. In this way a chain movement of girls develops from a particular community. These girls will find jobs for their brothers and cousins. The balanced sex ratio of migrants and the balanced sex ratio of the towns and cities favour stabilization and the trend towards more permanent movement − a factor observed by Nelson in classifying the stability of migration streams (1976).

Circulation and the migration transition

The principal feature of the population geography of Peru in the mid-twentieth century has been the rapid growth of urban places and most particularly of Lima-Callao. From a city of just over half a million in 1940 it had grown to almost 3.3 million by 1972 and its annual rate of increase between 1961 and 1972 was in excess of 5.4 per cent. This compares with a total population growth rate of 3.3 per cent per annum and a total urban population growth of 5.0 per cent per annum. In 1961 Lima-Callao accounted for 18.6 per cent of the total national population of Peru while by 1972 it was 24.4 per cent. Peru by 1972 was over 60 per cent urban and Lima-Callao represented two-fifths of this proportion.

In common with most of the world Peru has experienced rapid and massive urbanization which seems to be a 'universal, and to all appearances, uni-directional and irreversible phenomenon' (Friedmann and Wulff 1975: 26). Much of this urbanization has been caused by migration into the major cities. For example, in 1972 46.2 per cent of the total population of the provinces of Lima-Callao had been born outside these provinces. However, as will be clear from the earlier discussion this 'irreversible phenomenon' of urbanization is not characterized simply by irreversible migration. Circulation plays a fundamental role in the transition from a predominantly rural society to one in which the majority of people live in towns and cities.

The early cities in most developing countries were colonial enclaves eccentric to the distribution of indigenous populations. These colonial nuclei were characterized by labour shortage and it was the demand for labour that engendered seasonal and longer-term circulation from the native society. In Peru the colonial *mita* had its twentieth century counterpart in the *enganchador* system of labour recruitment, when recruiters scoured the highland communities for labourers for coastal plantations or the smaller subtropical intermontane estates of the eastern Andes. As the cities and other colonial and neo-colonial enclaves built up their own populations labour shortage developed into a labour surplus. This is the case with the plantations on the north coast, where now little seasonal migrant labour is required (Scott 1976), or with the cities where the involution and multiplication of services in the so-called informal sector bears testimony to a labour surplus economy (Mazumdar 1976). There is a decrease in opportunities for migrants in agricultural activities and they move into the cities. Within the cities the intense competition for jobs encourages a stabilization of population: having secured a livelihood people are reluctant to lose it. This reinforces the fact already noted that the participation of women in the migration flows encourages the trend towards stability or more permanent migration.

It is difficult to say just how permanent the movement to cities actually is. The 1972 census included a question on place of usual residence in 1967. Examining the department of Cuzco we find that less than 4 per cent of the 1967 outmigrant population had returned to their department of birth by 1972 − fewer than 3,275 out of an estimated outmigrant population of 86,000 from Cuzco in 1967. The 1970-1 urban population survey included a question on future intentions of the migrants in the major cities. Only 8 per cent of all migrants indicated an intention to migrate again, although the majority of these few appeared to want to go back to their home areas (Martínez, Prado and Quintanilla 1973: 36f). Census data and the sample survey data conceal a multitude of short-distance, short-term movements and it has been shown that return migration is still important in certain Cuzco communities. However, the trend towards more permanent long-distance migration was clear throughout the department and in other parts of the country.

In this paper and elsewhere it has been argued that there are distinct temporal and spatial forms of mobility that are transitional during the change to urban society. To call these circulation would be false, although certain forms, for example labour movements in the colonial and neo-colonial system, arose and declined as the system evolved. Circulation is the most persistent form of mobility with permanent residential shifts only becoming important during the transitional period as people move from village to town. If anything, it is migration, if defined as a permanent shift in place of residence, that may be one of the most important transitional forms, and even then these occur within a matrix of circulation. Circulation as a usual facet of human behaviour existed before the transition began in movement to different ecological zones, and it will persist after it is over. The migration has merely shifted the centre of gravity of circulation (Roseman 1971). The daily commuting or journey to work between the peripheral and primarily residential *barriadas* to industrial and service areas is perhaps the most obvious

119

example of this urban-based circulation. Obviously permanent residential shifts continue into a predominantly urban society but these are of small scale relative to the volume of oscillation.

There will be spatial variations in the way the circulation and permanent migration develop. For example, in the Mantaro valley in the Andes immediately east of Lima return migration seems to be persisting alongside the pronounced permanent outmovement to Lima (Roberts 1976). In this region the prosperous rural economy based on easy access to the market of the capital encourages migrants to return to their villages to invest in agriculture or village industry. It is from this type of region too, close to Lima, that we find weekly or monthly commuters similar to those identified in West Java (Hugo in this volume).

However, outside these favoured areas, as has been shown for southern Peru, the trend is presently away from circulation from the village towards a permanent shift to the towns. The rural population stagnates and where pronounced outmigration has developed it is actually declining. A similar process appears to have been going on in the densely populated Andean valleys of Colombia since the 1950s (Williams and Griffin 1978). Whether rural to urban residential shifts will decline in the future as commuting and other forms of circulation become dominant in a mainly urban Peruvian society is beyond the present concern. What does seem certain, irrespective of whether Peru tends towards a mobility situation that can be described by one of Zelinsky's advanced phases or variations thereof, is that continued circulation will be a basic characteristic of any future pattern (Zelinsky 1971; Fuchs and Demko 1978; Skeldon 1978).

Acknowledgment

Fieldwork on which this paper is based was supported by the Canada Council and the International Studies Programme of the University of Toronto.

Note

1 Each district comprises an urban sector, which includes the district capital and any other populated centre comprising 100 contiguous dwellings or more, and the remainder of the district is considered rural. In this part of Cuzco the district capital is usually the only urban centre, although Sangarará is exceptional as the urban sector also includes the village of Marcaconga.

Part II
Ecological perspectives

Introduction

Many, though not all, forms of circulation involve the exploitation of different sets of circumstances. This may be done from choice or may be due to pressures and sometimes there are elements of both. The four papers in this section are concerned with ways in which various aspects of the physical environment are the major constraints on and incentives for circulatory movements. They are set in a range of socio-economic conditions.

While it is pervasive the influence of the physical environment is not solely determinant of the forms and patterns of circulation discussed in these papers. The people involved may exercise choice within a range of what is environmentally permissive, and this choice they exercise in complex fashion. They are also influenced to varying degrees by external factors. While there may be little direct control possible over the external factors they may still be manipulated to achieve what is perceived at least to be advantage. However such achievement may result in significant changes in the nature of circulation.

In her discussion of the circuits of hunter/gatherers on the island of north Luzon in the Philippines Jean Peterson is concerned with a group which is much influenced by the physical environment with an economy which is marginal to the global capitalist economic system. Yet the activities of the Agta in their indigenous economy are most complex and the variety of circulatory movements involved must be explained in terms of both ecology and social organization. Agta mobility reflects a compromise between centripetal and centrifugal forces, between the need for individual mobility and for group cohesion. Like the

121

Hausa they employ circulatory strategies which are deliberately flexible and often inherently ambiguous. Recent changes which are being experienced are documented with precision since the discussion is based on original fieldwork in 1968–70 and a further study in 1978. Over the decades there have been alterations in the direction, range and seasonality of moves made by the Agta in search of food and to trade in food. These changes have been in response notably to disease, colonization of Agta land by settlers, the intrusion of logging operations and the introduction of primary education.

As yet the impacts on Agta circulation are producing modification rather than major change. Among the Duru' of the interior of Oman, traditionally involved in camel-trading with subsidiary but complementary economic activities, Stace Birks shows that the impact of external factors has been made greater. Traditional patterns of circulatory transhumance were controlled by seasonal variations in the harshest of physical environments. Response to these conditions produced a delicately balanced accommodation between men and animals in ways well-known throughout arid and semi-arid areas of the world. Recently, while there have been no major changes in the physical environment, the Duru' have effected major changes in their life-style through their response to alternative economic opportunities stemming from the oil wealth of Oman and adjacent Gulf States. Traditional circulatory movements have been adapted to accommodate these opportunities but the Duru' have exercised choice and have not been forced into making these adaptations. Birks is concerned with the progressive disintegration which is occurring in Duru' society and economy. This concern results not from a romantic view of the fast-diminishing traditional transhumant camel herder, but because of what will happen in the possibly not-too-distant future when the oil-based opportunities may come to an end. The intractable physical environment will remain but the ways for coping with it that have been built up over many generations of experience will have been lost.

Traditional Duru' circulation involves horizontal movement but much of the literature on transhumance is concerned with vertical movements made at different times of the year between environments at different altitudes. Studies of vertical transhumance have been mainly of movements associated with economies which are predominantly pastoral and keyed to the seasonal variations in the availability of forage. There has been some study of cultivators exploiting the potentialities of altitudinally-differentiated environments in the development of strategies for the spreading of risk.

Jim and Linda Belote have examined such an example for the Saraguro Indians in the Central Andes of southern Ecuador. Their agricultural system includes the raising of cattle and the cultivation of subsistence crops. The activities range over three altitudinal zones varying in average elevation from 1,700 to 3,200 metres. Two of these zones which are on the western slopes of the Andean chain are contiguous but the third, on the eastern side, is distant about 80 kilometres. The mobility between these zones is termed vertical circulation, drawing on the concept of vertical control favoured by Andean anthropologists whereby local populations use the resources of environments at different altitudes. The utilization of such dispersed landholdings by the Saraguro is possible because of great flexibility in the division of labour among family members, both adults and older children, who may work alone for days and weeks tending cattle, growing maize, hauling firewood and caring for younger children.

The first three papers in the group are concerned with forms and patterns of circulation of the majority if not all of the members of the communities involved. They are also concerned with circulations which are pivoted on the home places of the communities. 'Strange Farmers' in the Gambia, as their name indicates, have come from widely located origins, both inside and outside the country. They are almost entirely active male adults unaccompanied by dependants.

Strange Farmers are one of many groups who originate in the less well-endowed parts of West Africa and move to more precociously developed areas where there are demands for labour, in the Gambia for the cultivation of groundnuts. The majority of migrant labourers who come from the northern parts of West Africa move during the dry season when the labour requirements in their home areas are very limited. As Kenneth Swindell shows Strange Farmers move to work in the Gambia in the wet season when groundnuts are cultivated. They may circulate elsewhere at other times in the year but in doing so may not necessarily return to their places of origin. Contrary to previous thinking Swindell has demonstrated that the circulation of Strange Farmers pre-dates European administrative and economic contact with West Africa in the last hundred years. Like many of the labour movements in West Africa, and in contrast to those in southern Africa, this circulation is not recurring in a racially and economically plural society; Strange Farmers are employed on small farms owned by Gambians and not on large farms or plantations owned by expatriates.

6 Hunter mobility, family organization and change

Jean Treloggon Peterson

Mobility is perhaps the most striking feature of hunter-gatherer life, and has received a good deal of attention, particularly in the last decade. The stimulus for much of the work on hunter mobility, especially the ecological analyses, has come from ethnoarchaeology, which attempts to interpret the past in the light of data collected on contemporary hunter-gatherers. Recent work has corrected many false impressions about hunters: that they lived a hand-to-mouth existence, laboured long hours, and wearily wrested their living from the land as they wandered endlessly leaving exhausted resources in their wake. While hunters accept more environmental constraints than agriculturalists, they are not dependent on such a meagre subsistence and they put in a relatively short workday (three to five hours). Since 1968 we have more adequate descriptions of hunter mobility, and systematic investigation has addressed, directly and indirectly, the questions of why they move, the patterns of movement, and the frequency of moves (e.g. Yellen 1977a: 37-48; 1977b: 64-76; Williams 1974: 71-8; Yellen and Harpending 1972: 245-9; Harpending and Davis 1977; Lee 1972).

Because of the archaeological orientation, however, the focus of this recent work has been on the movement of groups from campsite to campsite; the ultimate archaeological concern is not the movement or social organization, but the site, contemporary or archaeological – how it came to be where it is, what population it represents, what subsistence activities were carried on there. This approach leaves largely unexplored a variety of movements that do not involve relocation to a new campsite, and motives for movement that are not materially measurable. Furthermore, there is a tendency in much of this work to extrapolate to the ethnographic present, ignoring recent changes among hunters, or acknowledging those changes without examining them in detail. This paper examines individual and group movement among one population of tropical hunters, interpreting the movement in terms of ecology and social organization, and accounting for recent changes.

The area and people (Figure 6.1)

Even today Palanan, Isabela, on the north-east coast of Luzon in the Philippines remains isolated, and life there is difficult. No road connects this section of the coast with either the Cagayan Valley to the west or other coastal communities. Military planes and chartered light planes fly in, at least in the dry season. Access to the nearest logging road requires at least two to three days of hiking in rugged forested terrain. The mean monthly dry season temperature is 82 degrees, and annual rainfall exceeds 254 cm, falling predominantly from September through January (Spencer and Wernstedt 1967: 54, 423). Thirty-two per cent of all typhoons reaching the Philippines strike this coast, taking a significant toll on life, property, and both the domestic and wild food supply. Most of the area consists of steep, forested hillsides cut by narrow winding river valleys. In 1978 a priest initiated para-medical training in Palanan; until then medical care consisted only of sporadic visits by government doctors. Tuberculosis, malaria, and pneumonia are especially problematic; infant mortality is 33 per cent among the Agta Negritos, and 19 per cent among Palanan farmers.

The Agta Negritos of Palanan Bay, who numbered about 800 in 1968-70, are dependent on a wide range of subsistence activities. They are usually characterized as the earliest modern inhabitants of the Philippines (Kroeber 1928: 18-19) and continue to provide their animal protein by fishing and by hunting wild pig and deer. They gather some wild fruits and vegetables, some plant small swidden gardens,[1] but they trade extensively with Malay-type farmers to obtain the vast majority of their carbo-hydrate staples. This diversity of economic activity has probably been characteristic of Philippine Negritos for at least thousands of years (Peterson and Peterson 1977; cf. Morris 1977; Bronitski 1977), in spite of the efforts of governments, from the Spanish to the present, to settle them on the land in less mobile and more easily administrated communities. They have achieved this remarkably stable adaptation to their environment by allocating personnel among resource activities, and the food and other goods obtained among personnel. To achieve this allocation a household typically moves every seven to ten days during the dry season, and somewhat less often during the rainy season. Camp groups demonstrate a constantly changing set of personnel. Changes are, however, beginning to occur in Palanan, as with Negritos elsewhere in the Philippines, and these are reflected in a somewhat changed Agta lifeway.

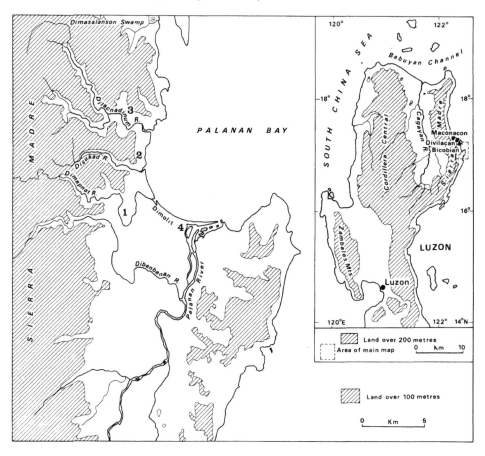

FIGURE 6.1 Palanan, Isabela, Luzon: study area

The Malay-type farmers in the area, who numbered about 10,000 in 1968-70, are referred to by the Negrito Agta as *puti* (light-skinned). The two populations speak a mutually intelligible language which is characterized as Austronesian (Headland and Wolfenden 1967; Headland and Headland 1974). In modern times, until World War II, *puti* settlement was confined to the lower Palanan River valley. Since that time *puti* have moved up and down the coast and up the Palanan, Dibenbenan, and Dimapnat Rivers, clearing and settling on the land. As farming settlements push outward, the Agta, moving ahead of them, clear tiny plots, which are then taken over, often usurped, by the advancing farmers. The Agta prefer to live on the fringes of farming settlements where they have easy access to the forest, trade, and unclaimed land. In addition to this internal migration, increasing numbers of immigrants, mostly Ilocanos, have been attracted to the area since 1971 to claim land. These farmers produce mostly corn, some roots and tubers (predominantly manioc), and little rice. They are unique in the Philippines for the small numbers of domestic animals they raise, depending instead on the wild animal protein provided by Agta through trade. Two-thirds of *puti* obtain from 30 to 50 per cent of their animal protein foods from Agta, who in turn acquire 70-100 per cent of their domestic carbohydrates from *puti* (Peterson 1978b: 342).

Within the area the Agta identify three bounded territories. Resources vary among these territories, and resource access within a territory is limited to those who are born there and their affinal and consanguineal kin. When seasonal variation in resource availability is juxtaposed with territorial variation, it is apparent that a very real potential exists for critical food shortages within a territory. For example, a territory with ready access to marine fishing, but very limited access to game, can and does experience a shortage of protein food when a typhoon tears up the reef. Most families anticipate these difficulties by manipulating marital alliances within sibling sets in part to maintain access to the diversity of resources represented among the territories. As one resource or another within their own territory fails seasonally, they are able to activate kin ties in other territories in order to gain access to resources there (Peterson 1978a: 45-63).

The basic division of labour among the Agta is by sex and age. Women collect wild vegetable foods and forest products, carry on most trades with *puti*, and generally can be characterized as 'carbohydrate producers', as opposed to men who are 'protein producers'. There is significant variation among men in the amount of time given to hunting as opposed to fishing. While all men know how to hunt and fish, most show a preference for one activity or the other. Sometimes the preference is strong, as in the case of a man generally identified as the best hunter in the area, who occasionally stream fishes, but will not go into the ocean for fear of sharks and large waves. Another, one of the best fishermen, hunts only in farmers' fields or on their edges lest he become lost in unfamiliar forest.[2] These preferences are established early and largely reflect those of a man's father, or other male who teaches him, and the nature of the resources most readily available within his territory. With advancing age, both men and women turn to planting instead of other activities, and old persons are responsible for the majority of domestic vegetable food produced by Agta.[3] Increasingly, however, young men exhibit a preference for working for *puti* in exchange for cash. Diversity of individual productive effort is one means of assuring a stable food supply; when fishers fail because of seasonal variation or other variables, hunters may enjoy success. Within any given segment of the population diversity of productive skills is therefore advantageous; it requires, however, a means of reallocating the diverse resources obtained. Clearly, some sort of exchange among the Agta is necessary to level this variation in individual productive activity and regional and seasonal availability of food.

As with subsistence activities, Agta modes of allocation exhibit unusual diversity. They exchange with farmers in formalized trading partnerships, they sometimes sell protein foods and other forest products for cash, they practise both generalized and measured reciprocity, and they widely share any critical food items among themselves. This diversity of economic activity may be interpreted as a particularly stable arrangement which has facilitated the persistence of their lifeway for so many thousands of years, and which has made it so resistant to change even in those parts of the Philippines where drastic environmental change has occurred (Peterson 1978a: 108-12). Within this diversity of allocation modes the single most common economic activity for the Agta is simple sharing among themselves (cf. Lee 1969). In this respect the Agta may be said to manifest the Marxist maxim: 'from each according to his means to each according to his needs.' In 1968-70 virtually the only privately owned goods were hunting and fishing gear, which were made and owned by the maker. Most families owned two or three lengths of cloth which were used as skirts and baby slings, and there was no need to share these items. Unusual clothing items, such as dresses, pants, shirts, and underwear, might be passed from one person to another several times a day. Cooking pots, bush knives, files, and plates are not owned by every household and are freely shared. Most notably, however, food is shared. Severe sanction demands that any food be widely shared; failure to share equitably is cause for enactment of black magic (Peterson 1978a: 18).

Food sharing occurs most commonly within the extended family or the camp group. Because extended family and camp group are not always coterminous, the basic food producing and sharing group has been termed the 'core cooperative group' (co-op group). The co-op group may often camp together, but some members will camp elsewhere on occasion, and members of other co-op groups may join a camp group. Core co-operative groups consist of an older male and female,[4] their unmarried children, some or all of their married children, their grandchildren, and possibly other families who are of their children's generation. Because some of their married children may live in another territory and not participate in their co-op group, and because orphaned or other families may join them, the group cannot simply be described as an extended family. All the skills essential to survival are represented among the members of a co-op group, and the diverse foods and goods they produce are shared within and beyond this group.

Structure of the core co-operative group

Kin diagrams and resource activity preferences for two co-op groups will demonstrate the structure of the groups and the diversity of skills represented within them (Figure 6.2).

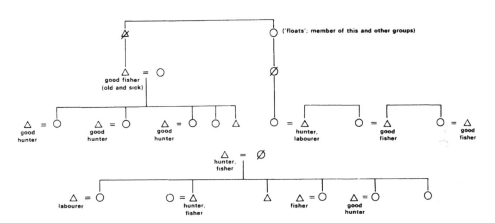

FIGURE 6.2 Kin structure and resource activity preferences for co-op groups

Two features of these co-op groups are striking, and characteristic of these groups generally. The first is that a diversity of resource skills is represented within them. A second feature of these co-op groups is the number and distribution of arranged marriages and child betrothals, indicating the operation of a deliberate strategy to establish this diversity of skills within a group through manipulation of marital alliances (cf. Peterson 1978a: 45-63 for a discussion of marriage as a strategy for maintaining access to a diversity of resources through establishing and maintaining ties with other territories). In twenty-one marriages in the adult children's generation of seven groups (the total universe of groups regularly occupying the Dimapnat, Disukad, and Dilacnadinum river valleys and contiguous coast) two distinct patterns emerge. Six of seven sets of parents arranged the marriages of the first children to marry, and nearly half of all marriages of first and second children to marry involved child betrothal or parental arrangement.

TABLE 6.1

| | First child to marry | | Second child to marry | |
	male	female	male	female
child betrothal	1	4	1	
arranged	0	0	1	1

n = 7 sets of parents; 17 marriages of first and second children to marry

Parents tended to allow 'free choice'[5] to children who married later; in two cases the last child to marry eloped. In each case the first or second marriages supplied a male to the woman's family who brought with him skills different from or markedly superior to those of the father-in-law, or brothers-in-law. Two families reversed this strategy, moving from the leniency of allowing their children free choice of marriage partners to controlling choice of marriage partners. The first of these cases is a very clear example; after two free choice marriages of children, and an elopement, a child was betrothed at age seven. In the second an arranged marriage followed an elopement and preceded a marriage by individual choice. Within this basic food producing and sharing group, diversity of subsistence endeavour is important for assuring a steady and diverse food supply in the event of failure of one resource or another, and as with access to extra-territorial resources, this essential diversity is maintained in part through management of marriage choice.

This diversity of effort produces a social group required on the one hand to tap scattered and often mobile resources, activities which may scatter personnel, and also to share those resources (Yellen and Harpending 1972: 246-7; Yellen 1977a: 66-7) and co-operate in domestic tasks, activities which are best served by co-residence of the group. Individual, household, and camp mobility effect a compromise between these two survival needs.

Core cooperative group organization and mobility patterns

Resources within any area utilized by Agta are not concentrated in a single place, and at least some of those resources are mobile (fish, game, and to a certain degree *puti* trading partners). Furthermore, resource availability varies seasonally. Allocation of personnel with diverse skills among these resources accounts in large measure for the mobility of Agta. Furthermore, the desire of Agta not to be separated for long periods from loved ones is another major variable in their movement patterns. These together account for the blending and reblending of personnel described above.

Agta mobility may be described in four categories: daily movements of individuals; the movements of groups of individuals (one or more households) from campsite to campsite; the movement of groups of individuals out of their territory; the movement of individuals out of their territory (cf. Williams 1974: 71-4). The most common is the daily movement of individuals as they perform various economic and social tasks. Sex and age variables, as well as specific subsistence skills, greatly affect the pattern of individual movement. The peak productive years for hunters are approximately thirty to forty-five. Male socialization to hunting begins seriously in the early teens. Younger boys are given miniature bows and arrows, and practise archery, but not until later do adult men begin taking youths hunting and instruct them in the vast store of Agta knowledge of the environment, including game habits and reproduction, plants and their uses, location, and reproductive cycles. A male in his twenties is still learning; by about age thirty he has acquired sufficient skill to hunt regularly and diligently on his own. By age forty-five to fifty his stamina and strength begin to decrease, he has grown sons and sons-in-law to assist him and he begins to decrease his hunting activity, and consequently his mobility. A hunt, once the site is reached, may involve walking as much as 30-40 km tracking game, climbing 90 per cent slopes, climbing large trees to await game, dangerous confrontations with wounded animals, and ultimately carrying animals weighing 40-60 kg back to camp. These activities require superb physical condition. In contrast, fishing is a skill taught and practised by young boys (approximately age seven and up). A male narrowly focused on fishing may therefore achieve maximum productivity, and consequently higher mobility, five to ten years earlier than a hunter. He might also extend productivity and mobility somewhat longer. However, men usually abandon underwater spear fishing for line or net fishing by age forty-five to fifty, and will fish near where they are camped, rather than making long walks just to reach a particular fishing site. Swimming, travel to fishing sites (as much as 60 km round trip in a day) are strenuous activities, but less so than hunting. Fishing activities are continued, therefore, to a later age than hunting activities.

Adult female economic activity occurs in a reverse pattern. Teenage girls exhibit considerable mobility, travelling as much as 35-50 km a day on errands for the household. This mobility decreases markedly for young women with the birth of a first child. A woman with young dependent children will spend all or most of her time within a 2-10 km radius of where she is camped. Young children tire easily on long walks under a tropical sun, grow weary of maternal attention to economic activities, encounter countless hazards if unattended, and if under about age five, have to be caried. Family size among Agta is variable ($r = 0-7$) and child spacing is equally variable ($r = 1-13$ years).

A woman is likely to spend at least six years with at least one child too young to walk. She might well have more than one child too young to regularly walk long distances. Mothers therefore limit their mobility to areas near the camp, though occasionally father, grandparents, or other relatives or friends are available in camp to care for young children (cf. Williams 1974: 71). A woman's mobility increases markedly as her children grow up, and once they are grown it will equal or surpass that of her husband as she moves about each day collecting forest products, trading at houses of *puti*, and working in her own or *puti* fields. Very old men and women may continue to walk as much as 60 km some days, but age, tuberculosis, and malaria reduce their mobility. Dry season mobility records of members of two co-op groups for selected periods illustrate this variation[6] (Figures 6.3 and 6.4).

These data show variation in the activities and mobility of individuals who camp together, with variation by sex and age. Individuals leave camp daily on various tasks, sometimes two or three together. Most nights they return to be with their families; occasionally younger males stay away one to three nights at a time. The Agta are, however, loath to be parted from loved ones for long. Homesickness was twice cited as the cause of death of individuals (one adult, one child) separated for a long while from loved ones. When resource exploitation draws one member of the group away from his family for prolonged periods, the household and perhaps the whole camp group will eventually join him. Household and camp mobility for one co-op group over a period of three months in the dry season illustrate these

CO-OP GROUP I

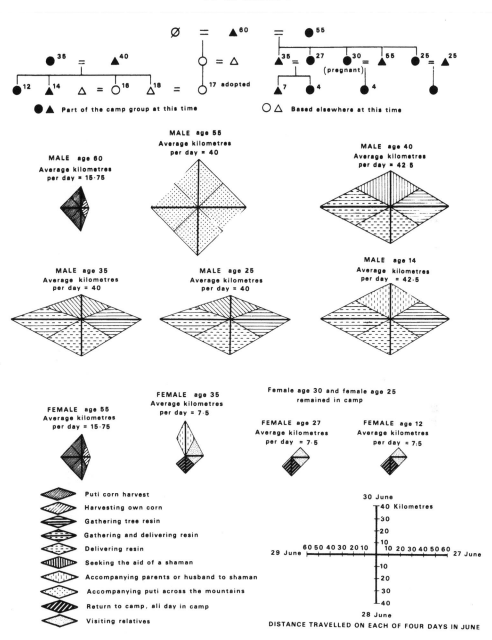

FIGURE 6.3 Co-op group I (June): kin structure and movement

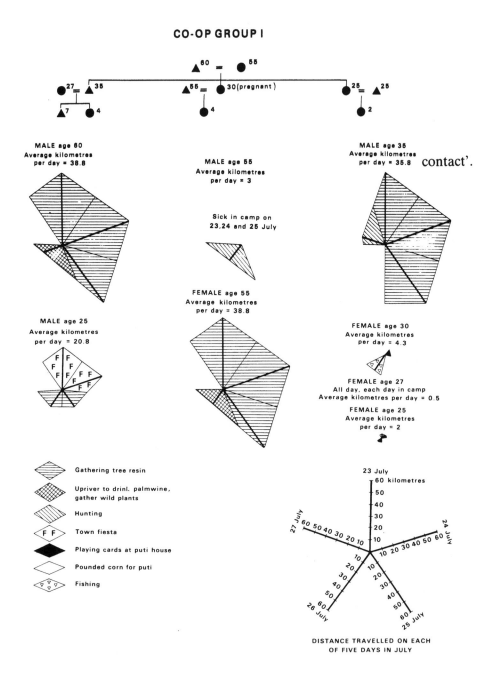

FIGURE 6.4 *Co-op group I (July): kin structure and movement*

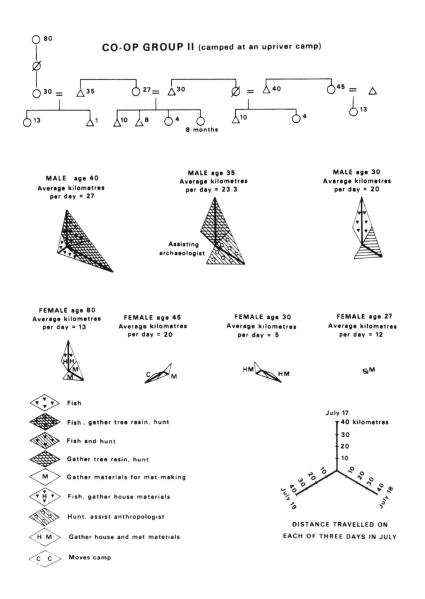

FIGURE 6.5 Co-op group II (July): kin structure and movement

135

centripetal and centrifugal forces[7] and the movement of co-op groups among several core areas exploited (Figure 6.1).

Area 1: offers hunting, riverine fishing, a small borrowed garden plot, trade, and work for cash.
Area 2: poor hunting, riverine and marine fishing, acces to trade.
Area 3: offers good hunting, riverine fishing, their own garden plot.
Area 4: marine fishing, trade, labour for cash.

5/1–5/19 – The entire co-op group camped at Area 1. The younger men during this period hunted at both Areas 1 and 3. Their hunting activities kept them away from their families a total of three nights during this period. They also went to Area 4 to fish.
5/20–5/27 – The co-op group split up, hunters and their nuclear families going to Area 1 to hunt and work their field there, and fishers going with their nuclear families to Area 4 to fish.
5/28–7/18 – Fishers and their families remained at Area 4; hunters and their families went to Area 2 to hunt, fish, and work. They are able to visit frequently between the two sites. 7/15 fishers returned to Area 1.
7/18–7/30 – All are reassembled at Area 1.

These movements illustrate the balance achieved between the centrifugal pull of scattered, mobile, and seasonally variable resources, and the centripetal pull of non-mobile resources and social and emotional ties. A compromise is achieved between the need for individual mobility and the need for group cohesiveness. Group cohesiveness reflects not only the values of Agta about family life, but also the domestic needs of co-op groups. Food procured by individuals cannot be stored for long and must be shared and consumed within the co-op group, or traded to *puti*, before it spoils. Game, particularly, affects mobility in this respect; repeatedly carrying heavy animals long distances back to camp is wearying even for the Agta. A second factor is that having more members in camp enables sharing of child care which in turn frees the mothers of young children for involvement in some economic tasks (collection of forest products, farm labour, corn and rice pounding).

The third type of significant movement is of groups of individuals outside their home territory for two purposes. Social reasons centre on life crisis events. Agta leave their home territory to attend weddings or invite others to weddings. They also leave to attend the various ceremonies surrounding a death, or to announce the death of one of their members and to escape the spirit of the recently deceased. On other occasions, having not visited relatives for a long time, they pay purely social visits. The groups involved in such movements are households, one to three moving together for periods of one to several days. Environmental variables also affect group movement beyond territorial boundaries. Whenever resources fail over a prolonged period of time, as they will within a territory seasonally, a household will visit kin in another territory to hunt or fish with them. Even in good years, when resources are adequate within the home territory, they will visit at least once or twice to maintain the ties (Peterson 1978a: 49).

Finally, individual Agta cross the mountains to the Cagayan Valley, serving as bearers for *puti*. Overwhelmingly these are men; nearly all Agta men have visited at least one of the major market centres in the Cagayan Valley; women and children rarely accompany them. One Agta girl, however, lived for a period of time in the Cagayan Valley, working as a housegirl. Panamin (Presidential Arm on National Minorities) took three Agta to Japan on a fund raising venture in 1968, and has sponsored several for medical care in Manila. These trips beyond Northern Luzon are almost uniformly traumatic for the Agta. They are often frightened of traffic, buildings, and crowds, and apprehensive about strange foods; some actually become ill as a result.

Sources of change

In the effort at reconstruction of the ethnographic present anthropologists have often ignored those populations of hunters who come into daily or near-daily contact with sedentary peoples, or dismiss such contact where it occurs, adopting what Wobst (1978) calls a parochial view of hunting life. In fact, hunters have probably experienced contact of this sort for millennia (Peterson and Peterson 1977; cf. Wobst 1978; Bronitski 1977; Morris 1977; Hutterer, ed., 1977) without altering their lifestyle significantly. On the other hand, in this century hunters everywhere are experiencing the impact of environmental change too profound not to affect their lives. Elsewhere (Peterson 1978a: 64-89) it is suggested that these changes stem from the influence of industrialization and hierarchically ordered social systems in colonial and neo-colonial states (cf. Peterson 1977). Change of this sort has begun in Palanan since 1970.

The two most obvious environmental changes in Palanan were the military occupation of the area following the declaration of martial law in the Philippines in 1972, ending in 1975, and a cholera epidemic in 1973 which killed an estimated 25-35 per cent of the Agta in one territory. In an effort to secure the area militarily by controlling the movement of Agta hunters, the Army encouraged Agta to settle together in two areas of Palanan. In the Disukad area several hundred Agta were concentrated on the beach, allowed to hunt once a week, and required to meet a 4 p.m. curfew.[8] Without benefit of instruction in the hygienic measures essential to a sedentary life, the camps became grossly fly infested and cholera broke out. When the epidemic subsided and the military left, the frightened Agta scattered up the coast, as far as Divilacan and Bicobian.[9] Nine co-op groups formerly resident in the Disukad area in 1968-70 now claim territorial identity farther north.

The immigration of farmers into the Dimapnat-Disukad area was an additional incentive to this move. In 1970 only nine farmers maintained homes in that area. Now there are thirty-one households and the first terrace of the Dimapnat River is continuously cleared and cultivated for five miles along the river from the mouth upstream. Gradual immigration by Palanan farmers began during World War II. It has been amplified by an influx of Ilocanos from the Cagayan Valley; nine of the households in this area are new immigrants from beyond the mountains; another is an Ilocano who immigrated to Palanan during World War II. They have taken over Agta land, forcing Agta up the coast if they wish to have access to land for garden plots. As one Agta woman expressed it, 'We moved from the Palanan, to Dimolit, to Dimapnat, Disukad, Dilacnadinum; soon we will fall off the land.' Ilocanos, in particular, have had other effects on the area. First, because they have brought with them more cash than the Palaneños, land has acquired a cash value far in excess of previous values. This has affected Agta claims adversely, and has stimulated a move to a cash economy. Previously most exchanges of goods were in kind; factory produced goods were minimally available, and labour was repaid with labour. Wage labour is now sought more readily. The Ilocanos have brought with them livestock and a fishing technology which give them access to animal protein without the traditional Palanan dependence on exchange with the Agta.[10] Finally, while some Palaneños were prejudiced and exploitative in their treatment of Agta (Peterson 1978a: 64-89), many Ilocano immigrants tend to be markedly so. Many Agta have left, choosing to avoid these changed circumstances in which they are enticed to drink to excess, induced to gamble, cheated of their money, raped, and openly mocked and chided for their dress and lifestyle.[11] Those who remain have more access to labour for cash, less access to trade in kind and to land of their own, and *puti* immigrant ridicule as an incentive to adopt a more settled lifeway with all the accoutrements of clothing, housing, and other material possessions.

Two other variables deserve attention as sources of change. Logging in the Sierra Madre is progressing at a break-neck pace. Vast areas of the western watershed of the Sierra Madre and areas north of Palanan are stripped of forest. Within the past eight years the Agta have noticed the effects of logging. They say there are now game trails high in the mountains where previously there were none, indicating a dependence by game on new resource areas, and that the overall quantity of game is diminished. Finally, a school has operated sporadically at Disukad since 1969 and regularly in 1977 and 1978 for Agta and farmer children. While only a few Agta children attend, this must sooner or later have some impact on their life. Aside from the eventual effects of education, schooling creates an immediate need for cash to purchase supplies and clothing. Furthermore, attendance at school restricts the mobility of a child's family.

The effects of change

As the natural and cultural environments of Palanan change so drastically, Agta lifeways must change as well. Traditional resources have diminished since 1970: the area of unclaimed land is shrinking, game and fish populations are decreasing, and trade in kind is becoming less common. At the same time cash is more readily available, and food and other goods for purchase are more abundant. These changes were reflected in Agta behaviour observed in 1978. The intense effort toward tree resin collection for cash sale to an increasing number of middlemen (mostly Ilocanos) is unprecedented. Similarly, while Agta always helped farmers during planting and harvest, this activity has greatly intensified in the past decade. Two young men now specialize in labour for cash, and rarely hunt or fish. Agta living near farmers now own much more: cloth, pots, blankets, radios, even phonographs. What is more, they are eager to own these items, whereas formerly they chose not to be burdened with carrying around too much when they moved. Probably Agta now eat less well; certainly eight years ago Agta children had strong, beautiful teeth, now many have deciduous teeth rotted out to the gums before their permanent teeth erupt, as a result of more refined sugar in their diet. An increase in skin diseases since 1970 may also be a result of deterioration in diet.

All of these changes have affected Agta mobility. The dry season used to be a period of high mobility, households moving every seven to ten days. In the dry season of 1978 some households remained permanently encamped from mid-June to the end of July, for the harvest and to gather tree resin. House forms have changed. In 1968-70 simple lean-to shelters sufficed throughout the dry season, and for many during the rainy season, as well, and were abandoned with each move. During the dry season of 1978, at any given time at least 80 per cent of the shelters at the Disukad encampment were the more permanent 'rainy season' type with raised sleeping platforms. One boasted a roof of fine nipa shingles which were taken along when the family finally moved camp. Upriver dwellings beyond farming settlement, still consisted of lean-to shelters.

The Agta anticipated difficulty in the coming rainy season, usually a more sedentary period. One immigrant from beyond Palanan who purchased land at the site of the usual Agta rainy season camp at Disukad has forbidden the use of the land. They said that if they must move their rainy season camp to Dilacnadinum, trade would be problematic and their diet would suffer. The distance is great to carry meat, and swollen rivers would isolate them from the farmers upon whom they still depend for a majority of their carbohydrate staples. Certainly, if these fears are realized, individual mobility in the rainy season may increase.

With the move to a cash economy and expansion outward, some Agta move on, but others remain, adopting a more settled lifeway and greater dependence on cash for their labour. This change has been apparent since World War II and is reflected in birthplaces and marriage places of adults as compared to areas where their children were born and where they are currently living (see Figure 6.6; cf. Yellen and Harpending 1972: 246-7; Yellen 1977a: 41-7). On the whole, both those Agta who move ahead of expansion and those who stay behind seem to be reflecting a trend to decreased mobility of groups (and more permanent encampments), and concomitant increased mobility of men and of older women as they range farther from 'permanent' camps to gather forest products, trade, hunt and fish.

Outward mobility and increasing sedentism will very likely effect changes in the present pattern of choosing mates. Marital ties have been a principal means of maintaining flexibility by providing access to resources in other territories. With outward expansion marital ties with former allies in territories within Palanan will become less efficacious because of the need to travel greater and greater distances in order to activate those ties for resource exploitation. The Agta of Disukad now speak of consolidating ties with the San Mariano area across the mountains, a former enemy territory. Others have moved north

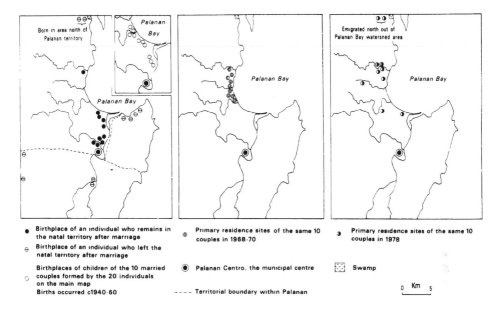

FIGURE 6.6 Palanan: birthplace and primary residence sites

to areas many Palanan Agta still regard as 'enemy territory'. Although too few marriages have occurred in the past eight years to reflect a true pattern, alliances appear to be shifting, and changes should be measurable in the future. Some concrete evidence already exists for such change. One feature of Agta marriage serving to maximize alliances and increase adaptive flexibility is an extremely broad definition of incest. Agta should not marry any known consanguineal *or affinal* kinsman. This too appears to be changing, if deviant behaviour can be interpreted as a harbinger of change. At least two cases of 'incestuous' marriage, one a case of sororate, now exist in Palanan. These may be interpreted as an effort to consolidate access to changing resources, rather than diversifying access to varied and mobile resources as exogamy does (Peterson 1978a; Lee 1972; Yellen 1977b).

Inter- as well as intra-ethnic relations are changing in Palanan as Agta either move away from farming centres, or settle near them in a changed lifeway (cf. Lee 1972). Agta abandon old trading partners as, with outward movement, the distance they must travel to trade becomes too great. Those who remain behind spend more time working in farmers' fields for cash or food, and less time travelling out to the increasingly distant forest beyond the expanding cultivated area. Those who precede the

141

frontier must avoid or adjust to a new set of social rules and a changed economic system introduced by ethnically different immigrants.

Conclusions

Yellen (1977b), applying a biogeographical approach to desert hunter mobility, argues for the adaptiveness of flexibility, which is certainly true of the tropical Agta (Peterson 1978a), and goes on to contrast desert and tropical hunters: 'Societies which rely on predictable tropical resources should, paradoxically enough, show some of the same characteristics of their desert counterparts: they should exhibit similar long-term stability; yet when change does occur among tropical groups, one may anticipate that the magnitude of the alteration will be greater, the effects more abrupt, and the pattern observed will be replacement rather than gradual alteration' (p. 272). Long-term stability has certainly been characteristic of Negrito hunters in the Philippines, and abrupt change is beginning to occur in Palanan. Yellen also indicates (p. 64) that subsistence needs, especially access to water, are foremost in determining camp moves. He notes, further, that they try to minimize the distance travelled each day, and that a desire for a varied diet also affects camp moves. These generalizations apply to the tropical dwelling Agta as well.[12]

Yellen, however, while he considers the relationship between individual and camp mobility, does not address the role of affective and social ties in influencing decisions relating to subsistence strategy and movement. Among the Agta both individual and camp movement seem to result from a combination of the need for successful resource exploitation and a desire to maintain easy access to the family on a daily basis. While minimal subsistence needs cannot be compromised, social variables can be met in conjunction with subsistence needs. Much of their movement can be accounted for in terms of quantifiable environmental variables and the need to allocate resources, but social variables play an important role, as well. To ignore these social factors would leave some movement unaccounted for, or inadequately explained.

The social and emotional factors that play a role in hunter mobility have not been acknowledged by ethnoarchaeological studies of mobility. Perhaps this is because it is the relocation of camps (or sites) that has concerned the ethnoarchaeologists, not the social organization or movements of people. An examination of individual movement, both long-term and daily, among desert dwellers might reveal important internal social, as well as external environmental, variables affecting both individual and camp movement (cf. Lee 1972: 143-4).

A second difference between the approach in this paper and an ethnoarchaeological approach is the examination of the effects of contemporary change. Wobst (1978) challenges the perspectives of salvage ethnographers and those who attempt to reconstruct the ethnographic present – 'the imaginary point in time when the studied populations were less affected by culture contact.' He points out that these approaches induce a parochialism which is not characteristic of either contemporary or prehistoric hunters, and which limits the development of anthropological theory. It is also true that ethnography produces a short-range interpretation. For example, an apparent outward expansion may be only one part of a traditional expanding and contracting cycle. Wobst urges an archaeological approach for correcting this spatially and temporally limited perspective. Nonetheless, dramatic change is affecting hunters in this century, probably disrupting traditional patterns. Acknowledgment of this change might also enhance anthropological theory; certainly it should command attention because of its implications for the peoples experiencing it. In Palanan change involves a very different economic system, diminishing access to critical resources, the imposition of non-traditional values, and increasing exploitation of the Agta. Certainly it behoves us, when a future without intervention or advocacy appears so potentially bleak for peoples like the Agta, to address the issues of change among hunters now.

Notes

1 In 1968-70, 12 per cent of Palanan Agta interviewed had never planted, 12 per cent were not planting in 1968 and/or 1969, and 25 per cent planted only a few roots.

2 The degree of this specialization is reflected in the fact that of an estimated 3000 kilograms of pig and deer killed and accounted for in May 1978 in one area of Palanan, 30 per cent was killed by the two best hunters. Success, they say, is dependent primarily on diligence and secondarily on skill. Neither fished during that period.

3 In one of the three Agta territories in Palanan one old man produced 95 per cent of the vegetable foods produced in that area by Agta in 1968-70.

4 If one of these individuals dies and the other becomes economically less active the survivor will most likely join the households of one or more married children. The grandchildren, by this time, are of marriageable age and a core cooperative group composed of different personnel begins to take form.

5 'Free choice' of a marriage partner may involve a good deal of

friendly persuasion. As children approach marriageable age they will be offered every opportunity, through attendance at social functions, life crisis events, and choice of campsite, to meet acceptable members of the opposite sex.

6 Because of the distances involved I could not observe a larger community, or smaller groups for continuous periods of time. The data used are based on interview and observation. Initially I attempted to select more 'typical' time periods, avoiding periods of tree resin collection, harvest, and the town fiesta. After nearly two months of observation and note-taking I determined that these intensive activities *were* typical of the 1978 dry season. Movements of persons were monitored as much as possible, and where dependent on informants' recall of activities and locations accounts were cross-checked. Distances were calculated from map measurements. In some activities, particularly tree resin collecting and distant hunting, the distance covered in a day was largely in travel to and from the site of the task rather than travel demanded by the task. Ages of individual Agta are estimates based on comparison with Palanan cohorts where ages are known.

7 Wilmsen (1973) discusses the effect of centripetal and centrifugal forces on hunter-mobility, referring only to the distribution of resources, not considering the attraction of social ties. Lee's (1972) treatment of campsite relative to resource location is similar to Wilmsen's in this respect.

8 My husband found it quite difficult in 1969 and 1970 to find archaeological labourers interested in a wage. In 1978, while the corn harvest still syphoned off a potential labour supply, wages were much more eagerly sought.

9 Griffin (personal communication) notes that the major consolidation of settlement occurred in 1973, and that typically Agta continued to move in and out of the settlement through 1974 and 1975, at times abandoning it altogether. Furthermore, he calculates relative to the epidemic, which he observed at its inception, that 'after about 11-13 Agta died, the Agta split up, some going up the coast, some down'. This might suggest a mortality estimate lower than that indicated.

10 Large fish traps were first used in Palanan the summer of 1978. Many Palaneño families adopted this technology, intending to store fish as *bagoong* (a salty, fermented fish paste) for the rainy season.

11 Agta men wear loincloths and women, skirts; with increasing immigration into the area they are beginning to wear cast-off *puti* trousers and dresses or blouses.

12 One old man I interviewed about the feeding habits of wild pigs noted that they like to eat farmers' crops. I asked then, why they moved around so much, why they did not stay always near the farmers' fields. The old man answered, 'Then they would be domestic pigs. They are not domestic pigs. They are just like Agta. They like to eat many different foods and must move always to find them.' Other Agta expressed similar motivation for mobility, particularly of pregnant women who may get hungry for specific foods.

7 Traditional and modern patterns of circulation of pastoral nomads: the Duru' of south-east Arabia

J. Stace Birks

The spatial mobility and circulation systems of pastoral nomads have long fascinated academics and other observers and commentators. Nomadic movement has also preoccupied administrators and politicians who have had to deal with pastoralists. Moreover, it is generally acknowledged that spatial mobility is so built into the social and economic life of nomads that no sense can be made of their social organization, or of their cultural outfit, without consideration of this parameter (Fortes 1971: 1-20). In view of the centrality of movement to pastoral life, it is perhaps surprising that nomadic patterns of circulation have not been evaluated more fully.

Given the scant systematic treatment of geographical movement of nomadic groups in the past, it is unfortunate that recent studies of nomads have chosen not to deal in particular detail with patterns of spatial mobility. For example, Asad (1970), Cole (1975), Cunnison (1966), and Irons and Dyson-Hudson (1973) all contribute little to either extra detail or analysis of the circulation of nomads. The lack of information on the spatial aspects of nomadic life is easily demonstrated by attempts to fill in patterns of nomadic circulation in, for example, the Arab world. At any but a banal level of generalization such efforts fall well short of completion because of a paucity of relevant knowledge. Attention has been drawn to the incomplete and simplistic analyses of nomadic movement by Gulliver (1975).

There would be value in more detailed descriptions of the processes behind the spatial element of nomadic life. The relative neglect in modern works of the detail of the movement of nomads has led to a continued over-simplification of the patterns and processes involved, also to an underestimation or ignoring of the degree to which the circulation of population reflects upon

145

the whole of nomadic life. This is demonstrated by reference to a nomadic tribe of south-east Arabia.

The Duru' are a bedouin tribe of Nizari descent, numbering about 6,000 (though no full census has been taken), inhabiting the eastern fringes of the Empty Quarter in an area which now falls into the Sultanate of Oman. They occupy an extensive tribal territory (locally called a *dar*, plural *dira*, *dawar*, etc.) between the lands of the Al Bu Shamis and Bani Oitab in the north, and the Wahiba in the south (Figure 7.1). The Duru' *dar* consists mainly of rolling gravel plains, with extensive sandy depressions and dune formations. Across this area of generally low relief flow the braided wadis from the western Hajar mountains of the Sultanate of Oman. Rainfall is irregular in incidence and distribution, probably averaging less than 30 mm per year. Large areas of the gravels provide an inhospitable plant habitat, featuring only low open scrub, but in the sandy areas and wadi courses growth is less restricted. Apart from *Acacia* spp bushes and low trees, there is a light cover of *Zygophyllum* spp and *Fagonia* spp. *Tamarix* spp occupies areas in the larger wadi beds, and occasionally *Peganum* spp occurs, with *Haloxylon* in the most favoured habitat.

The traditional pattern of circulation

Traditional Duru' economy, and the way of life of the men in particular, revolved around and was based on the camel, which was relied on for food, drink and transport. The Duru' supplemented their income by hunting, trading particularly in salt, and with revenue from the carrying trade. Duru' camels were used extensively on all trade routes from the Ibri area to the Gulf, interior Arabia and Muscat.

Their way of life derived essentially from efforts to husband camels in the local environment in the best possible way. This the bedouin sought to achieve by moving with their *dar* in a semi-regular transhumance pattern. The regular aspects of this circulation were determined by the march of the seasons and the need to harvest date palms, the irregular by the vagaries of rainfall, tribal disputes and celebrations.

Duru' families spent the high summer, June to early September, the period of the date harvest, living near to date groves. Almost 65 per cent of Duru' families own date palms, the fruit of which comprises a significant element of their diet. The date groves, situated in oases on the mountain fringes to the south-east of the Empty Quarter, are irrigated by *falaj* systems (Birks and Letts 1977a; Twisleton-Wykeham-Fiennes 1970; Wilkinson

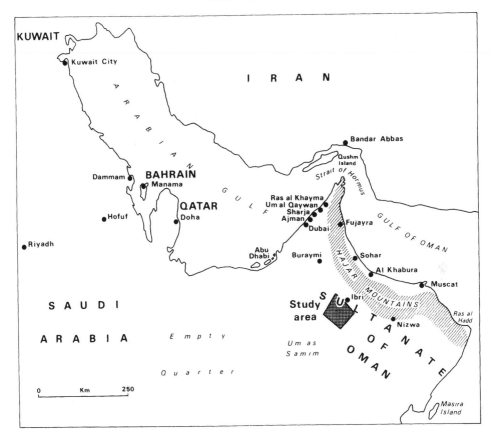

FIGURE 7.1 South-east Arabia: study area

1974). These oases acted as foci of many transhumance orbits, drawing in the Duru' from their dispersed winter sites in the pastures. After the date harvest, in early September, the tribesmen began dispersing again, leaving behind only the *bidars* to irrigate the dates. Most of the bedouin moved relatively quickly away from their summer residence, driving their animals directly to the area of wells near which they planned to spend the early winter. They departed usually for the same wells or area of pastures. During the early winter the Duru' normally made several moves of *fariq* site over short distances of about two or three kilometres. A *fariq* (plural *firgan*) is a temporary nomadic camp, occupied by a nuclear family, usually found in small groups of between three and seven. These local moves served to better use of local pastures, and provided clean sites, with more easily available firewood. Cole (1973 and 1975) mentions a

147

similar pattern amongst the Al Murrah of Saudi Arabia.

A longer move was often made to a new area of pastures for the second half of the winter and early summer. This shift of site was less predictable than that made immediately after the date harvest, depending upon incidence of rains, on the whereabouts of relatives and friends, as well as a general assessment of the browse.

The movement in May from the pastures in the peripheral areas of the *dar* towards the summer residence for the date harvest was slower than the movement away from it. This was because of the heat, the scarcity of browse, and the lack of dates with which to hand-feed the camels. The bedouin sometimes went short of food and milk during this period, especially those who were travelling with only part of the herd, for the milk camels often remained longer in the winter pastures.

The return to the oasis for the summer represented the completion of the annual cycle of transhumance. While fundamentally a regular circulation, it would be misleading to overstress an identical pattern of the movement from year to year. Each circulatory set of transhumance movements varied according to particular conditions, both in response to the limiting parameters of weather, especially rainfall but also temperatures, as well as the changing circumstances of each family group from one year to the next. Ownership of a different number of camels, a result of sales, loans or disease, would result in a different circulatory pattern from one followed the year before by the bedouin group concerned.

The bedouin's interest in their patterns of circulation has made it possible to create, by careful retrospective questioning of household heads combined with travel around the *dar*, a map of the traditional pattern of circulation of a sample of Duru' households (Figure 7.2). This shows in detail a sample of transhumance cycles out to winter pastures in 1956 and back to Tan'am for the summer date harvest of 1957. The 1956/57 transhumance cycle was chosen to re-create the historical picture because it was readily identifiable within a calendar of local political events, but it appears to have been made in a 'typical' year in terms of weather and pastures.

It was not possible to record the movements of all households which took place in this year, for apart from other problems of completing enumeration the sample was limited by the time available in the field. The houses of the *bidars* who irrigated the palms and lived in the immediate vicinity of Tan'am are excluded for they did not move with the animals. These sedentary households amounted to about 8 per cent of the total in the

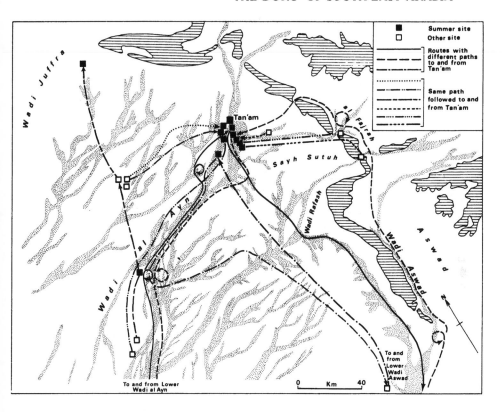

FIGURE 7.2 Seasonal movements of fariqs *1956/57*

1950s. The great majority of households were involved in transhumance movements; about 40 per cent of these mobile households that were in the area are shown (Figure 7.2). The seasonal shifts of *fariq* were made on foot and with baggage camels, the herd being driven slowly from well to well, deviating widely from the direct route in order to benefit from available browse.

This nomadic way of life, as represented by patterns of circulation illustrated, represented a system in which the camel was the over-riding interest of the bedouin. They lived in close relationship with their camels, striking a fine balance between them and the desert in this part of the Empty Quarter. Nomadism provided the basis for a relatively self-sufficient life augmented in a relatively minor way only with ancillary activities such as trade. Most significantly, this traditional pattern of circulation enabled the maintenance of the camel population without causing the long-term deterioration of the environment

149

in any way. The Duru' were a society in ecological balance.

The very basis of this system, the pattern of circulation linking winter pastures and date groves, is no longer a prominent feature of Duru' life. Change has been rapid and profound: it has had repercussions upon the external relationships of the tribe, both political and social, with neighbours and government; it has been of great impact upon the internal organization of Duru' society, altering deep-seated attitudes such as those towards agriculture and the role of women. Most critically, the relationship of the Duru' with their camels has been destroyed. Indeed the camel has been virtually discarded, to the extent that many Duru' youths today, sons of nomads famous all over south-east Arabia for breeding Omani racing camels, cannot ride competently.

The processes of change

Rapid change only began some two decades ago. The widespread exploitation of oil on the Gulf Coast and in Saudi Arabia introduced a new element into Duru' life − the possibility for men to travel outside their *dar* to obtain wage-paid work. The small scale of the early movement of labourers, and the nature of its organization meant that it did not radically affect patterns of animal husbandry; it only absorbed labour that was under-employed for much of the year. The absence of some male members from the household for purposes of trade or hunting was not uncommon. Migrant labouring simply replaced these pursuits. Birks (1978) discusses similar changes amongst the Bani Oitab, a neighbouring tribe.

Migrant labourers' travel was facilitated by the Duru' trading caravans. A second seasonal circulation was established, that of migrant workers, which was integrated with that of households on the transhumance orbits with the camels. These two circulations coalesced in the summer for the date harvest at the oases. The migrant labourers returned from their places of work in the more economically developed areas of the Arabian peninsula and Gulf at the same time as their families converged upon the date groves from the winter pastures on the periphery of the *dar*.

For some years in this way the bedouin gained a larger cash income that in the short term was not detrimental to pastoral life, which continued much as before. Although fewer of the men travelled the transhumance orbits with the camels, the pattern of circulation between the palm groves and the winter pastures was little changed. The withdrawal of labour from the traditional system as a result of migrant labour movements was compensated for adequately by extra efforts made by remaining men, and a wider role assumed by the Duru' women. Duru' migrant labourers at this time considered themselves to be temporarily away from home as wage earners; their cash income was designed to augment pastoral life, not to replace it.

In the 1960s, an ever quickening pace of economic development and commensurate increased opportunities in Oman and the nearby Emirates greatly increased the numbers drawn to cash employment. *Fariq* populations were depleted by the movement not of only one member away to work, but by the absence of several of the family menfolk. Once the Duru' became aware of the potential cash income from large-scale employment their desire for wages became paramount, and large numbers of men took work on a long-term basis. This larger-scale, longer-term absenteeism quickly had a deleterious impact upon the traditional pastoral economy; camel husbandry was extensively disrupted.

A basic change in Duru' philosophy had occurred; the men began to feel that their primary occupation was that of migrant labourer. They began to return home only temporarily for holidays and to visit the family. Their view of the animals, their traditional wealth, was thus transformed; men began to think of herding as only a secondary occupation, furthermore one which interfered with their major role in life, earning money as migrant workers. The more recent, originally secondary, circulatory system, of migrant labourers from the Duru' *dar* to obtain wage employment in the modern sector, was becoming dominant, displacing the pastoral circulation as the governing pattern of Duru' life. Boute (1975) gives details of a similar process in the Sahara.

The scale of migrant labour movements

The extent of the withdrawal of labour from traditional pursuits can be illustrated by reference to a sample enumeration of 655 of the Duru' (about 115 families) in 1976. Of the recorded population, over 16 per cent was absent from home at the time of enumeration. People were counted as absentees only if they had been away for at least ten days, and were not living in an adjacent *fariq*. The significance of this proportion of the population being away from home is clearer if the male population alone is considered, 59 per cent of adult males (those of over 14 years of age) were away working or in search of employment; over 72 per cent of males aged between 15 and 40 years were absent. Another 11 per cent had been at home for only six months or less. Thus over 70 per cent of the menfolk were either absent from home, or had just returned from working away. Only 13 per cent of those enumerated had not lived away from home for at least six months. These comprised mainly the young (those aged between 14 and 18 years), most of whom would depart as migrant labourers in the near future, those who were too aged to avail themselves of the new opportunities of employment; and the group which traditionally remained in the oasis to irrigate the date palms. So great is this movement away to work that only 29 per cent of Duru' nuclear families did not have at least one person absent at a place of work. Birks and Sinclair (1977) comment generally on the movement of menfolk away to work from this area of the Sultanate of Oman.

In 1976, some 47 per cent of Duru' men absent from home were employed in Abu Dhabi. A further 7 per cent worked elsewhere on the Gulf, and about 6 per cent in Saudi Arabia; most of the remainder worked with the local oil company. However, only relatively few complete nuclear families have moved away to these places of work. As yet, the population circulating between the Duru' tribal lands and the places of employment is almost entirely male.

The average duration of each trip to work was nine months. About one in ten of migrant labourers returned every month to their households and families. These were mostly either enlisted in the Abu Dhabi armed forces, or were employed in the Omani oil company. Some 14 per cent of the migrants were away for between one and four months on their most recent trips as migrant labourers − these comprise the regularly employed migrants. The unskilled, casually employed, could not return so frequently, having no formal periods of leave.

Over 13 per cent of migrant labourers had been away on their last trip for 12 months. Whilst this is partly a result of a 'rounding' of responses, it actually represents a common period of absence; many of the migrants have twelve-month contracts of employment. It is also a consequence of the desires of the tribesmen to return to their *dar* for the period of the date harvest. This annual return might ostensibly be ascribed to the desire of the migrant to help with the date harvest, and some do return with this in mind; but it is not too cynical to assert that the migrants return home not to help in the harvesting of dates, but simply to enjoy them. Many who are employed outside the *dar* only return in order to relax and 'take a holiday'.

About 16 per cent of migrants were away for between one and two years. Some of these are employed a considerable distance from home − in Saudi Arabia or Kuwait. Others are target workers, who plan to return home only when they have saved a certain sum. Most of the movement to work is more obviously periodic, and so clearly a circulatory movement.

The profundity of change

The extent of the withdrawal of labour from the traditional economy which such repeated periods of absence represent has been so extreme that the pastoral system has collapsed. Many herds have been sold off, others simply ignored. The organization of grazing and standard of husbandry has become so slovenly that, despite reduced numbers of camels which should in theory have provided those remaining with better pastures, their condition has deteriorated and they have become more prone to drought and disease. The camel has fallen from being the pivot of Duru' life to becoming a neglected element on the fringe of Duru' decision-making. Today over 55 per cent of Duru' families do not own camels; most do not consider them worth the trouble of keeping.

Through detailing some of the ways in which these profound social and economic changes have manifested themselves it is possible to further understand the rapid evolution of the new facet of society – the circulation of migrant labourers. As little historical data on the Duru' exist, this assessment of change is dependent upon information collected in the field, some of which is retrospective, with all its problems in such a society.

The camel

An obvious indication of the extent of this change would be the variation in camel numbers over time. It proved possible, though arduous because of the counting and cross-checking involved, to collect information about present numbers of camels owned by households. Unfortunately, though not surprisingly, it was difficult to collect useful data about past numbers owned. The Duru' are very aware of the decline in camel numbers, and are prone to wild exaggeration when giving estimates of how many they owned even two or three years ago. It is therefore not feasible to trace the decline in the numbers of camels.

It is possible, however, by comparison with other areas, to postulate what camel numbers might have been prior to their decline. In northern Dhufar, a ratio of four camels per person is the minimum viable number. Amongst the Duru' today the ratio is less than 1.8 per person, reflecting decline to only a marginal asset. Whilst there are now about 800 camels within the area studied, there were probably over 2,000 two decades ago.

Goats and sheep

Small stock have not been mentioned previously, because they did not feature large in traditional Duru' life. Although most households had a few goats and sheep, they were not an important consideration in decision-making, but were marginal in the way that the camel now is. However, it proved much easier to collect information about the numbers of goats and sheep owned in the past. The smaller numbers of small stock owned in the past did not lend themselves so readily to exaggeration as did the larger numbers of camels. Furthermore, the Duru', attaching less traditional social status to goat and sheep ownership than to camel possession, were less inclined to overestimate. The Duru' who were enumerated owned some 2,900 goats and sheep. This represents a large increase in goat ownership. Even a decade ago, they certainly owned less than 800 head and possibly as few as 600. This represents a rise from six or seven to about 26 goats and sheep per household.

The replacement of the camel by small stock is common amongst bedouin in Arabia. It is normally attributed to an increase in the number of watering points; to the bedouin's response to market forces, mutton being a preferred meat in the peninsula, and the fact that small stock require less attention. In this case, it is mainly the result of the enlarged role of women, who are responsible for the goats and sheep (Birks and Letts 1979b). The tending of small stock was traditionally the women's domain, but sheep were previously only secondary to the camel. As the menfolk have taken up migrant labouring on such a large scale, so the women have been able to expand goat and sheep numbers. There has thus been a marked change in pastoral emphasis, consequent upon the changed pattern of authority within the households of absentee males.

Whilst emphasizing the profound nature and speed of change, the increase in small stock is to some extent misleading. Goats and sheep remain only marginal in the modern Duru' economy, and discussion of them should not obscure one of the main facets of change − the overall decline in the time and inputs devoted to pastoral pursuits.

Farming and the changing role of women

The adoption of farming by the Duru' illustrates the decline in their interest in pastoral activities. Traditionally, farming was considered demeaning by the tribesmen, and was the task of a servant class (*bidars*). Traditionally, cultivation was limited to the *falaj* irrigated areas in the oases, only a small area of seasonal crops being irrigated by water drawn from wells by bulls. In contrast, today over 10 per cent of the enumerated households have established new gardens based upon pump wells, and there is every sign that the number of families establishing irrigated gardens is increasing rapidly.

The establishment of these gardens is a form of investment. Most Duru' families, because of the number of migrant labourers, have a substantial cash income from remittances, but only a relatively restricted range of consumer desires to satisfy with this new wealth. Once immediate consumer wants are satisfied they tend to use surplus cash to buy land, to have a well dug, and to have a pump installed. Once established, the garden is not run on a commercial basis, but it is often almost ignored by the men; its day-to-day running often falls to the women who work the pump, irrigate and in some cases even seed and manure.

The investment in farms is another example of the widening female role in Duru' economy and society; women run the gardens in large part to produce alfalfa for their goats and sheep. Increased economic activity on the part of women is producing a markedly different socio-economic system, and a new pattern of land and labour utilization in which irrigated gardens feature increasingly.

The modern pattern of mobility

The growth of migrant labour movements, and consequent erosion of the traditional pastoral system have resulted in a transformation of the pattern of household circulation that existed when camel numbers were larger. This evolution of the pattern of pastoral circulation is one of the most evocative measures of the profound change in Duru' life. The cessation of the movements designed to benefit the camel, at the core of the old social and economic order of the Duru', exemplifies the virtual eclipse of the traditional livestock economy.

Figure 7.3 shows the seasonal movement of households between September 1974 and August 1975. Completely sedentary households are excluded from the maps, but those families who made no seasonal move amount to 58 per cent of the total, compared to 8 per cent in 1956. All households in the study area which moved site during 1974/75 are included.

The changed proportion of sedentary households is not the

155

only comparison of the circulatory patterns to be made between 1956/57 and 1974/75. Equally important is the varying average distance moved by the *fariqs* in these two years of reference. In 1956/57 when camels were still an important aspect of Duru' life, the average distance moved by the *fariqs* in the annual cycle was 114 km. The smaller proportion of households which changed site seasonally in 1974 moved an average of only 15 km. The circulatory patterns of movement for camel grazing have broken down virtually completely. Comparison of the two different patterns of mobility suggests that the propensity of the Duru' to follow pastoral pursuits has reduced to 13 per cent of its former extent.

Furthermore, if the moves of *fariq* made in 1975 are examined in more detail, many are found not to be stimulated by concern for animals and are not at all connected with pastoralism. The three longest seasonal moves − to the Wadi Aswad from the immediate vicinity of Tan'am (Figure 7.3) − do not relate to livestock in any way, but were concerned with the tending of a well-garden and illegal trading. If some of the shorter moves are considered in detail, these too are found to be related not to transhumance nor to the requirements of any animals the families own. The majority are made so that the family can inhabit a clean site free from droppings and rubbish, usually within a kilometre of the previous one, and normally utilizing the same water source.

Few of the moves depicted (Figure 7.3) are the result of the complex of pastoral motives which lay behind the system of circulation in 1956/57. The traditionally stimulated moves that remain in 1975 are those of medium length to Tan'am from the areas of Biyar and Tawarish. Even these moves are not made in a traditional manner, by driving the animals (goats, mainly) in order that they benefit from pastures *en route*; most of the animals are now transported with the Duru' by lorry and landrover increasingly; families owning goats are abandoning the seasonal move to the site near Tan'am and are living all the year in what used to be the winter pastures. Previously, the depth of the wells in the peripheral pastures discouraged the keeping of animals there in the summer because of the effort involved in watering them. Water sources are near the surface in the area of the date groves.

It is the replacement of the camel by the landrover as transport that enables a family to live all the year in the more distant areas of the *dar*. The vehicle covers in a few hours journeys from the pastures to the oases, which used to take several days by camel. This enables parties to drive from the pastures to an oasis,

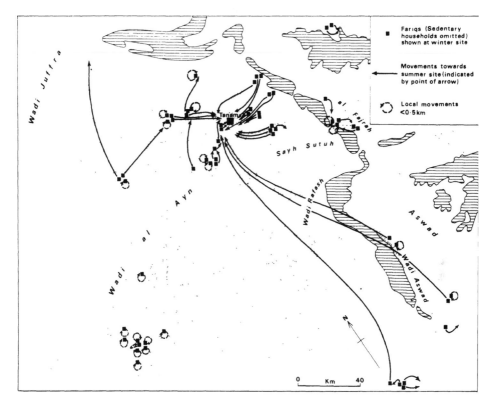

FIGURE 7.3 Seasonal movements of fariqs *1973/74*

harvest some dates, and return the same day. Thus the essential reason for the seasonal move – the need of the family to live near the dates in order to harvest them – is removed. The landrover superseding the camel has contributed to breaking down the traditional pattern of pastoral circulation.

The rate of introduction of the landrover amongst the Duru' has been high. Ten years or so ago, only the three major *shaykhs* had vehicles. Nowadays 20 per cent of households own one vehicle, and 7 per cent own more than one. Few families do not have at least the occasional use of a landrover. Its proliferation is thus making possible the logical extension of the Duru's disinterest in the camel leading to virtually complete sedentarization.

Other more trivial factors further change household mobility. As the Duru' collect more consumer goods their houses become both more substantial and cluttered, and so more difficult to move. The extra effort needed to shift house is all the more

157

significant because the absence of so many men results both in a shortage of labour needed to make the move and, more critically, an absence of authority to initiate the move.

Some wider implications of the modern patterns of circulation

In many respects, the Duru' have exchanged an ecologically determined pattern of circulation for one which is governed by the wider modern economy of the Middle East. The movement of households, once the dominating feature of life, is much reduced and still declining. The settlement pattern is progressing towards one of isolated sedentary households. The most important manifestation of increasing mobility has become the circulation of labourers.

Such a change of emphasis is having a considerable impact upon the difficult and marginal country in which the Duru' live. The reduction in mobility has caused a marked spatial concentration of their impact upon the environment. Areas from which the Duru', with their customary pattern of circulation, derived benefit are now not used by them. Moreover, the consequent greater concentrations of livestock, despite their reduced numbers, are causing overgrazing. In this sedentarization, combined with the changeover to goats and sheep from the camel, there is increased risk of the destruction of an important resource. Pastures may be marginal in world terms; within the Middle East they are significant. The importance of the pastoral resources in the Duru' *dar* in particular is enhanced by the limited future of oil in the Sultanate of Oman. Emphasis must be placed upon the development of non-oil-based activities within the Sultanate in the near future. Meat production could feature large amongst these.

At first inspection, there is little reason to suggest that the sedentarization which has occurred should prejudice adversely development of livestock production amongst the Duru'. Indeed, it might seem desirable to settle these erstwhile nomads before a modern fodder-based livestock exporting economy could be created.

There is, however, the question of the present-day overgrazing to set against this suggestion. Yet more fundamental, is the problem of over-extraction of groundwater needed to irrigate the cultivated fodder with which to hand feed the animals. Although careful evaluation has yet to be made, it appears increasingly unlikely that there are large supplies of groundwater available to irrigate the amounts of fodder crops necessary to support large numbers of stock. Indeed, unless careful control is exercised upon the increasing numbers of well-gardens at present being established by the Duru' and the rates of water extraction to irrigate them, it is likely that the hydrological resources will be threatened by over-pumping in the near future. In short, it would not be wise to advocate a marked expansion of the present-day trend towards goats and sheep fed by fodder grown within the Duru' *dar* which would be at the expense of exhaustion of groundwater resources. Animal numbers could only be increased if they were fed with fodder brought in from a less marginal area. Such a scheme would have many disadvantages.

It is when the future of livestock production amongst the Duru' is viewed in this way that the breakdown of the traditional ecologically-determined patterns of circulation appears to be a significant loss. Circulation was a particularly effective way of exploiting this marginal area in the long term rather than just the immediate term. However, the pastoral circulation cannot now be recreated. There is now a lack of inclination among the tribesmen to revert to a nomadic lifestyle. They see many advantages attendant upon sedentarization and also display individual inability to deal again with the traditional way of life. The structure of tribal authority which underlay the pastoral circulation system has also been destroyed with the settling of the population.

It is difficult to envisage a local economy that could be developed in the area which would be viable, and so prevent a permanent dependence of Duru' society upon the remittances resulting from the new circulation system of migrant labourers. Given that the remittances are even today insecure, being vulnerable to both the political and economic vagaries of the Middle East, the question of the form of such a local economy might well become more than academic. In this event, the loss of the pastoral circulation system would have profound implications for the Duru'.

Acknowledgment

Thanks are due to John Carter for discussion of many points of Duru' life, and for unpublished material relating to the tribe.

This paper derives from a study made in 1975, when the author was a Research Fellow at the Centre for Middle Eastern and Islamic Studies, University of Durham. The work was financed by Petroleum Development (Oman) Ltd. However, the views expressed are entirely those of the author.

8 Vertical circulation in southern Ecuador

Jim Belote and Linda Belote

The town of Saraguro, with a moist, temperate climate, lies at an altitude of 2,520 metres in the Andes of southern Ecuador. In a hard day's walk westward from the town, one can descend to a warm, dry desert area only 1,000 metres above the level of the sea. An even harder day's journey to the east would follow a gradually ascending route through cultivated fields, scattered montane forest and high, wet, cold *paramo* grasslands of the continental divide at elevations of over 3,200 metres − followed by a precipitous descent through the moss-bromeliad- and orchid-covered trees of the cloud forest − to arrive in the warm, sub-tropical rain forest of the Upper Amazon Basin at an altitude of around 1,500 metres.

Extreme altitudinal/ecological diversity of this sort, within relatively short distances, is common in Andean geography. This diversity has often given rise to adaptive strategies in which local or regional populations have attempted to attain economic self-sufficiency and strength through control of the resources of a variety of altitudinal/ecological zones. These adaptive strategies have been given the title 'vertical control' by the anthropologist and ethno-historian, John Murra (e.g., Murra 1968: 121-5; 1970: 57-8; 1972: 429-30). Vertical control as either a primary or secondary theme has gained considerable attention among Andean anthropologists. Brush (1977) and Orlove (1977) are good recent sources for this literature. Lambert (1977: 5-8) provides other sources and a summary discussion of the role of Andean households involved in vertical control strategies and Dillehay (1979: 24-31) gives an application from archaeology.

Vertical control and vertical circulation

Adaptive strategies of vertical control can take at least two basic forms. On the one hand, a population such as a community or an

160

individual that has direct control over only limited altitudinal/ecological zones may extend vertical control through patterns of 'reciprocity and exchange' with populations or individuals who have direct control over other altitudinal/ecological zones. Rhoades and Thompson, in an overview of Alpine adaptive strategies, have called the pattern which involves concentration of the productive activities of populations and individuals to single environmental zones, a *specialized* strategy (1975: 546-7). A *generalized* strategy is one whereby populations or individuals directly exploit a series of environmental zones themselves (Rhoades and Thompson 1975: 546-7).

In his recent analysis of vertical control models, Orlove claimed that there has been an overemphasis on the specialized strategy (with reciprocity and exchange being utilized to gain access to resources in various zones) due to a theoretically biased focus on systems of distribution rather than production (1977). We would suggest, however, that distribution and exchange patterns play a relatively greater role in specialized systems and are thus deserving as a focus of study. But we agree with Orlove in the case of generalized vertical control strategies. In these, patterns of production − the allocation of productive efforts to various altitudinal/ecological zones, the extent to which production in one zone is integrated with production in others, and the degree to which production in various zones constrains other activities − must be examined carefully.

The Indians of Saraguro have a generalized strategy of vertical control at the individual/household level. They own land and engage in productive activities in a number of altitudinal/ecological zones located in the region. In following this strategy they must frequently move from one zone to another and back again. They are thus engaged in patterns of what we call 'vertical circulation' in order to produce what they need to maintain a strong subsistence base and to engage in a cash economy. We have chosen the term 'vertical circulation' to distinguish the Saraguro patterns from the old world patterns of transhumance in mountainous regions which are determined by seasonal variations of available forage at different elevations. Seasonality is only a minor factor in Saraguro movement. These patterns of production-oriented vertical circulation followed by the Indians of Saraguro are discussed here.

While the most time consuming, vertical circulation is obviously not the only kind of circulation in which Saraguros engage. Among the others which will not be discussed, are regular

161

(usually weekly) visits to the towns of Saraguro or Yacuambi, movement between scattered agricultural plots in a single altitudinal zone, trips to cities or on regional or national religious/market pilgrimages, etc. Insignificant numbers of Saraguros from the communities studied engage in circulation to other areas for wage labour.

The people of Saraguro

The Saraguros are a distinctive group of highland Indians, numbering around 10,000, whose traditional homeland is in the northern part of Ecuador's southernmost province, Loja. Hair woven in a long single braid and homespun black woollen clothing are the primary ethnic identity markers of both sexes which serve to distinguish them from the non-Indian (*blanco*) population of the region. Other distinguishing features include linguistic facility in a local dialect of Quichua (the language of the Incas) as well as Spanish, and an elaborate religious festival system (Belote and Belote 1977b). The Saraguros live in substantial tile-roofed, wattle-and-daub or adobe-walled, three-roomed houses scattered about the agricultural fields of dispersed settlement communities. This study is concerned only with the 3,000 or so Saraguros associated with the communities of Quisquinchir, Lagunas, Ñamarin, Tuncarta, Tambopamba, and Oñacapa, all of which are located within 10 km of the town of Saraguro.

The Saraguros, for the most part, have a strong subsistence economy based on individual and family landholdings of fifteen to twenty or so hectares which is more than adequate to provide most of their food, clothing, shelter and fuel needs. In addition, the average Saraguro household (a nuclear family with four to six members) maintains a herd of ten to twenty head of cattle in addition to other livestock which provides them with an entry into the cash economy. The combination of a strong subsistence base with market engagement has provided the Saraguros with an economic situation which is far better than that of most Indian groups in Ecuador or in the rest of the Andes. The average Saraguro is also economically better off than the average town dwelling non-Indian of the area and is at least on a par with rural non-Indians. Because of their relative economic strength and independence, Saraguros do not suffer from the most severe patterns of indignity and discrimination common to most other Indians in highland Ecuador (cf. Burgos 1970; Casagrande 1974; Maynard 1965). Nevertheless, as part of a national system in which Indians are treated as less than first-class citizens, Saraguros are not by any means altogether free of these patterns of indignity and discrimination (cf. Belote 1978; Mason 1977; and Schmitz 1977).

As the largest town on the Panamerican Highway, between the provincial capitals of Loja (60 km. to the south) and Cuenca (160 km to the north), Saraguro is the market, administrative, social and religious centre of the region. With a population of over 1,600 (virtually all non-Indian) it is also a *cabecera cantonal* (county seat). Most of its inhabitants who include shopkeepers, artisans, money lenders, real estate dealers, priests and nuns, school teachers, thieves, labourers, cheese and egg dealers, bootleggers, cantina owners, beggars, a few landowners – depend directly or indirectly on Indians for their livelihood (see Belote 1978). On any day, but especially on Sundays, Indians visit the town to buy and sell, attend mass, meet friends, drink, attend to official business or seek medical care. Countryside-town circulation patterns are an important part of the life of rural *blancos* (whites) as well as Indians. However, vertical circulation patterns are quite different for the two groups. Country *blancos*, like Indians, are primarily engaged in agricultural pursuits including subsistence crop raising and market oriented cattle production. Unlike Indians, they have more access to other occupations such as bootlegging, storekeeping and government employment as well.

Altitudinal/ecological zones (Figure 8.1)

In very broad terms, five altitudinal/ecological zones of signifi-cance in this discussion of Saraguro vertical circulation can be distinguished: the community zone; the *cerro* (high mountain interior forests); the *paramo* (high mountain grasslands); the cloud forests; and the Oriente (foothills and lowlands to the East of the Andean crests). Three of these, the community, *cerro* and Oriente zones, are the primary loci of Saraguro production. The cloud forest and *paramo* zones, while important in the past as sources of cinchona (quinine) bark and pasturage for free ranging livestock respectively, are today of significance primarily as obstacles to easy circulation movement.

The community zone

The community zone is the area of both primary settlement and most subsistence food production. Located on gently sloping, moderately well-watered land at elevations of between 2,000 and 2,700 metres above sea level, the community zone is suited to the production of large-grained varieties of maize, the chief Saraguro staple, various beans and squashes which are planted intermixed with the maize, and other subsistence crops such as potatoes, wheat and cabbage.

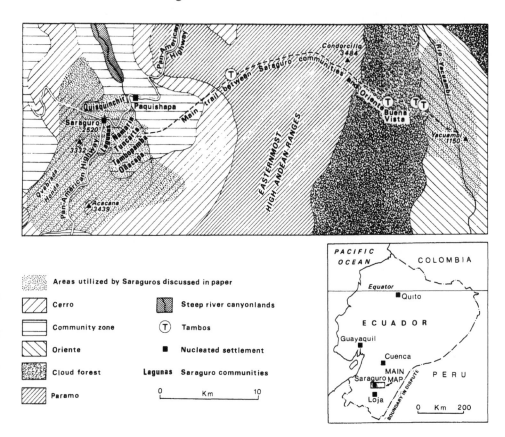

FIGURE 8.1 *Ecological zones in southern Ecuador: study area*

The community zone is characterized by dispersed settlement with houses distributed amongst agricultural plots and small pastures. Each household owns a number of small plots of land, totalling from one to three hectares, scattered throughout the community zone. Scattering is usually due, initially, to rules of equal inheritance regardless of sex or birth order. While some consolidation takes place, complete consolidation is inhibited by the Saraguro practice of maintaining subsistence security through the spreading of risks over a variety of micro-habitats each of which may have its own set of localized weather patterns, pest infestations and plant diseases. This is an important subsistence security strategy due to the absence of strong non-family based systems of social insurance involving patterns of sharing, reciprocity, redistribution or obligation networks (see Belote and Belote 1977a).

Finally, it should be noted that crops produced in the community zone are reserved for subsistence use. Surplus production does not enter the market place but provides seed for the next season's planting, goes into storage for lean years and may be distributed, mainly to relatives, through the religious fiesta system. By not having crops produced in the community zone be engaged in the vagaries of the market economy the Saraguros are also following a 'safety-first' subsistence strategy which has been described elsewhere (Wharton 1971; Scott 1976). The strength and security of the Saraguro's subsistence base underlies their ability to be successfully engaged in the sometimes risky but generally profitable business of raising cattle for cash.

The cerro

Adjacent to the community zone is the *cerro*. Located on the western side of the easternmost high Andean ridges at elevations ranging between 2,700 and 3,100 metres, the *cerro* consists of generally steep slopes with a natural cover of montane forest. Within the memory of older living persons this zone was almost entirely forested and utilized primarily as a source of wood for fuel and construction. Today the lower sections of the *cerro* have been largely cleared by Saraguros for pasture and some cropland while the upper and more distant sections still contain forest cover broken only by a scattering of pastures of from one to ten hectares in extent. Most Saraguro households own at least a hectare or so of *cerro* land, some have twenty or more. These plots are from one to fifteen kilometres from the community zone residence of their owners. While the *cerro* continues to serve as an essential household resource base for wood, and while it is utilized to supplement the production of some subsistence crops such as maize in the lower elevations, most Saraguro effort and time in the *cerro* is now oriented around cattle production. Especially in higher or more distant areas wood is taken as a by-product of clearing pasture and potatoes are planted only for a year or two in the freshly cleared land.

Many Saraguros have constructed one or more shelters on their *cerro* properties. These range from one-room huts to three-roomed houses similar to those in the community zone and make up what we call 'secondary settlements'. Secondary settlements serve to reduce the time and energy devoted to circulation by the Saraguros and provide a place to stay while guarding crops and cattle against theft. As indicated below, secondary settlements in some areas are in the process of becoming primary settlements for some Saraguros.

The Oriente

Most Saraguro occupation of the Oriente is concentrated in the Yacuambi River valley, the centre of which is some 50 kilometres to the east and across the Andes from the community zone. In the search for cinchona (quinine bark), gold and eventually, land, Saraguros and other highlanders began to enter the area before the turn of the last century – eventually displacing most of the native Shuar (Jivaro) Indian population to more remote areas. The current basis of Saraguro occupation is the raising of cattle on plots of land cleared of forest cover. Experience has led to the abandonment of clearings at elevations of above 1,700 metres (approximately marked by the upper limit of tall-growing palms as important components of the forest community). Most clearings are below 1,500 metres where various grass species planted as forage continue to produce indefinitely under good management, even on slopes of up to 100 per cent.[1]

With a population of 500, San José de Yacuambi is the administrative, commercial and communications centre of the area. A few Saraguros live in and around the town; most have established isolated homesteads scattered throughout the Yacuambi River basin. Shelter exists in a variety of forms, though almost all have wood or log walls and palm thatched roofs. Most representative is a structure with a living floor raised two metres above the ground on posts. The area beneath the floor is unwalled, used as a dry working space, and often includes an animal-powered *trapiche* (sugar cane grinding mill).

While most Saraguros prefer highland foods such as large grained maize, beans, squashes and potatoes, they all maintain mixed gardens which produce sugar cane, bananas, manioc, taro, small grained maize and other tropical crops in their Oriente holdings.

Like the *cerro*, the Oriente is primarily a zone of Saraguro secondary settlement. A few Saraguros, however, have disposed of their highland properties and have ceased regular visits to that area, thus making the Oriente their zone of primary settlement. In Murra's model of vertical control, well separated, discrete territorial units are called 'archipelagos' (1972: 464-8). This situation obtains in the Saraguro region where the Oriente on the one hand and the highland zones of community and *cerro* on the other, are not contiguous to each other but are separated by a region of little current productive utility which is traversed only with difficulty due to factors such as distance, cold, wind, rain, steepness, trail quality and, at times, the presence of armed bandits. This region contains two broad ecological zones: the *paramo* and the cloud forest.

The cloud forest

The cloud forest, located on the eastern Andean slopes between 1,700 and 3,000 metres, catches the full brunt of the moisture-laden winds blowing westerly across the Amazon basin. Because of the steepness of the terrain and density of the forest, travel within it is extremely difficult, if not quite impossible, without trails. Oral histories indicate that with pack animals in the early days of Oriente penetration it could take nearly a week to traverse direct the six or eight kilometres between the upper and lower limits of the cloud forest.

Over the years the trail system has been improved — largely through the efforts of Saraguro and other settlers organized in work groups by religious and political authorities. Today the entire trail system is maintained by a paid trail crew under the direction of Yacuambi county (*canton*) officials. Trails, which must withstand high rainfall and heavy circulation traffic (some days with over 100 people and 200 cattle and horses) are usually located on ridgetops where the drainage is facilitated. Switchbacks are not constructed to permit *gentle* grades but only to avoid *impossible* grades and to skirt obstacles. County officials also maintain a *tambo*, a Quichua word for the way-stations or inns maintained by the Incas and their Spanish successors on many Andean routes of travel in the cloud forest zone. A corral for animals in transit and barely adequate shelter for human travellers are provided free, and simple hot meals are available at low cost. Several private *tambos* are also located on the major route below the cloud forest and one is located in the *paramo* zone.

The paramo

The *paramo* lies above the *cerro* and cloud forest zones and is a region covered with grasses and sedges, mosses and lichens, brush, mud, rocks, lakes and bogs. Over fifteen kilometres of the main trail between the Oriente and the highland productive zones passes through the *paramo*. Depending upon wind exposure, human intervention and fire, the lower limits of *paramo* vary between 2,900 and 3,100 metres above the level of the sea. The *paramo* extends to the highest elevations in the region which nowhere exceed 3,500 metres. Unlike the steep, rugged underlying terrain of the cloud forest or upper *cerro* zones, the *paramo* consists largely of flat or gently rolling land except on its lower fringes. This has directly contributed to two problems for circulation patterns. Gentle terrain and high rainfall have led to extensive bog formations which block otherwise more direct trail routes. Secondly, the gentle terrain provides no shelter from the frequent wet, cold, strong winds blowing in from across the Amazon basin. When the weather is at its worst, highland/ Oriente circulation is severely curtailed. Though temperatures seldom dip to freezing, an average of one or two persons per year die from hypothermia (exposure) and many more claim to have barely escaped it. Only one *tambo* is located in the *paramo*, and being at the eastern edge it provides no haven for those travelling the most dangerous, middle section of the *paramo*.

Several decades ago the *paramo* was utilized by Saraguros and others as free range-land. Cattle were left to forage on their own for days and weeks at a time. While in other parts of Ecuador this is currently a common practice (cf. Acosta-Solis 1969: 26; C. Lopez 1961: 20) in the Saraguro *paramos* only a few very wild, ownerless cattle still roam the area. More intensive techniques of cattle raising (discussed below) that permit controlled breeding and grazing, utilization of milk products and greater protection from theft, disease and injury, have been developed to the point that *paramo* cattle raising is no longer considered worthwhile even though much less time-consuming.

Livestock and land management

Saraguro vertical circulation is now based largely upon the raising of cattle. Only the wood resources, particularly firewood, of the *cerro*, could maintain vertical circulation of any general significance in the absence of cattle raising. The only culturally defined essential resources of the Oriente other than cattle are such items as crude sugar and bananas which, unlike wood, can now be obtained easily and cheaply enough from storekeepers and traders who bring these goods into Saraguro by motorized transport.

The general principles of Saraguro cattle management are the same for all three productive zones. Cattle are always staked except when being moved − thus no fencing is required for pastures (to keep the cattle *in*) or agricultural plots (to keep cattle *out*). One end of a rawhide or fibre rope, three to five metres in length, is tied to the horns, the other to a stake pounded into the ground. Staking permits controlled breeding of herds with no sexual separation. It also permits fine-tuned pasture management — such as the prevention of over-grazing or trampling and the encouragement of the consumption of less preferred forages. In the highlands cattle must be taken to water (usually a nearby stream) and moved to a new grazing area twice a day at least three or four hours apart. In the Oriente the nutrient and moisture content of pasture grasses is high enough so that cattle need to be moved only once a day for new feed and do not always need to be taken to water at all. Pastures are always planted, usually with specific grasses, although in the highlands white clover and a succulent composite are also utilized. One household member, man, woman or older child, takes care of the cattle each day. While in the pasture area that person will cut firewood, clear new areas, sleep in the sun, visit with persons in neighbouring pastures, milk cows, dig drainage ditches and — very important in tropical pastures — chop out weeds with an ever present machete.

Pastures are very limited in the community zone and are used primarily for milk cows, for bulls used in ploughing fields, as a resting place for cattled grazed in nearby *cerro* land during the day and to hold cattle in transit to other areas for short periods. Maize fields are used for cattle grazing after harvest although maize stalks are sometimes gathered and stacked in piles (*calcha*) for later use. Because of the small area of community zone pastures most Saraguro cattle spend most of their grazing time in either the *cerro* or the Oriente.

Each Saraguro household owns at least one horse or mule, which are generally kept with cattle. Each household also maintains a subsistence herd of eight to twelve sheep (wool for clothing). These are sometimes taken to the *cerro* with cattle — more rarely to the Oriente — but are usually cared for by children near the home on otherwise useless land such as steep or rocky areas, or on fallow land, or on small sections of nearby *cerro*.

So strong is the Saraguro emphasis on the nuclear family household as an independent economic unit that there is rarely any reciprocal sharing of cattle management between different families. In any case, the use of dispersed private pasture rather than common rangeland would make exchange of cattle care duties difficult to arrange. Furthermore, the intensive nature of cattle management makes it hard for a single person to manage more than twenty head of cattle per day.[2] Potential exchange labour is thus limited by the fact that combined herds would almost always total well over twenty-five head.

169

Landholdings of a single Saraguro household involved in both *cerro* and Oriente utilization may be scattered over a linear trail distance of more than 80 kilometres. Fewer than half of all Saraguro households own no land in the Oriente but even their scattered landholdings are likely to be extended over a trail distance of more than eight kilometres. Sahlins (1969) has suggested that patterns of extended land utilization by members of the community of Keteira, Fiji, helped determine the existence and persistence of extended family organization there. In Saraguro, on the other hand, the difficulties inherent in the utilization of dispersed landholdings are moderated not by extended family organization but by great flexibility in the sexual and age based division of labour.

While some preference is expressed, both men and women, when alone, freely engage in such daily routines as caring for cattle and other animals, cutting and hauling firewood, taking care of young children, cooking, washing dishes and clothes, etc. Furthermore, children of both sexes are given responsibilities according to their capabilities which are considerable. Thus members of the nuclear family household − husband and wife, parents and children − are capable of living and working apart for days and even weeks at a time as is sometimes required by the dispersed nature of their productive properties.

Patterns of vertical circulation

The frequency and timing of Saraguro vertical circulation is determined by a multitude of regular and irregular individual, social, economic, religious, agricultural and natural factors. These factors operate in a context of two basic forms of Saraguro vertical circulation: 'daily' and 'periodic'. Daily circulation is the practice of travelling every day from a (usually primary) settlement to a non-contiguous pasture zone at a different (usually higher) elevation to take care of cattle. The cattle may or may not participate in this movement, depending upon whether they are left untended in the pasture or brought back to the settlement at night. One-way travel time ranges from twenty to ninety minutes; elevation change ranges between fifty to about 800 metres.[3] Periodic circulation occurs where people spend days, weeks or even months in the secondary settlements established in the pasture areas. While periodic circulation involves greater distances, it reduces the total time spent in circulation. In secondary settlements pastures are contiguous to, and at more or less the same elevation as, the residence area. Thus daily circulation does not occur for most people while engaged in a periodic circulation pattern. Like daily circulation, periodic circulation does not necessarily include the movement of cattle.

Daily vertical circulation is a common feature only between the community zone and *cerro* areas. Periodic vertical circulation occurs between the community zone and the more distant parts of the *cerro* and between the community zone and the Oriente. Periodic *cerro* circulation always requires less than 1,000 metres of elevation change and two or three hours of travel time; periodic Oriente circulation, on the other hand, requires a minimum of 3,000 metres of elevation change and one to three days of travel. Unless otherwise stated, the following discussion refers to periodic circulation, especially that between the highlands and Oriente.

Periodic vertical circulation in the Saraguro region is not determined by seasonal variations of available forage at different elevations – except for maize. The highland maize production cycle at times requires the presence of family members as well as a pair of bulls for ploughing in the community zone. Cattle are usually also brought to the fields to feed on maize stalks after the harvest. This results in a statistical (but not absolute) pattern of seasonal transhumance (especially for Oriente-highland circulation) which, however, varies according to localized maize production cycles. In most communities maize is planted in early October and harvested in late May – giving a 'double' peaked pattern of movement in and out of the Oriente. At the other extreme, in the communities of Tambopamba and Oñacapa maize is planted in September and harvested in July. This permits cattle to be maintained on maize stalks and other local feed in or near the community zone until ploughing is completed in September.

The only other annual, regular determining factor is the religious fiesta system. Saraguro men and women, independently and together, sponsor celebrations lasting for several days which involve the consumption by many people of large quantities of food and drink. The major fiestas all take place in the community zone and include celebrations of Christmas/Epiphany, Holy Week, Holy Cross, the Virgin Auxiliadora (a local event) and Corpus Christi. These all occur between late December and June – the maize growing season. Each of these fiestas involves ten or more sponsors, dozens of assistants and hundreds of participants (Belote and Belote 1977b). There is thus a bias in circulation movement towards the community zone just prior to fiestas, and away from the community zone just afterwards. An exception to this pattern is found in the communities of Tambopamba and

Oñacapa. The major fiesta for the inhabitants of these communities, who are the most heavily engaged in Oriente utilization, is for the Virgin of Mercedes, celebrated on 24 September – a time when most of them are in the highlands anyway because of their localized maize production cycles.

While crops and fiestas are the only bases for regular annual scheduling of circulation, there is a regular weekly pattern of movement. Saraguros claim that the heaviest movement *out* of the Oriente is geared towards arrival in the highlands on Saturday so that they can go to the town of Saraguro on Sunday for mass, market, visiting, etc. Monday and Tuesday, on the other hand, are claimed to be preferred for starting trips *to* the Oriente – giving people a last chance to go to town before setting out for an extended stay in an isolated area. Furthermore, Saraguros express reluctance to do heavy travelling on Sunday which is supposed to be a day of rest. Thus few Saraguros plan to be on the trail on a Sunday, but delays related to weather sometimes make Sunday travel unavoidable (see Table 8.1 for partial confirmation of the above).

We must re-emphasize that regular weekly or annual patterns of periodic circulation are relatively weak. Irregular or idiosyncratic factors probably account for most movement. As Table 8.1 indicates there is considerable day-to-day fluctuation in the volume of human and animal circulation and on some days movements both *to* and *from* the Oriente are approximately equivalent. Compare, for example, the movement on 28 August and 30 August 1971. On Sunday 29 August (not given in Table 8.1), the weather was so bad that only a couple of hours were spent in observation – no movement was observed. Weather conditions are, in fact, an extremely important short term determinant of movement to and from the Oriente. The sudden arrival of bad weather in the *paramo* causes most people en route to stay up to several days at a *tambo* or other sheltered area while those who had been planning trips will wait at their settlements. Subsequent weather improvement then releases a flood of circulation movement.

Among a host of other irregular factors affecting circulation are temporary exhaustion of pasture resources in one area; births, weddings or funerals; need to sell cattle; family problems; pressing legal affairs; illness, and so forth. Although important in overall influence, there is not space enough in this article to discuss these factors individually.

Leaving aside further consideration of factors influencing the intensity of highland/Oriente circulation, we will briefly examine some characteristics of that movement as revealed primarily by

TABLE 8.1 *Saraguro Indian highland–lowland periodic vertical circulation: six days of 'trail counts' made in paramo section of Saraguro–Yacuambi route*

Date and direction of travel	Weather conditions	Men	Women	Children*	Horses**	Cattle	Calves
19 Jan. 1971 (Tue.)	Early rain and hail						
to Yacuambi	followed by clearing	39	21	9	54	19	6
from Yacuambi		11	2	2	7	14	5
20 April 1968 (Sat.)	Partly cloudy						
to Yacuambi		4	3	1	6	0	0
from Yacuambi		17	3	1	21	3	2
20 June 1971 (Sun.)	Rainy cold morning,						
to Yacuambi	clearing afternoon	0	0	0	0	0	0
from Yacuambi		4	3	0	4	10	2
21 June 1971 (Mon.)	Partly cloudy with						
to Yacuambi	some rain	10	6	7	16	2	0
from Yacuambi		10	3	3	6	32	9
28 Aug. 1971 (Sat.)	Clear to partly						
to Yacuambi	cloudy	24	11	19	27	74	15
from Yacuambi		23	15	16	27	104	16
30 Aug. 1971 (Mon.)	Very windy, rainy and						
to Yacuambi	cold	10	0	1	9	5	3
from Yacuambi		5	1	6	8	28	9
Totals		157	68	65	185	291	67
Totals for non-Indian movement during the same period		51	3	1	47	11	3

Total number of animals other than those enumerated above (excludes guinea pigs, chickens, cats and very young dogs, sheep and pigs which are carried rather than allowed to travel under their own power).

	Sheep	Dogs	Pigs
with Indians	9	32	10
with non-Indians	0	3	0

* Estimated as under 15-16 years of age
** Used primarily as pack stock although a few are ridden. A small number are mules.

the limited data given in Table 8.1. As very rough estimates (multiplying the six day totals by 60) we can suggest that there are around 17,000 individual Saraguro crossings of the *paramo*, around 22,000 cattle and calf crossings and around 10,000 horse or mule crossings each year. About 75 per cent of this movement involves the 2,000 or so Saraguros and their animals from the communities under discussion who are engaged in Oriente utilization.

The sizes of the travelling units of people and animals are not distinguished in Table 8.1. There is no typical group. A unit may commonly vary in size from one person with one or two horses up to three people with eight head of cattle to six or seven people with three or four horses and eighteen or twenty head of cattle and calves. Only about half of the Saraguro travel units include cattle or calves.

A comparison of Indian and non-Indian travel along the Saraguro-Yacuambi route is quite revealing. The proportion of cattle to non-Indian travellers is much lower than the proportion of cattle to Saraguro Indian travellers. This reflects at least one aspect of non-Indian adaptive strategies. Unlike Indians, many non-Indians are engaged in occupations other than cattle-raising in the Oriente, which include store-keeping, government service, subsistence agriculture and the production and distribution of contraband alcohol.

The contrast in relative participation of women and children between the two groups is just as significant. Less than 10 per cent of non-Indian circulators are women and children. Among Indians nearly 45 per cent of the circulators are women and children. Non-Indians are thus engaged in a pattern of male circulation while Indians are engaged in patterns of family as well as male circulation. This difference is manifested, for example, in school attendance. A teacher in one Oriente school claimed that Indian attendance varied between five and fifty pupils in short periods of time whereas non-Indian attendance was relatively stable. The same problem exists to some extent in highland schools. However, increasing Saraguro interest in formal education is leading to modifications in the circulation patterns of some families to permit more regular schooling for their children.

Changes in vertical circulation

As part of an adaptive strategy aimed at both subsistence security and market engagement, vertical circulation has served the Saraguros reasonably well. But, like most human phenomena, vertical circulation is not static and unchanging. New conditions bring about new demands, new opportunities, new ways of achieving the goals of people. Periodic vertical circulation, in particular, is undergoing a process of change, some of which is now examined in conclusion.

Periodic Oriente circulation involves not only the movement of people and cattle, but also the movement of goods and messages. As the number of people engaged in periodic circulation has increased, the number of trips made per person or family has undoubtedly decreased slightly due to improved means of transporting goods and messages (cf. Zelinsky 1971: 232). For example, the population in the Oriente increased sufficiently to justify once weekly mail service and a daily 'telegraph' (ground-line telephone) service between Saraguro and Yacuambi. This service is, however, of use primarily to individuals living in or near the towns as there is no out-of-office message distribution system.[4] But the increase in the number of circulators has also provided a more easily manageable source of people who can transport messages or small amounts of goods for people who otherwise would have to travel to deliver them personally. The use of this informal system to transmit messages has been facilitated by a rising literacy rate among Saraguros – complex messages can be sent in written form without the danger that the carrier will forget important details.

While the frequency of periodic circulation may be diminished in some cases, in other cases periodic circulation may by virtually eliminated. A number of Saraguro families have withdrawn from Oriente circulation because of negative factors such as failure to establish a viable cattle management system in the Yacuambi area; intolerance for Oriente food, climate, isolation or other conditions; or limitations invoked by illness or age. Others withdraw for more positive reasons. They may achieve enough economic success in the development of their Oriente properties that they can sell out and buy enough good land in the highlands to maintain a good cash and subsistence system entirely in the highlands. Still others withdraw from periodic circulation by turning their secondary settlement into a primary settlement. In this case, they give up their community zone primary settlement either for negative reasons (e.g. owning too little land in the community zone) or for more positive ones (such as being well adapted to, and preferring the conditions obtaining in, what had been the secondary settlement). Several dozen Saraguro families scattered throughout the Yacuambi valley and adjacent areas have made this shift.

A smaller number, mainly from the community of Lagunas, are turning a section of the highland *cerro* called 'Quebrada

175

Honda' into a primary settlement. In Quebrada Honda, which is about eight kilometres from Lagunas, the land has been extensively cleared for pasture, agricultural fields have been established in lower elevations, and substantial houses have been built. Probably Quebrada Honda and, still later, other sections of the *cerro*, will become socially and politically recognized highland communities.

As periodic circulation is diminished through the transformation of secondary into primary settlements, new patterns of daily circulation radiating outward from the new primary settlements are likely to develop because of emerging shortages of contiguous land in the vicinity as populations continue to grow. At this point it would be too speculative to suggest that still later, new secondary settlements, tributary to the new primary settlements, would be created, thus continuing a cycle of spatial expansion of Saraguro adaptive strategies.

As we have indicated in this paper, production-oriented vertical control adaptive strategies have worked reasonably well for many of the Indians of Saraguro. Over a period of several decades it has enabled them to learn how to successfully, and sometimes creatively, manipulate and exploit new environments for the raising of cattle − all the while protected by their community area subsistence base. In addition to personal factors, changes, or the lack of changes, in population growth, availability of land, motorized transportation systems, political events, cattle prices and the expansion of desirable occupational alternatives for Indians in Ecuador will all influence the nature and intensity of vertical circulation among the Saraguros in the future.

Acknowledgment

The research on which this paper is based was supported by the University of Illinois (Department of Anthropology); Midwest Universities Consortium for International Activities, Inc. (Internship E-1-144); and the National Institute of Mental Health (Fellowship 1 FOI MH 48824-O1s1).

Notes

1 For details of Saraguro exploitation of the Oriente not given in this paper see Stewart, Belote and Belote (1976). For comparison with another nearby population also engaged in highland/Oriente circulation, see Ekstrom (1975, 1979).
2 Figures given by Strickon indicate the extreme labour intensity of Saraguro cattle management. On the northern plains of the United

States one herdsman was needed for every 1,000 head; in Argentina two to five herdsmen were needed for every 1,000 head of range cattle (1965: 245).

3 In this paper 'elevation change' refers to the total number of metres in elevation ascended on a trip to a higher area or descended on a trip to a lower area. Thus, for example, in going from one area with an elevation of 2,500 metres to one of 2,700 metres the elevation change may be 500 rather than 200 metres — due to the crossing of several ridges.

4 Many of the commercial radio stations in Ecuador transmit personal messages for a small fee during scheduled hours of the day. While an important aspect of communications in some areas, it is little used by Saraguros (most of whom have radios) as there is no powerful commercial transmitter anywhere near Saraguro or Yacuambi.

9 Seasonal agricultural circulation: the Strange Farmers of The Gambia

Kenneth Swindell

Circulatory movements are an important facet of the economic life of West Africa, which can be observed among young men leaving the Sudan-Sahel, to become daily farm workers, contract workers or share croppers in the better endowed and developed coastlands. Alternatively some men leave the rural areas in the dry season and find work in towns. Thus some migrants mix two types of farming, whilst others combine farming with work in the non-agricultural sector. Labour migration in West Africa received a great stimulus at the end of the nineteenth and in the early years of the twentieth century, when the colonial authorities encouraged the production of cash crops, standardized currencies, reformed taxation and abolished domestic slavery. In a broader context seasonal movements must be recognized as a vital aspect of pre-industrial agriculture, related to the uneven spread of farm workloads (either for cash crops or subsistence), together with geographical and structural imperfections in the farm labour market. Apart from the contemporary significance of seasonal migration in underdeveloped countries, it was a common feature of agriculture in nineteenth-century Europe (Collins, 1976: 38-59).

One important example of agricultural migrants in West Africa is the migrant groundnut farmers known as 'Strange Farmers' in The Gambia, and *navétanes* in Senegal. These men are wet season migrant cultivators who have been associated with the development of the groundnut trade since the beginning of the nineteenth century, when the crop was first exported from Senegambia. The Senegambia groundnut basin is a major crop zone where commercial cropping was integrated with the indigenous domestic agriculture well before the colonial balkanization of West Africa, although with the colonial presence it materially expanded.

178

The Strange Farmers are drawn from a wide area within the Senegambian and Upper Niger river basins, and comprise Gambians and non-Gambians, a distinction which is somewhat artificial in the case of short distance movements because of the shape of The Gambia and its enclosure by Senegal. In the day to day life of the people, the international boundary is something of a technicality and in common with other parts of West Africa it has little significance as a barrier to movement for those living either side. In the case of The Gambia it is difficult to speak of a Gambian population in view of the amount of circulation which occurs, although the government shows a concern about circulatory movements, especially as it may be a transitional stage leading to more permanent settlement. However, the control of border movements is often ineffective, with little effect on the volume of movements to and from Senegal, or from the more distant Guinea and Mali. Notwithstanding the above qualifications it is worth making a distinction between internal and international migrants, as the fact that a substantial number of Gambians move away from their home village within areas of agricultural similarity is of some interest.

Both internal and international Strange Farmer movements are representative of the seasonal circulation of agricultural labour in West Africa, where men leave home to farm and return after one or two years. Although circulation of labour is widespread in West Africa, such movements may be slackening and giving place to more extended stays from home, together with permanent settlement. Also, the development of local job opportunities in the source areas of migration is gradually slowing the rate of outward movements. To what extent the Strange Farmers fit the description of rural to rural circulants is one of the themes of the following analysis, together with observations on why men leave home to farm, involving them in journeys which can range from a few to a few hundred miles. To this end we must first define the Strange Farmer system and note the origins and distribution of these migrants within The Gambia.

The Strange Farmer system

A Strange Farmer is generally described as a seasonal migrant, who comes into the Senegambian groundnut basin to cultivate groundnuts from April to December (Labouret 1941; Jarrett 1948; Pollet and Winter 1969; Van Haeverbeke 1970). The system rests on a contractual arrangement between a host farmer and migrant, with an agreed number of days each week worked for the host (usually between two and four) and on the remaining

179

days the migrant is at liberty to cultivate groundnuts on his own farm provided by the host. The migrant during his stay is provided with food, a hoe, and if necessary the loan of seednuts, together with a hut within the compound which he may share with other Strange Farmers. Migrants search for a host amongst the villages, and in some cases hosts seek out Strange Farmers which may be effected by a variety of informal networks, sometimes with the leader of a group of migrants acting as intermediary. Repeated migration leads to a 'matching' system which builds up a relationship between host and client.

This system is quite different from share cropping with which it is frequently confused, and it essentially derives from a combination of labour shortages and land surpluses (Swindell 1978: 3-17). The advantage for the host is that he receives extra labour inputs without any need for cash payment of wages, whereas the migrant according to the size and quality of his groundnut farm will produce his own crop, the money from which accrues to him and to him alone at the end of the season. Groundnuts are a wet season crop, and unlike tree crops, have a quick production cycle, thus after approximately seven months the migrant has cash in hand, some of which he may spend on imported goods to take back home.

This particular migratory system is of long standing, and represents the oldest movement in West Africa associated with cash-crop cultivation. Strange Farmers have been coming into Senegambia since 1834, in numbers which at times have exceeded 100,000 per annum. Groundnut cultivation in Senegambia was initiated by the response of long-distance traders to the market opportunities provided by their European counterparts. The Serahuli (Sarakole) and Mandinka traders from the Upper Senegal and Niger river basins became interested in groundnut cultivation as the slave trade declined, and the labourers they brought into Senegambia represent the antecedents of the Strange Farmer migrations (Brooks, 1975: 52-4; Swindell 1980: 93-104). Subsequently, the local populations (especially the Wolof) of Senegambia became attracted to the cultivation of groundnuts, and eventually in the twentieth century the railway diffused its commercial cultivation inland towards Mali.

The number, origins and destinations of migrants

During the 1974-5 farming season, the Gambian government implemented its first agricultural survey, based on a sampling procedure devised by the FAO as part of the census of world agriculture. The 1974-5 Survey was the first attempt to estimate the number of farmers in any one season, although previously the tax returns from the Local Authorities had given some information on the number of migrants but without any indication of their national composition. One quarter of the Strange Farmers sampled were found to be Gambians, which was equivalent to 8,000 out of a total of 33,000 migrants; the remainder comprised almost equal proportions of Senegalese, Guineans and Malians (Table 9.1). The Survey showed that migrants were widespread throughout The Gambia, but with discernible concentrations in certain regions. The most important receiving area for strangers was in the western part of the Lower River North Bank Division, comprising three districts, Lower and Upper Niumi and Jokadu. Approximately one-third of all migrants were recorded there. This concentration of Strange Farmers is partly due to the configuration of the boundaries *vis-à-vis* the river-line, giving rise to one of the most extensive tracts of 'upland' with relatively good soils. Consequently, of the estimated 259,000 acres (117,727 ha) of groundnuts cultivated in the 1974-5 season, one-third were located in this region; also the area of groundnuts per farming unit was 11.7 acres compared with a national average of 8.0 acres. Basically, the high outputs of this area are a function of good groundnut land, and the presence of so many strangers, but analysis reveals that there are other attractions for migrants in this part of the Lower River North Bank.

Other important areas for Strange Farmers were in Western Division in the districts of Foni Brefet, Fini Bintang and Foni Kinsala, but there was a marked reduction in migrant numbers westwards towards the immediate environs of Banjul, the capital of The Gambia. The remaining areas with large numbers of migrants were MacCarthy Island South and Upper River Division, effectively the districts of Fulladu West and Fulladu East. The Fulladus accounted for just over 20 per cent of the migrants recorded in the 1974-5 season. Gambians formed a conspicuous element in the stranger population farming in the Lower River Division North Bank (one-third of total migrants) and Western Divisions (one-half of the total), and in general there was a reduction in their number as one moved up-river. But despite the regional bias in the distribution of Gambian farmers, they were to be found in twenty-seven out of the thirty-five districts of the country. An initial clue to why Gambians became 'internal' migrant cultivators can be discerned by examining the location of their declared home villages or towns with respect to their farming locations. For any given village, district or region, Strange Farmers may be generated firstly by non-locals moving into the area and secondly by locals moving *within* the area, but the fact that local men may be leaving to farm elsewhere must also be taken into account. Thus, whether a district or village has a net gain or loss of Strange Farmers is a function of these three variables.

TABLE 9.1 *Nationality of Strange Farmers by division*

Division	Gambia	Senegal	Guinea	Mali	Guinea Bissau	Other	Total
Western	48 (45)	35 (33)	9 (9)	4 (4)	10 (9)	—	106 (100)
Lower River South Bank	29 (29)	15 (14)	29 (29)	26 (26)	2 (2)	—	101 (100)
Lower River North Bank (West)*	100 (31)	79 (25)	57 (18)	85 (26)	2 (—)	—	323 (100)
Lower River North Bank (East)*	13 (15)	11 (13)	15 (17)	45 (51)	1 (1)	3 (3)	88 (100)
MacCarthy Island North Bank	19 (18)	28 (26)	46 (43)	10 (9)	2 (2)	2 (2)	107 (100)
MacCarthy Island South Bank	23 (15)	12 (8)	103 (66)	11 (7)	6 (4)	1 (−1)	156 (100)
Upper River	18 (13)	37 (26)	53 (37)	33 (23)	1 (−1)	2 (1)	144 (100)
Total	250 (24)	217 (21)	312 (31)	214 (21)	24 (2)	8 (1)	1025 (100)

* For purposes of analysis Lower River North Bank has been divided into west and east.
  Per cent in brackets.

Source: 1974/75 Sample Survey

Because of the elongated shape of The Gambia it is conceivable that internal movements may be anything from a few miles up to three hundred miles. For example, the Lower River North Bank attracted migrants from the length of the country from north and south banks, and migrants were recorded from twenty-six out of the total thirty-five districts excluding the receiving areas in question. Men were moving into the lower river chiefly from the central districts and from the peripheral area around Banjul, the capital. In both these cases groundnut land is restricted and population densities are over 70 per square mile, compared with a national average of 22 per square mile. Whilst there appeared to be a definite westward drift of migrants, a surprising number − almost one-third − of the men farming came from *within* Lower River North Bank Division. Further inspection showed that one-half of these men were moving within their home district, and are best described as local circulators. The distribution of districts having net gains and losses of Gambian migrants are shown in Figure 9.1, and this supports the contention of a general westward drift of migrants into the lower river areas. Thus, the Lower River Divisions exhibit local circulation and receive long-distance internal migrants, whilst the central and Upper River areas have local circulation and generate long-distance internal migrants.

From this analysis it would seem that the movements of Gambian Strange Farmers rest upon several factors. Firstly there is evidence that good groundnut land attracts inward movements, whereas areas of high population density and limited groundnut potential tend to promote outward movements. But this does not explain localized movements, often of short distances, between neighbouring villages. Such movements may be part of a general inclination of young men who wish to escape the various social constraints of farming either in their own compound or home village. As a stranger, a man has the opportunity to decide how he shall spend the proceeds of his season's work and if necessary can accumulate cash for specific projects of his own choosing. Such attitudes have been observed elsewhere as part of the migratory process, for example among the Hausa, where *Yawon duniya* ('the walk of the world') expresses the migrants' desire for liberation from social constraints (Olofson, 1976: 66-79).

Of the 250 Gambian migrants investigated in the Strange Farmer Survey, some 23 per cent found hosts within their own district, which means that they moved a maximum of ten miles. Some insights into the reasons for these movements can be discerned from the studies of Wolof communities and their household organization (Gamble 1957: 4461 and Rocheteau 1975: 4). Wolof households are polygynous with a double-descent system of lineage, which with the spread of Islam has gradually accentuated patrilinearity. In such circumstances the role of younger brothers, *vis-à-vis* the head of the family compound and the eldest son, is such that their socio-economic status is little

183

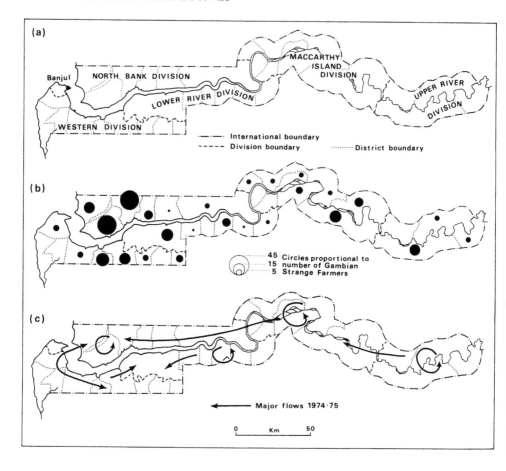

FIGURE 9.1 Gambia (a) administrative divisions; (b) proportions of Strange Farmers; (c) major flows of Strange Farmers 1974/76

different from that of strangers. Also, it has been observed that friction develops between the sons of the same father but different mothers, which may be accentuated by the differential allocation of groundnut plots amongst the younger menfolk of the compound. Thus there may be a strong incentive for young men to leave the household and become Strange Farmers in neighbouring villages, where they will be guaranteed a groundnut farm and complete control over the proceeds. This socio-cultural aspect of household organization within Senegambia, especially amongst the Wolof has also been cited as of considerable significance in the colonization and spread of groundnut cultivation by the Mouride brotherhood into the arid areas of eastern Senegal (Rocheteau 1975).

184

Although groundnut cultivation may have been started within the Senegambian area by migrants from the interior, it would seem that the emergence of the Wolof areas as the core of the groundnut basin may well have been assisted by the latent propensity for movement amongst young men who wish to become groundnut farmers on their own account. The successful introduction of commercial cash cropping into West Africa has been explained by some authors by reference to the classical 'vent for surplus' theory, which takes as a basic premise the release of previously under-employed elements in the local labour force, who respond to the introduction of new crops (Hopkins 1973: 231-6; Hogendorn 1976: 26-8). If this is so, it would seem that the introduction of groundnuts into Senegambia provided not only economic opportunities but also a resolution of the factionalism which marks many Senegambian households. Although factionalism within Mandinka and Fula households may be less than in those of the Wolof, similar situations obtain amongst these ethnic groups, and are a stimulus for migration within the more distant source areas of Guinea and Mali. The distinction being made here between economic and social factors is similar to that made by Mitchell between necessary and sufficient causes of migration and the rate and incidence of migration (Mitchell 1959: 12-47).

If non-Gambians such as the Tilibo[1] and Bambara from Mali, and the Serer from Senegal are added to the Strange Farmer population, then this migrant stream comprises a wider spectrum of ethnic groups than is found elsewhere in West Africa. With respect to ethnic matching of migrants and hosts, it is difficult to find strong evidence of partiality, especially in lower river areas where other cross-cultural factors may be more important. Also, in every region of The Gambia there are villages which contain households whose ethnicity differs from that of the dominant group.

Most Strange Farmers are aged between 18 and 35 years, although few of them know their ages with any accuracy. Most migrants are in this age range because hosts require able-bodied men capable of a good day's work, otherwise they are not accepted as Strange Farmers. Such selectivity effectively rules out young boys and older men. However, at harvest-time boys aged between 13 and 16 years appear in the villages as casual labourers, and they are paid by the field of groundnut lifted, or stack threshed. Such migrants are referred to as *m'baragnini* (Mandinka) or *firdu* (Fula), and they are local migrants moving amongst neighbouring villages. These casual workers were not included in the Survey, but when they are combined with the local movements of Strange Farmers, they collectively demonstrate the importance of small-scale intra and inter-village labour migration, which is of considerable value to groundnut farmers. Localized labour movements have received less attention than their long-distance counterparts, although the former frequently provide vital labour inputs for small-scale family farms.

If younger members of a household leave to become Strange Farmers elsewhere, they in turn may have to be replaced by other migrants depending on the household's demographic structure and labour consumer balance. This paradoxical situation which arises from the conditions noted above also explains why there is a general exchange of the existing labour units within the villages of a particular region, and the acceptance of long distance non-Gambian migrants.

The introduction of groundnuts as a cash crop also interacted with other aspects of indigenous social organization, which produced other incentives for young men to leave home and farm as migrants. In patrilineal societies bridewealth is common, but traditionally marriages were arranged by the senior members of families on behalf of their children or relatives. Formerly, bridewealth was paid in kind or through labour services given by the prospective bridegroom to his parents-in-law, but with the spread of the cash economy associated with groundnut cultivation bridewealth is now generally paid in cash. However, if the cash payment has been produced by the prospective bridegroom through his own efforts as a Strange Farmer, it is likely that he will wish to choose his bride rather than having one chosen for him. In this way there is an additional incentive for many young men to become migrant farmers for one or two seasons (Fouquet, 1958: 68).

The Sample Survey of Strange Farmers inquired into the specific reasons for migration, but these could not be examined in depth because of constraints of time and cost with a sample which covered the whole country. But it was argued that the motives and decisions to become a migrant farmer should not be dissociated from what a man was doing previously, since movement involves either permanently or temporarily abandoning that niche. Therefore, on the assumption that a knowledge of former economic activities or employment is pertinent to explaining the present role of a man as a Strange Farmer, the Survey inquired into the activities of migrants in the preceding dry season of 1973-74. The answers to these questions have proved most interesting, and furnish important insights into the workings of the migratory system and the associated patterns of labour mobility.

Dry season activities, 1973-4

The 1973-4 dry season activities of the migrants who were interviewed in the succeeding wet season of 1974-5 may be classified into six groups (Table 9.2). First, those engaged in the formal sector − that is in regular wage-earning employment, comprised one-sixth of the sample (Group A). As in most West African countries wage-earning opportunities are limited and are generally confined to the government or quasi-government sectors; in June 1974 some 80 per cent of wage-earners were employed in these sectors. Wage-earners in the Survey were, for example, involved in dock-work, where demands for seasonal labour are high with the beginning of the Trade Season[2] in groundnuts; also road and well repairing undertaken by the Public Works Department provided other dry season jobs. But the single most important employment for wage-earners was in the groundnut mills, the chief processing industry of The Gambia which derives 90 per cent of exports by value from groundnuts. There are two mill and groundnut-press complexes, one mid-way up-river at Kaur and a larger one at Denton Bridge on the outskirts of Banjul. In addition there are some 88 buying and loading depots distributed along the river.

It is possible to make an estimate of the average financial rewards for those combining groundnut farming with employment in the formal sector, since the basic wage rates in the latter are fixed by the Government. The daily rate for labourers in 1974 was 2.05 dalasis (£0.51) which, assuming a work period of four months in the dry season of 1973-4, could have given an average income of the order of 212 dalasis (£53). Combined with an average income from groundnut-farming of 240 dalasis (£60), this would have yielded a total annual income of 440 dalasis (£110). Compared with farming at home during 1973-4, migration as a Strange Farmer and factory worker would seem to afford considerable attractions as a means of satisfying either short-term needs, or of producing capital which might be invested back home.

A rather more diverse group of migrants had been involved in the informal sector, comprising petty trading, sewing, tailoring, baking, building and taxi and lorry driving (Group B). Overall this was the second most important group of dry season pursuits, accounting for 281 out of 1003 men interviewed. This category included a number of men whose motives for farming were overtly stated as the need to acquire money for business. These

TABLE 9.2 *1973/74 Dry season occupations/activities according to nationality*

Group	Gambia	Senegal	Guinea	Mali	Guinea Bissau	Others	Total
Formal sector	55 (22)	36 (12)	26 (9)	31 (15)	2 (7)	2 (25)	152 (15)
Informal sector	80 (33)	53 (25)	95 (31)	48 (23)	4 (13)	1 (13)	281 (28)
Agriculture/ fishing	65 (26)	61 (29)	116 (38)	83 (40)	9 (30)	2 (25)	336 (34)
Education	9 (4)	15 (7)	3 (1)	6 (3)	—	—	33 (3)
Miscellaneous	3 (1)	3 (3)	5 (3)	4 (2)	2 (7)	—	17 (2)
Nil	35 (14)	42 (19)	58 (17)	39 (16)	7 (43)	3 (37)	184 (18)
Total	247 (100)	210 (100)	303 (100)	211 (100)	24 (100)	8 (100)	1003* (100)

* The reduction in the sample size from 1024 is due to mis-recording of dry season occupations/activities

Per cent in brackets

Source: 1974/75 Sample Survey

men (some 16 per cent of the sample) insisted that they should not be recorded as farmers but either as businessmen or according to their particular trade. But this small number of migrants who were committed to the informal sector formed the nucleus of a much larger group engaged in this on a more casual basis. Unfortunately it was not possible to estimate the earnings of those in the informal sector, but there is no doubt these would show considerable variation compared with those in the formal sector.

Migrants in Group B, together with those in Group A, comprised 40 per cent of those interviewed and collectively they demonstrate the importance and diversity of off-farm employment in the dry season. Dry season employment of farm workers in the informal sector is widespread in West Africa and it has been argued that they, along with more permanent workers in this sector, represent the specialist substitution of non-agricultural goods and services formerly produced within the agricultural community or household (Hymer and Resnick 1969: 443-506). For example, increased income from cash-crop farming has led to a greater use of imported cloth which is now made up into clothing by small-scale businessmen-tailors frequently located in urban areas and the larger villages. But in the present case substitution is not necessarily achieved by releasing labour from the farming household into manufacturing and service industries; the Strange Farmer data demonstrate that it is the complementarity of the agricultural sectors which is so important. Also, in The Gambia the interplay of wet season farming and dry season trading has a long history and was observed in 1869 by the then British Administrator, who remarked on the seasonal influx of workers into Bathurst (Annual Report of the Gambia 1869: 14-16).

The largest group of dry season activities concerned those who were involved in agriculture or fishing (Group C). Just over one-third of the Strange Farmers spent the preceding dry season doing what is commonly termed compound work, which may be back on the family farm, on a local Gambian farm, or with their host of the previous wet season. This kind of work is subject to greater variations in the mode of payment than the other categories. Frequently it is in the form of daily payment, payment in kind, lodgings and food, or combinations of one or more of these. Dry season farm work, building and repairing houses, fences and granaries, together with well cleaning is rarely documented or measured in terms of time and effort, yet these activities are an important investment in the renewal or extension of capital works on the farm, simple and primitive though they may be.

The remaining three groups of dry season activities were of less importance compared with the three major groups and comprised those who were continuing their education (Group D), those who were doing a variety of things such as visiting relatives, seeking medical treatment etc. (Group E), and those who declared that they did nothing (Group O).

The fact that over 40 per cent of the sample were employed in the formal and informal sectors prior to becoming migrant farmers suggests the importance of an alternation between wet and dry season occupations for many men, which is an important element in Strange Farmer movements. In general, this alternation of employment is found in both past and present pre-industrial economies, because of the interdependence of agriculture and industry and the exchange of factors between them, especially of labour which may take place within rural areas, or between town and countryside. The concentration of large numbers of strangers observed in the Lower River may be related to this seasonal alternation of employment in town and countryside. For example, the drift of migrants into the western regions of The Gambia has been partly explained by the availability of good groundnut land relative to areas of land scarcity elsewhere, but Lower River also exerts an attraction on those who were previously employed in Banjul and Dakar. Such workers engaged in the formal or informal sectors during the dry season would be interested in farming in areas nearby the major towns should they wish to return in the next dry season, whilst others might be considering a first time move into the town to find seasonal employment. However, this hypothesis can be reversed; suppose some of these Strange Farmers in Lower River and Western Divisions were either permanent or semi-permanent urban-dwellers who farm in the wet season on the urban peripheries at a time when trade and jobs are in short supply. In other words, farming becomes a 'fall-back' mechanism for under- or unemployment in urban areas, when both labour and, to lesser extents, capital are diverted into the countryside. The problem of satisfactorily substantiating or refuting these propositions lies in the difficulty of securing longitudinal data on migrants. In the absence of a detailed inquiry the Sample Survey made certain inferences on which future research might be based.

Patterns of mobility according to previous dry and wet season occupations

Off-farm employment in the dry season in either rural areas or towns ideally integrates with wet season farming at home. Migrant groundnut farmers are semi-independent wet season cultivators, who subsequently may become employees, or self-employed workers, in towns or elsewhere for the duration of the dry season. Thus for long distance migrants after the initial move from home to become a Strange Farmer, it is possible to engage in an alternation between wet and dry season activities *within* the destination area, which may mean using the same village on successive seasons as a base from which to operate. For some migrants the strengthening of their relationship with a host may be cemented by marriage into his household, and the stranger may become a permanent settler, but until he is allocated land he may continue as a migrant farmer.

Alternatively, if migrants wish to integrate seasonal movements between farming and work in the town, they might become settled within the town, whilst continuing to farm in adjacent rural areas during the wet season. Thus for any one migrant or set of migrants there may be a sequence of moves extending over several years which gives rise to transitional mobility, whereby the migrant gradually transfers to a new permanent or semi-permanent location and becomes more involved in working in the formal and informal sectors. Within the Strange Farmer population as a whole it is possible to discern the elements in the sequence, as individual migrants reach different stages in the transition. The possible moves between town and countryside associated with migrant farming are given in a simple typology (Figure 9.2).

To investigate the above notions, the Strange Farmers were asked not only about the nature of their previous dry season occupations, but also *where* they had been specifically located. This information allowed some assessment of whether the migrant had been working away from home in the previous dry season of 1973-4, and more importantly where prior to his arrival in the village of enumeration. For example, an inspection of the data on Gambian farmers shows that only one-half were in their home town or village in the dry season, but 25 per cent – a substantial proportion – were in towns, notably Banjul, Dakar and Basse. Another 11 per cent were in other Gambian villages, with 12 per cent in their villages of enumeration having stayed over from a previous wet season. Very few Gambians, only 5 per cent, were outside their country during the dry season.

If the same analysis is applied to the 756 non-Gambians, it is equally apparent that a substantial proportion (39 per cent) were already within the country prior to becoming migrant farmers. Eighteen per cent were already in their villages of enumeration, the remainder were in Gambian villages and towns, with Banjul as the single most important location. But in contrast to the Gambian Strange Farmers there was a discernible element (11 per cent) who, although not resident in their home areas or The Gambia, were in another country which in the majority of cases proved to be Senegal. The analysis of the data on previous dry season occupations and their location showed that only half of the non-Gambian strangers were in their home countries, and therefore internal movements within The Gambia into the groundnut areas were of a much higher order than suggested by an analysis according to declared home town or village in a stated country (Table 9.1). Taking non-Gambians and Gambians together, approximately 49 per cent actually moved from their declared home areas, and of the remainder, 16 per cent were already in their villages of enumeration.

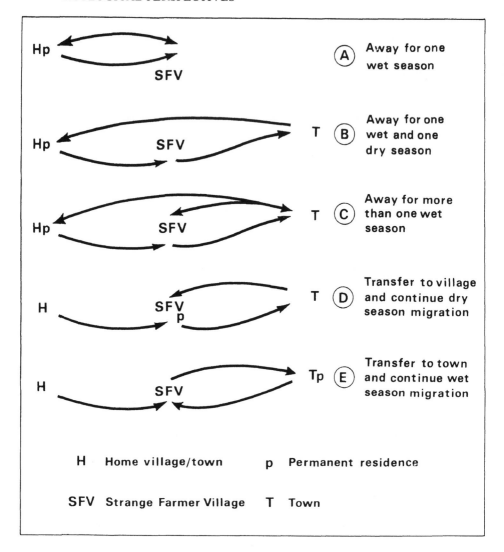

FIGURE 9.2 *Typology of movements of Strange Farmers*

Thus there were two distinct groups of Strange Farmers during the 1974-5 wet season, those who had come direct from home, and those who had arrived from some other location where they had spent the dry season. Examining what this second group had been doing during the dry season, shows an even stronger bias towards employment in the formal and informal sectors than is shown for all migrants irrespective of their dry season locations (Table 9.2). Of the Gambians who spent the dry seasons away from home 31 per cent had been in the formal sector employment and 40 per cent in the informal sector; the corresponding proportions for non-Gambians were 24 and 32 per cent.

If the non-Gambian strangers are examined by country of origin, then there appears to be an important difference between the migrants from Senegal and those from Mali and Guinea. The Senegalese displayed no interest in finding dry season employment outside of their own country other than in The Gambia. This fact emphasizes the particular attraction of The Gambia for them and it has been suggested that there is a net gain of population into The Gambia from Senegal, particularly of seasonal migrants involved in farming or trading and other forms of employment (Diallo, 1971: 1-22). The data from the Survey seem to support this view especially as there was very little evidence of Gambians taking either dry season or wet season employment in Senegal. Thus compared with Guineans and Malians who were scattered throughout Senegambia during the 1973-4 dry season, the Senegalese moved either from within their own country or from within The Gambia into their villages as Strange Farmers for the 1974-5 season.

In the case of the Guineans and Malians it would seem that, apart from those who were already in The Gambia (41 and 32 per cent respectively), a small proportion of both groups (13 and 16 per cent) were in Senegal. Taken together these figures show that many of the longer distance migrants moved relatively short distances into their farming villages and illustrate that those from the interior spend more than one season away from home. But there was one noticeable difference between Guineans and Malians with respect to the numbers already in the villages of enumeration; a greater proportion of Guineans (21 per cent compared with 11 per cent) spent the previous dry season in the villages in which they farmed in the 1974-5 season. This may be a function of their particular interest in the Fulladus and their settlement in these areas of The Gambia. The data on the previous employment of Strange Farmers have several implications, but in particular they make it necessary to qualify any inference made from the declared home–origins of migrants noted in Table 9.1. Whilst allowing that some migrants may have made trips back home at the end of the dry season, it would seem that in terms of occupation, approximately one-half transferred to their Strange Farmer villages from other places where they had also been migrant workers.

The evidence derived from questions on dry season employment and its location emphasizes the care needed in handling data on migration when it is sorted into simple dichotomous categories such as 'internal' and 'international'. Much of course depends on the definition of movement adopted and the time period used, and in the present case The Gambia is something of a geographical anomaly. But in West Africa movement is not always susceptible to generally accepted definitions, because of the manner in which people consider places of residence and the intermittent nature of their occupations. Clearly the data from the Strange Farmer Survey demonstrates the important wet-dry season differential in location of those involved in seasonal groundnut farming, and lends some support to the proposed typology of movements outlined (Figure 9.2).

Of the 1003 migrant movements recorded, 30 per cent spent the previous dry season either fully employed, intermittently employed or unemployed in urban areas, and this gives some measure of the outflow of migrants from urban areas into the countryside. These urban origins (albeit dry season ones) show that the Strange Farmer movement is not a simple rural movement of workers, depending of course on how or when the place from which the movement occurred is defined. It now remains to use what additional data the Survey provided on the mobility and circulation of these migrants starting with the last wet season up to their present location as Strange Farmers, together with their expected onward moves.

Once it had been decided to include in the Survey a question on previous dry season occupation and its whereabouts, it seemed opportune to ask the same questions about the previous wet season of 1973-4. It was hoped that this question would reveal whether the migrant had farmed at home or elsewhere as a Strange Farmer. In addition to these questions about previous occupations and movements, the migrants were asked about their expected moves in the coming dry season of 1974-5, after they had finished farming. Thus it is possible to build up a limited migration history going backwards from the point of enumeration to two previous jobs and their locations, and forward by one intended move. Included in this matrix of movements is of course the migrant's declared home town or village.

Patterns of mobility: two case studies

The migration history available for any one Strange Farmer is extremely limited, but for a sample of 1003 migrants even if their occupations are limited to the simple classification used earlier (Table 9.2), when these are combined with specific locations, the number of possible movements are of a higher order. Here a lack of space prevents a complete analysis and two selected enumeration areas will be examined as case studies. These examples are taken from areas identified as having important concentrations of Strange Farmers, and give some indication of the nature and range of their movements over two and a half farming seasons. One of the enumeration areas is in Lower River North Bank West and the other in MacCarthy Island Division South Bank. The movements of each stranger have been mapped showing his declared home village or town and his subsequent wet and dry season movements from 1973 to 1975 (Figures 9.3 and 9.4).

The first example from an enumeration area in Upper Niumi District (Lower River North Bank Division) comprised the two villages of Madina Sachebo and Pakauding. The random example of 15 *dabadas*[3] yielded 28 Strange Farmers. The range of movements was considerable, but two things attract the attention. First is the number of men whose declared home origins were in towns (32 per cent), and second the number of men (89 per cent) who had spent the previous dry season in towns before their arrival as Strange Farmers. Of this proportion of dry season dwellers, approximately one-half had also farmed away from home in the last wet season of 1973-4, with the locational emphasis being in villages in Senegal and The Gambia. Thus, for the 1974-5 wet season under investigation, they were *repeat* Strange Farmers, although not necessarily in the same villages.

It has been noted already that a good proportion of men appeared to be leaving towns to farm in the countryside, but the evidence in Figure 9.3 suggests that an important element are also moving back into the towns after farming, though these are different from their home town. Thus there appears to be some grounds for isolating an urban-rural-urban stream of migrants such as was contained in the typology (Figure 9.2). On the other hand, just over one half of those who spent the previous dry season in a town were originally from villages, and it would seem that there is another stream of migrants which may be described as rural-urban-rural. It would seem that Strange Farmers from rural areas might have been spending a few weeks or several months working or trading in a town before they returned home. At the risk of repetition, it must be stressed that groundnuts are a wet season crop, grown and harvested within a seven-month period. The complement to the agricultural activity of many Strange Farmers is a dry season occupation centred in the town, or at nodal trading points such as ferry crossings, during the Trade Season. Finally, a small number of men (14 per cent) had

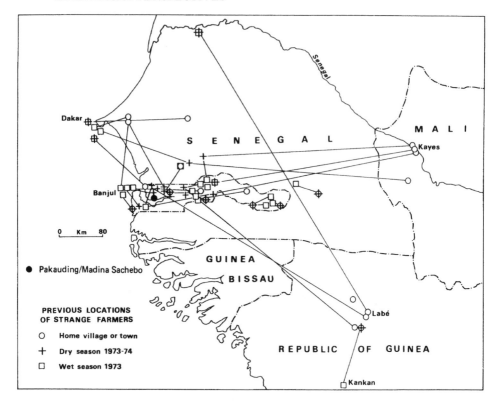

*FIGURE 9.3 Pakauding/Madina Sachebo: previous locations
of Strange Farmers*

spent the previous wet and dry seasons working in town, and
then moved into villages for the 1974-5 wet season. All of these
men indicated a desire to return to the town in the 1974-5 dry
season and they would appear to be illustrative of those town
dwellers using seasonal farming as a 'fall-back' mechanism.

The second example taken from MacCarthy Island Division
South Bank comprised one enumeration area, coincident with the
village of Sare Silere which had 21 Strange Farmers in the 15
dabadas sampled. Their origins and movements showed rather a
different pattern from those of Madina Sachebo (Figure 9.4).
First, their origins showed less geographical dispersal, with a
strong Guinean connection; almost all of the Strange Farmers in
Sare Silere were Fulas from the Fouta Djallon. Compared with
Madina Sachebo and Pakauding, few had their home origins in
urban areas, and a smaller proportion (40 per cent) had been
away from home in the previous dry season, although the

196

majority had been in towns. Turning to the previous wet season of 1973-4 even fewer men (25 per cent) had been away from their home villages. The Strange Farmers in Sare Silere exhibited less mobility than their counterparts in Madina Sachebo, and 49 per cent had been at home in both the previous dry and wet seasons and were possibly first time Strange Farmers. Whilst there was evidence of what has been described in Madina Sachebo as rural-urban-rural movements, there was more evidence of simple rural-urban circulation between the home village and the one chosen for a brief stay as a Strange Farmer.

The conclusions which may be drawn from these two examples emphasize once again that the Strange Farmers comprised several sub-groups who were using migrant farming in rather different ways. It would seem that what the migrants were doing in the previous dry season and where they were located are important clues to their patterns of mobility. For example, in the first of the examples described above, over 82 per cent of the migrants were engaged in the formal or informal sectors in towns before they

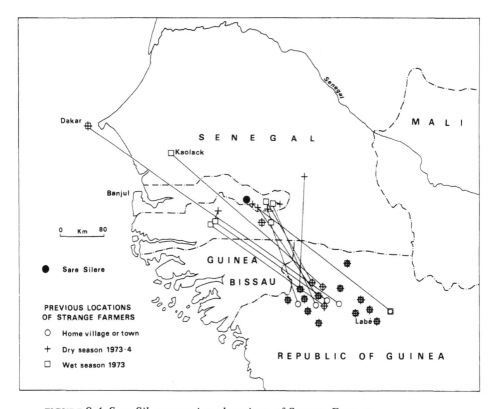

FIGURE 9.4 Sare Silere: previous locations of Strange Farmers

became migrant farmers; in the second example, 49 per cent were at home on the family farm. However, it must be stressed that whilst many strangers were economically occupied away from home during the dry season of 1973-4, the Survey did not provide data on whether they moved on directly to become Strange Farmers in The Gambia, or whether they had made short trips back home first. However, the cost of doing the latter would be relatively high for those migrants from the more distant parts of Guinea, Mali and Senegal.

Conclusion

The observed patterns of mobility discussed in the two case studies give some support to the proposed typology of Strange Farmer movements and they are reflected in patterns of movement observed in the whole sample. Figure 9.5 demonstrates the major patterns of mobility, comprising 70 per cent of the sample, and focuses on those farmers who came from home, from an urban area other than home, and a special group of 'repeat' migrants not considered hitherto. Some 16 per cent of the farmers enumerated had farmed in the same village in the previous wet season and two-thirds of these (Figure 9.5) had also spent the previous dry season there and showed no intention of moving onwards. On the other hand, simple seasonal circulation between a migrant's home town or village and the one in which he became a Strange Farmer formed the largest single group (49 per cent of cases examined), and nearly all these men had previously farmed at home and were intent on returning there. However, this group of migrants could be roughly divided into those who had spent the last dry season on the farm, and those who were involved in craft industries and petty trading in their home areas.

A more complex set of movements was displayed by 39 per cent of the Strange Farmers who had spent the last dry season away from home, working in the urban formal or informal sector before they moved into the village of enumeration to become migrant farmers. Furthermore, some 10 per cent of the total sample of Strange Farmers had also farmed away from home in the previous wet season and another 5 per cent had spent both the last wet and dry seasons in wage employment or trade. Likewise the majority of these men intended to move back into towns after they had finished farming. Apparently these two groups were in the process of shifting, or had shifted the centre of gravity of their economic activities away from their home areas, together with those Strange Farmers who had been in their

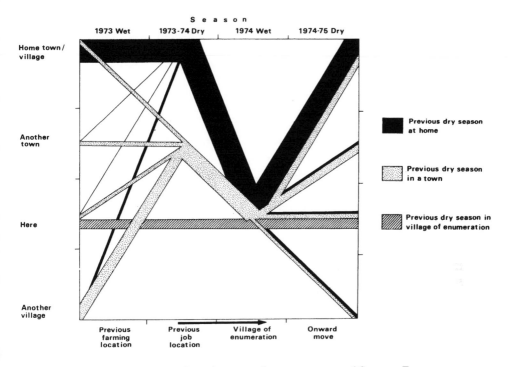

FIGURE 9.5 Time-space flow diagrams for movements of Strange Farmers before and after the 1974 farming season

village of enumeration for the previous wet and dry seasons.

The occupational and geographical mobility observed in the Strange Farmer Survey underlines the need for migration histories and longitudinal studies of employment to establish the migratory process and its modification. But in addition to an understanding of process, longitudinal data are required to classify correctly aggregate flows of migrants. The data produced by the Survey showed the differences between flows defined and measured between declared home area and destination, and flows between where the migrant spent the previous dry season and their destination as a Strange Farmer. In the 1974-5 Survey although three-quarters of strangers were non-Gambians, their migration histories showed that 39 per cent of them were already in The Gambia and working there during the 1973-4 dry season. Thus, the number of internal Strange Farmer movements were in fact of a higher order than initially suggested by considering Gambians as distinct from non-Gambians. The evidence from the Survey suggests that there is a need to carefully record small-scale localized movement, which is of considerable importance

199

both to farmers faced with labour shortages, as well as migrants and the strategies they adopt whilst they are working away from home.

The Survey also provided some comment on classifications of migration based on the dichotomy between rural and urban places, in pre-industrial agricultural societies. Whilst such a distinction is useful for aggregate inter-regional flows, it can divert attention from the interplay and interchangeability of urban and rural milieus for many migrants. The town and the village are not discrete, but economically complementary, as exemplified by the circulation of labour between them. In the Strange Farmer system, a migrant according to his preferences and the opportunities available may move in a manner described as rural to rural, urban to urban, rural-urban-rural, and if farming is part of maintaining an urban job commitment, urban-rural-urban. Much depends on the stage of economic development, and the objectives and characteristics of migrants, and it is apparent that the Strange Farmers are not a homogeneous group.

Unlike other major flows of agricultural workers in West Africa, Strange Farmers are concerned with wet-season farming, but they have many of the characteristics of other migrants, especially the seasonality of movement and the frequent change in economic roles. However, whilst simple circulatory migration forms a major element in the migratory system, it would seem that wet season farming as a stranger combined with some kind of dry season work is a powerful mechanism for effecting more permanent transfers either from one village to another, or from village to town.

Acknowledgment

The research on which this paper is based was financed by the Social Science Research Council and the Centre of West African Studies, University of Birmingham. It was associated with the first agricultural survey of The Gambia in 1974-5 based on sampling procedure devised by the FAO as part of the Census of World Agriculture. The sample used in the Strange Farmers Survey was devised by Mr D.Y. Lele of the FAO.

Notes

1 'Tilibo' is a term used by Mandinka to describe those who come from the Manding heartland centred on Kangaba in the Upper Niger valley.
2 The Trade Season usually runs from the middle of December until the end of March, commencing on a date announced by the

Government. During this period groundnuts can be purchased by the official agencies and licensed buyers at the producer price fixed by the Government.

3 A *dabada* corresponds to what may be called a 'farming household' in which those living and eating together pool their labour and other resources. A compound could contain one or more *dabadas* and a *dabada* one or more cooking units (*sinkiros*).

Part III
Social perspectives

Many of the papers in this volume discuss relationships between circulation and the social structures within which movements take place. Whatever may be the economic incentives and pressures to circulate cultural, social and political factors have influence on the nature and pattern of circulation. Cultures, societies and politics may in turn be influenced by circulation. The papers in this section illustrate some of these interactions with reference to differing forms of organization at a variety of scales.

Lynne Brydon considers relationships between circulation and society at micro-scale, focusing on family and community in part of the Volta Region in Ghana though the movements which take place involve other parts of the country. It is particularly important that she is concerned with the movements of women and children; many studies of circulation and other forms of mobility for the most part consider their movements as dependent on those of men. In many West African societies women are free to act both socially and economically independently of men. This needs to be recognized and attention given to the circulation which derives from this independence.

Circulatory movements occur both within and across cultural and political boundaries. People may adapt to moving from one cultural area to another when this may be for a limited period of time, or they may accept and tolerate the difficulties with which they are confronted since these are outweighed by the advantages of the economic gains which can be made. Movements across political boundaries may be allowed without restriction, or they may be permitted subject to formal arrangements, or they may be officially forbidden and yet take place clandestinely or with an official blind-eye turned to them. Often mobility involves several of these circumstances. Movements in island realms frequently cross internal and political boundaries and pose some problems which differ from movements within large land masses. Fragmentation does not inhibit inter-island circulation in the Pacific or in the Caribbean. Dawn Marshall shows that the people who circulate from the poverty-stricken island of Haiti to the more prosperous Bahamas cope with an amalgam of physical, cultural and political problems which are compounded by the illegality of this mobility.

Great religions act as major unifying forces among their adherents who are otherwise racially, culturally and politically distinctive. Religions may thus facilitate the movements of people. In addition zeal to proselytize and the need to escape from religious persecution have both been motives for movement. All great religions have holy places and shrines to which adherents are drawn for spiritual and sometimes physical benefit, usually involving movements of limited duration. Religion is thus a major factor in promoting circulation over long and short distances in many parts of the world.

Some of the movements are of inter-continental proportions, as in the great annual convergence of Moslem pilgrims on Saudi Arabia. Intra-continental circulation is common, as Bhardwaj shows to the Hindu shrines in India. These holy places are of varying importance and range in a hierarchy from the national to the local scale. Religious piety manifests itself in different ways at these different scales and, furthermore, the Hindu caste system exercises constraints. Both scale and social stratification influence the patterns of circulation. Bhardwaj sees circulation as more than the repetitive movements of people in time and place; it involves also the reciprocal movement of ideas, values and other socio-cultural elements. Constant pilgrimage reinforces the Hindu religion and enhances feelings of ideological community among those who participate. The broad perspective of circulation which Bhardwaj adopts is in the humanist tradition of French geography, inspired notably by Vidal de la Blache, which was more important earlier in this century than it has been in recent research.

Like religion, education, in the various ways in which it may be defined and as it is variously practised, has traditionally influenced people's movements. The 'wandering scholars' were an important element of the intellectual life of medieval Europe, and in the present day in the Moslem areas of West Africa religion and education combine to produce very considerable movements of Koranic teachers and their students (to which Olofson refers). Such movements developed without deliberate planning and organization. The provision of Western-style education, which is being expanded in all parts of the Third World, requires deliberate planning and organization. It is in great demand but the resources available to meet this demand are scarce. To meet the demand most effectively requires the exercise of various possible ways of allocation which are the subject of substantial differences of opinion.

Since there is not universal provision of education in Third World countries movement will be necessary for many of those who are seeking the resources which are available. Much attention has been directed to studying the way that education promotes the movement of people after it has been acquired, but little attention has been given to the mobility which educational facilities promote. William Gould examines the circulation of schoolchildren and students to various types of schools in East Africa. Among the three countries considered − Uganda, Kenya and Tanzania − there are differences of political attitudes and ideology which influence significantly the ways in which educational institutions are located and the ways in which places in them are allocated. These differences are reflected in the patterns of circulation of schoolchildren and students. Gould stresses that circulation for education is no passing form of social behaviour despite the fact that stage-type models suggest that such behaviour is somewhat transitory.

The papers in the section which have been introduced so far range in the scale of their considerations from local to national and international. Mukherji in his paper on labour circulation in India combines a number of scales, from local to national, to show how circulation at these various scales is interrelated. He combines data from his own fieldwork with those from other sources including the national census. The picture he paints is depressing, of society in dependence and immiseration. The main endeavour of those who circulate must be directed towards survival, and their prospects of achieving something better are severely limited. Thus the theme which runs through the several levels of enquiry and the future scenarios outlined in Mukherji's paper is that through circulation upward social mobility is not necessarily achieved.

10 The Avatime family and circulation 1900—1977

Lynne Brydon

Polly Hill published *Migrant Cocoa Farmers of Southern Ghana*, in 1963. It looked at the movement of Ghanaian peasant farmers in the Eastern Region to acquire land on which to grow cocoa. She showed how the distribution of land of farmers differed among groups having different systems of inheritance and descent and she emphasised the circulatory nature of movement. Although the farmers spent considerable periods of time in the cocoa-growing areas, they built magnificent houses in their home towns, and their formal familial ties were focused around these towns. Funds from booming cocoa sales meant that children of migrants could be educated, an advantage in the increasingly bureaucratised and white-collar oriented society in the towns and cities of Ghana. It is in this sense of the maintenance of enduring links with a natal area and the eventual, hopefully triumphant, return to the natal area that circulatory movement is best understood in Southern Ghana. Polly Hill's analysis did not however, extend to groups trying to participate in the cocoa boom in other areas of Ghana. In the centre of the Volta Region is Buem, another fertile cocoa-growing area. Like those west of the Volta, it attracted in-migrants from the surrounding areas. Some of these migrants were Avatimes whose traditional land is in the hills of the Togo Ranges, about twenty miles north of Ho, the regional capital.

This movement was by no means the first the Avatimes had known. Their oral history includes extensive stories of wandering from their traditional homes in Ahanta before they settled at their present site, probably at a similar time as the Ewes were drifting into the area from the east, in the middle years of the eighteenth century. However, prior to the establishment of a colonial presence in the area movement, in the sense that it is used here, was not found. There was some movement of people: inter-marriage with surrounding groups, taking of captives in skirmishes (to be sold as slaves), pawning of children in times of scarcity and visits to established markets in more distant areas. But, the voluntary movement of people over a longer period than market trips or to work to earn money did not occur. With the entrenchment of colonial authority this pattern changed, until today almost a third of the population of Amedzofe (one of the Avatime villages) is away and migrants from all the other villages are to be found in the large urban centres of Accra, Kumasi and Ho.

This paper examines change in family structure in Amedzofe-Avatime throughout the colonial period, and particularly looks at the relevance of movement for change in family structure in more recent years. Most of the detail is based on data collected from Amedzofe in 1973-4 and 1976-7 and the findings are relevant for Avatime as a whole.

Avatime

Some background information on Avatime ethnography and structure is given here but a more detailed account can be found in Brydon (1976). The Avatime are one of a number of small groups who live in the hill and more remote areas of the Volta Region of Ghana (Figure 10.1). Their language is closely related to but not mutually intelligible with the languages of some of the other groups in the area: Westermann and Bryan (1952) lumped together these languages into the residual category 'Restsprache'. There are seven Avatime villages, each having its own chief and formal authority structure. The paramount chief's village is Vane.[1]

The first colonial influence in the area was German, Avatime forming part of the colony of Togoland. This began in the mid-1880s, but the Bremen Mission had been working in the area generally since 1853. European traders were also familiar with the area since the Volta River was a major trade route connecting the coast with the hinterland. A mission station and seminary were established in Ho and the missionaries had their first Avatime convert in the 1870s in the villages at the foot of the mountains. In 1890 a mission station was established in Amedzofe, the highest Avatime village, and in 1894 the Teacher Training College and Seminary were moved from Ho to Amedzofe. The climate of Amedzofe, relatively cool and mosquito-free, was one of the major factors in this move. After 1911, Africans began to be ordained as priests and the early part

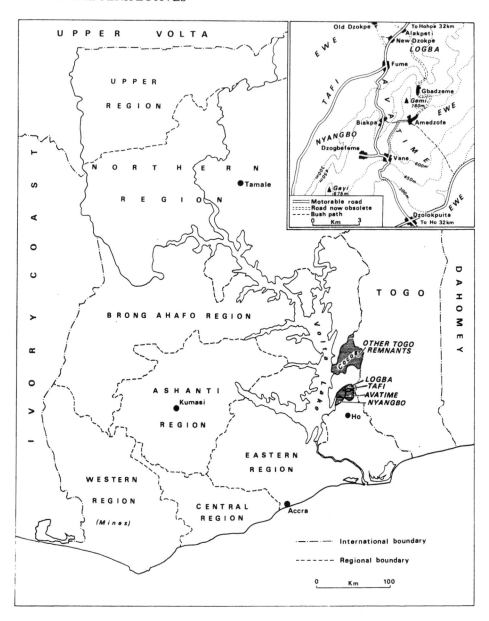

FIGURE 10.1 Avatime, Ghana: study area

of the First World War saw an emphasis on the ordination of
native pastors. After the war the former German colony came
under the mandate of the League of Nations (and later was a
Trust Territory of the United Nations), divided for adminis-

tration, between the British and the French. Avatime came under British authority and was administered from Koforidua in the Gold Coast. Before the war the focus of administrative and commercial activity from Avatime was in the east (Palime and Misahöhe); after the war, the focus shifted towards closer ties with the Gold Coast to the west.

In addition to training teachers and catechists, the Germans also taught practical skills; men were trained as carpenters, masons, bricklayers, blacksmiths and sawyers and women were taught to sew and to read the vernacular. Although the Avatime language was and still is spoken in the village, the written vernacular is Ewe, into which the Germans had translated the Bible and which was used for Church services. Women as well as men went to school and in 1902 a day nursery was established in the village. Between the coming of German authority and 1914 the colony prospered economically. Timber and palm products were exported, rubber and cotton growing were introduced and Togo became the only self-supporting African colony. The Avatime area was too wet for cotton growing and unsuitable for rubber and so European influence was confined to that of missionaries and administrators, and not traders. At least from the turn of the century onwards, educated and skilled men could find work for cash both in Togo and in the Gold Coast. The importance of cash increased with the introduction of imported goods and taxes.

Traditional social organisation

To understand movement it is necessary to have some idea of the structure of the community. In the absence of documentary evidence for societies like Avatime the anthropologist has to resort to oral evidence and any structural pointers to suggest the nature of past family forms. Fortunately, the period relevant to this paper is within the memory of the oldest living people in the villages and they are very willing to reminisce about their youth and old forms of rituals. The old forms of the nubility and marriage ceremonies provide corroborative evidence for the ideal 'normal' type of family structure in the very early stages of the colonial period. The particular forms and functions of the ceremonies considered as an abstract system meant that logically there are constraints on forms of residence pattern and family structure (Brydon 1976).

Descent in Avatime is patrilineal. A person belongs to a nesting series of groups from the narrowest in range, the *oku*, a minimal descent group consisting only of three or four generations, through a putatively agnatic (male-descended) clan, to the widest group which is all the Avatime people. Traditionally on marriage a man should be able to provide a new house for his bride, a new hearth, clothes to wear and cooking utensils. The nubility and marriage rituals formed the complementary parts of what was effectively a single cycle of ceremonies. A girl could not be married unless she had had the nubility ceremonies performed for her and marriage followed immediately. The later ceremonies in the marriage rituals focused on the establishment of the new residence: the walls of a new house were smeared with a fine grained clay, water was brought ceremonially to the new house and the lighting of a fire in the new hearth for the first time was also an occasion for ritual. The emphasis in these and other ceremonies was on the establishment of a new residential unit, distinct from the houses of either the husband's or the wife's parents. In keeping with the patrilineal ideology, however, the new house was always close to the house of the man's parents; the *oku* is a localised group. The study of the old forms of marriage customs therefore indicates that residential units contained only two generations; three-generation, extended or expanded groups were not the norm. Evidence collected from old people in the village also points to this kind of nuclear family-based residential pattern.

Headship of the residential group was vested in men, although women might wield considerable power in the everyday running of affairs. In the traditional jural system, however, they were not recognised as heads of houses. The practice of widow inheritance meant that a woman whose husband died moved to live with one of his patrilineal relatives. If a woman refused to marry a relative of the husband then strong pressure was put on her to marry someone else. Women who remained adamant either stayed in their affinal group areas under the protection of a deceased husband's *oku*, or returned to their natal *oku* and lived with a brother. Such cases were rare, the status of single adult female was anomalous. Even today women are not recognised as formal household heads in the traditional jural sphere of village life, but now *de facto* headship has assumed far greater importance separate from and relative to *de jure* headship. Women are now the *de facto* heads of 64 out of a total of 212 residential units in Amedzofe.

Early patterns of movement

With the establishment of German authority in Togo and the subsequent increasing importance of cash, Avatimes began to travel outside their own locality to work. On one hand were the ideologically motivated migrants, the pastors, catechists and teachers, mainly men, and on the other, mission-trained craftsmen, again usually men. Education and religion were closely connected until the 1950s. Barbara Ward (1950) states that the Germans had noted an emigrant flow from Togo as early as 1900, and the repressive nature of the German regime has been cited as one reason for the movement of people at this time (Amenumey 1964). After 1918, cocoa began to be grown in Buem, about seventy miles north of Avatime. Avatimes went there and acquired land on which to grow this crop, the land around the Avatime villages being unsuitable for cocoa production on a commercial scale.

These early types of movements gave rise to different patterns of visiting and eventual return to the home areas. The literate migrants were posted from station to station often with their wives and visited home when leave or school vacation permitted. Eventually on retirement they returned to the village and settled there. The skilled workers travelled around looking for work. Many of them crossed the Volta to the Gold Coast, some going as far as the mines in the Western Region. These migrants were often itinerant, only working for a short time in each place. Visits home were confined to times between jobs and short periods of annual leave. Wives did not usually accompany husbands in such cases, and periods of itinerant migration were often terminated on marriage. Such a case is Kwasi Bansah. He was about 15 when he left home (about 1923) and went to Accra, wanting a job which paid cash. The pay was not sufficient in his first job in a store, so he left and went to the mines in about 1926. He was laid off and went as a fitter to Bodua (1927-30). Again, he was laid off and went as a fitter and an engine driver to Takoradi. The reason he gave for leaving this job was the low pay. Next he became a gold miner (1932-3) and left after a year because the work was too hard to become a sawyer. After two years he managed to go to Buem to buy a cocoa farm, and once it was established he came back to Amedzofe and married. He was 39 when his first child was born.

Some of the itinerant workers settled in the places to which they went and married women there. However, most of them returned home either on retirement or when they had enough cash to buy a cocoa farm in the more fertile areas. The cocoa farmer's pattern of maintaining contact with home was different and depended on the season of the year. Also, once a cocoa farm had been established the time spent on the farm could be limited provided that a suitable caretaker would oversee the farm other than at harvest times. Distance was also a factor in maintaining contact with home; cocoa farmers had a relatively short distance to travel from their farms to home villages. Those who were teachers or mission workers or who went to the Gold Coast had much longer distances to travel. The Germans had made several laterite roads in the Volta Region and had intended to bring the railway from Lome to Kpandu. Roads uniting the Volta Region and the Gold Coast were few; there was no transport in the early days of movement and people walked.

What made these people return home? The idea of 'home' is complex in any culture. For Avatimes there is an emotional attachment to 'home' (*kepa*) where Avatime (*siyase*) is spoken. 'Home' is where you come from: your relatives and your rights to land, until recently the main source of livelihood, are there. 'Home' is also where, ideally, you should die, but if this is impossible, every effort is made to bury you there. 'Home' (*kepa*) is explicitly contrasted with 'abroad' (*igbodoleme*) where Avatimes are strangers and have no rights to land or support from kin. Similarly, strangers as such have no rights in Avatime. Avatimes say of strangers 'he is a log' (*onu kesegu*), because they do not understand the language and can take no part in conversation. Alternatively, a stranger is defined as one 'who doesn't eat green leaf stew' (*o na sigase*), a popular traditional food in Avatime.

For the most part people return to Avatime because it is 'home'. Ideally they return on retirement or before, having financed the building of a fine house on family land in the village. They take up a role suitable to their genealogical or political position (which they should be fully conversant with because of regular visits home), make fine farms on family lands and should be ready to help and advise the people in the village in the light of their experience away. If a migrant has the misfortune to die suddenly away from the village, his body should be brought home to be buried. Traditionally a person had to be buried on land belonging to their clan section, *oku*. Now, the main funeral ceremonies take place in the deceased's *oku* area and burial takes place in a cemetery. Even women who have been married and resident for many years in another clan area or village will be buried from their natal group area, the body is laid in state and the funeral ceremonies are performed and the meal is cooked in a house belonging to a member of the deceased's *oku* group. The attitude of people towards 'home' is an indication of the strength of attachment of the members of the group to their villages in the traditional area.

Changes in movement patterns

The patterns of movement discussed were prominent in the early years of this century. Later patterns of migration (pre-1960) may be examined using data collected from returned migrants in Amedzofe, Gbadzeme and Biakpa in 1976 and those of Ward from a fourth village, Vane, collected in 1946.[2] Some inter-village differences are present, which can be explained in terms of Amedzofe's early introduction to education and the presence of European missionaries in the village.

Ward's data (Table 10.1) are adapted so that they are directly comparable with those collected in 1976 on range of occupations of returned migrants (Table 10.2). Table 10.3 shows the destinations of migrants from Vane and in Table 10.4 Ward's destination groups are used to show the destinations of the returned migrants in Amedzofe, Gbadzeme and Biakpa in 1976. The occupations and destinations of migrants from the four villages are compared in Tables 10.5 and 10.6 respectively. These data all indicate movement patterns certainly before the time of the intensive fieldwork (1973-4) and in most cases before 1960.

Field data from Amedzofe, Gbadzeme and Biakpa show that there were more Amedzofe people than those from Gbadzeme and Biakpa who worked further afield than in the Volta Region. This is also shown in the occupations of returned migrants from the three villages. More male migrants from Amedzofe were in occupations which are not found frequently in rural areas. Before independence in 1957 there were no large urban centres in the then Trans-Volta Togoland. Hohoe was the main commercial centre, and after union with the Gold Coast Ho became the

TABLE 10.1 *Occupations of Vane migrants by sex in 1946*

Occupation	Men	Women
Farm/cocoa	24	23
Marriage/trader	0	50
Skilled	9	7
Vocational	0	0
Unskilled	13	9
Government/teaching	4	2
Other/clerical	6	0
Total	56	91

Source: Ward 1950: 131

TABLE 10.2 *Occupations of returned migrants: Amedzofe, Gbadzeme and Biakpa*

Occupation	Amedzofe		Gbadzeme		Biakpa	
	Men	Women	Men	Women	Men	Women
Farm/cocoa[1]	4	1	9	9	12	11
Marriage/trader	0	15	0	4	0	3
Skilled	12	0	5	0	5	0
Vocational[2]	0	1	0	2	0	2
Unskilled[3]	4	2	4	4	3	2
Government/ teaching	5	0	0	1	0	0
Other/clerical[4]	2	4	2	0	0	2
Total	27	23	20	20	20	20

[1] Some of the men included in this category also said that they were carpenters or masons or sawyers
[2] Includes seamstresses and nurses
[3] Includes nursemaids, housegirls and labourers
[4] Includes prostitutes

regional administrative centre but was not a major commercial centre. Fewer of the Amedzofe men were cocoa farmers and even of those who had spent some time in the cocoa areas, five said they were craftsmen rather than farmers.

The diversity in range of occupations of Amedzofe men and their greater tendency to go away from the Volta Region reflects a higher standard of education than that of men from Gbadzeme and Biakpa. This is a function of the long entrenched position of the mission and its associated schools in Amedzofe, giving Amedzofe men an advantage in terms of the scope of their occupations over those from Gbadzeme or Biakpa. There are no data on education available from Ward's article, but the pattern of destinations and occupations of Vane migrants is similar to that of the Gbadzeme and Biakpa rather than to that of the Amedzofe migrants.

The data on destinations from returned women migrants are similar to those for men, which is not surprising since many of the returned women cite joining a husband on marriage as their personal reason for movement. For most of the returned women from Amedzofe, Gbadzeme and Biakpa the first marriage, if not subsequent marriages, was within the village. The range of returned women's occupations supports the suggestion that more Amedzofe women migrated to the urban areas. Of the returned

TABLE 10.3 *Destinations of Vane migrants by sex in 1946*

	Destination	Men	Women
British Togo	Amedzofe and local villages	31	34
	Ahamansu, Buem (Cocoa)	40	55
	Hohoe	0	2
	Ho	1	4
	Keta and Coast	0	3
	Sub-total	72	98
French Togo	Palime	3	2
	Other Togo	7	10
	Sub-total	10	12
Gold Coast	Accra	9	10
	Kumasi	1	3
	Koforidua	1	3
	Tarkwa and Konongo (mines)	4	2
	Elsewhere in Gold Coast	3	4
	Northern Territories	1	0
	Overseas	5	0
	Sub-total	24	22
Total		106	132

Source: Ward 1950: 132

TABLE 10.4 *Destinations of returned migrants: Amedzofe, Gbadzeme and Biakpa*

Destination[1]	Amedzofe		Gbadzeme		Biakpa	
	Men	Women	Men	Women	Men	Women
Avatime/local	1	1	1	5	2	8
N. Ewe	12	7	6	7	6	7
Hohoe	0	3	2	2	2	2
Ho	1	3	2	1	1	1
Cocoa	8	2	11	6	10	3
Coast (V/R)	0	2	0	0	1	0
Sub-total	22	18	22	21	22	21

Destination[1]	Amedzofe		Gbadzeme		Biakpa	
	Men	Women	Men	Women	Men	Women
Togo	6	1	1	2	2	0
Sub-total	6	1	1	2	2	0
Accra	10	8	4	4	4	5
Kumasi	0	0	2	0	0	2
Koforidua	3	2	3	0	3	0
Mines	2	5	0	0	2	1
Elsewhere	10	4	6	4	2	0
North	0	1	2	1	1	0
Sub-total	25	20	17	9	12	8
Total	53	39	40	32	36	29

Sub-totals correspond to 'British Togo', 'Gold Coast' categories in Table 10.3.
  1 Each destination of each migrant is recorded here. Hence the total of
    destinations is greater than the total number of migrants.

TABLE 10.5 *Occupations of migrants from Amedzofe, Gbadzeme, Biakpa and Vane (percentages)*

	Vane		Amedzofe		Gbadzeme		Biakpa	
	Men	Women	Men	Women	Men	Women	Men	Women
Farm/cocoa	43	25	15	4	45	45	60	55
Marriage/trader	—	55	—	65	—	20	—	15
Skilled	16	8	44	0	25	0	25	0
Vocational	—	0	—	4	—	10	—	10
Unskilled	23	10	15	9	20	20	15	10
Government/ teaching	7	2	19	0	0	5	0	0
Other/clerical	10	0	7	17	10	0	0	10

TABLE 10.6 *Destinations of migrants from Amedzofe, Gbadzeme, Biakpa and Vane (percentages)*

	Vane		Amedzofe		Gbadzeme		Biakpa	
	Men	Women	Men	Women	Men	Women	Men	Women
Volta Region	70	74	42	46	55	66	61	70
Togo	10	9	11	3	3	6	6	0
Gold Coast	22	17	47	51	42	28	33	29

Amedzofe women, only one was a farmer during her period of migration, while fifteen can be classified as 'married/trader'. This category means that they worked as traders, (small goods, cooked food, bread, cloth) as an adjunct to their marriages and possibly in combination with food growing on a small scale. The other returned women had jobs as unskilled labourers, seamstresses or were said to be prostitutes. The ranges of occupations of Gbadzeme and Biakpa women are similar; a much higher proportion of returned Gbadzeme and Biakpa women than of Amedzofe women gave their principal occupation as farmer (again carried out as an adjunct to marriage: Gbadzeme 9/20, Biakpa 11/20, Amedzofe 1/23). The range of occupations for Vane women appears to be more akin to that of Amedzofe women than for women from the other villages. Twenty-three women are categorised as farmers, fifty are in a 'married/trader' category (N = 91). It is likely that because of the lack of strict comparability in occupational categories, more of the Vane women would, in the present scheme, have said they were farmers since in the distribution of Vane women migrants by destination, fifty-five women were in the cocoa areas, while only twenty-two were in the Gold Coast. Women can farm within the framework of their marriages in the cocoa areas, but not in the urban areas of the Gold Coast.

Migration from Avatime: post-1970

The types of migration from Avatime from the beginning of the colonial era to the 1950s indicate that the range of occupations was similar throughout although Amedzofe had greater advantages in terms of education. Different occupations of migrants gave rise to different patterns of contact with the home areas. A census carried out in 1974 showed that out of a total population of 2164 in Amedzofe, 588 over the age of 20 were away.[3] The occupations of those absentees in rural areas were predominantly not farming, but were teaching and government employment. This re-inforces the pattern revealed in the examination of the occupations and destinations of returned Amedzofe migrants; the majority are in salaried jobs rather than cash crop farming. Migrant cocoa farmers from Amedzofe today are rare.

Urban migration accounts for many current Avatime migrants, not only those from Amedzofe. Those who are in rural areas are usually teachers or employed in some aspect of government service. Factors such as the decline in cocoa prices in the 1950s and 1960s, swollen shoot disease in cocoa, the increase in availability of education, the prestige attached to white collar

217

rather than to manual occupations and the increasing standards of technology introduced in Ghana mean that the scope for urban employment has increased. Data from Amedzofe in 1974 show that the proportion of migrants in farming is small and there is no evidence to indicate that the pattern of movement in the other villages today is any different from that of Amedzofe. The larger proportion of migrants is less than 35-40 years old and the provision of primary and middle schools in the other villages has meant that the advantage that Amedzofe had in terms of education has been nullified. 'Push' and 'pull' factors, qualifications and opportunities, are similar for people from all of the villages. What is significantly different about movement today concerns the roles and importance of women.

Information from returned migrant women shows that before the mid-1950s the main reason that women left the villages was to accompany a husband or to join a husband on marriage. Now this has changed. Women say that they move away from the village to look for work and not specifically to be with a husband. Change in reasons for women's movement is shown in Figure 1~.2. There are three stated reasons why women leave the village: to join a husband, to accompany a relative and to work. The proportion of women who do not leave for work has decreased in the period between the time of return of the sample of 'returned migrants' and the present time. For the most part, now women do not move away from the village because their husbands are away, they move before marriage to look for a salaried job on their own account. Movement in youth with an adult, also means that by the time women who leave in this way are old enough to work they may well already be in the urban areas. As with male migrants, the range of jobs available to women has increased although some of the current migrants can still be classified in the 'married/trader' category. These women may have left the village originally to look for work but now, because of marriage and the chores of child-rearing and housekeeping, they find it difficult to hold a regular salaried job. Petty trading from her own house allows the woman to set her own hours, to be free to look after her children and to retain some financial independence (Peil 1975).

What do these changes in the pattern of women's migration mean? First, they mean that most women who emigrate are not married; they do not leave the village to join a migrant husband. Migrant women who work in the urban areas now do not necessarily work within the framework of marriage and child-rearing. A job is not regarded only as a source of supplementary income or a way of passing the time.

218

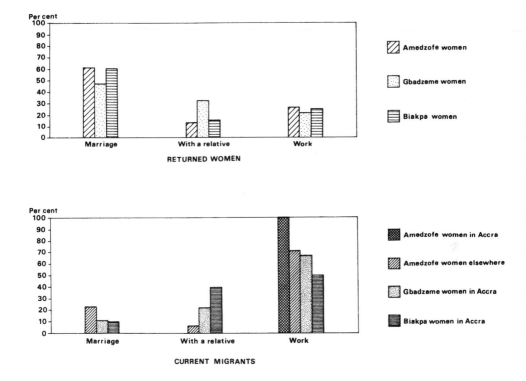

FIGURE 10.2 *Changes in reasons for women's movements*

Family structure: transition

Having traced the pattern of migration up to 1976, what effects do the introduction of and changes in this pattern have on those who stay in the villages? Ward (1955) looked at family structure in Vane in 1946, making the point that her data could be generalised for the whole of Avatime. The data collected in Amedzofe, Gbadzeme and Biakpa in the 1970s are also typical of Avatime as a whole, more so since all the villages now have schools, and suggesting that earlier information for Amedzofe was perhaps not typical of Avatime as a whole.

Ward's analysis is in terms of consumption groups (which she calls 'households') and not in terms of residential units. However, her figures do show that more than 70 per cent of consumption units are centred on a conjugal pair, while only 19 per cent are headed by a woman (N = 167). Some of these households are

219

combined to form what she terms 'dwelling groups', residential units. Her data show that there was departure from the 'ideal' type of traditional Avatime residential unit in Vane in 1946, although she says of households composed of the 'head's own simple families only': 'This was clearly the normal residential unit in a statistical sense' (Ward 1955: 36).

She notes that adult children usually formed residential units separate from their parents (which conforms with the traditional pattern) but she also notes several factors at variance with this. In Vane, there were women living with their sons and families as members of the son's consumption groups, which was not the pattern in Amedzofe. Old women did not form single consumption units with their sons and families unless they were physically incapable of cooking for themselves. Ward also noted that widows who were not remarried must return to their natal *oku* area. Again, the data from Amedzofe differ, showing that twice the number of widows stay in their marital homes than return to their natal homes. Finally, Ward notes that there are a number of what she calls 'illegitimate' children, children whose parents are not married and living together. All of these indicate some shift away from the traditional ideal pattern. Although Ward's data indicate that there was some deviation from the traditional ideal residence pattern in Vane in 1946, data collected in Amedzofe in 1974 indicate a much greater divergence from the traditional ideal. Specifically, the incidence of female-headed residential units (30 per cent) in Amedzofe is much higher as is the incidence of three-generation residential units (Brydon 1976: 228-41). While Ward's data show that these deviations are present in Vane, her conclusions emphasise the importance of patrifiliation as a structural principle in residential group composition, that is, that the nuclear-type family group is still the norm.

Family structure: post 1970

Figure 10.3 shows the proportions of males and females in the migrant and non-migrant populations of Amedzofe. Between ages 25 and 40 there are proportionately more females than males resident in the village. An examination of why this is the case leads to a discussion of family structure in Amedzofe (and Avatime) today.

Who are the women in the village in this age group? Some are married and settled, their husbands are mostly farmers in the village and older than themselves. Cases where the husband works away while the wife and children are resident in the village, as in some Ewe groups (Verdon 1975), are rare in

Amedzofe. There are, however, a number of unmarried women in this age range in the village.[4] They have usually spent some time away and have borne children in the urban areas. Some of these women were interviewed (N = 16) for their migrant and child-bearing histories. Although several of them had spent long periods away and had worked in a range of jobs, they found it difficult to support themselves and their children and at the same time to care for young children on their own. In some cases, the women had been married for a time and had borne children in the framework of the union. The marriages having ended, the women found themselves alone and with children to support in the urban areas. These women chose to come home to the village where they could both work (farm) to feed their children and would have help in the care of their children from relatives in the village, two channels of support not available away from home.

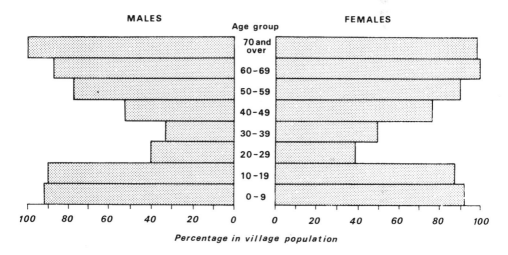

FIGURE 10.3 Age-sex structure in Amedzofe

How do these women fit into the traditional pattern of family structure? In the past, it has been argued, nuclear family units were the norm, two-generation rather than three-generation family units. Women who return home with children and without a spouse usually live with their parents. A three-generation residential unit is thus formed. However, the frequency of three-generation residential units in Amedzofe in 1974 was too great to be accounted for by the return of daughters from urban areas. There are at least 67 out of 212 residential units with more than two generations (Brydon 1976: 216).

Although it is impossible to know what the actual composition of residential units was in the past, residence norms and the structural constraints of marriage customs militated against great leeway in the range of residential unit composition. Now there are so many different forms that it is a futile task to try to classify residential units into types: the range is so great that when the simpler forms have been accounted for, a large number of unique 'other' and more complex family groups remain. Now the old forms of nubility and marriage ceremonies are no longer performed, widow inheritance is no longer practised, and a lack of space in the village among other things means that there is not such a high degree of localisation in residence as there appears to have been. These factors can be considered as having been constraints against diversity in residential unit composition.

What part does movement play in the wider range of residential unit composition in the village? Single women with children who return home live with their parents and form a three-generation unit, but this movement is not sufficient to account for either the number or the diversity in composition of multi-generation residential units. The data from current migrants provide an answer. Now, both men and women leave the village to look for salaried jobs. They want to continue to work until either they have enough money for a specific project or they retire and return home to the village with the prestige of returned successful migrants. On the other hand, having children is important. Men want children to continue their names and for help in old age, and women want children particularly for help in old age. In addition, bearing children is important for Avatime women as women. An older woman who has not borne children, while not being openly stigmatised in any way is regarded with sympathy, and reasons for her lack of children are a topic for rumour and gossip. Bearing children in the urban areas means that the woman must have financial support both for herself and her children, and she must be prepared to care for her children herself since there are no members of her kin (usually an older relative) who are near at hand and willing to care for them. A woman who continues to live away must resolve these problems.

Resolution is easier if women are married. If the husband is earning a high salary the wife can stop work to look after very young children. She may return to work as the children grow, or may turn to work that can be done as an adjunct to her domestic roles, such as trading (Peil 1975). If the wife is not willing to give up her job, she may, after a period of maternity leave which is long for women in Government service and in teaching, hire a baby nurse for the child or send the child to a day nursery, providing money is available. Alternatively, the child may be sent back to either the husband's or wife's parents or other relatives to be reared in the village. This explains, for the most part, the frequency of residential units in Amedzofe (37 per cent) in which there are sons' children or daughters' children of the head regardless of the presence of their parents. Where parents of both migrant spouses are dead or too old to care for young children, the children may be reared by another relative.

Bearing children and being married are not necessarily linked in Avatime today. Young girls (either in middle school or soon after completing middle school) may become pregnant and have their children in the village. This does not prevent them from then leaving the village. The children are usually left with parents and the girls leave to find jobs. Again, the result in the village is a three-generation residential unit.

Migration is not alone in influencing current family structure in Amedzofe. We cannot say that only because Avatime leave their traditional area to work away for a time has family structure become so diverse. Migration is one of a complex of factors which have effected the diversity in residential group structure. Other factors include the influence of Europeans (as colonial administrators and as missionaries, educators and traders) and the demise of the traditional values and practices associated with nubility and marriage. Avatimes have certainly been migrants for all of this century. If Ward's data on family structure are taken to be applicable to Avatime as a whole then, remembering the traditional model outlined above, we can see that changes in family structure have been taking place gradually throughout the period of migration, tending towards the diversity revealed in Amedzofe in 1974. Further evidence for this gradual shift comes from returned older female migrants who were interviewed. The reason that most of them gave for migration was 'marriage', and if they had any job in the migrant areas the job was secondary to their roles as mother and wife. Only in the samples of current migrants do the majority give 'work' as the actual reason for migration.

Now migrant men stay away for most of their working lives, returning to the village on retirement to farm, to look after family lands and to play an active role in the affairs of the village. Women must now be seen as an independent category of migrants. They do not migrate within a framework of marriage, they migrate to look for work to enable them to support themselves in a nation where the importance of cash and manufactured goods is rapidly increasing. When women migrate and money and work are the most important factors, their traditional roles as wives and mothers must alter. Increased

223

diversity in residential unit composition reflects both the fact that women migrate separately from men and the increased importance of continued employment for the women: children of migrant parents are reared in the village with their grandparents and single women may choose to return to the village as the least difficult way of supporting both themselves and their children. Three-generation units are formed in both cases.

Only two aspects of change in residence group structure in Amedzofe have been discussed, both related to migration. Cases where men migrate for long periods leaving their wives in the villages, as in southern Africa (Murray, 1976) are not found in Amedzofe. The pattern described by Verdon (1975) for the Abutia Ewe − where, although men and women migrate together, after a period in the migrant areas the women (as wives) and children are sent home because of lack of money in an entirely cash-based situation − is not found among Amedzofe migrants. Traditional residential units were based upon the nuclear family. It is only recently, especially since Ward's work in 1946, that the residential unit has ceased necessarily to be based upon a nuclear family or to contain a nuclear family unit. This assertion is contrary to Goode's hypothesis (1963). His general thesis is that the emergence of what he calls the conjugal family type is positively correlated with the increased importance or inception of the complex of variables constituting 'industrialisation' and 'urbanisation' and in which migration is included. In Amedzofe there is increasing diversity in residential unit composition, a shift away from the traditional nuclear family ideal. This diversity can be seen in three ways:

(i)   a deviation from the old norm of nuclear family based residential units;

(ii)   as representing a stable state, so that the present variety of residential units will be tolerated by the society and will persist over time;

(iii)   as a transitional state, leading to a new 'ideal' state which is not yet crystallised.

The first possibility implies a return to the status quo ante. To conform to the nuclear family model and also to fit Goode's hypothesis, there must be emphasis on a strong formal conjugal bond. Although space does not permit discussion of this in full, it has been shown elsewhere that there is less and less emphasis on the formation of a strong and durable conjugal bond (Brydon 1976). Bearing children and being married are not necessarily linked and now women have status in the society as adults in their own right. The second possibility is unlikely because Ghana is changing and evolving so rapidly. The third possibility is the most likely, but we are left with the question, 'transition to what?' It does not seem as though Goode's model of increasing frequency of conjugal families is pertinent in the short term, at least not until migrants live with their spouses and raise their children away from the villages in the migrant areas, and the practice of early pregnancies for unmarried females is discontinued. The current pattern of residential group diversity in the village is one reflection of the fact that Avatime men and women as adults want to participate in the developing society that is Ghana. Movement for Avatimes, in the sense of leaving the villages to work for a period of time, followed ultimately by a return to the village is now a regular feature of life. Any move towards a nuclear family residential norm must pose constraints on the women migrants particularly and emphasise their roles as mothers and wives. Their problems are not unlike those faced by working women with children in western societies. At the moment, the Avatime women are making use of their extended family ties and a closely knit social structure to which their western sisters have no access.

Notes

1 Fieldwork was carried out in the Avatime area in 1973-4 and in 1976-7. Data were collected from all of the villages, but the most detailed data come from Amedzofe. The second period of work was devoted to interviews with and about migrants from three of the villages: Amedzofe, Gbadzeme and Biakpa.
2 Ward's data are used in direct comparison to my own data from returned migrants. These returned migrants are usually old people (over 60) and were migrants at the time Ward collected her data (1946). The comparability of the two data sets validates to some extent the retrospective data from returned migrants.
3 Two questions were used in enumerating. The first, 'Who slept here last night?' was intended to give a *de facto* enumeration of the Amedzofe population, and the second, 'Who usually sleeps here when they come home on leave or at Christmas and Easter?' to give a *de jure* enumeration.
4 Marriage in the village can be defined functionally as a co-residential commensal and conjugal union (Brydon 1976). There is no single major ceremony now which can be called 'the marriage ceremony'. A woman must have the nubility ceremony performed for her before she can live in a co-residential union in the village. Children are born to women whether or not they have had the nubility ceremony performed for them; bearing children and marriage now have no necessary connection.

11 International migration as circulation: Haitian movement to the Bahamas

Dawn I. Marshall

It is likely that there has always been some kind of interaction between the Bahamas and Haiti, for Great Inagua Island, the southernmost island of the Bahamas chain, is only fifty-five miles away from the Ile de la Tortue, off north-west Haiti. Until tourism became important to the Bahamas in the 1950s interaction would have been mainly in the form of trade: small scale trade, an extension of the coastal schooner trade of Haiti and the Out Island trade of the Bahamas. Some Haitians would have stayed in the Bahamas, but this would not have been common since opportunities for jobs were so limited before tourism was developed that Bahamians themselves were leaving the islands in search of employment. However, by 1948, a few Haitians had begun to move to the Bahamas.

This movement of Haitians to the Bahamas is an illegal one and very few Haitians on their first arrival have entered the Bahamas legally. Because of its illegal nature, very little is known about the movement. Since May 1957 the Bahamas Government has recognized it as a problem, for despite their efforts at control illegal entries have continued, and at least until 1974 apparently increased. Estimates have grown from 1,000 in 1957, to 10,000 in 1962, 14,000 in 1967, 20,000 in 1969, 25,000 in 1970 and 40,000 in 1974 – significant numbers in a country whose total population was only 168,838 according to the 1970 census. From newspaper reports, however, it is clear that these are indeed estimates and that no consensus about numbers has existed even among government officials concerned with the problem. No one really has known or knows, how many Haitians there were, or are, in the Bahamas.

A history of the Haitian movement, based on data from Bahamian newspapers covering the period January 1955 to

226

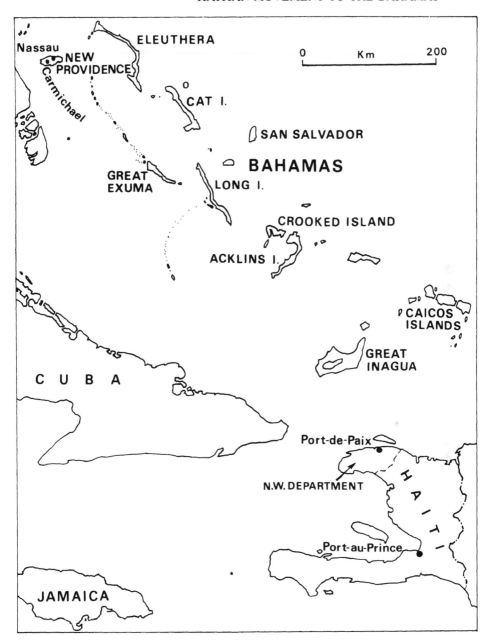

FIGURE 11.1 Haiti and Bahamas

December 1971, proved to be an essentially one-sided account of the development of a rather narrow Bahamian immigration policy towards the Haitian movement. Controlling the illegal entries, raids and round-ups like those of the 1963 'operation clean-up' and the 1967 'crackdown campaign', and an eventual solution by wholesale deportation, were the predominant concerns of the Bahamian Government. Because of the increasing numbers of Haitians resident in the Bahamas, the Bahamian Government saw the movement as a permanent one. The opinions of the public expressed in the press also indicated a perception of the movement as permanent, with the end result of 'Bahaiti' rather than a Bahamas (*Tribune*, 24 May 1976). Nowhere in the newspaper reports during this sixteen-year period is there any indication, explicit or implicit, that Haitians were returning voluntarily to their homeland after a successful stay in the Bahamas.

In going to the Bahamas, Haitians not only cross an international boundary, but also move from an economically deprived, rural culture speaking a creole patois based on French, to a more metropolitan, tourism-based, English-speaking group of islands. Although it is always referred to as a migration, this paper will show that the movement has some of the characteristics of circulation (Zelinsky 1971: 225).

Background data on the Haitian movement

Haitians from all parts of Haiti can be found in the Bahamas, but the North-West Department seems to be the major source area. It is a rugged area, particularly vulnerable to drought. Thus, in a country dependent on agriculture, it is an environment of economic deprivation, lacking opportunity for the Haitian peasant. Little is known about the characteristics of the Haitians moving into the Bahamas except for a case study on which this paper is based carried out in 1971 among Haitians living in Carmichael, thirteen miles south-west of Nassau, the capital of the Bahamas. Data were collected on seventy-one households and their 135 adult members, about 85 per cent of the Haitians living in the study area.

Clearly this is only a small proportion of the total number of Haitians in the Bahamas, and any generalizations made refer only to the Carmichael Haitians. The essential criterion was quite simply the nature of the question (Brookfield 1973: 11). Because of the illegal nature of the movement (a practical problem) and the nature of the understandings which were sought (questions about the reasons for the movement and its effects) a micro approach was inevitable: it was necessary to know a lot about a little. It is tempting to carry Brookfield's argument even further. Because of the way in which circulation is defined, detailed data needed to be collected on the movers' intentions to return home as well as on the repetitive nature of their movements. This type of data is best collected at the micro-level. Until comparative studies of other Haitian communities in the Bahamas become available (although there is no indication that any such studies are being carried out) at least some understanding will have been achieved of the movements of the Carmichael Haitian.

A profile of the Carmichael Haitian can be drawn from the data collected in 1971. It is one of a man from the rural parts of the North-West Department; three out of every five respondents were men. He is almost certainly a Roman Catholic; he is likely to be young, less than 30 years old, and illiterate. In Haiti, he was a farmer owning his own small farm, but he was not among the poorest. He lived in the place in which he had been born, but he was very mobile, often travelling within the North-West, and even as far as Port-au-Prince. As he travelled such signs of affluence as he saw around him were related to movement to the Bahamas. From 'Nassau men', men who had worked in the Bahamas and then returned to the North-West, he heard of the 'ultra-modern cities' of Nassau and Freeport. He also heard of raids and round-ups, deportations and unemployment, but these seemed small risks in the context of the hardships and hopelessness of his everyday life in Haiti.

However the Bahamas could seem to be the promised land only in contrast to what Haiti had to offer. The range of economic activities available to Haitians in the Bahamas is severely restricted, not only by competition from Bahamians and immigrants from other islands besides Haiti, but also by their limited experience in economic activities other than peasant farming and petty commerce, their poor schooling, by having to learn to speak English, and by the fact that they have entered the Bahamas illegally. Haitians therefore obtain jobs mainly as unskilled, casual labourers.

The Haitian in Carmichael particularly, exchanges an environment of very limited job opportunities in the North-West of his island for an environment of somewhat different, but hardly less limited, opportunities. Only eleven of the respondents had full-time jobs at the time of the survey. All of the other respondents were either unemployed or under-employed: housewives who wanted jobs but could not get them, caretakers whose employment was simply living on the premises, female casual labourers who worked for one or two days a week washing and/or ironing clothes, and casual labourers who went from house to house and from job site to job site taking anything they could get. Their incomes reflected the uncertainty of these jobs. Income depended on the number of days' work which could be found each week, the usual wage for a Haitian being US $10 per day. More than half of the respondents put their incomes at less than $15 per week.

Data on the employment histories of the male respondents show that although opportunities for employment were particularly bad in 1971, they had not been much better during previous years. Almost 60 per cent of the male respondents had arrived in the Bahamas before 1965, but less than 40 per cent of them had held three or more steady jobs during that time, even though the majority of the jobs were of short duration, of a year or less. Periods of unemployment, including that immediately after arrival, were both frequent and long-lasting. Respondents were not always able to remember how long the initial period had been, but they seemed to think that a maximum period of two years was acceptable: 'I came in October 1970 and I've only had two weeks' work with pay since then. I intend to spend another ten months, to make it two years. If I get nothing by that time I shall go back.' Two years is a long time to have to depend on others for support.

Despite this dismal employment situation, remittances from Haitians in the Bahamas seem quite substantial. Sources in Port-de-Paix stated that in 1969 the bank in that town received about a $100,000 a month in remittances. In addition to money remitted 'officially' through banks, many Haitians send home money via friends: for instance a priest travelling to Haiti in 1971 carried $5,000 for families in Port-de-Paix. Ahlers (1978: 47) estimates that between $5,000 and $10,000 dollars were remitted annually to Le Borgne. The value of remittances from Haitian men in the Bahamas was made from data collected in a random survey of 10 per cent of the Haitian men employed in a government department in Nassau in 1969. According to these calculations, the value of remittances from a population of 10,000 Haitians would have been three million dollars. Although the reliability of this estimate is very low, and the calculation was made from remittances made by Haitians in steady jobs, it nevertheless gives some idea of the scale of remittances from the Bahamas to Haiti.

The economic situation of the Haitian in the Bahamas is particularly important to discussion of whether the movement is temporary or permanent. Money is not only the main reason for the movement, it is one of the main requirements for a return to Haiti. Returning Haitians are expected to carry back gifts as well as money which will be used to improve houses, buy land, send children to school or support families if they return again to the Bahamas. The chronic unemployment of the Carmichael Haitian should therefore be constantly borne in mind in the discussion which follows.

The intention to return

In the North-West Department of Haiti, three types of movement seem to be taking place: a relatively unimportant seasonal movement in search of well-watered, arable land; a rural-urban movement to the departmental towns which involves the majority of the movers; and the movement to the Bahamas (Gayot 1971: 67-72). It is generally accepted that economic considerations are predominant in both the rural-urban movement and the movement out of Haiti. Gayot (1971: 75) described the attraction of the Bahamas in graphic terms: 'the word Nassau is a magical term in the North-West Department, Nassau stands for the Bahamas . . . "Nassau" is the country where the streets are paved with gold.' But, according to a creole saying in the North-West, the Haitians intend that the riches should be spent in Haiti. ' "Nou vin Nassau, nou pa vin rété sé g-in-n dola nou vin chaché" (we come to Nassau, we don't come to stay, we come only to look for dollars)' (Gayot, personal communication, August 1981).

Returning Haitians tend to follow a pattern in the investment of their savings: after the first successful stay in Nassau they build a house; they get married after the second stay, and after the third stay they invest in commerce or agriculture (Gayot. 1971: 87). To Haitians a corrugated zinc roof and masonry walls are signs of affluence, so improvements in houses tend to incorporate these two characteristics. In the summer of 1971 along a dusty paved road in Port-de-Paix, there were ten or twelve concrete houses, which it was said had been built by 'Nassau men'. According to sources in Port-de-Paix, the construction business there was booming in 1971. One contractor, who previously used to visit Port-de-Paix only occasionally, then had a permanent representative in the town and his business was extending credit to a total of US $18,000, in addition to making cash transactions – this in a deprived region of a country with a per capita income of $70 per year. Ahlers (1978: 4) noted a similar investment in Le Borgne in the North Department. At the time of his survey in 1976 there were six concrete houses under construction, five of which were being built with migrant remittances from the Bahamas. Ahlers explained that movement from Le Borgne to the Bahamas was generally considered to be temporary, in order to build up cash savings, with the migrant returning to his area of origin. Thirty-six per cent of the households in his sample had relatives in the Bahamas (Ahlers 1978: 47).

Data collected from respondents on their reasons for going to the Bahamas also indicated that no permanent move was intended. Gayot (1971: 75-6) quotes four respondents interviewed in Haiti, all of whom implied that they intended to return to the North-West. For instance, one stated 'We shall do like X. . . . The first trip made it possible for him to build a house. Now he wants to come back to ensure his children's education.'

Of the reasons given by the respondents in Carmichael for coming to the Bahamas on their first visit almost a quarter of the respondents gave reasons which indicated an intention to return to Haiti (Table 11.1). These included going back to children left in Haiti, to build houses and to take home money which they hoped to make in the Bahamas. The most common reason given indicates that a climate of movement had been established in the North-West: 'everybody was going to Nassau'. While this reason does not actually indicate an intention to return, it could be argued that the signs of affluence in the North-West which resulted from the investment of savings by 'Nassau men' formed a part of that climate. Even if it is argued that the push factor of economic difficulties in Haiti and the purpose of joining relatives in the Bahamas indicated a permanent stay, these reasons were given by only a third of the respondents. Certainly no respondent indicated an intention to remain in the Bahamas permanently.

TABLE 11.1 *Reasons given for first visits to Bahamas*

Reasons	*Respondents % (N = 135)*
Reasons indicating intention to return	24
'Everybody going to Nassau'	39
'Things hard in Haiti'	17
To join/accompany relative/spouse	16
Other	4

Source: 1971 Carmichael Survey

Another indication of the intention to return was given by mothers of children born in Carmichael, as to whether they wanted their children to live in the Bahamas or Haiti. The results were not conclusive. The answers of twelve of the twenty-six mothers indicated uncertainty. They either did not know where they wanted the children to live; or they wanted the children to live wherever they themselves were going to be, but could not say where this would be. Seven of the mothers wanted their children to live in the Bahamas because that was where the children had been born, and eight of the mothers wanted their children to live in Haiti because they, the mothers, had no intention of remaining in the Bahamas. Among these eight mothers there was a high degree of certainty: 'I will never allow my child to reach eighteen in Nassau, because Nassau is not her home', and the long period of time over which the intention to return had persisted. At the time of the study, three of them had been in the Bahamas for nine years, had never visited Haiti during that time, but still intended to return because Haiti was their home.

No one bit of evidence is conclusive in itself, but together the climate of movement in the North-West and in Le Borgne, the investment of savings by returning Haitians, the reasons for moving given by respondents both in Haiti and in the Bahamas, and the wishes of mothers for their children, indicate that the movement to the Bahamas is not intended to be permanent and that those who move intend to return to Haiti.

Realizing the intention to return

Although the essential characteristic of circulation is the lack of any declared intention of a permanent or long-lasting change of residence, some evidence of the realization of this intention is needed. Moreover, implicit in the definition of circulation as repetitive movement is the recurrence of the movement at intervals. Data on return visits to Haiti by the Carmichael respondents in 1971 are impressive given the illegal nature of the movement and the very uncertain nature of the employment in Carmichael. However, because the survey took place in the Bahamas rather than in Haiti, it was impossible for the data to include those movements which terminated in the home country. The results from research carried out in the North-West would obviously be complementary and more conclusive.

As would be expected, more visits were made by respondents who had been in the Bahamas longest (Table 11.2). Forty-five per cent of all respondents had returned to Haiti at least once, while almost a half of those who had made no trips had been in the Bahamas only since 1970 (i.e. an eighteen-month sojourn at the time of the survey). In contrast, only 16 per cent of those who

TABLE 11.2 *Respondents making return visits to Haiti (%)*

Date of first arrival	No visit	One visit	Two or more visits	(N =)
Before 1960	16	32	55	(19)
1960-4	43	27	30	(44)
1965-9	51	46	3	(37)
1970 and after	97	3	—	(34)
All respondents	55	28	17	(134)

Source: 1971 Carmichael Survey

had been in the Bahamas before 1960 had never been back to Haiti. Thus the data also suggest that time (more than eleven years) had not eroded the links with home, at least not to the extent that movers no longer wished to return for visits. The main reasons given for returning to Haiti after this first stay in the Bahamas were to be with their families, to work on their land, because of sickness and deportation, while some had even intended to remain in Haiti and never return to the Bahamas.

Two factors, other than the financial one, also affected the respondents' will to return. Some respondents felt that they needed the security of a work permit before they could take the chance of travelling. Several respondents said that they had made no return visits until they had been able to get a work permit; then they returned to Haiti each year. The illegal nature of the movement across international boundaries is a definite constraint on the realization of intention to return − a powerful centrifugal force which must be added to those which normally affect internal migration (Chapman and Prothero 1977: 2). Other respondents felt that they should not take a trip to Haiti until they were ready to stay there. In fact 14 per cent of those who returned to Haiti had intended to remain there permanently. But their savings were soon exhausted, or their land did not provide a satisfactory living, and so they made their way back to the Bahamas.

The data indicate that a substantial number of the respondents were able to carry through their intentions to return to Haiti. There were individuals who returned to Haiti regularly, like a respondent who first came to the Bahamas in 1958 and who returned to Haiti each year to work on his land for two or three months. But Table 11.2 also shows that only the respondents who had first gone to the Bahamas before 1965 seem to have had sufficient time to make two or more returns to Haiti. This possibility is further supported by the fact that the average length of time spent in the Bahamas by respondents before their first return to Haiti was three years. It is therefore reasonable to argue that the movement is not yet 'old' enough for the data to show recurrence. However, the data do seem to indicate that once certain conditions are met the Carmichael Haitian would make return trips to Haiti.

The strains on previous social bonds

Although the evidence is not incontrovertible, the Haitian movement to the Bahamas does seem to satisfy two of the more important characteristics of circulation: a declaration of the intention to return and the realization of this intention. These strongly imply that the movement is really a circulation of labour and not a permanent migration. Nevertheless, there is also need to examine the movement to see whether it satisfies the characteristics of migration: a spatial transfer from one social unit to another which strains or ruptures previous social bonds.

Most Haitians try to maintain contact with their place of origin. In the North-West, this contact is maintained in three ways: by written correspondence between the mover in the Bahamas and his family at home, by the frequency of the traffic between the North-West and the Bahamas which permit these contacts to be maintained; and by the mover's investment of his savings in the North-West.

Gayot states that the Presbyteries in the Diocese of Port-de-Paix handle about 1,000 letters per month to Nassau, as well as the receipt of a similar number of letters from the Bahamas. He adds that this is obviously an underestimate of the correspondence which goes on since letters are also carried by the regular postal services as well as by sailors and passengers on sloops which travel between the two countries. This correspondence, he feels, maintains the close bonds between the mover and his family (Gayot 1973: 85-90). It is also true, however, that most of the Haitians in Carmichael, and their families in the North-West, are illiterate and therefore would have to find someone both to read and write letters, hence the use of the clergy in the Presbyteries. This illiteracy would inhibit correspondence to some extent, but because of the frequency of traffic between the two places, *telediol* (the grapevine) is just as effective between Haiti and the Bahamas, as within the Bahamas, and within Haiti.

Once the Haitian has left home, two sets of factors begin to work against the fulfilment of his intention to return. Because of his absence, one set of factors operates to erode those ties which bind him to his home, while the mover himself, in his efforts to create a satisfying life for himself in the Bahamas, generates a new set of ties which commit him to this new life. Thus, correspondence cannot take the place of the migrant in the family. Gayot tells of the gulf which develops between the father and his family. When he returns, the father tries to regain control of his family who resent this: 'they think it better if he left again and the sooner the better, all they need and want is their father's money' (Gayot 1973: 89). Moreover, Gayot states that many men in the North-West profit sexually from the husbands' absences, and that the women give in without much difficulty because they fear the evil with which the men threaten them if they do not co-operate.

Given that the illegal nature of the movement can be considered a constant in this context perhaps the most important of the dynamic factors which work against the return of the Haitian is his economic situation. The mover needs to have money in order to return: to pay his fare and to give to his family and friends who expect him to return wealthy. But the economic situation of the Carmichael Haitian is very uncertain. Over ninety per cent of the respondents were either unemployed or underemployed at the time of the survey; only casual labouring jobs were available to them; they faced the constant possibility of raids and round-ups by police which could either bring their jobs to a sudden end, or would inhibit an employer's tendency to employ them. Jobs were of short duration and separated by relatively long periods of unemployment. Moreover, male respondents perceived themselves to be at the mercy of Bahamian employers who, they felt, either refused to pay them, or underpaid them, fired them arbitrarily, and mistreated them sometimes physically. As a result, cash accumulation which is the primary objective of the movement, is fraught with difficulties and is possible only over a long period of time.

In addition, the Carmichael Haitian also forms new ties which bind him to the Bahamas, or rather to Carmichael, and which because they are more immediate probably exert more force than those binding him to the North-West. Forty-six of the seventy-one Haitian households in Carmichael included married or *plasaj* (common law) unions. Only in a few instances were these couples who had migrated together, or unions which were the continuations of relationships formed in Haiti. The majority of the unions were formed in Carmichael. Indeed, it is the practice of Haitian men in New Providence generally to meet the Haitian sloops as they arrive to 'look over' the female arrivals in search of potential partners. The Haitian male seems to have a strong desire to establish a stable union in Carmichael, while for the Haitian women it is almost a necessity. Most of the Haitian women in Carmichael remained unemployed for most of the time they were in the Bahamas, half of them had never worked despite an expressed desire to do so. It is therefore essential for them to find someone who will provide support.

Inevitably these unions produce children and the ties to the Carmichael community are strengthened by these new family commitments. In the households surveyed in 1971, there were fifty-five children who were 14 years or younger, all of whom were born in the Bahamas. Thirty-nine of these children were younger than 5 years, another indication of the youthfulness of the Carmichael community. The obligations to this new family must take precedence over the obligations to the family left behind in Haiti, simply because the mover is an active member of the family in Carmichael. The Haitian in Carmichael not only has to support his new family, but he is often called upon to support other Haitians as well. Until a mover gets a job and is able to support himself financially, his fellow Haitians will house him, feed him and even clothe him and this initial period can lengthen into two years. Moreover, opportunities for employment are so few and shortlived that respondents alternate between periods of employment when they can play the role of supporter, and periods of unemployment when they need to be supported. No stigma is attached to the unemployed Haitian in Carmichael, unemployment is the norm and is seen as the result of chance, or of 'Bon Dieu Bon'.

These financial and emotional commitments to persons in the Bahamas may be reinforced by changes in the individual, changes which will make themselves felt when the mover returns to Haiti. Gayot indicates some of these changes in mental attitudes. The mover becomes aware of progress, he needs to seek more efficient means to improve his living conditions, he acquires a certain sense of time – he wishes to move faster, he no longer walks as before, he takes a bus, a truck, sometimes even a plane, just to save time. He acquires a sense of rationality: 'you can't just fold your hands and say "Bon Dieu Bon" if the harvest is bad. We must get away from such mannerisms, especially we, the youth of this century, else we shall perish' (Gayot 1973: 96). When the returning Haitian also realizes how limited opportunities are for the investment of his savings, the need to go back to the Bahamas and the life to which he has become accustomed grows stronger.

Circular or permanent movement?

This paper has examined the Haitian movement to the Bahamas in order to determine whether it is circulation, when circulation is defined as a movement in which there is a declared intention to return. It is obvious, both from the increases in the numbers of Haitians in the Bahamas and from the data collected from the Carmichael Haitians, that for many individuals the movement becomes a permanent one, despite their declared intentions. Thus, at times, we have felt that we have been forcing the movement into the mould of circulation into which it fits only partially. However we do not conclude that our fault has been in forcing the fit. Rather, the extent to which the movement does fit suggests that the essential characteristics of circulation and migration, as generally accepted, are not mutually exclusive. The straining and rupture of social bonds is not a once and for all act which can be precisely located in time. Rather it is a gradual process which takes place over a period of time during which the intention to return persists, and during which the equally gradual forging of new social bonds away from 'home' also takes place. It is not enough to define circulation essentially in terms of the intention to return.

To a large extent this definition seems to be an attempt to avoid the problem of defining permanency. The ultimate solution is not usually operable, that is to suspend judgment until the mover's life-span is complete. The usual solution in migration studies has been for the researcher to define permanency individually (or arbitrarily), for a particular movement. Because of the differing concepts of, and different values placed on, time – particularly between the developing and developed worlds – this individual resolution of the problem does not contribute towards a universal definition. In fact it has been suggested that such a universal definition is probably impossible (Gould and Prothero 1975: 42-3). The alternative suggestion only takes us back to the intention to return.

What is the significance to the understanding of mobility of the intention to return? At one level it is of no significance. For instance, the Bahamian Government, on the few occasions when it has considered the effects of the movement on the Bahamas, has discussed this in terms of competition for jobs and the additional burden on public social services. Within the context of these specific concerns it really does not matter whether the movement is seen as circular or permanent. The length of time spent by the Haitian in the Bahamas is long enough that these

238

services would have to be supplied in any case. If, however, the Bahamian Government was concerned about the integration of the Haitian into the Bahamian society, as it should be, then the Haitian's intention to return is a very crucial fact. Inherent in the intention to return to Haiti is a lack of commitment to the Bahamas, and a lack of motivation to attain the skills which are necessary to cope with life in the Bahamas; for example the ability to speak English. Only seven of the respondents in the 1971 Carmichael Survey could speak English and only twenty-seven of them had made a deliberate effort to learn. One would expect that Haitians intending to make the Bahamas their permanent home would make a greater effort. On the other hand, the declared intention to return implies a continuing commitment to the North-West which is expressed in remittances, the maintenance of links with home and in return visits, effects which are assessed as positive and desirable in the North-West.

Chapman and Prothero (1977: 8-10) seem to accept the significance of this sense of commitment, for they claim that one of the basic principles of circulation is the territorial division of activities and obligations and the consequent development of a system which extends outside the homeplace, and, as in the Haitian case, across national boundaries. This territorial division can only be sustained by the maintenance of contact between the two 'extensions'. Chapman (1976: 132) certainly feels that links with home are an important aspect of circulation.

But is this extension of a system achieved only, or even predominantly, by circulation? From their discovery by Europeans the islands of the Caribbean, including both Haiti and the Bahamas, were both perceived and utilized as an integral part of a larger colonial system. Since emancipation from slavery the West Indian has been moving from limited opportunities, chronic poverty and deprivation to what are perceived as better conditions, both within and without the Caribbean. As a result the West Indian perceives this extended system as a legitimate area in which to make choices. Thus the system in turn extends the alternatives and opportunities available, and mobility becomes merely an additional cost paid for opportunities available away from home, while the intention to return is frustrated not only by the forging of new social bonds, but also by the persistence of limited opportunities at home − as the sense of commitment also persists.

The argument can be taken even further. Wolf (1966: 14) states that the maintenance of links with the home society is characteristic of open societies where kinship ties are not lost after migration but instead become valuable assets for the transmission or distribution of goods and services. This leaves a basic question about cause and effect: are the intention to return, the sense of commitment, and the maintenance of links with home merely features of the form of mobility which characterize an open society? This would certainly seem to be the case in the Caribbean. Is this form of mobility the same as that which is generally called circulation, and among which Zelinsky (1971: 226), for example, includes vacation travel, trips by business executives, and migratory (sic) farm workers? We feel that they are not the same, that implicit in these examples of circulation are parameters which do not characterize the Haitian movement and which are not adequately expressed by the existence of an intention to return. With Zelinsky (1971: 226), we are forced to conclude that there is no realistic alternative to treating all territorial mobility as a single continuum. If circulation is to be accepted as a distinct form of mobility, we must also recognize that to locate it along this continuum is an extremely hazardous exercise.

12 Religion and circulation: Hindu pilgrimage

Surinder M. Bhardwaj

Hindu peregrination is a type of religiously motivated 'circulation'. It thus focuses upon but one strand of human mobility, manifested primarily as transeconomic behaviour which tends to establish man's connectivity with forces transcending his own power and authority. The minimal dimension of pilgrimage includes the human individual, a believed suprahuman entity or 'force', and the spatial *act* of attempting to bring about their relational proximity. The relational proximity thus achieved may be considered by some pilgrims as a point in time when desired suprahuman intercession by the 'deity' becomes meaningful for the mundane life. For some other pilgrims the act of traversing space may symbolize such material transcendence which is not a mere escape from the phenomenal world, but rather a desirable 'higher' state of existence in sacred space.

Although this essay is conceived within the general framework of geographic (spatial) circulation, an attempt is also made to examine the phenomenon of pilgrimage from some other dimensions to appreciate better significant if diverse scholarly insights and thus to avoid what otherwise could indeed be 'disciplinary chauvinism', to use Victor Turner's phrase (Turner 1977: 75). The spatio-religious aspect of pilgrimage is illustrated by taking specific examples of Hindu pilgrimages.

Circulation and pilgrimage

Hindu pilgrimage as a spatial activity partakes of the concept 'circulation' both as an example of religiously generated spatial process and as part of the totality of societal circulation. Gould and Prothero (1975: 42) have suggested 'intentionality' as constituting the core of circulatory as distinguished from migratory processes: 'if there is a specific desire on the part of the individual or group of individuals who are moving to return to their place of origin, and when before leaving in the first place this intention is clear, then the movement may be considered as circulation rather than migration.' Within the religious domain there is no more prominent process than peregrination which comes closer to the above definition of circulation. Geographic literature dealing with the economic basis of circulation is abundant and growing (Kosinski and Prothero 1975). Circulatory human processes which are non-economically motivated, even though explicitly spatial, have tended to be neglected by social scientists until recently. Even so, such studies generally have analysis of the phenomenon as their main objective rather than explication of its meaning in the life of the participants. Tourist activity for example, may be a non-economic leisure time behaviour so far as the tourists are concerned, but its analysis, rather than meaning, is usually the objective of the social scientists. The fact that London has become the mecca of wealthy Arab tourists does not mean, however, that tourism is non-economic in its structural totality nor is pilgrimage circulation 'non-economic', for example, in so far as the traders and mechants of the holy city of Banras (Varanasi) are concerned.

The concept of circulation employed in the Vidalian tradition of French human geography has some interesting implications for understanding the meaning of pilgrimage circulation. Circulation in the French tradition is double edged − on the one hand, 'seen as a destructive force transforming traditional regional equilibria and stable *genres de vie*, and also as a creative process promoting the diffusion of ideas, the emergence of areal comparative advantages and the radiation of sociocultural influences from nodal centers' (Buttimer 1971: 190). Sorre (1963: 408) has cogently stated that 'circulation carries elements that renew *genres de vie.*' Many famous pilgrimage centres such as Makkah and Jerusalem can and do perform this function at least symbolically through pilgrim circulation. The newly built Sri Venkateswara temple at Pittsburgh in the United States is an excellent example of an incipient Hindu pilgrimage centre outside India. This temple is a smaller scale but authentic Western Hemisphere seat of the famous Tirupati temple of India. Already, several hundred Hindu pilgrims visit this deity every month from many parts of the United States and Canada for the performance of religious rites in the strict Indian Sanskrit tradition (Figure 12.1). The distribution of Hindu donors to this temple may give some idea of the potential pilgrims to this temple (Table 12.1). The author's informal interviews with this

TABLE 12.1 *Sri Venkateswara Temple Pittsburgh, Pa. USA Donors (families) 1977 4th qtr*

Origin	Donors	Origin	Donors
Pennsylvania	113	North Carolina	7
Illinois	104	Kentucky	5
New York	104	Louisiana	5
Ohio	99	Delaware	4
Maryland	56	Rhode Island	4
Michigan	55	South Carolina	4
New Jersey	52	Colorado	3
California	29	Connecticut	3
Virginia	27	Iowa	3
Massachusetts	26	Mississippi	3
Ontario (Canada)	22	New Hampshire	3
West Virginia	21	Arkansas	2
Indiana	20	New Mexico	2
Texas	17	North Dakota	2
Wisconsin	15	Alberta (Canada)	1
Alabama	11	India	1
D.C.	10	Manitoba (Canada)	1
Georgia	10	Newfoundland (Canada)	1
Minnesota	10	Oregon	1
Missouri	10	Quebec (Canada)	1
Tennessee	10	Utah	1
Florida	8	Vermont	1
Kansas	8	Washington	1
Oklahoma	8	No address	2
		Total	906

Source: Sapthagiri Vani, vol. 3, no. 1, 1978, first quarter. The data have been classified from the list of names and addresses of donors published in the above publication of the SV Temple. Donors receive this publication.

temple's visitors and several family visits leave little doubt that this temple is beginning to create a sort of renewal of long dormant and unfulfilled religious feelings including feelings of religious security in the minds of many theistic Hindus in the United States and Canada. This, in spite of the fact that most Hindu heads of households in the USA belong to scientific professional and managerial classes, whose views on Hinduism and religion in general would be considered highly liberal were they to be understood as expressed in India.

Hindu pilgrimages in the spatial behavioural sense clearly fall in the category of circulation as the latter is defined by Gould and Prothero (1975: 42). At the same time, in the functionalist sense, peregrination belongs to the *circulation* of the Vidalian tradition, for it seems to fulfil a role of 'renewal', of bonding and of helping to maintain a system by repetitively emphasizing some of its properties. Hindu pilgrimage as such a circulation phenomenon has been elegantly analysed by David Sopher in his 'Pilgrim Circulation in Gujarat' (Sopher 1968). The reinforcing of regional as well as all-India identity through pilgrim circulation has also been suggested by Sopher (1968: 425). Bhardwaj (1973) has also examined Indian pilgrimage as a circulation phenomenon both diachronically and spatially at various 'levels' of Hindu places of pilgrimage.

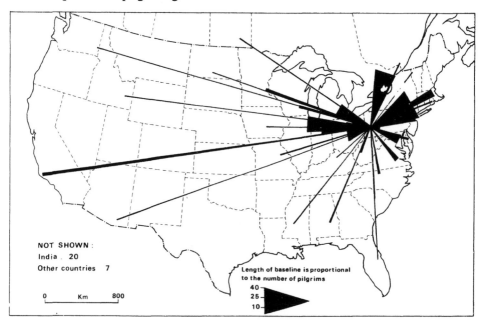

NOT SHOWN :
India   20
Other countries   7

0   Km   800

Length of baseline is proportional
to the number of pilgrims
40 —
25 —
10 —

FIGURE 12.1 Origins of pilgrims to Sri Venkateswara temple

Pilgrimage: concept and bases

The spatial circulatory aspect of peregrination can assume more meaning if we understand what pilgrimage is in the first place for without it peregrination may be simply reduced to its dictionary definition. Pilgrimage is a spatio-temporally complex process for which the English word 'pilgrimage' helps to provide only a general referent. In the Islamic tradition, for example, the word *hajj* (pilgrimage to Makkah) refers in reality to 'observance of specified acts at specified places in or near Mecca in Arabia, at a specified time' (Al-Nagar 1972: xv). *Hajj* furthermore is obligatory performance, yet the obligation is tempered by the directive that 'the pilgrim be able to afford the rite; we are not to make *Hajj* if it brings hardship to those dependent upon us' (Kamal 1961: 9). Religious visits by Muslims to places other than Makkah are not *hajj* and are instead characterized as *ziarat*. Victor and Edith Turner have characterized Catholic pilgrimages to Jerusalem and Rome as 'liminoid' (voluntary) undertakings in the beginning, but becoming prescriptive, and extensions of ecclesiastical control later on (Turner and Turner 1978: 232). In Christianity as a whole, pilgrimages are not a requirement in the same sense as in Islam, although, the 'journey of the ideal pilgrim could be presented, as Franco Sacchetti presented it at the beginning of the fourteenth century as an elaborate allegory of the life of Christ from the Nativity to Resurrection' (Sumption 1975: 93). In spite of its non-obligatoriness in contemporary Christianity, pilgrimage is widespread and extraordinarily rich in content and symbolism, particularly where the population is dominantly Roman Catholic (Turner and Turner 1978).

In Sanskrit, the word *tīrtha yātrā*, literally tour of the sacred river fords, connotes taking a holy dip at the various sacred places. Visitations to the goddess shrines are rarely covered under the idea of *tīrtha yātrā*. Thus, when the word pilgrimage is used to describe peregrination in the Hindu context, it can obscure the considerable differences in religious circulation with reference to sacred places which may be 'fords' or male gods' temples or seats of the female deities. In addition, a 'holy man' may be described as a *tīrtha* (Bharati 1970: 89) in the Hindu tradition.

It was mentioned in the introductory section that there is probably an attempt on the part of pilgrims to create relational proximity between them and the 'deity' or suprahuman force, through the spatial effort which they make. This idea has special meaning in Hinduism because of the concept of 'interdependence' between humans and gods – a relationship of 'reciprocity' (Schoep 1968: 31). The following two verses from the *Bhagavadgita* illustrate the idea (*Bhagavadgita* 1977: 137):

By this (sacrifice) foster ye the gods and let the gods foster you; thus fostering each other you shall attain to the supreme good (*Bhagavadgita* 3.11).

Fostered by sacrifice the gods will give you the enjoyments you desire. He who enjoys these gifts without giving them in return is verily a thief (*Bhagavadgita* 3.12).

At the sacred places of specific deities, the pilgrim feels spatially as well as emotionally closer to the deity he believes in. By traversing the physical distance between his own place in the world and the place of the deity the pilgrim also is in effect *transcending* that distance and comes 'close' to the otherwise unapproachable deity and may virtually assume identity with it.

The spatial behaviour of the pilgrims is simply the manifestation of ideas and beliefs which pilgrims hold about pilgrimage. One such idea − transcendence of space − is symbolized by actual traversing of space to achieve proximity − both symbolic and 'real' (i.e., manifest). Another dimension of pilgrimage is explained by Victor Turner in a most thought-provoking essay where he has characterized pilgrimage as the 'ordered anti-structure of patrimonial-feudal systems' (Turner 1973: 204). He argues that 'Pilgrimages seem to be regarded by self-conscious pilgrims both as occasions on which communitas is experienced and journeys toward a sacred source of communitas, which is also seen as a source of healing and renewal' (Turner 1973: 217). It is not possible to discuss in this essay the extraordinary richness of Turner's symbological argument but the great Hindu epic *Mahabharata* suggests Hindu pilgrimage (as then conceived) a lonely quest for religious merit, particularly for the poor who cannot afford sacrifices (van Buitenen 1975: 373-4). On the other hand, modern Hindu pilgrimages, particularly to the goddess shrines, leave little doubt about their 'communitas' character. Imbued with the spirit of goddess pilgrims from villages − men, women, children − march toward such hilltop shrines at Naina Devi and Chintpurni in the Siwalik hills. When they arrive at the sacred place with flags raised high and dancing and singing in loud chorus about the might of the Mother Goddess, there is no distinction of age, caste, sex, or wealth. All of these individual and social attributes become utterly meaningless in the sacred precincts. These same attributes are the very basis of Hindu social structure − outside the sacred walls. Thus, pilgrim circulation may be considered as an occasional liberation from social structures.

Many Hindus consider the everyday world as a web, a routinized necessity from which time taken for piety and deity is desirable sacral activity. This activity could assume great importance after the *dharma* ('duty') of the Hindu householder has been duly carried out to its completion. Thus, it is not uncommon to find individuals or couples undertaking pilgrimage for an extended period of time. In such instances, the pilgrims symbolically transcend the 'world web' for sacred space. Such symbolic transcendence may occur on several occasions during householder's life, for a short or an extended period of time when the pilgrims visit sacred places. Pilgrimage thus conceived is not an 'escape' but a temporally short or long actualization of certain ideal behaviour patterns expected in the culture.

Temporal cyclicity is a fundamental presupposition of Hindu eventing. With such a conceptual framework events, particularly of cosmic import, reactualize periodically. Thus, it is considered possible to participate in such events. They include the massive twelve-yearly *Kumbha* bathing festivals at places such as Hardwar and Prayaga (Allahabad), the first one on the banks of the Ganga and the second at the confluence of the Ganga and Yamuna. These gatherings are not commemorative of the event but are participatory in the reactualized event. A pilgrimage such as this is neither obligatory in the Hindu tradition nor contractual (deity-pilgrim relationship) in character. Instead, it seems to be a quest for eternality. Outwardly, and in popular mind, the festival merely involves a holy bath at a special occasion which because of its twelve-yearly cycle may not be possible next time for a pilgrim, given the uncertainty of human life.

Pilgrimages for the purpose of seeking cure for health, for the washing away of sins, for fulfilment of a vow or promise to the deity in lieu of a favour from him or her, and for many other obvious reasons are, and have been, popular in Hinduism as also in Christianity (Sumption 1975; Turner 1978). The growth of population, the spread of the cult of certain deities and increased facilities and ability to travel have meant an intensification of pilgrimage activity in India. As devotees of a particular deity of a holy place migrate, they may continue to patronize their old place of pilgrimage giving the impression that the 'draw area' of the place has increased.

Pilgrimage circulation and pilgrimage 'levels'

It is extremely difficult to estimate the number of pilgrims to the numerous shrines and sanctuaries of India ranging from the local to those of national importance. For the sacred places which are situated in large cities, it is difficult to separate 'pilgrims' from other visitors. Also, the author has frequently noticed the tendency among many white collar visitors to holy places to call themselves just 'tourists' rather than pilgrims. In addition, there are numerous sites where pilgrims do not use any vehicular transportation, thus making the job of enumerators even more difficult. Then, too, certain massive bathing festivals on the occasion of solar or lunar eclipses, and the gigantic twelve-yearly

Kumbha bathing fairs may attract from one to four or five million pilgrims (Bharati 1970: 103), thus making annual counts somewhat meaningless. Nevertheless, considering a modest average of 100,000 pilgrims visiting each of the 142 shrines of some popularity Bhardwaj (1973: 81) gives an annual figure of over fourteen million. Numerous local pilgrimage shrines not counted in the above could conservatively add further about half of the above number. This reckoning gives a rough but conservative estimate of about twenty-one million pilgrims annually, not considering double counts, for India's Hindu population, and not considering the gigantic *Kumbha* fairs every twelve years.

Hindu pilgrimage system

The Hindu pilgrimage supersystem is composed of several underlying systems due to the very nature of the syncretic character of this religion. Bharati (1970) suggests a three-fold classification: all-India, trans-sectarian sites; regionally important sites usually with sectarian emphasis; and sites of purely sectarian importance. Hindu religious corpus recognizes a broad four-fold classification of sacred places or *tīrthas* (Aiyamgar 1942: lix).

(a) *Daiva*; places revealed/sanctified by gods;
(b) *Āsura*; presumably holy due to the destruction of demons (*asura*) by gods;
(c) *Ārṣa*; places sanctified by the saints;
(d) *Mānuṣa*; places 'made holy' by certain ruling dynasties.

The author has found that a two-fold classification of *tīrthas* is also recognized in the Hindu mind, places associated with temples (*mandir tīrtha*) and those with sacred water (*jala tīrtha*). In Gujarat in spite of cult preferences among the Hindus there is almost no exclusivism toward pilgrimage to the shrines of other deities (Sopher 1968: 397). Nevertheless, in the Dravidian part of India distinction between the worshippers of Vishnu and Shiva is significant (Nilakanta Sastri 1963) while in northern India such distinction is in practice minimal. The most celebrated shrines of these two traditions do differ (Bharati 1970: 100). To add to this complexity are the places sacred to more specific cults such as the *Bhakti* (devotion) focusing upon Krishna – an incarnation of Vishnu. Shrines of Mother Goddess (called *pīthas*) constitute virtually an autonomous tradition in Hinduism, and pilgrimage is considered in it to be an important practice (Bharati 1965: 85). Burton Stein has convincingly argued that 'goddess worship, from the thirteenth century marked a significant universalization of folk ritual' in south India. This process also resulted in the full emergence of the temple as a popular pilgrimage centre (Stein 1973: 75). Kinsley (1975) has elaborated the symbolic aspect of the cult of Krishna and Kali, the Mother Goddess, suggesting the prominence of the latter since medieval times in India. The many shrines of the goddess have been enumerated and (as far as possible) identified by Sircar (1948). Apart from the holy places of major male deities (Shiva, Vishnu) and the goddess in her multifarious forms, there are many sacred places of the lesser deities who locally or even regionally may assume considerable attractive power for the pilgrim.

The tradition of bathing for ritual purification is very old in India going back to perhaps the Indus valley civilization. In the ancient vedic lore, many rivers are considered sacred. A large number of Hindu sacred places are thus associated with the numerous rivers and sacred lakes and ponds. The confluences of streams are generally considered sacred. These add a sub-system of 'fluvial' sacred places to the above described variety.

As 'Hinduism' diffused from its north Indian core, it absorbed many other cultures and their deities and through a slow but gradual process of accommodation transformed such deities to the ones more widely recognized. The net result of this convergence and accommodation of all these traditions and 'systems' has been that Hindu places of pilgrimage do *not* form a single unified religious hierarchy but are systems operating within the supersystem of pilgrimage. Future research on peregrinology could seek to identify and clarify the systematic interchanges, overlaps and other yet unclear dimensions. Considering its diversity it seems that at least the following systems may be active within the Hindu pilgrimage supersystem.

1   Spatially specific places of deities and saints − mostly at the very localized level (excluding goddess shrines).

2   Shrines of other male gods of 'lesser' stature than the trinity (Shiva, Vishnu and Brahma).

3   Goddess shrines (*Pithas*) having within this system places of 'highest' sanctity for all the *Sákta* cult (goddess cult) down to the local village shrines of female deities.

4   Sacred centres associated with the life and activities of the major recognized incarnations (mostly of Vishnu). Examples include Ayodhya the birthplace of Rama, the hero of the epic Ramayana and Brindavan associated with Krishna and the cult of Bhakti (devotism).

5   *Tírthas* (mostly temple centred) of the deities of the Hindu trinity known by their generic names (Brahma, Vishnu, Shiva) or other descriptive appellations.

6   *Jala tírthas* − places associated with sacred water such as

rivers, certain ponds and lakes. Such sacred places usually assume high sanctity on specified auspicious astrological occasions, such as *Kumbha* (when Jupiter enters Aquarius), and are mostly 'trans-sectarian'.

Each of the classes identified above (except 1 and 2) could have places with very localized fields of pilgrim circulation, as well as those which draw pilgrims from the entire Hindu universe.

Pilgrimage levels

Interviews with over 5,000 pilgrims at eleven sacred places in north India (most of the places were visited more than once during 1967-8) have yielded some interesting results which need to be verified by further studies (Bhardwaj 1973). These results may be briefly stated and their meaning examined in the religious circulation, though there are several limitations in the analysis.

1 There are some fairly clear 'levels' of Hindu pilgrim circulation − local, sub-regional, regional, supra-regional, and Pan-Hindu.

2 Levels of pilgrim circulation seem to have identifiable attributes with respect to

(a)   social strata that participate at a given level,

(b)   the nature of religiosity expressed at each level,

(c)   the motives of pilgrims and the degree of 'symbolic emphasis' (to use Turner's phrase).

In the vast and dynamic interaction manifest of India the numerous Hindu places of pilgrimage form the foci of its syncretistic belief pattern. Several scholars have commented on the role of pilgrimages in promoting a sense of identification with the spatial extent of India. 'Thus the institution of pilgrimage is undeniably a most powerful instrument for developing the geographical sense in the people which enables them to think and feel that India is not a mere congeries of geographical fragments, but a single, though immense organism' (Mookerji 1960: 47). Mookerji was obviously speaking about the cultural unity of India at the highest level, even though he probably exaggerated the role of pilgrimages. David Mandelbaum (1970: 401) writing about wider identification, makes a very similar observation: 'There is a traditional basis for the larger national identification. It is the idea, mainly engendered by Hindu religion but shared by those of other religions as well, that there is an entity of India to which all its inhabitants belong. . . . That sense was and is continually confirmed through the common practice of pilgrimage.' Sopher (1967: 53) noted an 'informal hierarchy' of pilgrim circulation. Mandelbaum (1970: 402) speaks about the range of sacred centres, 'From those that attract visitors from a few score miles . . . to the great supercenters that draw pilgrims from all parts of the land.' Similarly, Turner (1973: 202) recognized a pattern of national, regional, district and intervillage 'pilgrim catchment areas' in Mexico.

To appreciate the dimensions of pilgrim circulation better a simple criterion, average distance travelled per pilgrim, was computed for each selected sacred place on the basis of pilgrim samples taken at specific climactic occasions, and the places were accordingly ranked (Table 12.2). The criterion used suggests some natural groupings of the sacred places here termed 'levels', but also raises questions regarding such groups. Badrinath is clearly distinguished from Hardwar. However, both Hardwar and Kangra would appear to belong to the same category despite the fact that the former is a 'trans-sectarian' site while the latter is specifically a centre of mother-goddess worship. The pilgrim samples at Hardwar were taken as the six-yearly fair of Ardhkumbha. On this occasion, Hardwar attracts pilgrims mostly

TABLE 12.2 *Ranks of selected Hindu sacred places on specific occasions*

Sacred place (and occasion)*	Number of pilgrims: sample	Average distance per pilgrim (miles)**	Rank
Badrinath (AY)	400	475.1	1
Hardwar (AK)	800	175.8	2
Kangra (NC)	450	173.5	3
Jwalaji (NC)	500	122.8	4
Naina Devi (SA)	400	72.8	5
Chintpurni (SA)	300	71.7	6
Mansa Devi (NC)	250	53.5	7
Rewalsar (B)	100	14.3	10
Baijnath (SR)	100	27.4	9
Shiv Bari (J)	100	35.5	8
Bhagsunag (SR)	85	1.5	11

* AY = Annual Yātrā; AK = Ardha Kumbha; NC = Navrātrās of Caitra; SA = Srāvana Astamī; B = Baisākhī; SR = Sivarātri; J = Jātrā
** Straight line distances from each sacred place to the *home-district* headquarters of pilgrims

Source: The data in this table were collected by the author and his assistants during 1967-8

from north India. If samples are taken for the year as a whole, this sacred place will show a much greater diversity of pilgrim origins by regions (see later discussion). Similarly, this criterion sets Kangra and Jwalaji rather wide apart even though both places according to literary accounts are considered *major* goddess shrines. Kangra, on the basis of average pilgrim distance has a higher rank largely because the pilgrims of western Uttar Pradesh consider the goddess (Vajresvarī) as their patron deity even though the place is in distance closer to the Punjab. The central supposition in the average pilgrim distance as a measure of rank is that if people consider a particular place 'more' sacred, they are probably willing to travel longer distance to it.

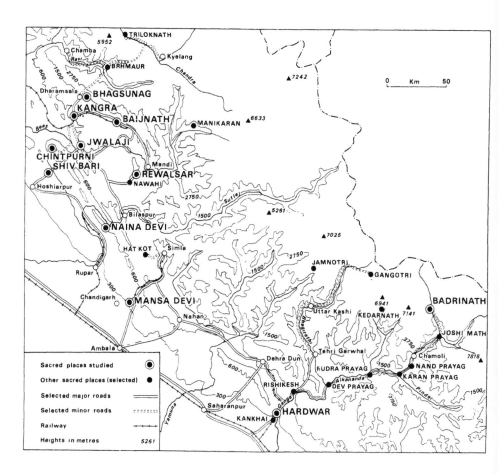

FIGURE 12.2 North-west India: study area

Unfortunately for social scientists, 'sanctity' cannot be easily quantified. Nevertheless, the distances travelled by sampled pilgrims do give some idea about the 'field' of sacred places of different levels at specific occasions (Figure 12.2).

A possibly useful criterion to rank sacred places could be the *diversity* of assembled pilgrims, on the premise that places considered sacred by Hindus of all areas in India will reflect this through the pilgrim body. Language or dialect could be used as a measure of diversity. The use of such criteria would also be hazardous because a sacred place situated close to or in a linguistic transition zone could be considered higher level even though people from short distances may have made the effort to go there. Such arguments can be multiplied, but the real issue is that even if there were sacred centres of statistically higher or lower levels, of what consequence are they for either the pilgrims or the social scientists' understanding of peregrination? Identification with a given region may be of trivial importance from the viewpoint of the devotee of a particular deity. It is consequential for the devotee to share in the religious symbolism of the given sacred centre, thus expressing his identification with a belief. Since the beliefs do have a spatial dimension (apart from psychological), we can speak of a regional identification but only in the sense of a shared belief. There is no logical necessity that pilgrims to a particular shrine hold other ideas in common also.

The full discussion of assignments of 'levels' to different sacred places studied has been reported elsewhere (Bhardwaj 1973: chapter VII). It must be emphasized here that the 'field' of the sacred places, particularly the goddess shrines and where bathing festivals are held in different seasons, varies for different occasions. Thus, for example, at Hardwar during October, Bengali pilgrims tend to predominate, while in January, pilgrims from the Himalayan districts of Uttar Pradesh and Himachal Pradesh are prominent. In fact, it is possible to enjoy at Hardwar the spectacle of different regions of north India by watching the seasonal succession of pilgrims in their distinctive regional dress.

The sacred places studied were classified into levels as shown in Table 12.3.

In order to examine whether the 'levels' of sacred places are at all meaningful in terms of the attributes of pilgrim circulation, a comparison is made below of the major caste groupings represented in the sample of pilgrims at selected places of different levels (Table 12.4).

In general, the Brahmans and Mercantile castes make up a substantial part of the pilgrim circulation at all levels. Certainly, these castes do not constitute such high proportions of total

253

TABLE 12.3 *Levels of sacred places studied*

Places	Levels
Badrinath (Badrinarain)	Pan-Hindu
Hardwar	Supra-regional
Kangra, Jwalaji, Chintpurni	Regional
Naina Devi, Mansa Devi, Rewalsar	Sub-regional
Baijnath, Bhagsunag, Shiv Bari	Local

population in any cultural region of India. Thus, these relatively affluent and socially so-called higher castes have a disproportionately high propensity for pilgrimages. This has inviting possibilities for research on the relative mobility of different castes and diffusion of ideas and institutions. It also seems, leaving aside the local level places where only local caste composition may be reflected, that there is an increasing proportion of Brahmans and Mercantile castes with the 'higher' level sacred places. The reverse is true when the proportion of scheduled castes and cultivating castes is compared for each level. Relatively few members of these castes are represented at the higher level shrines. The relatively low participation of farming castes in pilgrimage is particularly noteworthy and tends to stress the socially differentiated rate of participation in religious circulation.

The 'levels' of places were also compared with respect to the chief motives of the devotees for making the pilgrimage (Table 12.5). The very specific motives indicate a relation of reciprocity between pilgrim and the deity as discussed earlier while the more general motives might suggest the pilgrims' 'higher' religious quest, without the expectancy of a tangible benefit in return. Specific motives included the performance of certain life-cycle activities, visits for fulfilling certain vows and promises (*Sukhna*) such as the birth of a son, job security, victory in a legal case, and numerous other mundane problems of existence. Overall, it seems that at the regional and sub-regional level, the specific motives are important, whereas, at the supra-regional and Pan-Hindu levels more general motives predominate. The general motives would include just *darsan* (to 'behold' the deity) or a holy bath without any contractual relationship. A strict relationship between the higher level sacred centres and the increasingly general motives of pilgrimage is not implied; rather there seems to be such a tendency.

TABLE 12.4 *Levels of Hindu sacred places and caste groupings (percentage of sample)*

Place	Occasion*	Level	Brahmans (a)	Mercantile castes (b)	Total of (a) & (b)	Scheduled castes (c)	Cultivating castes (d)	Total of (c) & (d)
Badrinath	AY	Pan-Hindu	30.0	49.5	79.5	0.5	4.5	5.0
Hardwar	AK	Supra-regional	26.5	50.6	77.1	3.8	4.3	8.1
Chintpurni	NC	Regional	26.2	33.2	59.4	11.8	8.0	19.6
Mansa Devi	NC	Sub-regional	7.2	28.8	36.0	28.4	15.6	44.0
Shiv Bari	SR	Local	25.0	37.0	62.0	13.0	3.0	16.0

* For explanation of abbreviations, see Table 12.2

Source: Data collected by author and assistants 1967-8

255

TABLE 12.5 *Chief motives of Hindu pilgrims at selected places of different levels*

| Place | Occasion | Level | Percentage of pilgrims who came with | |
			specific motives	general motives
Badrinath	AY	Pan-Hindu	2.5	97.5
Hardwar	AK	Supra-regional	0.6	98.4
Chintpurni	NC	Regional	45.6	54.4
Mansa Devi	NC	Sub-regional	56.0	44.0
Shiv Bari	SR	Local	17.0	83.0

Source: As in last table

Note: The specific motives column may also include small proportion of 'no-response'. For explanation of specific/general, see text.

Whether or not a pilgrim goes to a certain holy place for a general or a mundane material (specific) motive, is obviously dependent upon his or her perception of the deity. Such perceptions may have been formed as a result of the 'experience' of other individuals regarding the 'power' of the deity to 'grant' the desired object. The likelihood of a devotee's crossing linguistic or other significant cultural boundaries to seek a deity's intercession in his or her everyday affairs would seem to be limited. A given sacred place could be just an object of sanctity for a pilgrim who is bound for a general pilgrimage of Hindu sanctuaries, but its principal deity could be 'approached' by a devotee seeking help in personal problems and woes. In the Hindu context, at least a distinction must be made between a pilgrim and a devotee. Such distinction is assumed by the use of word *bhakta* (devotee) of a particular deity, and *yātrī* (pilgrim) to any shrine. Thus, understood we could at least for analytical purposes differentiate between the stream of devotees visiting *their* deity for temporal motives and a group of pilgrims partaking in the sanctity of different pilgrimage centres as they move to the various points in the sacred space having symbolically transcended their mundane secular space by the act of undertaking pilgrimage. Understood in this fashion a 'high' level place would be one where the highest ideals of religion are expressed, where the central tendencies of the ideology rather than the geographic or sociological dimensions assume prominence, where spiritual rather than the material dimension prevails, and where quest rather than fulfilment is the goal.

At successively higher levels of pilgrim circulation, through the operation of a 'filtering process' reduction in the parochial elements of the religion probably takes place. At local level places, e.g. Shiv Bari, localized parochial motifs dominate the 'pilgrimage'. Although the deity is Shiva, he is perceived to be intimately associated with the local rural milieu. Pilgrimage to this temple is made for thanksgiving after the *rabi* (spring) harvest and collective prayers are made to Shiva for rain to occur at the proper time. The occasion of pilgrimage which results in a local fair is often used by the local *Rajput* (landowners) to stress their dominance over the other castes in the area. In a very real sense the Shiva of Shiv Bari is a highly particularized deity of a small area in Himachal Pradesh who is used for sacred and secular purposes.

The next higher level (sub-regional) sacred place may be illustrated by Mansa Devi near the modern city of Chandigarh. Its field is nearly coextensive with what the linguist Grierson called the *Malwi* and *Powadhi* sub-dialects of Punjabi. The temple of Mansa Devi is of relatively recent origin, yet the goddess has an appeal that transcends the immediate environs and caste boundaries. The *Bania* (traders) devotees of this goddess come to perform several life-cycle ceremonies at this place. Scheduled caste devotees make pilgrimages for many vows and sacrifice goats to the goddess. In either case the goddess is *not* associated with the immediate *milieu* but rather with the religious beliefs of people of a more extensive area.

The goddess temple of Chintpurni in Himachal Pradesh illustrates a regional level shrine (Figure 12.3). Pilgrims from all over the Punjab converge to this shrine. During the main pilgrimage occasions, some Punjabis who have settled elsewhere in India also appear in the pilgrim streams. Certainly many pilgrims of Punjabi origin settled in Delhi make it a point to visit their favourite *devi* (goddess). The proportion of scheduled castes and farming castes there is substantially less as compared with the sub-regional shrine described above. On the other hand, Mercantile castes and Brahmans are in much greater proportion. At this shrine the sacrifice of animals is expressly forbidden. The priests of the shrine are Brahmans and they try to perform the worship of the goddess following the appropriate literary style. In general this shrine, in spite of its specific goddess cult, is much more expressive of the Punjabi Hindu religious tradition. Pilgrimage here tends to be motivated by specific vows and promises although with somewhat less intensity (Table 12.5). Several pilgrims from Uttar Pradesh visit this shrine on their way to their own goddess further up in Himachal Pradesh at Kangra.

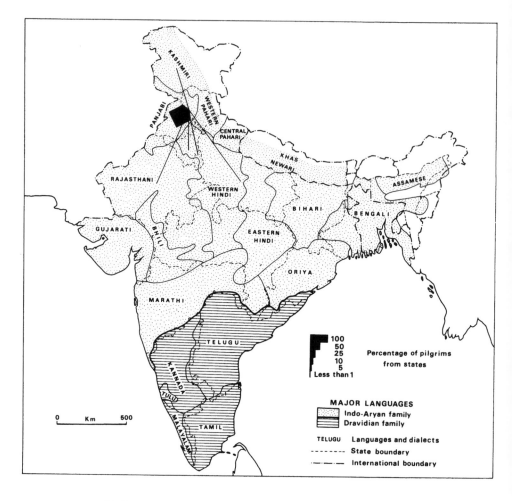

FIGURE 12.3 Origins of pilgrims to Chintpurni Shravan Ashtmi 1968

Hardwar represents the 'supra-regional' level (Figure 12.4) attracting pilgrims from all over northern India – from Kashmir to Bengal; pilgrimage to Hardwar is rarely made for a vow, and although there are numerous temples the worship of deities is only incidental to pilgrimage. At Hardwar the ashes of the deceased are consigned to the holy water of the Ganga. The place is thus symbolic of the dissolution of mortal beings and their absorption in the eternal cosmic flow. Purification by bathing, one of the most universal religious practices in Hinduism, finds its full expression at the super-climactic times of the *Kumbhamelās* when the reactualization of a life-giving cosmic event occurs. Pilgrimage is made here to earn merit, and

258

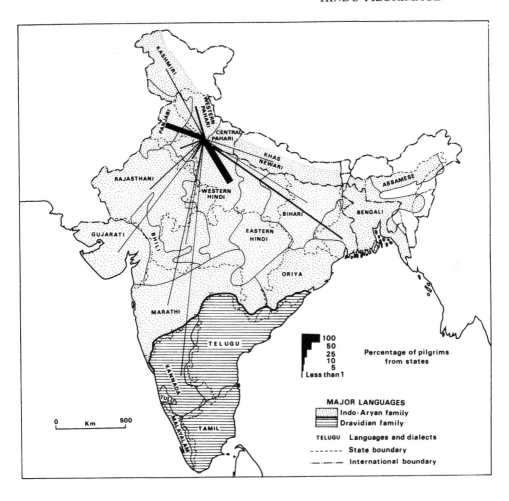

FIGURE 12.4 Origins of pilgrims to Hardwar Ardha Kumbha 1968

experience sanctity rather than to pray for material gains.

Finally, there is pilgrimage at the pan-Hindu level, exemplified by Badri *yātrā*, centring around some of the most fundamental ideals of Hinduism (Figure 12.5). Pilgrims from different parts of India transcend the regional linguistic barriers of the secular world to reach this *dhāma* (the abode) of bliss. *Yātrā* to Badrinath (also called Badrinavain), as (we believe) to other pan-Hindu sacred centres, is rarely undertaken with a view to fulfilling any promise to a deity or with an expectancy of receiving a material benefit from the deity. To undertake *yātrā* to Badrinath is symbolic of eternal quest to achieve identification with rather than expect material gain from the deity. It is not a mere purification of the soul by bathing in the sacred (and icy) waters of the Alkananda, but rather transcending this to merge with *parmātmā*, the ultimate reality, above and beyond the physical world. Temple worship (*Pūjā*) and other ritualistic paraphernalia at Badrinath adhere clearly to Sanskritic, Brahmanic mode rather than to any specific regional motif or a regional language or dialect. Cultivating castes and scheduled castes make up only a minuscule proportion of the pilgrims. The pilgrim stream is dominated by the more literate, religiously more conscious and economically more affluent people such as the Mercantile castes and Brahmans.

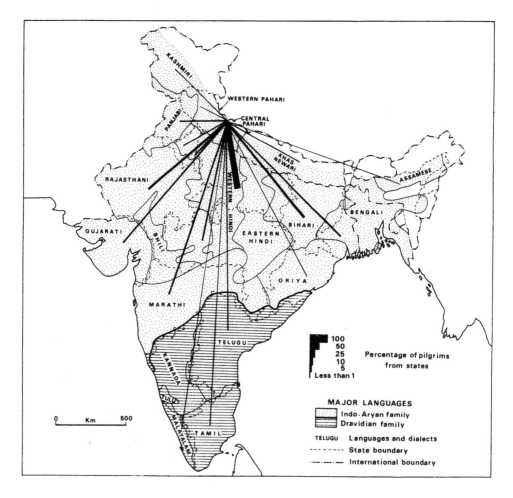

FIGURE 12.5 Origins of pilgrims to Badrinavain 1968 Yatra

Envoi

'Peregrinology' is beginning to be enriched through studies of scholars in several disciplines such as comparative religions, history, anthropology, sociology, and geography. There is clearly the need for a comparative understanding of pilgrimage phenomena. Within the Hindu pilgrimage super system it appears that increasing symbolic universalization is reflected at higher level centres and particularization at the lower levels. That this needs further extensive research is obvious. From the geographic angle research is needed to more clearly determine the diachronic spatial dimension of the fields of Hindu sacred places and intensification of pilgrimage within these fields. The impact of increased mobility on pilgrimages needs to be understood.

The interlinkages and flows between the various Hindu pilgrimage sub-systems are as yet mostly unexplored. The sociological, economic, political and even medical consequences of Hindu pilgrim flows are also largely in a speculative stage at present. It may be hoped, however, that the 'go and see' tourist ethos will not be so propagated as to undermine totally the profound sanctity of a phenomenon which arose out of devotion and quest.

Acknowledgments

The author wishes to thank the University of California Press for permission to use materials from *Hindu Places of Pilgrimage* (Bhardwaj 1973). Michael Dougherty's help in drafting maps, and Mrs Steigerwalt's help in the typing of the manuscript is gratefully acknowledged.

13 Circulation and schooling in East Africa

William T.S. Gould

The social characteristics of individuals affect the form, frequency and periodicity of their spatial mobility in all societies, and one of the most widely recognized of these characteristics is education. The educated tend to be the most mobile in any society, socially as well as spatially, both while they are in school acquiring an education and after they have left it. The close relationship between educational attainment and migration (identified by enumeration in an area other than a previous place of residence) is a familiar phenomenon in developed (Shryock and Nam 1965) as in developing countries (Conroy 1976), but the data and methodology used in most studies of the educational selectivity of migrants assumes a permanent migration rather than circulation. A close relationship between school enrolment and mobility, particularly into towns, has also been noted in many countries of the Third World, e.g. Sierra Leone (Swindell 1970), Ivory Coast (Saint-Vil 1975), Ethiopia (Gould 1973a), Thailand (Sternstein 1974), much of which involves absence from home for periods of a few months and may be therefore identified as circulation (Gipey 1978). This paper seeks to further identify the circulation generated as part of the process of acquiring a formal education. It does so with specific reference to East Africa (Kenya, Tanzania, Uganda), countries where circulation is widely recognized as an important feature of population mobility (Elkan 1976, Parkin 1975).

Formal education, as measured by actually attending school or the level of attainment in years or some formal qualifications before they leave it, is a characteristic among people that is easily identified. Rapid expansion of education in all three countries of East Africa since independence in the early 1960s from previous relatively low levels has given education greater value as a criterion for economic and social differentiation within each

262

community and society as a whole. High demand for schooling suggests that education has an economic and social value to the individual who acquires it. The willingness of governments to meet that demand by devoting large expenditures to education suggests the value which they place on having an educated population as a factor in development, and on the potential of education to promote broad social objectives. Rapid expansion of places at school, much in excess of the rate of expansion of jobs for the products of schooling, has created many problems associated with unemployment among those who have been to school (Dore 1976). But the expansion has also affected the patterns of population mobility associated with school attendance. With more educated people for each available job the mobility of the educated has been altered; with more schools, more evenly distributed throughout the country, the patterns of journey to school have altered. This paper focuses on the latter, examining the factors affecting the periodicity and frequency of movement to school, and how the spatial structure of the movement has been affected by rapid expansion in recent years.

Schools are nodal service points. The school is normally and ideally within daily commuting range of the child's home. Since this will not involve absence from home for more than twenty-four hours, movement should be considered as commuting rather than circulation. The desirable and actual length of the daily journey to school is a matter of considerable practical importance for planning the delivery of education (Gould 1978); but planning must also take note of the fact that many journeys to school in developing countries involve distances which are longer than are reasonable for daily commuting, and require absence from home for a period of at least one night up to the whole school term, or in extreme cases even longer. The amount of circulation is largely a result of there being relatively few schools and poor transportation to overcome the friction of distance, such that many children, perhaps a majority in some poorly served areas, live beyond reasonable commuting distance of a school. An increased probability of needing to leave home to attend school comes with higher levels of education, as there are likely to be fewer schools. However, this paper argues that the circulation generated by school attendance is not simply a response to the lack of schools, but is maintained by important social and policy considerations.

Mobility of young people in pre-colonial East Africa

The practice of young men leaving home for 'education' was

familiar in some pre-colonial societies in East Africa, particularly those with large-scale political and social institutions. Sending children to spend some of their formative years with influential kinsmen or chiefs was a familiar feature in the traditional Kingdom of Buganda:

> it was common for a child to be sent away from his own parents to the household of some relative of the father . . . a boyhood spent in a chief's household was the surest way to advancement in life, and boys might be sent to quite a distant relative if he was a chief (Mair 1934: 60).

Children were the joint responsibility of the clan, but since the clan had no territorial basis and members were widely spread throughout the kingdom children could leave home for fairly distant destinations. The reasons for this mobility included essential socialization with the kinship group, but involved social as well as spatial mobility. The pinnacle of the hierarchy of chiefs was the Court of the King (the *Lubiri*) to which boys, notably chief's sons, came from throughout the Kingdom to live for some time as pages (Watson 1969).

This traditional mobility among boys assumed a significance for school attendance in Buganda when formal Western schools were introduced by Christian Missionary groups in a major way from the turn of the present century, at about the same time as colonial control was being established. 'A promising child is no longer sent to a chief's house to serve, and be trained; rather he is sent to the home of a relative who lives near a good day school or who is wealthy enough to pay his fees at a boarding school' (Fallers 1960: 58).

Lucy Mair also noted the change within the twentieth century, that 'in every village where there is a state school there is hardly a household without one or two relatives' children living in it for the purpose of attending school' (Mair 1934: 63). She was, of course, writing at a time when there were far fewer schools than there were when Margaret Fallers was writing, but both emphasize the continuity of pre-colonial mobility into the present century. Then, as now, the linkage between spatial and social mobility and the need to leave parents' home to acquire specialist training for economic and social advance was well perceived.

The case of Buganda stands in considerable contrast to the situation observed among the Kikuyu of Kenya. This large group has an acephalous political structure and strongly patrilinear social structure with nuclear homestead groups associated with sub-clans which tend to have considerable geographical cohesion.

None of the standard ethnographies of the Kikuyu suggest circulation of young people of the kind observed for the Buganda. Education in its widest sense was essentially a family matter, with evidence of much greater use of child labour than was the case in Buganda (Kenyatta 1938, ch. V). When formal schooling was introduced, rather later than in Buganda but with a much more rapid early spread away from the earliest centres, the links between school and community were much stronger than in Buganda. Parents looked to and sometimes built the local primary school rather than seeking a distant option for their children (Anderson 1970: 116). The mobility of young people was correspondingly lower than in Buganda, and daily commuting to school was much more common.

These major, but sharply differing, examples of the traditional mobility of young people represent opposite ends of a continuum of frequencies and periodicities of circulation. The great variety of social structures in East Africa would suggest a great variety in patterns of traditional mobility of children, and would be expected in themselves to affect current patterns of journeys to school. However, policy differences over space and through time between Governments, rival mission groups and local communities in the establishment and type of schools have further complicated the patterns of mobility generated by them. These variations in traditional mobility, in educational policies and in ease of daily access to schools have combined to create a complexity of mobility patterns that may be separately considered in detail for primary and secondary levels.

Primary schools and circulation

The majority of children of primary school age may be expected to live at home and commute daily to school. Access is constrained by distance, and in most of East Africa the journey to school is made on foot. School catchments are small, and the evidence from an area of highly dispersed rural populations at varying overall densities in Western Uganda indicates that very few children commute further than 5 km to the school (Table 13.1) (Gould 1973b: 31-37). Ideally the distribution of schools would allow all homes to be within 5 km of a school, and children would not have to walk for more than one hour from home to school. This is certainly achieved in some of the more densely populated areas (e.g. Western Province, Kenya; the coastal belt of Tanzania; Bukedi in south-east Uganda) and in the richest areas (e.g. Central Province, Kenya; Kilimanjaro, Tanzania; Buganda, Uganda), but only in Central Province,

Kenya, is there near universal enrolment in primary school. Since education is not compulsory in any of the three countries some children may not attend school even if they live within daily commuting, access being constrained by shortage of places or teachers, lack of school fees or simply a lack of demand. In other areas, however, children live beyond reasonable daily commuting range, and if they wish to attend school they are obliged to leave home during term-time to live at or near a school.

TABLE 13.1 *Journey to primary school in Ankole, Uganda*

Distance	High density area (181 psk)		Medium density area (86 psk)		Low density area (45 psk)	
	No.	%	No.	%	No.	%
Primary 1						
less than 1 km	78	40.8	48	27.9	21	31.8
1-2 km	56	29.3	51	29.7	16	24.2
2-3 km	36	18.9	40	23.3	21	31.8
3-4 km	19	9.9	20	11.6	5	7.6
4-5 km	2	1.1	5	2.9	3	4.6
over 5 km	0	0.0	8	4.7	0	0.0
Total	191	100.0	172	100.1	66	100.0
Primary 6						
less than 1 km	51	38.9	15	10.6	1	2.8
1-2 km	35	26.7	26	18.4	7	19.4
2-3 km	30	22.9	39	27.7	9	25.0
3-4 km	14	10.7	29	20.6	7	19.4
4-5 km	1	0.8	17	12.0	9	25.0
over 5 km	0	0.0	15	10.6	3	8.3
Total	131	100.0	141	99.9	36	99.9

Source: Gould 1973b

If distance were the only factor affecting the patterns of journey to school then, as the schools system expands and schools are built in previously unserved areas, the incidence of circulation would decline in favour of commuting until all journeys to school were on a daily basis. It is certain that there is proportionately more commuting now than in the early days of education in East Africa when many of the schools were boarding institutions. Dubbeldam (1970: 12-13) cites a case from Sukuma-land in northern Tanzania in the 1920s at a time when there were less than eighty primary schools in the whole country:

> I was born in M. village in about 1913, grew up in the village and at about eight years of age I was sent to Bukambi to start schooling. I was in the school for three years up to 1923. By 1924 I was taken to Mwanza School, now known as Mwanza Boys. By then people from all over Lake Province brought their children to this school. People from each chiefdom had their hut (round one) which was built by the chief for this purpose. . . . By the end of the year 1924 all sons of chiefs were transferred to Tabora school. I remained in Mwanza and took my standard 4 examination in 1926 and was selected to go and attend the first (one year) training course at Mpwapwa.

Most of these early schools have either been up-graded to boarding secondary schools or else have remained as primary schools, but no longer provide boarding accommodation for most pupils live within daily access.

However, not all children attend the school nearest their home even if one is within the daily range. In the same area of Tanzania as that cited above there were very many more primary schools in the late 1960s than in the 1920s, and daily access to standard 1 was possible for most pupils. Yet 18 per cent of a sample of 377 children in urban and rural schools were not living with their parents, and over 10 per cent of those who were with their parents had been living with others before entering school. 'It is not uncommon for children in the area to stay with relatives, often grandparents for at least some years' (Dubbeldam 1970: 108). As in Buganda, finding accommodation with relatives or friends is common at the primary school level. The sending of children to live near a school is particularly valuable in areas where the network of schools is less than complete, but occurs for other reasons. At this level it is less common in urban areas, not only because urban populations in East Africa are a small proportion of the total population, but also because those who live in urban areas, either temporarily or permanently, are more likely to be limited in their accommodation and ability to provide space and food for a young child whose economic contribution to the household will be less than it would be in rural areas, and for whom growing up in an urban environment can bring problems. Gutkind records for the 1950s '[A] number of parents [in Mulago, a peri-urban community of Kampala] reported that they sent their children to their rural relatives, not because of the high cost of looking after children in town, or because it was considered the traditional thing to do, but simply because they failed to be able to control them in the urban setting' (Southall and Gutkind 1957: 132).

Given this tradition of high mobility among children of primary school age, it is hardly surprising that many children do not attend the school nearest their home, even if it is within daily commuting distance. The overlapping of the catchment areas of schools is further intensified by the differential attraction of schools, for reasons of real or perceived quality as measured by a record of success in having passes in the primary leaving examinations, or of religious affiliation or foundation, or of single sex schools. Each or all of these factors can and do operate to undermine any assumptions about distance-minimizing behaviour and 'optimizing' models of spatial analysis that would allocate students to the school nearest their home, and promote commuting where possible. Children commute daily to a school other than that nearest their home, as happens in Ankole, Uganda (Gould 1973: 35) or may become circular migrants.

Nevertheless, the distance-minimizing model must be the starting point of proposals to improve access to primary schools. It has been shown that children who stay at home to go to primary school in Buganda are likely to perform better in school than those who are away from home (Wallace 1974). Expansions in all three countries have been designed to bring more potential students into the catchment areas, either as in Kenya and Uganda through a better distribution of schools in unserved or under-served areas, or exceptionally as in Tanzania by engineering change in the distribution of population in the villagization programme to ensure that daily access to schools and other facilities is universally possible (Kuhanga, 1978). At the same time, however, other planning decisions have ensured the continuation of circulation. By continuing the provision of fairly large full primary schools with one teacher per grade the extension of provision into areas of low population density has been impeded, as there will not be sufficient potential students within the catchment area. Small village schools are held by Government to be inferior educationally and more expensive to build and maintain than complete schools with high pupil/teacher ratios. The inevitable consequence of maintaining the established size norms for schools ensures that access in many areas can only be obtained by children leaving home (Gould 1979).

The existence of schools which offer only part of the cycle is also a cause of leaving home to attend upper levels of primary education. Even if the early classes are accessible daily, enrolment in the upper levels may require transfer from one school to another. Dubbeldam (1970: 108) found that a higher proportion of standard 8 students than of standard 1 were living away from home. The high incidence of repeating the final class in order to improve one's grade in the primary leaving examination to allow admission to secondary school may account for further mobility. Since repeating is frowned upon but not forbidden in Kenya, it is often done in a different school.

> In for instance the Elgeyo-Marakwet region, it is apparently accepted practice for many repeaters from the better schools on the top of the escarpment to go down to the valley floor, and take a year or two in the less populous schools before returning to their original area. Often however, because of the constraint of having to live with family or kin, repeating relationships will be worked out amongst four or five neighbourhood schools in a single locality (King 1974: 134).

This trend in Kenya is also evident in Tanzania where it is further complicated by the existence of regional quotas for passes in the primary leaving examination. This encourages the movement of some children from the better provided regions, notably Kilimanjaro, to take or repeat their final year in less well provided provinces with lower pass requirements, thereby enhancing their prospects of gaining a place in secondary school (Morrison 1976: 182).

It is clear that the circular mobility of primary school children in East Africa is not solely a response to the lack of schools and the problem of reasonable commuting access. These factors are still important but less so than in earlier years when there were fewer schools. Circulation is associated with a variety of other circumstances, notably traditional social relationships and educational policies, where many of the financial and social costs of leaving home temporarily to attend school are outweighed by the assumed benefits to be derived by each student by attending a particular primary school and subsequently gaining a place in secondary school.

Secondary schools and circulation

In East Africa there are far fewer secondary schools than primary schools, for they are not only larger than primary schools but the selectivity of the educational pyramid in all three countries means that a much smaller proportion of the age group remains in the system to reach the secondary level. Despite high rates of expansion since Independence only 13 per cent of the age group attended secondary school in Kenya in 1975, and this proportion was considerably higher than that for Uganda (6 per cent) and Tanzania (3 per cent) (World Bank 1978). Inevitably, therefore, since selection is based on a national primary examination and those who pass are reasonably well distributed throughout the country, the majority of students will live beyond reasonable daily commuting distance of even the nearest school. Even in Tanzania in 1978 after villagization there were 7,000 villages but only 80 government secondary schools, so that each catchment area would need to be large even if the schools were evenly distributed and if those passing the examination were to attend the school nearest their home. Use of public transport or availability of bicycles (Marvin 1977: 23) can usefully extend the range especially in areas of high population density, but these can make only a marginal impact on the number and length of daily commuting distances. Even if school catchment areas were optimized and students went to the school nearest their home there would be need to be circulating rather than commuting.

The possibility of living at home and attending secondary school as a day student is further reduced in all three countries by the system of choice of and selection for secondary school. Although the details differ from country to country, in principle selection for each school is based on national catchment areas, with a deliberate attempt to promote inter-regional and, thereby, inter-ethnic mixing in the schools as a contribution to nation-building. Despite political instability and educational changes of recent years, the admissions arrangements and implications described for the early 1970s remain unchanged in 1979 (Gould 1974). Such policies rest on the assumption that accommodation is to be provided for the student by the school, and the formal boarding school is the norm.

Boarding schools were the earliest formal educational institutions in East Africa, introduced by the various missionary societies and modelled internally on the classic English examples. More importantly, however, they attracted students from a wide area, and although the schools themselves were unevenly distributed in each country they ensured the early spread of access to education. In Buganda they were quickly associated with the traditional power structure, notably King's College at Budo built on the site of the royal coronation ceremonies as the school for the children of the major chiefs (McGregor 1967). The Ugandan example was copied in Kenya by an alliance of Protestant Missions in the 1930s (Anderson 1970: 22) and by the Government in Tanganyika in Tabora High School in the 1920s (Listowel 1965: 88-94). By the 1950s there was a network of secondary boarding schools in all three countries established in the main by mission groups, but by independence co-ordinated and controlled within the public educational system. Going to secondary school was associated with absence from home for each school term.

Expansion based on this model was undermined by the end of the 1960s by the high cost of building and maintaining boarding schools. Governments were under great pressure to provide many more places with financial resources that were not expanding sufficiently, and, since typically the cost of a boarding place was roughly equivalent to the cost of maintaining two places in a day school, expansion was disproportionately in day schools. In Tanzania the Government was able to resist the political pressure for expansion of the secondary sector much more successfully than in Kenya or Uganda, and the emergence of day secondary schools was not as marked. In Kenya and Uganda, however, there was a rapid expansion of enrolments in public and private secondary schools, but the impact on patterns and extent of movement to school was very different in each country.

In Kenya most of the expansion was in the lowest tier of the selection hierarchy in the public sector − mostly schools with a localized catchment area but including many boarding schools − and in the private sector in *harambee*, self-help schools that are almost entirely day schools, and disproportionately found in the densely populated areas of Central, Western and Nyanza Provinces (Somersey 1974: 70-5). There is sufficient demand for day secondary schools to operate successfully in these areas, especially since *harambee* schools are not obliged to select on the basis of a pupil's performance in the Primary Leaving Examination. The *harambee* element of the schools implies a close link between school and community. Daily commuting to school from the local area would be consistent with such a development, as it would with the pre-colonial pattern of relatively limited mobility of young people. However, the Government tried, largely without success, to resist the unplanned development of *harambee* schools, preferring to concentrate expansion in larger three-stream schools (Furley and Watson 1978: 368-70).

In Uganda, however, the expansion of day secondary school places in the public and private sectors was not accompanied by a proportionate shift from circulation to commuting, although there was a large shift from boarding to day schools. There were some public day schools before Independence, but all were in urban areas and provided initially for the heavily urbanized Asian communities, which preferred to have their children at home rather than in boarding school. Very rapid expansions of enrolments in urban schools, primarily through double use of facilities in separate morning and afternoon schools, brought large numbers of Africans into these schools for the first time. Whereas in 1962 5 per cent of national enrolment in the public sector was in day schools in Kampala, this had risen to 18.6 per cent by 1970. The number of students in day secondary schools in Kampala was further swollen by the disproportionate number of large private schools also being in the capital (Gould 1975).

Some of the details of the movement into Kampala to attend secondary school are indicated in Table 13.2. These data are derived from a survey of all students in the first form of the nine day secondary schools in the capital as part of a wider survey of 23 government secondary schools in Uganda in 1971. Only 31 per cent of the boys and 50 per cent of the girls attended primary school in Kampala or in West Mengo, the surrounding district, an area slightly larger than the reasonable daily commuting distance even allowing for use of public transport. The majority were living away from home and were attending schools that they may not have selected as one of their six ordered choices. The form on which the pupils made these choices from the complete list of over 70 government secondary schools in Uganda at that time did indicate which of these were day and boarding schools, and advised students to bear the accommodation problem in mind when selecting day schools. Some students from up-country districts opted for day schools in Kampala, but many did not. However, many achieved grades sufficient to entitle them to a place in a secondary school but not sufficiently high to allow them to attend one of their chosen schools, and they were allocated to one of the large and generally under-subscribed Kampala day schools. Some of these students, recognizing the accommodation problem, opted not to take up the place; but the majority, anxious to have a much coveted secondary education, came to Kampala and faced the problem. Students came from all parts of the country, and the expected decline of numbers with distance from the capital is not clearly demonstrated, though it is more noticeable for girls than for boys. When numbers in the sample are related to the populations from which they come, the high proportions from all four Districts of south-west Uganda and from tiny Madi in the north are clear and might suggest that these districts may be underprovided with locally available places (Table 13.2). However, these are all districts from which general rates of migration to Kampala are high (Masser and Gould 1975: ch. 4) and the high rates of movement to school may be related to the better possibilities of having accommodation with relatives or friends.

TABLE 13.2 *Africans in S.1 in Kampala Government day schools, 1971, by District in which Primary Leaving Examination was taken*

| | Boys | | Girls | | Pupils per 1,000 resident population of District |
	No.	%	No.	%	
Buganda					
East Mengo	108	9.6	21	12.1	.182
West Mengo*	345	30.8	87	50.0	.634
Masaka	25	2.2	7	4.0	.059
Mubende	34	3.0	6	3.4	.141
Eastern					
Bugisu	11	1.0	4	2.3	.037
Bukedi	53	4.7	7	4.0	.116
Busoga	29	2.6	7	4.0	.042
Sebei	3	0.3	—	—	.050
Teso	23	2.1	4	2.3	.048
Northern					
Acholi	54	4.8	—	—	.125
Karamoja	15	1.3	1	0.6	.055
Lango	12	1.1	—	—	.024
Madi	15	1.3	1	0.6	.198
West Nile	32	2.9	1	0.6	.061
Western					
Ankole	119	10.6	8	4.6	.155
Bunyoro	50	4.5	7	4.0	.168
Kigezi	91	8.1	7	4.0	.156
Toro	100	8.9	5	2.9	.206
Others**	1	0.1	1	0.6	—
Total	1,120	100.0	174	100.0	—

* including Kampala
** including foreigners and 'not stated'

Source: Field survey

Accommodation in Kampala was the responsibility of each pupil and not the school. There was some official hostel provision but this was very limited in relation to overall demand. Living with relatives or friends was clearly desirable but was not always possible, and the alternative was to find a rented room or to be

273

TABLE 13.3 *Present accommodation of S.1 boys in selected Kampala day schools, 1971, by region in which Primary Leaving Examination was taken*

	At home	With relatives/ friends	Other	Total
School A				
Buganda	34	28	23	85
Western	0	3	44	47
Eastern and Northern	0	2	19	21
Total	34	33	86	153
School B				
Buganda	17	5	5	27
Western	1	8	44	53
Eastern and Northern	0	11	19	30
Total	18	24	68	110
School C				
Buganda	24	6	10	40
Western	0	1	6	7
Eastern and Northern	0	2	8	10
Total	24	9	24	57

Source: Field survey

provided with a room in return for work, such as cleaning or carrying water. Some indication of the accommodation of pupils, differentiated by the region in which they sat the primary leaving examination, is given for three Kampala day schools (Table 13.3). School A is a fairly large, old-established school, of mission foundation and well respected in Buganda, but only recently upgraded to official secondary school status. Hence its bias towards students from Buganda. School B is a newly established secondary school associated with a teacher training college, but drawing a large number of students from Western Uganda. School C is a private school in the centre of the city, charging fees that are considerably in excess of those of Government Schools, and admission to which could be gained only by direct personal application. This would account for the small numbers from the poorer and less accessible parts of the country. Many of the students from Buganda in all three schools were able to live at home and commute daily. Others were able to find accommodation with friends or relatives, which is hardly surprising given the traditional mobility of children in Buganda and the presence of a considerable population of relatives and kinsmen in or near the capital. A roughly equal number from Buganda found accommodation by renting a room or getting a room in return for some work.

The pattern for students from other regions was markedly different. Only one student out of 176 said he was living at home and a very small proportion were living with friends or relatives. Most students were living in rented rooms, probably shared with other students, but often in difficult circumstances. In urban areas accommodation is very expensive, even for the employed, and presents severe problems to non-earning school pupils. In general they are obliged because of their weak economic support to take particularly unsuitable accommodation, and their school work inevitably suffers (Weeks 1967). A few may co-operate to organize self-help hostel accommodation, often with the assistance of their school-teachers or charitable organizations.

The procedures for allocating pupils to secondary schools in Uganda continue to assume the boarding school as the norm and that accommodation is available for all, but it is clear that the expansion of the urban schools has made attendance difficult for many. Nevertheless, pupils are willing to accept the place offered to them in urban day schools, as means to the education they need to get the modern sector job they want.

There is only one government day school in a rural area in Uganda. This is some twelve miles east of the capital in the heart of the banana/coffee farming area of Buganda, but near a small trading centre. Boys and girls in the first year of study at this school were also surveyed in 1971 by the present author. Two-thirds of the 129 in the sample had been to primary school in Buganda, of whom approximately one-third were living at home, another one-third with friends or relatives, and the rest in other accommodation, mostly a private hostel provided by the mission near which the school is situated (Table 13.4). Almost all the 42 students from elsewhere in Uganda lived in this hostel, though a few who could not be accommodated were in rented rooms in the trading centre. The nationally open admissions system also applies to this school, but the problems of providing accommodation for students from a distance have been eased by the provision of a dormitory by a voluntary agency. Without it

275

accommodation for schoolchildren from other regions or tribes would be even more difficult than in urban areas. Private rural day secondary schools, however, are more likely to operate without provision of school accommodation for, as with *harambee* schools in Kenya, they can admit local students who have failed to gain places in the Government schools. Marvin (1977) in a survey of two private rural day schools in Busoga District, an area with a social structure similar to that of Buganda (Fallers 1960), showed that 48 per cent of the sample of 407 students were living at home. All but 22 of these students had been at primary school in Busoga, but many students had moved from home to live with relatives within daily commuting distance of the schools. There is also some renting of accommodation, mostly by boys, for whom it is almost as important as living with relatives (Marvin 1977, Table 3: 17). Here, as in a private school in Ankole (Gould 1973: 70-1), the catchment area is much more circumscribed than catchment areas of Government schools, and a higher proportion of students live at home and commute daily to school. Those who do not commute are more likely to find accommodation with relatives than is the case in the Government schools.

TABLE 13.4 *Accommodation of S.1 students in a rural day school by region in which the Primary Leaving Examination was taken*

	At home	With relatives/ friends	Other	Total
Buganda	29	31	27	87
Western	0	0	25	25
Eastern and northern	0	2	15	17
Uganda	29	33	67	129

Source: Field survey

Overall, the distribution of secondary school places has become more biased towards towns, and therefore towards the distribution of job opportunities. Finding an education and finding a job are closely linked in parents' and students' minds. Moock's analysis of the role of the school in a poor rural community in Western Kenya goes as far as to directly equate labour circulation with secondary school places in urban areas:

The extended family and class group still play important roles in Maragoli's social organization. One such role which bears directly upon the educational system is the accommodation which town relatives provide to school leavers in search of employment or secondary school places. Since the network of almost every Maragoli family extends into the major towns of Kenya, the mobility of youngsters seeking jobs and school places is greatly facilitated (Moock 1973: 304).

The evidence for Uganda, however, suggests that social networks are not necessarily valuable for school pupils, even from areas of heavy labour migration such as south-west Uganda, and that a pattern of circular mobility can exist that is not dependent on kin or clan linkages. The shortage of secondary school places in these peripheral districts where there have been relatively rapid expansions in primary school enrolments has created an imbalance that can only be met by pupils leaving home to live in an unfamiliar social and economic environment.

Conclusion

The journey to school can be circulation as well as the more normal commuting, and both are important for primary and secondary schools throughout East Africa, with the relative importance of circulation increasing up the educational pyramid. Almost all tertiary level institutions offer residential accommodation as most, if not all, students will be living away from home. Going away from home to attend school or college and the circulatory mobility involved in it is a major component of population mobility in East Africa.

The mobility of children leaving home to attend school should be seen as circulation, for the principal spatial and temporal features of other mobility phenomena normally described as circulation are evident. However, rather different issues to those in the main stream of circulation research are raised. These do not focus on the relationship between circulation and migration, between temporary and permanent absences and on the way in which the relative importance of each of these has changed over time, but rather on the relationship between circulation and commuting, between temporary absence during school terms and absence less than twenty-four hours. Many studies have shown the inapplicability of the simple conceptualization of the circulation of workers as a temporary, transitional phase in the early stages of development from low levels of traditional mobility to high rates of permanent migration; equally the

277

available evidence must question the assumption that high levels of circulation in the journey to school represent a transitional phase between there being no schools and no mobility associated with acquiring an education and the universal availability of schools within daily commuting distance.

There can be little doubt that the relative importance of circulation has fallen over the last twenty years as educational provision has become more widely distributed, but it is likely, even in Kenya where the day school movement is most advanced, that there are absolutely more children than ever before leaving home to go to school. The persistence of this form of circulation arises from internal causes associated with the traditional mobility of young people as a means of social interaction and social mobility, and the wide range of social networks that arise as a result of more general population movement especially the growth of towns. It arises also from external causes associated with the institutional framework in which education is delivered and from policies imposed by governments to facilitate social engineering in the schools; policies which are maintained despite financial pressures to promote day schools and to oblige students to live at home wherever possible. Leaving home to go to school is not felt by parents or students to be a problem in itself, but rather something to be prized. It is almost a 'rite de passage', an indication of current success and the likelihood of a job in the modern sector in the future. It is the first step on the ladder to expected affluence and influence. For the individual pupil, circulation may be a matter of choice rather than necessity, and governments have been both unwilling and unable to prevent that choice being exercised.

14 The syndrome of poverty and wage labour circulation: the Indian scene

Shekhar Mukherji

'Did you ask how many years I have been pulling rickshaw? Twelve years! I was only thirteen then . . . when village money lender took away my father's little land. How could I buy this rickshaw? It costs 1500 rupees. I earn only seven or eight rupees daily, after 14 hours of sweating. But its owner takes away four rupees. I don't mind this terrible heat . . . if only I could feed my parents and my wife in village . . . last time I saw her was three months back when I went to the village . . . soon rainy season will come . . . the time for union . . . she weeps all through the rain, alone, separated, agonized and humiliated. . . .'

Halku, A rickshawala in Varanasi City,
India (May 30, 1977)

[A]ll tell the same story − a picture of rapidly increasing labour force within both rural and urban areas, increasing rates of unemployment, and absorption into low-productivity informal activities in urban areas which will accelerate in the decades of the nineteen seventies and eighties in most of the Third World countries.

McGee (1976: 13)

Fundamentally, it is poverty that must be eliminated . . . A comprehensive anti-poverty policy would thus include social assistance schemes, concessional input supply schemes, militant trade unionism and land and property reform, [and] the core of a rural unemployment relief policy would now be a massive rural works programme.

Krishna (1975: 240)

These three quotations encapsulate the main lines of argument of

279

this study. Halku vividly narrates the sad story of all circulating rickshaw-pullers and other low-grade operatives in India who have been uprooted from the countryside and have come to eke out a miserable living in the towns. It is the story of pauperization of labourers in the village, of dirt and filth of the slums in their urban 'eldorado', and of back-breaking hard work and exploitation. It is a tale of disrupted families and the dual responsibilities of circulators both in the village and in the town. 'Circulation or circular migration' is an insipid term for such an agonizing process!

The second quotation indicates some reasons for this situation: population explosion, abject rural poverty and stagnation, urban growth without development, limited employment opportunities generated by capital intensive industrialization and lack of capacity of parasitic towns to provide full productive employment for incoming labourers. Consequently, they are being absorbed only into the low-productivity urban informal sector as rickshawalas, porters, road-pavers, domestic servants, hawkers and petty shopkeepers. McGee (1978: 199-224) finds that both circular mobility of labourers and their absorption only in the urban informal activities will accelerate in future in highly populous countries of south and south-east Asia like India, Bangladesh and Indonesia.

The third quotation provides one possible answer to Halku. Here is a reference to abject rural poverty, widespread unemployment and increasingly inequitous distribution of land ownership due to the operation of usurious landlords in rural India. From these stressful conditions a great number of marginalized sharecroppers, agricultural labourers and the unemployed try to escape by crowding into the cities, leading to increase of unemployment in the urban informal sectors. Programmes are suggested to ameliorate poverty and generate mass employment in both agricultural and non-agricultural sectors of the economy, but these have to be supported by necessary structural and institutional measures.

This introduction identifies the three interrelated aspects of this paper: the true nature of wage labour circulation that is occurring between rural and urban areas in parts of India; actual socio-economic condition of the wage labour circulators in the towns; and at the more generalized all-India level the likely shape of things to come if the present-day trends of increasing circulation of labourers and their absorption only in urban informal activities continue. These aspects are briefly examined with the help of a variety of substantive empirical data. The conclusion indicates briefly the measures necessary to alleviate the problems of wage labour circulation which are induced by poverty and under-development.

An example of wage labour circulation in India is revealed from sample survey data on 1940 cycle-rickshaw pullers, known as rickshawalas, in Varanasi city (formerly Benares), Eastern Uttar Pradesh, which were collected during January-May, 1977. Varanasi (0.8 million population in 1978), one of the oldest cities in the world, is a great centre of pilgrimage, learning, commerce, trade and handicrafts, but it has few modern industries. The sample comprised a 10 per cent simple random selection of the city's rickshawalas. Very detailed information was collected on their movements (both migration and circulation), reasons for moves, socio-economic condition and stresses both in village and in the city, and other related data. Data are also used from the Indian population censuses (1951-71) and various National Sample Survey reports (1953-4 to 1961-2; 1961, 1969a, 1969b) on occupational classification of workers and unemployment. On these the more generalized discussion on migration, circulation, urban involution and sequences of development of India in the future rests.

Rickshawalas as migrants, circulators, and non-circulators

Out of the total 1940 rickshawalas sampled, 1258 (65 per cent) have moved from the surrounding rural districts of Eastern Uttar Pradesh into Varanasi and 682 (35 per cent) were locally born. Ninety-five per cent came from the countryside, mostly from a zone of 100-150 mile radius. According to the conventional definition of migration (crossing a pre-determined administrative boundary and a permanent change of residence for one or more years), these 1258 displaced persons might be called permanent migrants. But only 256 (13 per cent) may be so designated. The remaining 1002 regularly circulate (involving an absence of 24 hours or more) between the city and the home villages, even after staying one to five years (46.7 per cent of 1002 persons), ten to twenty years (18.8 per cent), or more than twenty years (11.3 per cent) in the city; and they have no declared intention to settle there permanently. These 1002 rickshawalas are circulators, as distinct from 938 rickshawalas (48.4 per cent) who do not circulate (256 permanent migrants and 682 locally born), and who are termed as non-circulators. One objective is to compare the relative socio-economic position of circulating rickshawalas who have to maintain two separate establishments in the village and the city with that of non-circulating rickshawalas.

Half of the 1940 rickshawalas belong to *harijan* caste or

untouchables, and another 34 per cent to low castes. All rickshaw-pullers are male. Most are young (61 per cent in age group 15-34), married (85 per cent), illiterate (67 per cent) or with 1 to 5 years' schooling (22 per cent), and either landless (59 per cent) or own less than 0.04 hectare per household (21 per cent). Fifty-one per cent belong to extended families and the rest to nuclear families. Thirty-five per cent have to support 5 to 6 non-earning dependants, and another thirteen per cent feed 9 to 16 dependants. Such a major dependency burden is a compelling reason for moving out and taking up whatever manual work is available in the city.

The nature of wage labour circulation in Varanasi region

The magnitude of problems of the labour circulators, constantly moving between rural poverty and urban poverty in order to perform dual responsibilities both in village and town, deserves much more attention than is usually given. According to Mitchell (1961a: 278) the wage labourer responds to two conflicting sets of forces: centrifugal (economic) which induce him to leave his tribal community and centripetal (social) which draw him back again. Repetitiveness in circulation is greatly emphasized by Chapman (1976: 132) for tribal mobility in Solomon Islands. In the Indian context, wage labour circulation has also been occurring for more or less similar reasons, but with certain

TABLE 14.1 *Repetitiveness in circulation, Varanasi sample, 1977*

Frequency of circulating from city to home village	Number of rickshawalas circulating	Percentage	Repetitiveness in circular mobility per person per year (average)
Once a week	112	11.1	52
Once within 15 days	394	39.3	26
Once within 1 month	224	22.4	12
Once within 6 months	140	14.0	2
Once in 6 months and over	69	6.9	1
Incomplete information	63	6.3	—
Total	1,002	100.0	20.3

Source: Field Survey

differences. These differences are briefly indicated in subsequent discussion.

Repetitiveness in circular mobility is a characteristic of rickshawalas in Varanasi City who each perform on average 20.3 circular moves per year to visit their home villages (Table 14.1). Seventy-three per cent circulate at least one to four times per month.

Unlike circulation which begins and terminates in the village, the circulation of wage labourers, such as these, both originates and ends in the city. Two components of movements emerge: an urban to rural circulation, for a short duration mainly for visiting family, and rarely for social commitments, festivities and harvesting; and a rural to urban circulation, a quick return to city to resume rickshaw-pulling (Table 14.2).

TABLE 14.2 *Duration of stay in the home village, Varanasi sample, 1977*

Duration of stay in the village	Frequency	Percentage
Less than a week	521	52.0
Between one week and a fortnight	261	26.0
Between a fortnight and one month	90	9.0
One month and above	61	6.1
Incomplete information	69	6.9
Total	1,002	100.0

Source: Field Survey

Thus, the nature of wage labour circulation here somewhat differs from that studied in the tribal contexts in Zambia and Solomon Islands, in the sense that the labourers' stay in the tribal domicile until 'they once again feel the necessity to seek wage earning occupations' (Mitchell 1961: 278), is reduced to a very short duration of less than a month, even a week. Their staying power in the village has considerably diminished due to the influence of the market economy on the peasant economy, but with limited industrialization. Detailed questioning shows that in the face of limited available land, expanding population has led to fragmentation and the growth of minifundia, increasing inequality in land ownership, and consequently a great rise in the number of pauperized migrants. Rural peasants and workers cannot afford to stay in villages where local employment opportunities, which used to exist previously (like weaving, black-smithing, carpentry, cottage industries, etc.), have fast disappeared due to the competitive market. Now they must stay in the city for much longer duration to eke out a living through urban informal activities like rickshaw-pulling or porterage. Such circulation occurs within the syndrome of poverty and mobility. Although 'circulation as a form of mobility is a time-honoured and enduring mode of behavior', a view Chapman and Prothero rightly hold (1977: 5-10), the nature of particularly wage labour circulation in a peasant-cum-market economy, as in India, probably has undergone many more changes (in quality, intensity, process and consequences) than could be fully described by the term 'accommodation' which they have used.

The most important purpose of urban-to-rural circulation of rickshawalas is to visit families left behind (85.5 per cent), and compared with that other purposes are insignificant (Table 14.3). The data show that out of 1002 circulating rickshawalas, 86.5 per cent are married; almost 100 per cent of all married rickshawalas live alone in the city, and 90 per cent live in crowded rooms in the city slums, sharing one room with 8 to 23 persons. They circulate on average 20.3 times per year per person not because of social bonds with the village community, but rather because they can never afford to bring their families to the city even after 10 or 20 years urban residence! If families could have been brought to the city then the picture would have been different, but this happened with only 256 permanent migrants. How far the so-called centripetal pull of the village (i.e., kinship ties, belongingness to the village, social commitments) is really responsible for inducing such circulation, and to what extent urban housing shortages, insecurity and a stressful life in urban *bastees* are the real reasons, needs to be further investigated.

TABLE 14.3 *Purpose of urban to rural circulation of rickshawalas, Varanasi sample, 1977*

Major purpose	Frequency	Percentage
Visiting family	857	85.3
Other familial-social commitments	45	4.5
Harvesting/other agricultural work	40	4.0
Illness	11	1.1
Incomplete information	49	4.9
Total	1,002	100.0

Source: Field Survey

TABLE 14.4 *Persistence of urban-to-rural circulation over time, within the context of rural-to-urban circulation, Varanasi sample, 1977*

Duration of residence in the city in rural-to-urban circulation	Number of circulators	Mean frequency of visiting home village per year per person (urban-to-rural circulation)
Less than 1 year	85	21.9
1 to 4 years	277	19.3
5 to 9 years	175	20.8
10 to 14 years	114	18.5
15 to 19 years	64	18.4
20 years or more	224	22.0
Incomplete information	63	—
Total	1,002	17.5

Source: Field Survey

Table 14.4 shows persistence in the frequency of urban to rural circulation of rickshawalas over time, even after 5, 10 or 20 years continuous stay in the city. From this, a number of things can be inferred. First, intention to return to home village persists as the commitments to meet the wives and children left behind also persists. Second, however, intention to continue wage earning occupations in the city also persists without any rising urban social commitments. Third, while urban poverty prevents the wage labourers bringing families to settle, rural poverty and lack of opportunities preclude return to the villages. Fourth, as a result, short-term urban-to-rural circulation is found to be enmeshed with longer term rural-to-urban circulation of the wage labourers, with the two kinds of mobility more or less inseparable. Although different kinds of circulation (e.g., marketing, pilgrimage, social purposes) exist as a distinctive form of mobility, as Chapman and Prothero rightly emphasise (1977: 5-9), so far as wage labourers in the study area are concerned, no clear distinction could be made between their urban-to-rural circulation (and return journey) and rural-to-urban circulation, as the former is contained within the latter, and both are performed by the same group of persons.

Circular mobility and social mobility

Social mobility is usually measured in terms of occupational mobility and income mobility. Both are employed here for assessing what scope for upward social mobility is available to the circulating rickshawalas in an Indian urban setting. Their previous occupations in villages before taking up rickshaw-pulling in the city tell the tale of the same process of pauperization, uprooting and rural exodus as stated earlier. There are three sub-populations who have gone to pull rickshaws: formerly skilled and semi-skilled, the unemployed, and the landless and unskilled workers. As many as 36.2 per cent were previously engaged in skilled or semi-skilled occupations: cultivating their own farm (13.7 per cent), weaving fine silk *sarees* (6.3 per cent), government service (2.0 per cent), private service (4.3 per cent), own business (5.0 per cent), and other semi-skilled work (4.9 per cent). The small farmers were uprooted due to mortgage, litigation, debt and land grabbing tendency of big landlords. Weavers were displaced due to excessively low prices given for their products by big silk merchants controlling the market. Others lost their village jobs for a variety of reasons. All these were more skilled and more desirable occupations than the hard manual work of rickshaw-pulling. A certain degree of downward social displacement of these skilled and semi-skilled workers is thus evident. Only 9.6 per cent were previously unemployed and for them some improvement has occurred. As many as 53 per cent were working as landless agricultural labourers and other unskilled wage labourers, but who, under crushing pressure of circumstances (manipulation of tenancies, bonded labour, debt, etc.), could not withstand further and were also uprooted. For them there was no change in the socio-economic status.

Data also reveal that absolutely no income gain has occurred for as many as 34.3 per cent of all circulators, and very little improvement (less than Rs.50 per month) of another 18.8 per cent (roughly Re.1 = 12 US cents or Sterling £0.05, but in terms of purchasing power in the local market one rupee is equivalent to one US dollar). Thus, more than half do not benefit by their spatial mobility and occupational change. Marginal improvement (Rs.50 to 149) may be noticed for 25.3 per cent, and only 18.8 per cent have gained more than Rs.150 per month. Hence, in contrast to a number of the optimistic assessments of the role of circulation in mitigating individual poverty and fostering rural development (e.g. in Greater Bombay, Zachariah 1968: 338-9), the evidence accruing out of this field is strong enough to suggest that this movement only maintains their poverty situation. Circulation of wage labourers is occurring within, and in turn, reinforcing, the syndrome of poverty and mobility, and upward social mobility is insignificant.

It is, however, not implied that the condition of the peasants and workers was much better in the village and that it further worsened in the city. They have come because they had no choice. Once uprooted, choice was limited between slow starvation and quick death. They take up back-breaking hard work of rickshaw-pulling (or road-paving, etc.) because these are the only low-grade informal activities in which they may be employed in the city and survive. The crux of the matter is that they were uprooted in village; they moved from one low-grade rural informal activity to another low-grade urban informal activity – characterized by very low levels of skill, technology, wages and per capita productivity, cut-throat competition, and extraction of surpluses from human labour at severely competitive wages. Consequently, there has been little vertical social mobility, and sometimes, they have actually slipped back from skilled to unskilled work; their income and levels of living have not improved much in the city, except in helping to avoid starvation.

Relative condition of circulators and non-circulators

Figure 14.1 shows the economic balance sheet of circulating compared with non-circulating rickshawalas. Among circulators, 0.5 per cent earn below Rs.60 per month, 17.7 per cent between Rs.60-150, 61.3 per cent between Rs.151-240, 14.2 per cent between Rs.241-330, and only 7 per cent above Rs.330. For non-circulators these proportions are 0.9, 16.3, 61.9, 15.8 and 5.1 per cent, respectively. Although the mean monthly income levels of the circulators and the non-circulators do not differ much, the mean monthly subsistence expenditure of the former exceeds that of the latter in almost all income groups, mainly due to their erratic existence and a lack of established foundation within the city. Compared with the non-circulators (who are locally born or permanent migrants), they are forced to spend more for the same minimal level of consumption. Consequently, their monthly remittances to home villages are substantially less in almost all income groups. These remittances are the main motive force behind their work. Non-circulators are also remitting to their blood or marital relations living in the village. Given this aim, circulators appear to be less successful in fulfilling it. The proportion of remittances to total income decreases as income level increases. For non-circulators, these proportions are 222, 78, 63, 54, 38, 43 and 31 per cent, respectively, for income groups of less than Rs.60, 60-150, 151-240, 241-330, 331-420, 421-510 and above Rs.510. However, for circulators these proportions are much lower; 130, 47, 53, 49, 31, 40, and 42 per cent, respectively. The proportion sometimes exceeds the monthly income, because a certain minimum amount must be remitted to the village, even

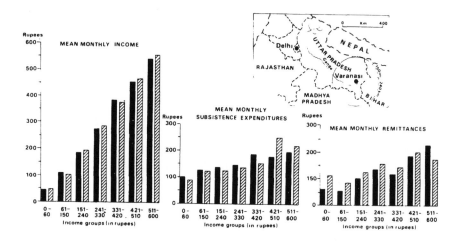

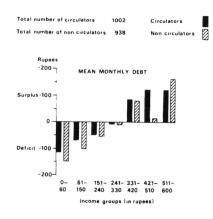

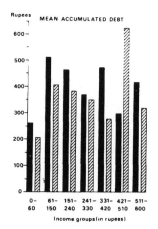

FIGURE 14.1 Varanasi rickshawalas: circulators and non-circulators: income, subsistence expenditure, remittances, debt and accumulated debt

288

by incurring debt. In spite of such high proportions, since remittances are very small, families in the village live on a pittance, and hardly any amount is available for productive use or technological change. Thus the immiseration of the rural poor continues.

Ninety-three per cent of circulators and ninety-five per cent of non-circulators are in monthly debt. More circulators than non-circulators are burdened with accumulated debt in almost all income groups (five times the mean monthly income in the lowest two income groups and two to three times in the next two groups (Figure 14.1).

Since the sum total of remittances over a life-time of a circulator is substantially less than that of either a migrant or a city-born, the former is less capable of raising the per capita productivity of his family or its level of technology in the village (Figure 14.1). Compared with the non-circulators, the circulators are much more handicapped. Fewer circulators than non-circulators are without any accumulated debt (thirty per cent compared with forty per cent), and more circulators are burdened with greater amounts of accumulated debt (between Rs.200 to 1400 per person) than their counterparts who appear to be relatively well off (Figure 14.2).

Compared with the permanent migrants (or non-circulators), the circulators are compelled to spend more in the city for barest sustenance; cannot afford to remit a substantial amount though remittance is their sole purpose of rickshaw-pulling; are more burdened with debt; and their remittances are not sufficient for productive use. The reasons are that circulatory migrants: have dual responsibilities to perform; have to maintain two separate establishments; frequently visit home village to meet families which means incurring heavy expenditures; maintain connexions with the stressful rural life, are exposed to its vicissitudes and vagaries, are prone to fall preys to the village money-lenders. Consequently, they incur more expenditure and debt than those who have settled permanently in the city.

Towards a generalized picture

The story of the rickshawalas is strongly corroborated by the findings of a previous sample survey that was made in Varanasi in 1973 on mobility of both general communities and all kinds of wage labourers (Mukherji 1975a: 296-7). A final linking canonical analysis (a higher form of regression analysis) was performed between the three matrices of mobility behaviour, place utility considerations, and the socio-economic attributes of the

(a)

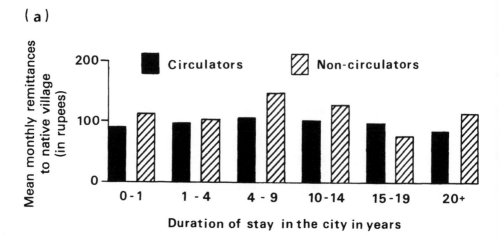

(b)

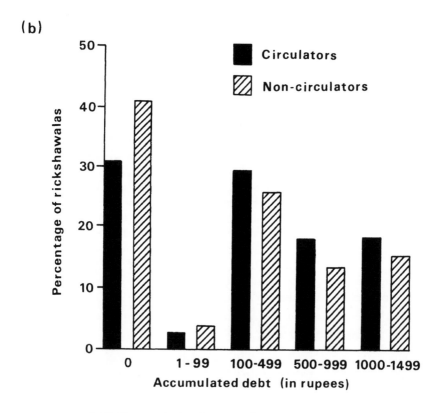

FIGURE 14.2 *Varanasi: circulators and non-circulators (a) duration of stay; (b) accumulated debt*

individual movers. As a result, the following six different patterns of relationships were found between them. The foremost pattern was that the poor, economically disadvantaged peasants and workers were found to be searching for any manual jobs and moved to towns that provided greater job-urban utility gain. Secondly, the former peasants and workers in the city circulated to the home villages for visiting family or harvesting. Thirdly, the landless and unemployed moved for gainful employment in the city. Fourthly, the unemployed, economically dissatisfied, and indebted people temporarily migrated to the city in the hope of employment and security. Fifthly, people in debt and familial stress frequently circulated between rural and urban places. Sixthly, the untouchables were frequently oscillating under conditions of severe drought and debt. Thus, rickshawala represents a microcosm of all low-grade wage labourers.

Now, it remains to be seen whether or not what is happening in the large city of Varanasi holds more or less true for other Indian cities. Direct study on circulation is lacking in India, yet a general picture can be drawn on the basis of abundant fugitive materials on the condition of labour migrants in urban areas, their absorption in poverty-induced tertiary sectors, return migration and related aspects. Based on the 1961 census, Mitra (1967: 57-63) studied internal migration to 101 Indian cities (with more than 100,000 population), and noted the overriding roles played by services and poverty-induced tertiary sectors in absorbing the urban peasant migrants who are found doing things which only the sheer growth of population creates, as distinct from jobs created by capital and expansion of production. In 1961 more than one-half of the working population of Calcutta was non-Bengali (i.e., migrants), and each of them was found remitting on average Rs.46.1 per month to home villages against Bombay's Rs.44.6, Delhi's Rs.42.9, and Madras's Rs.32.2. These figures also indicate how the wage labourers get along without the barest minimum of housing, sanitation, comfort and privacy.

Bose (1967: 1-20) noted that while 2.4 million people were recorded as different kinds of migrants during the year preceding the 1961 census, the total number of such migrants during 1951-61 was only 15 million, as against 24 million expected. This indicates a prevalence of return migration in India. Prabhu (1956: 85-95) also found that an extensive amount of return migration characterized migrants to Bombay, and circulation compounded the poverty of the movers because of their dual responsibilities both in the village and in the city. In a study of rickshawalas in Lucknow city, Gould (1974: 98-100) has described the same situation as that in Varanasi. Utilizing the 1971 census data on

291

migrants to 147 large cities (with more than 100,000 population), Premi (1978: 30-33) has found that most migrants come from far-flung rural areas (from 300 to 600 miles), are semi-literate and are absorbed either in the service sector or in very low-grade production process activities.

The trends in 1971 strongly corroborated those in 1961. There is growing evidence everywhere in India of the persistent influx of the poor labourers into urban areas, the proliferation of urban informal tertiary activities, and circulatory or return migration. The situation must have deteriorated further in the period 1971-78, when there have been signs of deepening rural and urban poverty (Planning Commission 1978: 3-7). If the trends continue, then what shape the future will take is within an intelligent guess which will now be discussed.

The process

Why is circulation happening on a large scale in an under-developed country like India? The Varanasi survey found rickshawalas to originate within a range of 100-150 miles. Supplementary evidence indicates that for a large number of cities the low-grade workers (like rickshawalas, porters, vendors, road-pavers) originated from far-flung rural areas (from a distance of 300-600 miles), and their story was very much akin to that of Varanasi rickshawalas. In attempting to progress from the micro-level to the macro-level, this circulation process may now be tentatively generalized for India as a whole, on the basis of the discussions made so far, supplemented by other information of a historical nature.

According to the Reserve Bank Survey (1972: 1-20) the poorest 10 per cent of rural households in India owned only 0.1 per cent and the richest 10 per cent owned more than 50 per cent of total assets (mainly agricultural land) in 1971-72. During 1961-71, while the population of India grew by 22.5 per cent, the number of agricultural labourers increased by 50.7 per cent, indicating the ongoing process of alienation from the land. Small-scale and cottage industries and handicrafts, which formerly used to provide employment opportunities, are now grossly neglected, and discarded village operatives are forced to find their way to the city. There has been no real vigorous attempt to ameliorate the condition of rural poverty, unemployment and village stagnation (Bardhan and Srinivasan 1974: 1). This is the rural side of the picture.

To the urban side, on the other hand, the investment and growth efforts are concentrated only on a few nodes and ports (like Calcutta, Delhi, Bombay and Madras) which grow very rapidly at the expense of the vast rural countryside and smaller towns (Planning Commission 1967: 2-35). These nodes are imperfectly related to their hinterlands, stunting their tendencies for development (Berry 1966: 8-9). Locational discontinuities in the distribution of production units, services and amenities, mentioned by Chapman and Prothero (1977: 7-9), are thus maintained and accentuated. These nodes, cities, and towns themselves have very limited employment-generating capacity under capital-intensive industrialization. As a consequence the only option left to the villagers is to move to take up any manual work available in the urban informal sector. Frequently they circulate to home villages but for a very short duration, mainly to visit families left behind, and quickly return to the urban ghetto.

Therefore, the process of wage labour circulation must refer to many interrelated macro factors – land inequality, pauperization, uprooting, rural exodus, conditions maintaining both rural and urban poverty, disarticulation of links between village and town, spatial-economic disorganization, urban polarization of resources, the parasitic character of urban areas and possibly many more. Collectively these may be called the working of a syndrome of poverty and mobility. Wage labour circulation is just one spatial manifestation of this syndrome. This brief outline of process only indicates that a great deal of penetrating research would be necessary to understand the complexity of factors that lead wage labourers to circulate in India and in the Third World generally. For one obvious corollary is that if these macro processes of the syndrome continue to operate, then there would be much more increasing, not decreasing, circulation of wage labourers in the future in India, especially when accompanied by a situation of population explosion.

Rural-urban migration, circulation and urban involution in India: the likely situation in the year 2001

This section provides a macro view and is concerned with India as a whole, where a characteristic feature of the urban economy is its lack of proper absorptive capacity. It maintains most of people at a minimum level of wages and consumption and keeps absorbing more migrants, but at still lower levels of per capita productivity and consumption. As more people move in, they are absorbed not in the organized secondary sector, but rather in a bazaar-type informal or tertiary sector. An increasingly greater number of workers perform a decreasingly smaller amount of work, and poverty is shared among them. Urban growth occurs

293

without development, and urban areas are dominated by characteristics of a peasant economy, by a large poverty-induced tertiary sector. Often this process is termed an urban involution (McGee 1971: 64-94).

Set within this context, what would be the future shape of rural-urban migration, circulation and urban involution in India in the year 2001? These phenomena were investigated in a recent ESCAP study (Mukherji 1977: 8-14) and its findings are summarized here as they bear directly on the magnitude of circulation to be expected in the future.

India's urban population has grown from 62 million in 1951, to 79 million in 1961, and to 109 million in 1971. Only 19.9 per cent of the population is urban, because rural population is also growing rapidly and rural to urban transfer is occurring slowly. About 8.2 million migrated during 1941-51, 5.2 million during 1951-61 (Zachariah and Ambannavar 1967: 95-100), and an estimated 8.5 million during 1961-71 (Mukherji 1978: 41-2). Even then, this is creating enormous human problems, and its dimensions probably will increase in the future. The census data do not reveal the actual magnitudes of in- and out-migration that occurred during the inter-censal period, nor record circulation. Beset with these limitations, the future magnitude of circulation can only be inferred indirectly from other phenomena, discussed in connection with the process of circulation, and especially as follows.

Based on census reports of India (1951-71) and National Sample Survey Reports on occupational classification of workers and unemployment (1953-5 to 1961-2), the following tendencies were revealed during 1951-71. The rural peasant sector is persistently large (increasing from 90 to 94 per cent of total workers during 1951-71). Growth in the rural organized sector has been negative (from 10 to 6 per cent during 1951-71). The organized urban sector is declining (from 57.5 to 50.2 per cent of total urban workers during 1951-71). Paradoxically on the other hand, the urban peasant sector is steadily increasing (from 42.5 to 49.8 per cent during 1951-71). All of these have occurred in spite of a succession of Five Year Plans for rural and urban development. Villages remain stubbornly peasant in character and the urban peasant sector is continuously on the increase.

Based on 1951-71 trends, four alternative projections were made for India up to the year 2001, out of which the two most probable ones are briefly discussed. Actual time series data were employed in the calculations of birth and death rates, migration and urbanization rates, and trends in growth of labour force, employment, unemployment, and growth of urban and rural peasant and organized sectors. Projections were based on different sets of assumptions. Assumptions in structural setting A were: that fertility is being reduced from 39 births per 1000 in 1971 to 26 by the year 2001; a continuation of 1951-71 trends in urbanization-migration; a continuation of 1951-71 trends in growth of rural organized sector and peasant sector; accompanied by growth of the urban organized sector at 1.4 per cent annually.

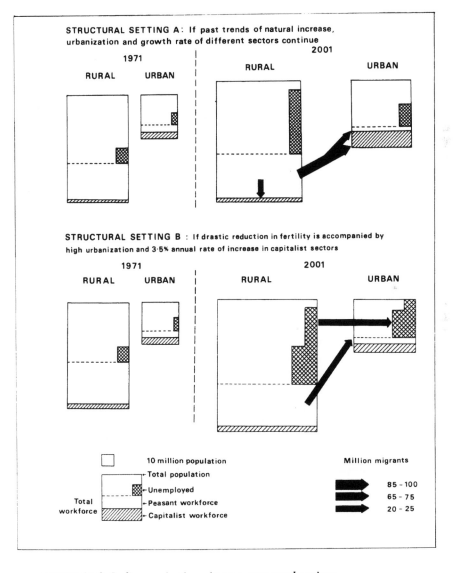

FIGURE 14.3 India: projections in two structural settings

Assumptions in structural setting B were: very slight reduction in fertility, little change in urbanization (2.25 per cent annually), no changes in organized/peasant sector of economy, equal rate of growth of urban/rural work force. These assumptions can be criticized and projections based on them simply show broad differences in trend patterns if the country follows different sequences of development. Detailed calculations are given elsewhere (Mukherji 1978: 40-7).

In structural setting A out of 162 million additional workers, a majority (92 million) would have to remain within the peasant rural sector, and only 4 million would be absorbed by the urban peasant sector. There would still have to be an expansion of jobs in the organized sectors in urban areas (49 million) and rural areas (17 million). Thus, there would be some improvement in the volume of movement from peasant-rural to urban organized sectors but movement from peasant-rural to peasant-urban would also continue. According to this setting, open unemployment would exceed 70 million in 2001, most of which would be compelled to remain in rural areas (50 million). Total rural-urban migration during the 1971-2001 period would be 89 million, of which 49 million would have migrated in the 1991-2001 decade alone. Most people would have to be content with very low levels of per capita consumption in all basic human needs.

Structural setting B represents a dismal situation in which neither the level of urbanization nor proportion of workers in the various sectors changes over the thirty year period. Total population would have doubled and crossed the billion mark, but the country would still have a predominantly rural character (80 per cent) and unchanged urban proportion (20 per cent). Open unemployment would have reached an alarming 145 million, of which 93 million would have to live in rural areas while urban unemployment would grow to 52 million. Overflow of un-employed from rural to urban areas would continue and raise the involutionary level alarmingly. The peasant sector would have to absorb a majority of the labour force: out of total 172 million additional labour, 135 million would have to find employment within the rural peasant sector and another 14 million in the urban peasant sector. Even then the organized sector would have to provide an additional 23 million jobs in a situation of very limited economic growth. In such a situation there would be little scope for rural-urban migration, only 21.7 million during the entire 30 year period (1971-2001). Since all the economic sectors would be stagnant, people would be forced to remain where they are. Almost no migration would be possible between rural peasant sector and organized urban sector and the situation would only allow increasingly 'circulatory movement' from rural peasant to urban peasant sectors and vice versa.

It is very sad to state that in all likelihood, the situation described in structural setting B is the one most closely approaching the present-day situation in India in 1978. The alternative structural setting A was based on past trends but only up to 1971; the overall economic situation in India has stagnated during 1971-8. For instance, 40 per cent of population were below the poverty line in 1971, but according to some estimates this has increased to 68 per cent in 1978. National income is growing by only 1 per cent annually. Distribution of income and wealth is increasingly concentrated among the privileged classes. The urban peasant sector has been rapidly growing but not the organized sector, and many big cities (like Calcutta) have already indicated net negative migration showing that they are saturated and overflowing. Unfortunately, the overall situation is fast approaching the involution described in setting B.

Conclusion

Many optimistic assessments have been made of the role of circulation in alleviating individual poverty and promoting rural development (e.g. Hugo 1977: 32-5), in diffusing modern urban values (Zachariah 1968: 338-44), or in relieving the pressures on towns (Dias 1977: 5-9). The findings of the present study in northern India reveal, on the other hand, that such wage labour circulation occurs from rural poverty to urban poverty, from one low productivity-cum-low wage rural peasant sector to another low productivity-cum-low wage urban peasant sector, and such movements do not permit escape from destitution-cum-downward social mobility. Neither are remittances adequate for relieving rural indebtedness (setting aside the question of rural development!), nor does one week's absence relieve the pressure in urban areas (putting aside the issue of diffusing modern values!). The crux of the matter is first to have an understanding that such widespread wage labour circulation in India is taking place as a spatial symptom of poverty and underdevelopment. It begins in poverty and ends in poverty, compounding further involution and underdevelopment. Referring back to the story of Halku, narrated in the beginning, a rickshawala remains at the same lowly position even after twelve or twenty or thirty years of urban residence. In the meantime, his sons and grandsons join him in the city to re-enact the same miserable drama of life. In short, such circulatory movement results in a massive waste of human potential both at the places of origin and destination, and both at the level of the individual movers themselves as well as for the country as a whole. If short but effective training was given to them, and if they were properly utilized they could have been transformed into an army of skilled workers to raise both per capita productivity and national productivity.

This paper makes dismal reading but concludes with an optimistic note. There must be a way out of this vicious circle of poverty and mobility. Answers to these problems do not lie simply in promoting other kinds of circulation (for instance, commuting from far-flung rural areas is unthinkable), but rather lies in alleviating some of the limiting conditions discussed in connexion with the process – especially in relieving village stagnation, rural-urban disparities, rural indebtedness, and concentrated land ownership patterns. It is in this context that Krishna's suggestions for land reforms, massive rural work programmes and employment generation in agricultural and non-agricultural sectors (both in rural and urban areas) are to be seen.

Some of the strategies which can be suitably adopted and implemented, if there is a political will and economic discipline, are elaborated elsewhere (Mukherji 1978: 60-90). Briefly these are land reforms, co-operative farming, rural reconstruction, massive employment generation, adoption of indigenous methods of production, labour-intensive industries, urban decentralization, restructuring of the space economy for a more even distribution of production units and services, low-level manpower utilization, migration restriction, expansion of internal domestic markets, and a more equitable distribution of income, wealth and levels of consumption among various strata of the society. Finally, strenuous efforts have to be made for rural industrialization (cottage, small scale and agro-industries) which would succeed in creating employment opportunities within the countryside, in restricting large-scale rural-urban migration and circulation, and absorbing the manpower locally. Only these will break the vicious circle of poverty and mobility.

Part IV
Economic perspectives

Most economic activities, domestic and otherwise, involve some element of circulatory movement for those participating in them. Circulation for domestic need is not illustrated in this section. For the most part it involves absence from home or from place of residence for a few hours and normally within one day, though within these times there may be movement over considerable distances. Activities such as fetching water and collecting firewood absorb considerable amounts of time and energy in Third World countries, particularly for women and children.

This section was planned to include a contribution on circulation for agricultural work, a form of rural-rural mobility to which little attention has been given. One of the few examples is the work of Ojo (1970, 1973) in south-west Nigeria on the movements of farmers from villages which are their permanent place of residence to farm settlements which vary in size and in their degree of permanence. Movements are made daily or weekly and sometimes absences are of longer duration.

While it was not possible to include a paper on this particular theme, that by Adrian Wood is concerned with movements which are made mainly for agricultural work. These movements to a pioneer fringe in the forest country of Illubabor in south-west Ethiopia are not of a commuting character; people have been drawn from near and far, the movements over longer distances being influenced by drought in the northern parts of the country in the early 1970s. They have come primarily to farm but also to trade and often these activities are combined. The paper is based on case materials for individuals and illustrates the problems of defining their intentions at the time when moves are made initially and these intentions as they are interpreted some time later. Wood has provided a rare example documenting these changes over time, making it possible to evaluate stated intentions, the use of which is one of the most controversial aspects of the present literature which is concerned with distinguishing circulation from migration.

In the last twenty years increased attention has been focused on research into the mechanisms for internal exchange at local, regional and national levels in Third World countries. Through markets indigenous and imported products are distributed. They absorb fully the time and energy of many people and part-time they involve a very large proportion of the population. Not only are goods exchanged but information and ideas are transferred through contacts made at markets; economic innovations and political opinions are diffused. Markets are important social as well as economic occasions.

In urban places exchanges take place in formal markets and even more through informal transactions, contributing to the processes of urban involution through which increasing numbers of people obtain economic support without comparable increases in resources. Through these exchanges there is much intra-urban circulation to which a number of papers in this volume refer. Research on market systems in rural areas has focused especially on their temporal characteristics, on the cycles and the rings which characterize the periodicity of market calendars. Rural markets result in the daily movements of large numbers of people who are drawn to them to sell and to buy; where there are regular periodic markets there are considerable movements of traders from one market to another extending over longer periods of time. Ray Bromley illustrates the periodic pattern of markets in the highlands of Ecuador and how they are arranged hierarchically. The higher-order markets offering wider ranges of goods and services, draw both traders and customers from more extensive catchment areas, and thus the spatial and temporal dimensions of circulation are increased. Modes of transport are related to the distances which people travel.

Occupations generate varying amounts of movement and many different types of mobility associated with them. Often those engaged in a particular occupation originate from a particular place from which they have diffused widely; for example, many of the grocers throughout Tunisia come from the island of Djerba, and many engaged in the same business in Morocco are from the Sousse valley in the south-west of the country. These are large-scale examples of occupation-specific mobility. Guy Ashton discusses the circulation of shoemakers (*zapateros*) who come from a small town in the Yucatan of Mexico and move to work for limited periods of time in neighbouring Belize. He traces the origin of this movement, and the economic and social advantages of going away to work as they affect both homeplace and place of employment. Young *zapateros* have learned to handle difficult situations in which they have been exploited to achieve advantage for themselves. They return from Belize with economic gains, socially more experienced and with a stronger sense of identity and attachment to their home place.

Within the last two decades movements between countryside and town have received the attention they deserve, but it may be argued that this has been to some extent at the expense of consideration being given to mobility in rural areas. The emphasis in rural-urban movement has been on migration, implying if not stating permanent changes in place of residence. The papers by Walter Elkan on Kenya and by Sidney and Alice Goldstein for Thailand examine aspects of the permanency of rural-urban movement.

Elkan worked at the micro-scale on circulatory movements in East Africa in the 1950s and 1960s, drawing attention to the policy implications of these and showing that circulation assisted and subsidized the growth of towns by reducing demands on services which could be ill-afforded if moves were permanent. Here he examines retrospectively semi-longitudinal evidence of varied character available for Nairobi. This shows that links between rural and urban areas remain strong. However the nature of these links and the form of circulation through which they are maintained have changed over time.

Conventional census data for the most part yield little information on movements which are circulatory. This deficiency results from census schedules which are based largely on experience derived outside the Third World. In recent years Sidney Goldstein has been stressing the need for fresh thinking and the development of new concepts in studying the movement and re-distribution of population. Here he and Alice Goldstein show how the existing data for two censuses in Thailand may be used to provide evidence of mobility associated with temporary absence rather than with permanent change of residence as might be assumed. The Thai censuses are unusual though not unique in providing data for such analysis and interpretation. They also permit a rather different emphasis than have other papers in this volume. It is valuable to be able to demonstrate, as the Goldsteins have done, the broad statistical patterns of circulation for a whole country.

This volume has been limited to studies of circulation in the Third World. However it is important to provide some examples of mobility which link countries of the Third World with one which is economically more developed. On the non-permanent movements of workers from countries in North Africa to Western Europe there is a substantial literature. Edward Douglas examines the movements between small island countries in the South Pacific and economically developed metropolitan New Zealand. The relative needs of each for the other are examined in the context of labour supply and demand, mediated by legislation and regulations of the New Zealand government. Such official sanctions are dealt with more specifically than in any other paper in the volume. When changes in political control and immigration regulations are placed in historical context it is possible to classify Pacific Islanders in New Zealand into various categories − visitors, guestworkers, sojourners and settlers. Given the extent to which political decisions have influenced this classification it is instructive to make comparisons with field typologies presented in other papers, where movement is more voluntary and less affected by official sanctions.

15 Settlement and circulation in a frontier region: Illubabor Province, south-west Ethiopia

Adrian P. Wood

Introduction

The expansion of settlement and the development of economic activity in a frontier region will stimulate a great variety of human mobility. Some people may move into a frontier zone with the intention of permanent settlement, fully committing themselves to their new area of residence. In these cases the movers are termed 'settlers'. Others may visit a frontier zone for only a few weeks; where this is so and the intention to return home is dominant, they may be called 'circulators'. Between these two a great variation exists in the intended length of residence in the frontier zone and the degree of commitment by the mover to the frontier zone and his home area. There may be further complexity because movers may alter their residence intentions from experience in the frontier zone and consequent adjustment of their material goals.

This study is concerned with the variety and alteration of residence intentions and material goals among persons who had moved into an expanded clearing on the forest fringe in the eastern part of Illubabor province, south-west Ethiopia. Discussion focuses upon the relevant importance of circulation in the frontier zone and its role in the settlement and economic development of the area.

The setting

Eastern Illubabor is part of the south-west highlands of Ethiopia. It is an undulating plateau, lying between 1,600m and 2,200m, dissected in the north by a number of deeply incised river valleys. Rainfall over most of the area exceeds 2,000mm and the wet season extends from March to November. Only January receives less than 50mm of rain. The natural vegetation is tropical montane evergreen forest in which the most important economic species are coffee (*Coffea arabica*) and the spice cardamom (*Afromomum angustifolium*). Both of these grow wild and are found in scattered localities. The forest, which covers two-thirds of eastern Illubabor, is most extensive in the south where it comprises part of the largest area of closed forest in the country, with only occasional clearings and agricultural communities. In the north clearance is extensive, although parts of the plateau and most of the river valleys remain forested (Figure 15.1).

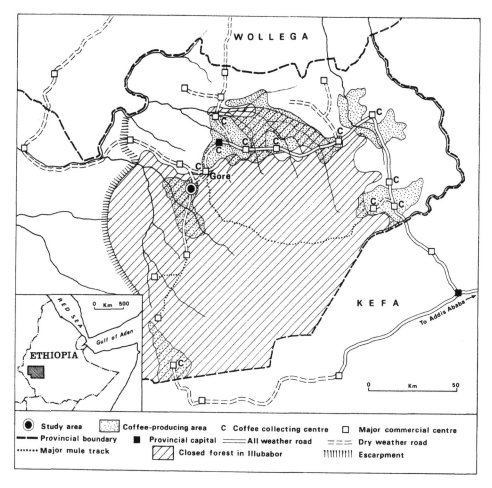

FIGURE 15.1 *Illubabor Province, Ethiopia: study area*

Rural population densities in eastern Illubabor range from 42 per sq.km in the north to 4 per sq.km in the south (Last 1965:

5). In the north the population is predominantly Oromo (Galla) while in the south the Shekatcho are the major group. There are also a number of Amharas from the northern highlands of Ethiopia who have settled in or near the urban centres of the province since its conquest in the late nineteenth century by the Emperor Menelik II. This conquest incorporated Illubabor into the Amhara-dominated empire and led to the alienation of land by the emperor primarily for distribution to those involved in the conquest and to the indigenous elite. In this way the majority of the farming population became tenants, although often their landlords were indigenous leaders. At the same time the state originally through the person of the emperor, became the holder of extensive areas of unallocated forest land (government land), which until 1974 were available for granting or sale.

The predominant economy of Illubabor is subsistence agriculture. Maize is the major staple with *teff* (*Eragrostis abyssinica*), the staple of the Amharas, of increasing importance. Despite the forested nature of much of eastern Illubabor, the ox-drawn scratch plough is used for cultivation. Crop rotation and fallowing are practised but there is no systematic manuring of fields. Consequently farmers often seek forested land to clear because it produces high yields, and also in some cases because this land does not require ploughing in the first years of cultivation and could be rent free for up to three years. Over the last three decades the clearance of forested land has increased as a result of population growth, rising aspirations and growing opportunities for the sale of surplus produce. At the same time as this has led to an increasing movement into the forest, the greater ease of access to markets and services which exists in the north of the province has attracted farmers from within the closed forest block to move towards the forest fringe. These two directions of spontaneous movement have led to a concentrated demand for agricultural land at the forest fringe and in clearings near the edge of the closed forest.

Thus a frontier of intensive clearance and relatively dense settlement can be identified which is moving predominantly southward in the north of the province and westward in the east. It is located on the edge of the closed forest (Figure 15.1), although the detailed pattern of the agricultural frontier is more complex with some expansion of the larger clearings within the closed forest. This pattern of recent clearance results from three influences. First, predators make crop protection difficult in isolated clearings. Secondly, prior to the land reform in 1975, many owners of forested land were absentees who were difficult for local farmers to contact and who for tax reasons did not want tenants. Finally, growing preference for access to urban centres for markets and services makes areas near to routes into the forest particularly attractive. Consequently, in the period before the revolution, clearance took place primarily in areas already partly settled, and/or on land owned by locally resident landlords, and only along major routes were extensive new clearings established.

While Illubabor is a frontier zone in the physical sense as a result of forest clearance for agriculture, the development of the collecting economy further highlights its frontier nature. Coffee, spices, and to a lesser extent honey have long been collected for sale to traders from outside the region (Abir, ch. 3 and 4). Rising prices and improving communications since the Italian occupation (1936-41) have facilitated the increased use and development of these resources. Today coffee is the most important forest product, its production having been expanded considerably through the transplanting of wild coffee bushes to form manageable plantations, often on formerly unused government land. This development of the collecting economy has increased penetration of the forest, with the coffee harvest in particular attracting large numbers of mostly seasonal labourers and traders from both within and outside the province. The frontier of settlement and resource utilization has been reinforced both directly through the temporary and permanent residence of these labourers and traders, and indirectly through them disseminating information concerning settlement opportunities there.

Perhaps of greater importance is the way in which the income generated by these forest products, and the trade and employment associated with them, have led to the rapid material and spatial expansion of the monetary economy. In 1950 monetary trade in the province was restricted to clothes, salt and a few other necessities, with permanent shops mainly in the 'coffee towns' in the north of the province where they were supported by the coffee plantation owners, their labourers and coffee traders. By 1973 monetary exchange in a wide range of commodities was established in the rural areas in the north of the province and was expanding into other areas. Thus a commercial frontier existed which was difficult to define but which was advancing primarily southward into the closed forest. Its progress was particularly rapid along the major trading routes, in the areas of coffee production and trade, and around the major centres of government employment.

The study area

Field study was carried out in 1973 and 1974, before the revolutionary changes which have since affected the rural areas of Ethiopia, in a village market centre and its surrounding clearing. This lay just inside the closed forest block some 30 kilometres south of Gore, the major centre of the coffee trade, to which it was connected by a dry-weather road (Figure 15.1). The cleared area was roughly star-shaped, at its maximum some six kilometres from north to south and eight kilometres from east to west. It contained 423 households, the majority living independently or in groups of two or three homesteads. Towards the northern edge of the clearing was the market place around which were clustered 72 buildings, mostly the homes of traders or craftsmen. The village contained one clothes shop, three small shops or kiosks (*suqs*) selling limited ranges of groceries and hardware, three drinking houses (*tej bet*) and one rest house for travellers. There were also a primary school and an Ethiopian Orthodox church.

Thirty-seven per cent of the heads of households (155 out of 423) had not been born in that area but had been resident there for over a year. They may be called 'frontier people' because through movement they had created a frontier in both physical and commercial senses. Frontier people were particularly important in the village community clustered around the market where they accounted for 76 per cent of the 51 household heads compared with 29 per cent in the other parts of the study area. This numerical importance was reinforced by the occupations they pursued which indicated their role in commercializing the rural economy, particularly through their capital and skills. Frontier people accounted for all who were in permanent employment as storekeepers, mill managers, coffee agents and the like (nine persons), and for 7 out of 8 of those with temporary employment, mainly in the coffee harvest. Among the self-employed they comprised 91 per cent (20 out of 22) of the traders and shop owners, and 3 out of 4 of the craftsmen, primarily tailors. In contrast only 30 per cent (110 out of 370) of the farmers in the study area were frontier people.

The majority of frontier people came from neighbouring areas to that studied; few came from more distant localities within Illubabor (Figure 15.2). However, 39 per cent (61 out of 155) were born outside Illubabor, most coming from areas in the northern highlands such as south-eastern Begemder, north-eastern Gojam and southern Shoa (Gurage), but also from neighbouring Wollega (Figure 15.3). All these areas have

307

traditional trade links with Illubabor (Abir 1968) and, with the exception of Wollega, more recent links as a result of the conquest and alienation of land in Illubabor to soldiers and administrators from them. Again with the exception of Wollega, these were rural areas where population pressure upon resources had become most severe as a result of Imperial neglect, rapid population growth and serious soil erosion.

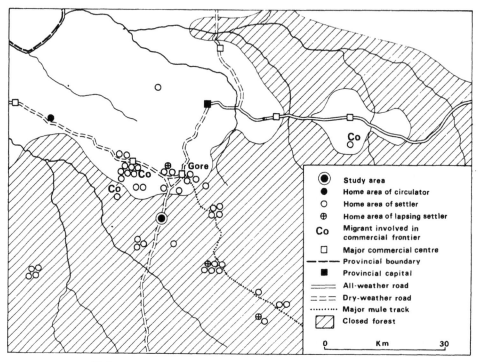

FIGURE 15.2 *Home areas of short-distance migrants*

Among frontier people 85 per cent (131 out of 155) of the heads of household were interviewed. However, as a number of these were children when they moved and had not been involved in the decision to do so, they are excluded from the following discussion. This reduced the study population to 96, of whom 47 were from within Illubabor (short-distance movers) and 49 from outside the province (long-distance movers).

The dates of arrival show that movement into the study area began in the late 1950s but was particularly marked in the late 1960s and early 1970s, although the arrival of short-distance movers is somewhat less peaked. This pattern primarily reflects improvements of the route south from Gore through the study area which were made in the early 1950s and the mid 1960s. The

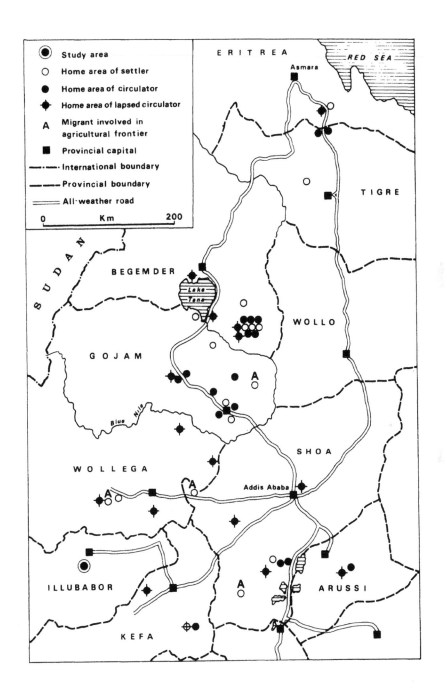

FIGURE 15.3 Home areas of long-distance migrants

309

less concentrated arrival of short-distance movers is a result of the differences in motivation between the two groups which are closely connected to their personal characteristics and circumstances at the time of moving. Among short-distance movers, who were primarily Oromo, all but three were established farmers when they moved and 70 per cent were married and moved with their families. Some of their movement was caused by the start of the commercialization of agriculture in the late 1960s and early 1970s, but other causes were social and ecological problems whose incidence is relatively constant and hence the less concentrated pattern of arrival. In contrast to the short-distance movers of whom only 64 per cent were in the 15 to 35 age range on arrival, long-distance movers were predominantly young, single men; 84 per cent were in the age range 15 to 35, only 37 per cent were married and only 2 of these brought their wives. They were mainly interested in trade and employment opportunities in the commercial frontier, and hence their movement was concentrated in the periods of most rapid commercial development which followed the improvements of communications.

The intended mobility of frontier people

Information concerning the residence intentions of frontier people on arrival was obtained as part of an interview schedule which focused on their migration histories, motivations for moving and adaptations and establishment. The information concerning movers' intentions at time of arrival was obtained through questions concerning the objectives or goals which they sought at the frontier and the methods of obtaining them. These questions were asked in association with others concerned with the decision to move. This focus upon the time of movement, together with the fact that many goals determined the form of mobility pursued, helped to ensure the accuracy of responses. However, in answering questions concerning decisions and intentions which in many cases were more than ten years old there must have been some element of *post facto* rationalization of the influences on the decision to move, the objectives sought and intended mobility in the light of the movers' experiences in the frontier. In a few cases anomalous answers revealed this tendency and clarification was obtained but it is doubtful if all such cases were identified. Further, although in many cases intended mobility was explained by movers' goals and their methods for achieving them, in other cases this depended on personal traits, family relationships and cultural ties about which it was difficult to obtain adequate information.

Bearing in mind these qualifications, the responses obtained do allow generalizations to be made concerning the motivations, objectives and intended mobility of frontier people on arrival. These are discussed with respect to the agricultural and commercial frontiers of Illubabor (Table 15.1 and Table 15.2).

The agricultural frontier

Among frontier people 50 per cent (48 persons) had moved with the objective of obtaining agricultural land and, with one exception, permanent resettlement was intended. The majority of these movers (44 persons) were born in Illubabor (Table 15.1, columns 1 and 5; Figure 15.2).

To most of the farmers from within Illubabor, who were moving from small clearings in the closed forest with declining populations, the frontier offered opportunities for cultivation where more extensive clearance facilitated crop guarding and reduced predations by wild animals. It was also attractive because with more tenants on a *gasha* (40 ha.) each person's share of the land-tax (which landlords passed on) was smaller than in remote clearings with few tenants per *gasha*. Similarly farmers from the north of the province sought relief from agricultural problems by moving to the frontier where high crop yields could be obtained through the clearance and cultivation of forested land, and the reduced competition for land resulted in lower rents and greater security of tenure. While 56 per cent (24 out of 43) of the short-distance permanent movement to the agricultural frontier was undertaken to solve specific farming problems 16 per cent (7 persons) was in search of opportunities for economic advancement (Table 15.2, columns 1 and 2).

To some farmers moving out of the forest the frontier's attraction of better communications and easier access to market were crucial pre-conditions for the more commercially-orientated farming they sought. In other cases the frontier contained the most accessible forested, and hence low-priced, land which was available for granting or for purchase. The remaining twelve short-distance settlers moved either to fulfil kinship obligations (2 cases), for marriage (2 cases), or to obtain assistance from friends and relatives in old age, ill health and times of difficulty (8 cases) (Table 15.2, columns 1 and 2). In these cases the direction of movement was determined by the location of friends and relatives rather than by the characteristics of the frontier. In fact this location of friends and relatives is of more general importance as most of the other short-distance movers chose their precise destination, within the general direction determined

311

TABLE 15.1 *Intended mobility and frontier involvement of frontier people on arrival*

Intended mobility / Frontier involvement	Frontier people								
	Short-distance migrants			Long-distance migrants			Total		
	No.	% a	b	No.	% a	b	No.	% a	b
Settlement, total	46	97.9		16	32.7		62	64.6	
Agricultural frontier	43	91.5	89.6	4	8.2	8.3	47	49.0	97.9
Commercial frontier	3	6.4	6.3	12	24.5	25.0	15	15.6	31.3
Circulation, total	1	2.1		33	67.3		34	35.4	
Agricultural frontier	1	2.1	2.1	0			1	1.0	2.1
Commercial frontier	0			33	67.3	68.8	33	34.4	68.8

(a) is percentage by origin of migrants – short-distance, long-distance or total
(b) is percentage within total migrants to each frontier – agricultural or commercial

TABLE 15.2 *Objectives of frontier people on arrival*

Objectives	Short-distance migrants			Long-distance migrants			Total		
	No.	%a	%b	No.	%a	%b	No.	%b	%c
Settlers									
Agricultural frontier									
Solution of agricultural problems	24	55.8	51.1	1	25.0	2.0	25	26.0	40.3
Economic advancement	7	16.3	14.9	3	75.0	6.1	10	10.4	16.1
Assistance and social obligations	12	27.9	25.5	0			12	12.5	19.4
Commercial frontier									
Independence from parents	1	33.0	2.1	5	41.7	10.2	6	6.3	9.7
Advancement in trade	2	66.0	4.3	4	33.3	8.2	6	6.3	9.7
Improved returns for employment	0			3	25.0	6.1	3	3.1	4.8
Circulators									
Agricultural frontier									
Capital for agriculture	1	100.0	2.1	0			1	1.0	2.9
Commercial frontier									
Independence from parents	0			16	48.5	32.7	16	16.7	47.1
Capital for agriculture	0			7	21.2	14.3	7	7.3	20.6
Advancement in trade (by traders)	0			4	12.1	8.2	4	4.2	11.8
Advancement into trade (by farmers)	0			4	12.1	8.2	4	4.2	11.8
Contract employment	0			2	6.1	4.1	2	2.1	5.9

(a) is percentage within sub group, e.g. short-distance settlers in agricultural frontier
(b) is percentage by origin of migrants – short-distance, long-distance or total
(c) is percentage within total settlers and total circulators

313

by their goals, on the basis of information concerning the availability of land from friends and relatives, their offers of introductions to landlords and other assistance.

All but one of the short-distance agricultural movers reported their moves to be permanent; partly because many of their goals could only be achieved, or were most easily achieved, by permanent settlement; and partly because established farmers with families were anxious to avoid facing again the difficulties of moving and obtaining land. Having moved only short distances most of the settlers were able to maintain regular links with friends and relatives in their home areas, thus reducing the social disruptions and perhaps facilitating permanent settlement. The only circulator was from a Moslem community in the north of the province to which he was intent on returning because he disliked living in a predominantly forested area among non-Moslems. He had been prepared to move into the frontier for only a few years in order to accumulate capital for the purchase of oxen (Table 15.2, columns 1 and 2).

The four long-distance agricultural movers were settlers who appeared to have moved more in response to information concerning the availability and quality of agricultural land in Illubabor than as a result of land shortage and other difficulties in their home areas (Table 15.2, columns 4 and 5). Their movement to the frontier seems to have been a speculative search to satisfy rising aspirations and with the intention of permanent settlement provided land was obtained. All but one of these settlers were single at the time they moved, presumably because of the distance and high risks involved. Only one moved to the frontier to solve an immediate agricultural problem; because of famine in his home area he moved with his family, helped by his knowledge of the frontier before moving and the relatively short journey from his home in neighbouring Wollega.

The commercial frontier

Fifty per cent of the frontier people (48 persons) had moved to take advantage of commercial and employment opportunities. In contrast to the agricultural movers, 69 per cent of those moving to the commercial frontier were circulators and 94 per cent were from outside Illubabor (Table 15.1, column 8; Figure 15.3). All those moving from within Illubabor were settlers, hence all the circulators associated with the commercial frontier were from outside the province (Table 15.1, columns 1 and 5 respectively).

Among the 15 movers who intended to settle permanently in

the commercial frontier three were from within Illubabor (Figure 15.2). They had moved into the forest in response to the growing opportunities for trade resulting from the commercialization of the rural economy and increased rural incomes associated with the development of the coffee forests. All three had chosen to settle at one locality rather than engage in lucrative itinerant trade because of family commitments or limited knowledge of the frontier. Two were established traders who also moved because of increasing competition from immigrant traders in their home areas, while the third, a young single man, had chosen to trade as competition for land had made it difficult for him to obtain a tenancy in his own right in his birth-place (Table 15.2, columns 1 and 2).

The twelve long-distance settlers had also responded to opportunities both for advancement in the occupations they pursued and for establishing themselves independently (Table 15.2, columns 4 and 5). Four among these were traders or farmers with trading experience wanting to settle in the Gore area after receiving detailed information about the favourable trading situation there. Another three were skilled and semi-skilled workers, mostly from Gojam, who also found attractive openings in the frontier where higher wages were offered for skills such as milling, and where posts of responsibility could be obtained with entrepreneurs and landlords from their home province who had interests in Illubabor. The largest group was of five young men who in their home areas had been dependent upon their parents or relatives for support for land and farming equipment. For them trade and employment opportunities in the frontier were means of obtaining economic independence.

All these movers envisaged permanent settlement in the frontier because of expected high returns from trade and employment. Among the long-distance settlers, permanent settlement was facilitated by the facts that 75 per cent were single when they moved and that 67 per cent had had travel experience outside their home areas before moving permanently to Illubabor. The latter fact was particularly important in helping the settlers realize that permanent settlement outside their home areas was possible and it indicated an important change of opinion in view of the strong traditional regional ties in Ethiopia (Levine 1965: 49-50).

Among the 33 long-distance circulators the most important attraction of the frontier was the prospect of obtaining economic independence. Sixteen of these circulators were young men who had been dependent on their families (Table 15.2, columns 4 and 5). Primarily through trade, particularly in spices, secondly

315

through employment in the coffee harvest, and, for a few, through tailoring, they planned to accumulate funds with which to establish themselves independently on their return home. Half of them planned to invest their savings in trade or tailoring, a quarter intended to farm and the remainder had no specific plans. Choice of occupation on returning home was apparently influenced by the agricultural situation in their home areas. Those from areas of severe population pressure upon farming resources had a higher preference for trade than those with similar agricultural backgrounds from other areas.

The second largest group among these circulators were seven established farmers, who through employment in the coffee harvest or trading sought capital, mainly to replace oxen killed by disease (Table 15.2, columns 4 and 5). Smaller groups of farmers and traders, each of four persons, sought to improve their standards of living by accumulating capital through trading in the frontier. The traders planned to increase the scale of their operations when they returned home, while the farmers, disillusioned with agriculture and seeking larger incomes, hoped to take up trading. A further two circulators came to the frontier on contract employment arranged outside Illubabor.

In all these cases circulation rather than permanent settlement in the frontier was planned; partly because limited travel experience among the younger long-distance movers caused concern over conditions in the frontier and a lack of confidence in permanent settlement there, and partly because of agricultural, trading and family commitments in their home areas.

The alteration of intended frontier residence and associated goals

While the opportunities in the frontier as perceived by different movers produced a range of mobility this variety was increased by the alteration of material goals and/or residence intentions after arrival. Change occurred partly because increasing length of residence in the frontier altered movers' knowledge and perception of the frontier and their home areas, and partly because of changes in personal circumstances and aspirations. Alterations were investigated by comparing intended mobility on arrival with that given in response to a question concerning future mobility in the light of movers' evaluation of the area at the time of the survey. The data obtained are limited by mis-reporting of goals and residence intentions held on arrival by movers who, influenced by the mobility they had actually pursued and the goals they had achieved by the time of the survey, had 'forgotten'

TABLE 15.3 *Intended mobility and frontier involvement of frontier people at time of survey (1973-4)*

Frontier people

Intended mobility / Frontier involvement	Short-distance movers No. (1)	% a (2)	a (3)	b (4)	Long-distance movers No. (5)	% a (6)	a (7)	b (8)	Total No. (9)	% a (10)	a (11)	b (12)
Settlement, total	43	91.5			30	61.2			73	76.0		
Agricultural frontier	40		85.1	66.5	15*		30.6	24.2	55		57.3	88.7
Commercial frontier	3 (all original)		6.4	8.8	15**		30.6	44.1	18		18.8	52.9
Circulation, total	4	8.5			17	34.7			21	21.9		
Agricultural frontier	4 (1 original + 3 lapsing settlers)		8.5	6.5	3 (originally commercial frontier circulators)		6.1	4.8	7		7.3	11.3
Commercial frontier	0				14***		28.6	41.2	14		14.6	41.2
Onward movement within frontier, total	0				2				2			
Commercial frontier	0				2 (lapsing commercial settlers)	4.1			2		2.1	5.9

(a) is percentage by origin of migrants – short-distance, long-distance or total
(b) is percentage within total migrants to each frontier – agricultural or commercial

*   4 original + 3 commercial settlers + 8 circulators
**   7 original + 8 circulators
*** Remaining commercial circulators out of 33

Note: the two circulators considering settling are included among the settlers their original plans. Similarly, responses concerning future mobility only record movers' stated intentions. However, the responses which were obtained show some clear trends in the alteration of goals and residence intentions which qualify the previous discussion above (compare Table 15.1 and Table 15.3).

Circulators

At the time of the survey, among the 34 movers who had intended circulating, 14 per cent had settled permanently in the frontier and another two were considering this. All were long-distance movers (Table 15.3, column 5). In general they had been away from their homes longer (average 21 years) than those who intended still to circulate (average 8 years), and their average age was 47 compared with 30. Although there was little difference between the two groups in the proportions having wives in their home areas, the majority of those who were settled had taken local wives in the frontier as compared with just over a half among those who remained circulators. Change to permanent settlement would seem to be associated with the lengths of absence from home and residence in the frontier, but ethnic origin and access to land in home areas also appear important. 86 per cent of the Oromo circulators decided to settle in the frontier, compared with only 33 per cent of Amhara circulators. This is explained partly by the fact that the former speak the same language as the resident population in the frontier which facilitates integration into the local community. Integration for Amharas is difficult, not only because of language difference but also because they are disliked by the Oromo who still recall the conquest and the subsequent alienation of land. Amhara circulators may also have been discouraged from settling in Illubabor because before the 1975 land reform many of them held *rist* rights to land in their home areas, rights which were not lost by a period of absence (Hoben 1973: 23). Only 25 per cent of the circulators from areas of *rist* tenure settled permanently in the frontier compared with 69 per cent of those from non-*rist* areas.

Three main groups of reasons can be identified for circulators who had settled permanently in the frontier. In two cases settlement was adopted after a number of years because of failure to accumulate the capital sought. Rather than return home in such circumstances both goals and residence intentions were altered with lower status occupations than those they had hoped to pursue if they had returned home. However, for the majority (9 persons) permanent settlement was chosen because of their economic success in trade, agriculture, or in other

318

employment. Many of these had carefully used the knowledge they gained while living in the frontier, moving from one locality to another as they learned of opportunities for their skills and acquiring capital. Most progressed from employment in the coffee harvest, through trade in spices which needs little capital, to finally establish themselves as traders or farmers. The four who had decided to stay because of trading opportunities had previously planned to invest their capital in farming on returning home. The two contract employees were attracted by the high crop yields in the frontier, although one had not taken up farming as his major occupation by 1976. Three who had planned to farm on returning home were encouraged to stay because they had obtained farm land in the frontier. The remaining three appeared to have drifted into permanent settlement; they had been encouraged to prolong their intended stay by their success in accumulating capital, by the presence of friends from their birth-places, and by marriage. Although they had maintained for many years their intentions of circulating in the end they found that they had too many commitments in the frontier and too much to lose by returning to their home areas, about which, by the time of the survey, they knew less than they did about the frontier.

Of the circulators who had changed their intention and settled, none had visited their home areas since arriving in the frontier, but one-third of those who still professed to be circulators had done so. These were visits by recent arrivals primarily to take money to their wives and families, and by persons who had been resident in the frontier for many years to renew social and kin ties which would facilitate an eventual return. As only one of these circulators had married since arriving in the frontier these visits appear to be a clear indication of intentions to return home eventually. Among the remaining twelve who still intended circulation but who had not undertaken such visits, 62 per cent had married since arriving in the frontier and 46 per cent had started farming. It appeared that a proportion of these circulators were in fact drifting into permanent settlement and only vaguely retained the intention of returning home in the event of economic hardship and ethnic or political conflict.

Settlers

While the identification of true circulators is difficult, the permanency of residence in the frontier by a number of settlers is also questionable. Among the settlers, five out of 62 reported that they were considering moving. Although this alteration of

319

residence intentions is smaller than that among circulators, it may be a considerable underestimation as settlers who had decided not to settle permanently in the frontier would no longer be found there. Of the five settlers planning to move, three were farmers from within Illubabor who planned to return home to be near relatives who needed assistance or from whom assistance was expected (Table 15.3, column 1; Figure 15.2). The other two were long-distance settlers who were considering moving to other localities in Illubabor in search of better trading opportunities and facilities respectively (Table 15.3, column 5). These five cases re-emphasize the role of mobility in the frontier areas as a means of adjustment to changing environmental and economic conditions, of satisfying rising aspirations, and of meeting individuals' needs and social obligations.

These benefits from mobility suggest that despite original mobility intentions it would be unrealistic to expect all settlers to remain at their destinations. Indeed, among short-distance settlers there was a considerable potential for circulation and resettlement in their birth-places. This results from the fact that relatives are the only persons from whom to request assistance and who are also a major source of information concerning the availability of land. The likelihood of circulation is increased by the visits to relatives and friends in their home areas which 26 out of 43 of the remaining short-distance settlers made at least once a year. Although such visits may facilitate permanent settlement in the frontier by reducing the disruptions to movers' social lives, it is more probable that they reduce their commitments to the new area of residence, and the links which they create facilitate circulation in the event of movement proving necessary in the future.

There appeared to be a similar, but smaller, potential for circulation among settlers from outside Illubabor. An unexpectedly high proportion of them, 7 out of 16, had visited their home areas since settling in the frontier, and another two proposed to do so. Most of these visits had been undertaken to fulfil social obligations − attending funerals and other celebrations and assisting parents. In these cases in view of the considerable distances involved (Figure 15.3) and the interest which these settlers expressed about their home areas, it is clear that such visits represented a reduced commitment to the frontier. Such a supposition is supported by the fact that all these settlers found it difficult to adapt to some aspect of the frontier, particularly the forested terrain and its remoteness. Those engaged in trade were also aware of the violent fluctuations in their fortunes which could occur and leave them destitute away

320

from the assistance of relatives. Some traders, particularly Amharas, were conscious of the friction with the local community caused by their accumulation of wealth. Thus it appeared that despite their stated intentions a number of these settlers doubted the viability of permanent settlement in the frontier and sought security by maintaining sufficient ties with their home areas to allow them to return there should the need arise.

Circulation and the frontier

In 1973 movement into the frontier zone in Illubabor was an important phenomenon. Among movers who had resided in the frontier for over one year circulation had been the intention on arrival of 35.4 per cent and was at the time of the survey the intention of 21.9 per cent (Table 15.3, column 10). There was also a considerable potential for circulation among those intending to settle permanently in the frontier. However, this is only part of the circulation which occurred in the early 1970s for the survey excluded circulation which involved less than a year's residence in the frontier and which took place within the study area.

Of these omissions the most important is the seasonal circulation associated with the coffee harvest. In Illubabor in the early 1970s this probably involved some 30,000 persons, given that neighbouring Kefa with a higher coffee output is thought to have had 50,000 seasonal coffee pickers (Bondestam 1972: 9). These circulators were mainly coffee pickers and traders but also included coffee plantation owners, and prostitutes. The majority came from within Illubabor but possibly up to one-third were from other provinces, especially Begemder, Gojam and Shoa. Circulation connected with the coffee harvest varied considerably; that by local farmers to pick coffee usually involved movement over limited distances, often with daily circulation to coffee plantations in forest near their farms. Such circulation was preferred partly because the coffee harvest coincides with the preparation of land for maize, the food staple in eastern Illubabor, and partly because lucrative share-cropping arrangements rather than wage employment could be obtained only where a farmer was able to tend the coffee bushes throughout the year and was trusted by the plantation owner. Circulation by long-distance coffee pickers involved their movement first to the 'coffee towns' in the north of Illubabor where they were recruited by plantation owners or their agents before moving to the plantation where they camped during the harvest. The owners who recruited their pickers in this manner were mainly from

321

outside Illubabor and appear to have had some preference for employing people from their own home areas. Most of the traders, plantation owners and prostitutes who circulated during the coffee harvest came from outside Illubabor. The latter stayed in the 'coffee towns', while the plantation owners divided their time between the towns and their land, and the traders spent most of their time visiting markets and farmers to buy coffee.

Also omitted from this study is the regular circulation of traders within Illubabor in the seven-day market cycles in the forest fringe, and the more irregular circulation of traders from the grain-surplus areas in the north of the province to the grain-deficit coffee-producing ones. There was also much local circulation by farmers visiting markets and relatives and engaging temporarily in trade following the coffee harvest.

Conclusions

Circulation in the frontier in Illubabor resulted from the opportunities provided in trade, employment and farming, and the relatively good returns offered. These were attractive because of the growing perceived needs for income supplementation and capital accumulation in many parts of the country as a result of population growth, rising aspirations and the stagnation of peasant agriculture. However, the majority of movers attracted by these opportunities did not stay permanently. This was for three reasons. First, the repelling characteristics of the frontier, including problems of animal predations, the 'strange' forested environment, the high rainfall which can make itinerant trading difficult and hazardous, and the potential for ethnic conflict given the political history of the area. Secondly, circulation was caused by the social and economic ties of movers to their home areas. These prevented the consideration of goals which required permanent settlement, and caused intending settlers to return home in search of, or in response to relatives' requests for, assistance. Finally, circulation occurred because some of the opportunities in the frontier could only provide a seasonal livelihood. This, combined with the difficulties in obtaining supplementary income for the rest of the year, caused movers who could cope with the repelling characteristics of the frontier and who had no ties in their home areas nevertheless to stay in the frontier for only a few months.

Despite their temporary residence, circulators played important roles in the frontier with both their labour and skills and through the dissemination of information. The development of the coffee forests in the late 1950s and 1960s was particularly rapid because, through the circulation of traders, soldiers and administrators earlier in the century this potential was well-known before rising coffee prices and improvements in communications made the establishment of plantations attractive. Traders also created widespread awareness both within Illubabor and beyond of the trade and employment opportunities and this led to a plentiful supply of traders and pickers at low wage rates to further encourage development. Long-distance circulation of traders and coffee pickers was also instrumental in consolidating the commercial frontier by providing information about conditions to traders and skilled labourers who were prepared to settle permanently. Conversely, short-distance circulation played the major role in the expansion of the agricultural frontier through the dissemination of information concerning the availability of land, although it also contributed to the expansion of the commercial frontier through the involvement of farmers in the coffee harvest.

Postscript

The circulation described in this paper occurred in south-west Ethiopia before the 1974 revolution and was influenced by the pre-revolutionary social, economic and political conditions. Changes since 1974 have affected population mobility in the area and have led primarily to a major reduction in long-distance circulation. This has been due mainly to a revival in ethnic rivalry and a desire among indigenous groups to control the economic resources of Illubabor. Immediately after the revolution these led to the expulsion of many alien landlords and traders from the rural areas. Long-distance circulation has also been discouraged by the nationalization of rural lands and the formation of Farmers' Associations (Ethiopian Government 1975). In Illubabor the coffee plantations are now operated by the Farmers' Associations who in the early years after the revolution mainly used their members to harvest the crop. Whether this was due to the absence of circulators because of the situation for aliens in the province, the shortage of funds to employ pickers, or 'economic nationalism', is not clear. The last influence together with a socialist drive against 'exploitative' traders has encouraged Farmers' Associations to establish trading concerns and market their own coffee, thus further reducing the opportunities for long-distance circulators.

Short-distance movement by farmers within Illubabor has also been affected by the nationalization of land and the control of its distribution by the Farmers' Associations. They are charged with

323

redistributing land to ensure equality of holdings among their members and have been unwilling to allocate land to people from outside their Association until this redistribution is completed. As a result local mobility, including circulation for social obligations and the like has probably been reduced.

The prospects for circulation in the frontier in Illubabor are uncertain. Revived ethnic rivalry has reduced the attractions of the frontier for long-distance circulators, while economic nationalism has reduced the opportunities. However, as Farmers' Associations with coffee lands become wealthy some employment of coffee pickers may take place; the ethnic bias of the past which ensured the recruitment of persons from outside Illubabor will probably be reversed. At the same time the need for circulation may decline if the rural development schemes can offer effective means whereby those who would otherwise be long-distance circulators can increase their incomes in their home areas. Long-distance circulations seem likely to remain below the 1973 level, but the volume of short-distance movement, including circulation, may rise back to or even above pre-revolutionary levels once Farmers' Associations complete the redistribution of land. Although charged with the preservation of the nation's forest resources, the Associations are also to allocate land to farmers in need and no longer will mobility be constrained by the problems of contacting absentee landlords or finding other tenants with whom to share the land tax for this is now abolished.

16 Circulation within systems of periodic and daily markets: the case of Central Highland Ecuador

Ray Bromley

Market-place trade is an important component of internal commerce in most countries, and is particularly significant in the commercial activities of low- and middle-income households in much of Africa, Asia, and Latin America. The gatherings of buyers and sellers of commodities which take place regularly in a public market-place are usually known as 'markets', and the settlements in which one or more markets are held each week can be described as 'market centres'.[1] On the basis of their periodicity, markets may be divided into two groups; 'daily markets', which take place on every day, or at least on every working day, of the week; and, 'periodic markets' which occur regularly on one or more fixed days each week. When a centre has more than one periodic market day each week, the day with the highest level of activity is the 'major market day'. In many market centres, small daily markets are supplemented on one, two or three days each week by more substantial periodic market gatherings, and even in those centres which have major daily markets, there are usually regular small day-to-day variations in market activity, adding a periodic element to the daily gatherings.

The majority of persons in a market-place are either 'consumers', who are buying goods or services for consumption or use, or 'traders', who are buying and/or selling goods or services for business purposes. Traders who deal only in one market centre are 'fixed', while those who regularly deal in more than one centre are 'mobile'.

Systems of periodic and daily markets

The market centres of a region can be visualized together as a hierarchical central place system articulated by flows of people

325

and commodities between producing, consuming, bulking, distributing, transit and exchange points. Within any given market system, there are pressures both for the foundation of new centres, and for the concentration of activity in some of the existing centres with a corresponding decline in other centres. The key variables in this situation are the sizes, populations and levels of consumer demand of the trade areas of the existing market centres, the nature of the transport system, and the costs of movement for passengers and goods. At each level in the central place system, therefore, an approximate equilibrium is reached between two conflicting pressures: a pressure to concentrate activities in fewer and larger centres so as to achieve greater scale economies and variety of goods and services at the expense of increased travel for many consumers; and, a pressure for the proliferation of small centres so as to reduce the distance travelled by most consumers, at the cost of forgoing many scale economies and reducing the variety of goods and services available in most centres (Symanski and Bromley 1974).

In conditions of rudimentary transport technology, the numbers and sizes of centres in the upper reaches of central place hierarchies are likely to be limited by the effort and cost of moving people and commodities long distances to, and from, large markets. Modern communications, and particularly road transport, have greatly reduced the friction of distance in many parts of the less developed countries, facilitating the restructuring of internal market systems. It becomes cheaper and easier to visit the larger centres, consumers concentrate their purchases in these centres and neglect the smaller ones. The larger centres increase in size and number while some of the smaller centres decline and eventually lose their central functions. In most less developed countries, this tendency towards a restructuring of the hierarchy of market centres is reinforced by rapid population growth and urbanization, and also by increasing division of labour and consumption of higher-order manufactured goods.

Within systems of periodic and daily markets, there are a wide variety of cyclical movements by both traders and consumers. All traders are also at times consumers, and the two categories may sometimes effectively merge into one. In general, however, a distinction between traders and consumers is a useful one and it has important implications in terms of circulatory mobility and total time spent in the market-place. Traders tend to spend more time in the market-place, to travel further in order to trade, and to visit more different market centres on a regular basis, than do consumers.

326

Central highland Ecuador

Central highland Ecuador, an area of about 22,000 sq. km, ranges in altitude from 1,500 metres to well above the altitudinal limits of cultivation at around 3,500 metres, with a few peaks rising to over 5,000 metres. The region was studied in 1970-2 a wider research project on 'periodic and daily markets in highland Ecuador' (Bromley 1975).

In 1972 the Central Highlands had an estimated population of 1.05 million, with an average density of 48 per square km, and 16.7 per cent living in urban areas (nucleated settlements with over 5,000 inhabitants).[2] About 82 per cent of the population lives in the Inter-Andean Valley between the Eastern and Western Cordilleras, in the basins of the Rivers Patate and Chambo which join to form the Pastaza and drain eastward to the Amazon, or in the basin of the River Chan Chan, which drains westward to the Pacific. Almost all of the remaining 18 per cent of the region's population live on the outer, western slopes of the Western Cordillera in the basins of the Rivers Toachi, Angamarca, and Chimbo which drain to the Pacific. In such mountainous terrain, population distribution is very uneven, dense clusters of population in the more fertile and level basin, plateau and terrace areas are separated by sparsely populated gorges, mountains, and montane forests and moorlands.

The region includes all of the provinces of Cotopaxi (capital Latacunga), Tungurahua (capital Ambato), Chimborazo (capital Riobamba), and Bolívar (capital Guaranda), above an altitude of 1,500 metres. It is separated from the neighbouring regions (the Northern Highlands, the Southern Highlands, the Coastal Lowlands, and the Amazonian Lowlands) by substantial tracts of sparsely populated or uninhabited mountain and forest terrain. Commercial links between the Central Highlands and neighbouring regions are strong, particularly with the capital city of Quito (1974 population 599,828), in the Northern Highlands, and the port city of Guayaquil (1974 population 823,219) in the Coastal Lowlands. The towns in the Central Highlands (defined as nucleated settlements with over 5,000 inhabitants) and their 1974 populations (INEC 1976-7) in rank order are: Ambato (77,955), Riobamba (58,087), Latacunga (21,921), Guaranda (11,364), Alausí (7,137), and Guano (5,389). The region is located within 3° latitude of the Equator and has little temperature variation from month to month. It is usually somewhat rainier during the coastal wet season (November to May), but only in areas west of the Western Cordillera with dry-season roads does this produce any major reduction in levels of participation in markets.

The Central Highland population is divided ethnically and culturally into 'whites' and Indians. 'Whites' are Spanish-speaking and notionally of European descent, while Indians are notionally of indigenous Amerindian descent and may speak only Quechua (the only surviving indigenous language in the region), or be bilingual in Quechua and Spanish. However, processes of miscegenation and cultural interaction over more than four centuries since the Spanish conquest of the region have led to a blurring of both ethnic and cultural distinctions, though ethnic 'labels' and stereotypes are still used to make what are now essentially socio-cultural distinctions (Bromley 1975: 80-8; Pitt-Rivers 1967: 549). To be 'white' is generally considered of higher social status than to be Indian, though both 'white' and Indian societies are stratified by differences in wealth, income and power. In general, 'whites' are more prosperous than Indians, are the majority of the populations of the towns and villages, and control most of the main economic activities and resources in the region. The Indians make up the majority of the rural population though they own only a small proportion of the farmland, mainly in small peasant farms of under two hectares.

In 1970-2, there were moderately high correlations between the populations and administrative status of nucleated settlements and their importance as market centres (Bromley 1975, 153-73). The importance of each market centre on each day of the week is measured in terms of total trading units, and the overall importance of each centre is calculated by adding the totals of trading units for each of the seven days to produce a weekly total.[3] Market centres are ranked on a logarithmic scale in terms of total trading units per week; first-order 10-99 units; second order 100-999 units; third-order 1000-9999 units; and, fourth-order 10000-99999 units. Of the 74 market centres in 1971, 39 were first-order, 23 were second-order, 10 were third-order, and only two were fourth-order (Figure 16.1). Only five centres, all of them first- or second-order and located in fairly remote areas, were not served by at least one all-weather road, and only one of these did not have even a dry-season road. There were roughly 8,600 motor vehicles in the region in 1972, one to every 122 inhabitants (INE 1973). However, most of these vehicles were owned and exclusively used by the wealthier members of the urban population. Only about 2,000 vehicles were even occasionally used for 'public' goods and passenger transport to, from and between market centres.

All 74 market centres had produce trading (in goods and

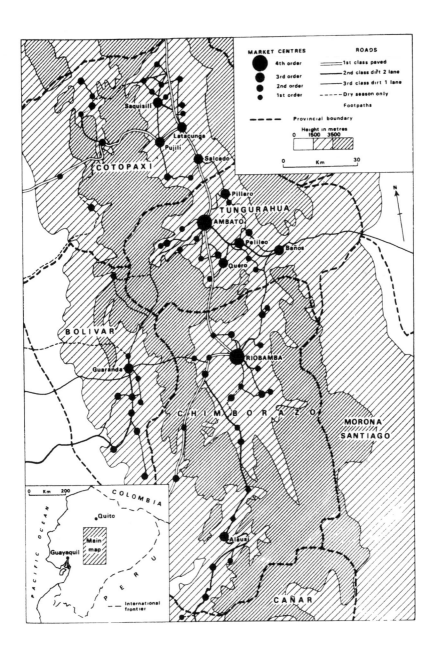

FIGURE 16.1 Central Highland Ecuador: market centres and road network

329

services other than livestock) and 35 of them also had livestock trading (in cattle, pigs and sheep, and in a few cases also goats, horses, mules, donkeys, or llamas). A great variety of produce was traded from basic consumption items such as potatoes, flour, meat, cooking fat, clothes and shoes, to more exotic and luxury goods like transistor radios and touristic folk weavings, and personal services such as shoe-shines, hair-cuts and knife-grinding. The complete list of goods and services in any of the larger market centres would run to several thousand items, reflecting the variety of local production, and to a much greater extent the diversity of local consumption and the significance of imports or products from outside the region, particularly tropical foodstuffs from coastal Ecuador and manufactured goods from North America and the Far East. Produce trading was about double the importance of livestock trading and was the main concern of the great majority of persons in the markets, and calculations of the importance of different centres are based on studies of produce trading.

Market movement censuses

Market movement censuses conducted in twelve centres on major periodic market days, and sometimes also on some or all of the remaining days in a week, show how circulation is oriented around the cyclically changing patterns of produce market activity on each of the seven days of the week (Figure 16.2), and the day-to-day variations in produce market activity of third- and fourth-order centres (Figure 16.3). Centres were chosen for study by purposive sampling; two were fourth-order (Ambato and Riobamba), five were third-order (Saquisilí, Pujilí, Latacunga, Pelileo, and Quero), three were second-order (Zumbahua, Penipe, and Salarón), and two were first-order (Huambaló and Tanicuchí).

The censuses measured the flow of people, vehicles and livestock into each centre during the build-up period of market activity, commencing in most centres between 4 a.m. and 6 a.m. on the major market day and finishing between 12 a.m. and 2 p.m. on the same day. In the largest centres, the censuses began on some entrances earlier in the morning, or even on the preceding day. Pedestrians, livestock, vehicles and bicycles were recorded. As many pedestrians as possible were asked in Spanish and/or Quechua where they had come from on that day. Their answers gave data on 20-40 per cent of pedestrians, and these data were projected to give approximate information on origin for all pedestrians. Persons riding cycles, horses, mules or

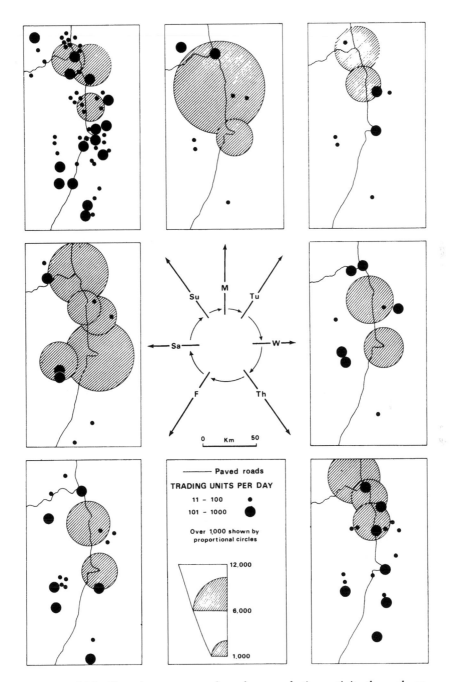

FIGURE 16.2 *Changing patterns of produce marketing activity throughout the week*

331

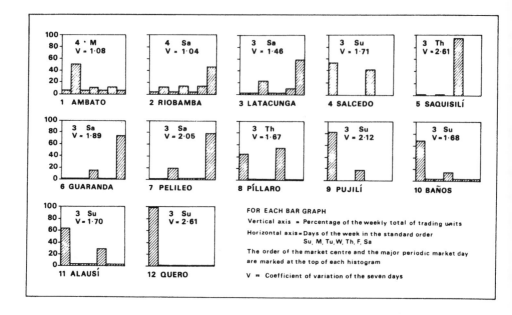

FIGURE 16.3 Day-to-day variations in produce marketing activity for third- and fourth-order centres

donkeys were recorded as pedestrians, and their mounts were recorded separately.

Motor vehicles were counted and classified under four categories: lorries, buses, cars, and pick-ups. They were stopped by the policemen or soldiers assisting with the census, and their drivers or conductors were asked where the vehicle had begun, and would end, its journey. Passengers were counted roughly, excluding the drivers and conductors of commercial vehicles, but no attempt was made to determine the place of origin of each individual passenger. Various checks made during journeys on local buses and lorries, and in unstructured interviews with drivers and conductors, revealed that the overwhelming majority of passengers board a vehicle travelling to market within 2 km of the beginning of its journey.

From each census, the people and vehicles passing through the settlement and not stopping for the market were eliminated, as were people entering the market centre for domestic service, construction work and other routine jobs unconnected with the market. This regular flow never exceeded 10 per cent of those entering the settlement on the major market day.

The composition of population entering market centres
for major periodic markets

A number of conclusions can be drawn from the market movement censuses (Table 16.1). In general, the larger the centre in population and market activity, the more people were attracted from outside for the major weekly periodic market, and the greater the proportion attending who came by vehicle rather than on foot, on horseback or by bicycle. Larger central places attracted people from greater distances than smaller central places, and long-distance modes of transport (vehicles) were more important for journeys to larger centres. The ratios of outsiders to inhabitants of the market centres tended to be low in the largest centres, high in the medium size centres, and low in the smaller centres.

Age/sex data were noted for all pedestrians, and for a 20-40 per cent sample of vehicle passengers, showed that 75-80 per cent of the persons entering each centre on its major periodic market day were over 15 years of age. In most cases, over half were women, reflecting their numerical predominance in most market activity. The proportion of women was particularly high in the smaller market centres where most trading is in foodstuffs, and in areas with a predominantly white population. The proportion of men was highest in the larger centres with considerable livestock trading (a predominantly male activity) and in areas with a mainly Indian population where drinking of white rum and maize beer on market-day is especially notable.

Between 12 and 16 per cent of the persons entering the market centres for the major periodic markets were aged 6-15. Many of them helped elder family members in selling, buying, or carrying loads, and some were independent traders in their own right. Males generally predominated in the 6-15 'age range because many girls are expected to remain at home on market day to guard the house and care for younger brothers and sisters, and because many parents wish to keep the eligible daughters out of the public eye. Persons aged under 6 generally made up 6-11 per cent of those attending market. They normally played no economic role in the markets, and were there because their mothers and sisters were attending market. The proportion of men was higher among pedestrians than among vehicle passengers, while the reverse was the case for women and children. Men are generally faster walkers, and so are more likely to prefer to save money in this way, and riding horses and bicycles are viewed as manly activities. Differentiation between pedestrians and vehicle passengers occurs not only by sex and

TABLE 16.1 *The main results of the market movement censuses*

Market centres (rank order by data in column 'A')	'A' 1971 average weekly number of trading units	'B' 1974 population of the market centres*	Percentage of weekly trading units on major market day	'C' Number of persons coming from outside for major weekly periodic market	Percentage of 'C' coming in motor vehicles	'C'/'B'
Ambato	21,634	77,955	48.9	49,740	84.9	0.64
Riobamba	13,610	58,087	46.4	27,552	72.7	0.47
Latacunga	7,898	21,921	58.9	25,894	74.5	1.18
Saquisilí	3,205	2,715	98.8	16,041	56.4	5.91
Pelileo	2,318	3,754	78.9	11,503	51.0	3.06
Pujilí	1,338	2,510	81.4	8,683	46.1	3.46
Quero	1,049	921	98.9	6,594	38.2	7.16
Penipe	529	578	100.0	3,672	35.9	6.35
Zimbahua	497	225	94.0	3,372	12.5	14.99
Salarón	239	65	100.0	2,138	0.0	32.89
Huambaló	88	1,067	100.0	1,027	3.2	0.96
Tanicuchí	28	505	100.0	334	1.5	0.66

* *Sources:* INEC (1976-7) and Bromley (1975: 157)

age, but also by social class and ethnic group. Lower status, poorer people characteristically walk to market, while higher status, better-off people are more likely to travel by vehicle.

A substantial proportion of pedestrians and vehicle passengers travelling to market carry farm produce, handicrafts and other goods to sell, and most return home with factory-processed foods, fruit, vegetables, hardware, clothing and other purchases. Many pedestrians carry loads on their backs or in their hands, and horses, mules, donkeys, and occasionally llamas, are used for additional burdens.

Because of the bulky loads carried by many passengers and the weak application of official regulations on vehicle use, most commercial vehicles and some private vehicles are used for both cargo and passengers. The concentration of movements to major periodic markets on a few days of the week, and on a few hours in the mornings of those days, puts local transport systems under considerable strain at these times. Most vehicles travelling to a market centre during the build-up of the major periodic market are full, and many buses, lorries and pick-ups are seriously overloaded. A substantial proportion of the transport services to any given market centre only run on market days. Most commercial vehicles have a different set of routes and destinations on each day of the week, depending on the distribution of periodic market activity. Only a minority of buses and a very small proportion of lorries run regular, timetabled services between the same places throughout the week, and many lorry and pick-up drivers work as transporters only on local market days.

Censuses in Ambato and Latacunga on four sample vehicle entrances and a corresponding number of pedestrian entrances on every day for a week, gave an indication of movement to market centres on secondary periodic market days and on days with only a minimal amount of market activity. They show a high correlation between the inflows of pedestrians and vehicle passengers and the day-to-day variations in trading activity (Figure 16.4). A small and fairly constant number of pedestrians enter the towns for work, shopping or education on five or six days each week, and do not participate in the markets. However, clearly day-to-day variations in market activity are the major determinants of the day-to-day variations in rural-urban and inter-urban movement. Proprietors of shops, offices and other service establishments frequently find it advantageous to open on days of peak market activity, even if these occur at weekends and to close on days of low market activity.

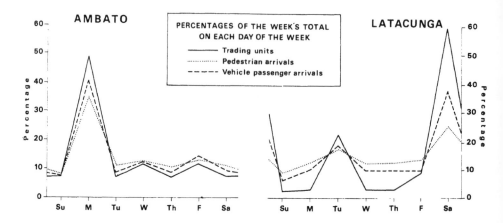

FIGURE 16.4 Trading units, pedestrian arrivals and vehicle passenger arrivals to Ambato and Latacunga markets

The spatial pattern of movement to market centres for major periodic markets

A cluster of four centres in Cotopaxi Province was examined in detail – three third-order centres, Latacunga, with a Saturday market, Saquisilí, with a Thursday market, and Pujilí, with a Sunday market, and one first-order centre, Tanicuchí, with a Sunday market. The other centres in the zone were so small as to not significantly affect the spatio-temporal pattern of movements (Figures 16.5 and 16.6). Straight or curved lines are used to link the market centres to the points of origin of those attending them, with no attempt to trace the actual routes followed, and all distances discussed are straight-line radial distances.

The trade areas of the different centres were relatively discrete, and most pedestrians travelled under 10 km to market (Figure 16.5). Pedestrian flows were particularly important in populated areas with the worst road systems, for example west of Saquisilí and east of Latacunga. Most pedestrian movements were to the nearest second-, third- or fourth- order centre, and there were relatively few pedestrian flows between different second-, third- and fourth-order centres.

Vehicle passenger flows show a strikingly different pattern (Figure 16.6). Most were for distances of over 8 km, many were for over 20 km, and a few exceeded 50 km. These flows mainly originated in towns or villages, and there was a considerable amount of movement between second-, third- and fourth-order centres. Unlike pedestrian flows, many vehicle passenger flows

336

were not to the nearest second-, third- or fourth-order centre, but to more distant centres, so that there was considerable overlap between the trade areas of different centres. It is also clear that there was an element of nesting in the hierarchy of centres, and that some communities were intermediate between the trade areas of two or more different centres. For example, more people travelled from Tanicuchí by vehicle to the markets of Latacunga and Saquisilí than travelled into Tanicuchí on foot or by vehicle for the market there. Similarly, the marketless villages of Poaló and Once de Noviembre, located in the triangle between Saquisilí, Pujilí and Latacunga, had substantial vehicle passenger flows and small pedestrian flows to all three centres, indicating a considerable overlap in trade areas.

Flows of vehicle passengers to market centres were particularly important along the axes with good road communications, and especially along the north-south axis of the paved Pan-American Highway. Further improvements in the density, quality and traffic flows of the transport network are likely to stimulate further increases in the proportion of persons travelling to market by vehicle, and in the relative importance of long-distance movements. However, even in areas with good road communications, a proportion of the population prefer to walk to the nearest market centre rather than travel by vehicle. In most cases people either cannot afford or do not wish to spend money on the vehicle fare. In other cases, they are driving livestock to market and are unable or unwilling to take their animals by vehicle. Vehicle drivers are prohibited from carrying livestock unless they have a special permit, although many ignore this regulation and carry pigs and sheep illegally.

The great majority of pedestrian movements to market centres and most vehicle passenger movements to nearby centres are of consumers, and of peasant farmers, artisans and producer-traders wishing to sell their products directly to the public or to collecting wholesalers. In contrast, most longer distance vehicle passenger movements are made by retailing intermediaries who live and trade in one centre, but trade in one or more other centres. Distance decay functions around market centres were examined for the four centres in the cluster in Cotopaxi Province (Latacunga, Saquisilí, Pujilí and Tanicuchí) and combined with data for a comparable cluster of four centres in Tungurahua Province (Ambato − 4th order; Pelileo and Quero − 3rd order; and, Huambaló − 1st order). It is clear that the larger centres attracted people from greater distance than the smaller ones. For example, while some people walked over 15 km to the major periodic markets of Ambato, Latacunga and Saquisilí, the three

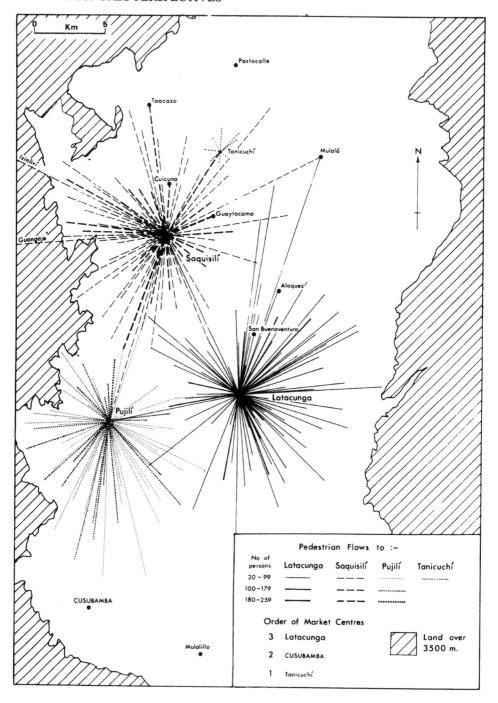

FIGURE 16.5 Pedestrian flows to markets

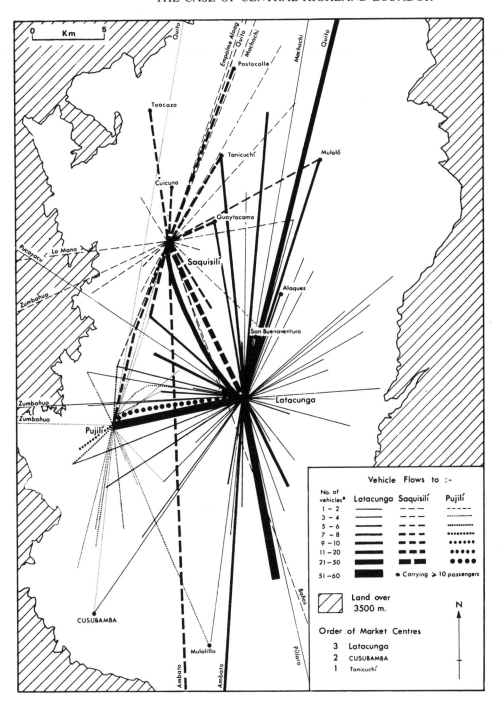

FIGURE 16.6 Vehicle flows to markets

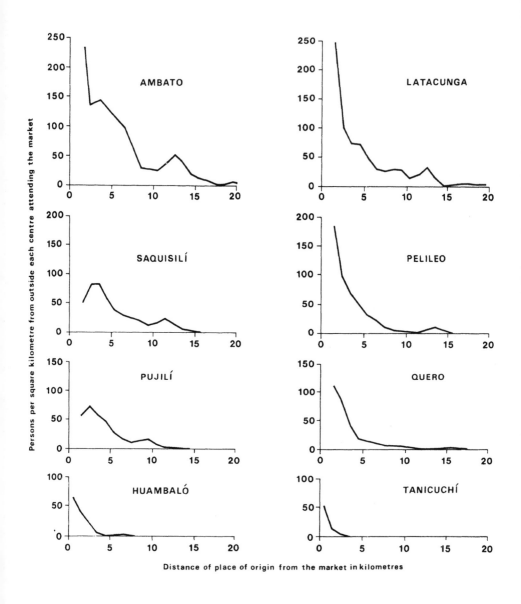

FIGURE 16.7 Relationship between population density and distance from place of origin

largest in the sample, no-one walked further than 3 km to the two smallest markets at Huambaló and Tanicuchí. Graphs plotted for the number of people per unit area visiting each centre, show a clear exponential decline in market participation with increasing distance from the centre; anomalies are due mainly to variations in population density and transport availability (Figure 16.7). In general, at any given distance from a market centre, the number of people attending its market is directly related to its total size in terms of weekly market activity. Steep distance decay is exhibited by the smaller market centre while the larger centres have much gentler distance decay curves.

Levels of market participation in rural areas are closely related to position within the Andean basins. Towards the middle of an Andean basin, rural areas are usually within 15 km of three or more different market centres, often with both major and minor periodic market days. Thus, a relatively high proportion of the population attends at least one periodic market each week. Towards the basin peripheries, however, some rural areas are over 15 km away from any market centre, and most have only one centre within a 15 km radius. In these more remote areas, levels of market participation tend to be much lower, both in the frequency of visits to periodic markets, and in the proportion of the population travelling to market.

Market visiting behaviour in five sample rural communities

Data from a random sample of thirty household interviews[4] in each of five rural communities in Tungurahua Province gave information on the market visiting behaviour of the rural population (Table 16.2). The communities were chosen because of the availability of local co-operation and all five have a predominantly 'white' population. The villages of Patate and Huambaló have their own small markets, while the hamlet of Montalvo and the dispersed rural settlements of Florida and Placer are all located 1-3 km from the nearest market centre (Figure 16.8). Surveys were conducted in July during weeks when there were no local festivals or other special public occasions. Family members who were absent from the house for the whole of the week preceding the survey were excluded.

Households ranged in size from a single adult to as many as 10-12 persons. The number of adults (aged 16 or over) in a household varied from 1 to 8, while the number of children (aged under 16) varied from 0 to 8.

In all five communities, average household size was in the

TABLE 16.2 *Main characteristics of the households studied in five sample rural communities*

Community	Av. no. of adults per household	Av. no. of children per household	Percentage of households mainly engaged in agriculture	Av. no. of market centres visited per household per week	Av. no. of periodic markets visited per household per week	Total no. of different market centres visited in one week by the 30 households	Total no. of different periodic markets visited in one week by the 30 households
Patate	2.8	2.6	30.0	1.7	2.5	4	10
Huambaló	2.8	2.6	63.3	1.6	1.7	4	6
Montalvo	2.8	3.3	86.7	1.2	1.6	2	4
Florida	3.2	3.3	83.3	1.5	1.7	5	8
Placer	2.6	3.6	86.7	1.3	1.9	3	6

Note: The five communities are listed in rank order of size and no. of services. Only visits to market centres which include some market-place trade are included.

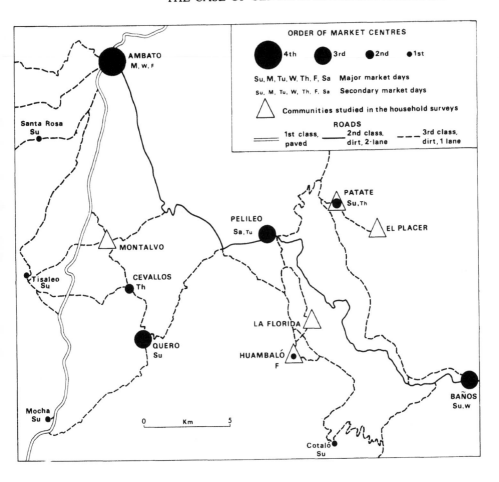

FIGURE 16.8 Market centres and communities studied in household surveys

range 5.5-6.5, and from 30 to 87 per cent of the households had agriculture as their main source of income, generally owning or renting smallholdings of $\frac{1}{2}$-10 ha. The average number of different centres visited per household per week for market-place trade range from 1.2 in Montalvo to 1.7 in Patate. As some households were represented in the same centre on two or more different market days, the average number of periodic markets visited per household per week was higher, ranging from 1.6 in Montalvo to 2.5 in Patate. In all five communities, over three-quarters of the households were represented in 1-3 different markets each week, but a minority of households (3-17 per cent)

343

usually the poorest, had no members visiting markets in any particular week, while a contrasting minority (3-10 per cent) were represented in as many as 4-5 different markets each week. These averages take into account only those visits to market centres which involved at least some buying or selling in the market-place. Many of these journeys were in fact multi-purpose, involving not only market-place purchases and/or sales, but also purchases in shops, visits to friends and relatives, visits to church, business at public offices, or private business relating to loans, debts, and property transactions. A substantial number of household members also made additional journeys to market centres and other communities each week for social, educational or business reasons without purchases or sales in a market-place.

Except in the smallest households, only a small proportion of the household members visited any particular market. In most households, there was a clear division of responsibilities: market visits were made by one or two of the adults, sometimes accompanied by one or two of the smallest children who could not easily be left alone at home. Women tended to be more frequent visitors to markets than men, and their predominance was particularly notable in the small village markets in Patate and Huambaló. There was little variation between the five communities in the number of household members visiting a market. Aggregating the five communities, 62 per cent of all market visits were made by lone adults, 10 per cent were made by one adult accompanied by one child, 16 per cent were made by two adults, and 6 per cent were made by two adults accompanied by one child.

The reasons given for trips to market varied somewhat from community to community. Within the market-place, household members can engage in one or more of three main types of commercial activity: buying food, clothing and other goods for household consumption or use; selling crops, handicrafts and other household produce; and, buying and/or selling goods as commercial intermediaries. In all five communities, over three quarters of market visits were made to buy goods for household consumption or use (Table 16.3). Most of the remaining visits combined such purchases with the sale of household produce and/or work as retailing and/or wholesaling intermediaries. The work of market-place commercial intermediaries was most important in Montalvo, the closest of the five communities to Ambato, but no instances of such work were recorded in Placer, the most remote.

In each community, 2-5 different market centres and 4-10 different periodic markets were visited for market-place trade

TABLE 16.3 *Reasons for market visits by household members in five sample rural communities*

Community	Percentage of market visits for one or more of the three main types of commercial activity							
	1 only	2 only	3 only	1 and 2	1 and 3	2 and 3	1, 2, and 3	Total
Patate	78.7	0.0	0.0	13.3	6.7	0.0	1.3	100
Huambaló	80.8	0.0	1.9	9.6	5.8	0.0	1.9	100
Montalvo	81.2	0.0	2.1	6.3	10.4	0.0	0.0	100
Florida	82.4	0.0	1.8	10.5	5.3	0.0	0.0	100
Placer	91.1	0.0	0.0	8.9	0.0	0.0	0.0	100

Note: 1 = buying goods for household consumption or use
2 = selling household produce
3 = buying and/or selling goods as commercial intermediaries

during the week under study by the total of members of the 30 households. The centres and periodic markets visited varied widely in size and in distance from the community. Distances travelled ranged from a few metres for the households adjacent to the market-places in Patate and Huambaló, to 32 km by road from Placer to Ambato, and 161 km by road from Patate to Quito. The majority of market visits were made on the major market days of the market centres visited, but a substantial minority of visits occurred on secondary market days, and in the case of Ambato which has a substantial daily market, visits even occurred on days without much periodic market activity. Visits to local first- and second-order market centres were usually made for the purchase of foodstuffs, and particularly of fruit, vegetables, meat, grain, potatoes, flour and salt. Purchases of clothing, hardware and other durable goods were usually made in larger, more distant centres, and foodstuffs were sometimes purchased on the trips to higher-order centres. Rural consumers tended to patronize a local, lower-order centre for limited purchases of perishable goods, and one or more distant higher-order centres for purchases of durable goods and bulk purchases of perishables. There was a tendency for consumers to by-pass middle level centres altogether, and to go directly to the largest available centre for their main purchases. Thus, for example, far more Montalvo households patronized Ambato a fourth-order centre 12.5 km away by road, than Cevallos a second-order centre only 3.5 km away by road.

The variations in market visiting behaviour between different households in the same communities can be partly attributed to the considerable variations in household size, wealth and economic activities. Equally important were variations between households in social connections, the timing of household activity, and knowledge and perceptions of market size, composition and accessibility. Almost all of the adults and many of the children were aware of the relative importance of most of the main market centres in the Province, and of the market days of these centres. Many of the adults were also familiar with the approximate bus fares and travelling times to several different centres, and with the availability of public transport on different days of the week. Although such knowledge was widespread, there was no uniformity of opinion as to which centre should be visited to buy or sell specific commodities. Indeed, because most trips to market involve visits to relatives, churchgoing or other non-commercial activities as well as the purchase and/or sale of several different commodities, the choice of which centre to visit was difficult to make, and opinions varied considerably. The decision was further complicated by the spatio-temporal distribution of periodic market activity and transport services to markets, and by varying constraints upon different household members' time. Not surprisingly, rural dwellers had no clear or rigid conception of hierarchies of market centres and trade areas. They simply had a more approximate idea of market sizes and locations and some perception of alternative markets to visit on different days of the week.

Conclusions

Market-place trade plays an important role in the economic, social and spatial organization of human activity in the Central Highlands, a region of great physical and cultural diversity with marked variations in population density, settlement patterns and economic activities. The spatial distribution of market centres is very uneven, and, taken together, the centres fit rank-size models of systemic organization much more easily than rigid hierarchical models. Because of this, hierarchies have been treated simply as classificatory tools based upon the fact that there are more small centres than large ones. Functional hierarchical organizations of market centres do exist in the context of bulking and distribution processes, and of consumer behaviour in seeking lower- and higher-order goods. However, the nature and interpretation of these functional hierarchies varies considerably through space and time, and according to social and economic status and scale. Such functional hierarchies should be viewed as highly flexible, and they can only be adequately defined in the context of specific localities, social groups, products, and scales of production and consumption.

After the sharp 'break' of the Spanish conquest in the sixteenth century, the systems of market centres in highland Ecuador have evolved and expanded gradually over several hundred years. Many colonial features of market location and organization are still important, but changes have occurred at an accelerating rate since the second half of the nineteenth century as a result of transport improvement, increasing urbanization and regional integration, and growth in population, production, consumer demand, and exchange. These processes have led to a degree of concentration and centralization of market activity in the more urbanized and accessible 'core areas' of the highlands, to a proliferation of new market centres in 'peripheral areas', and to the decline and eventual extinction of some small market centres close to larger expanding centres (Bromley 1978).

Particularly in the twentieth century, the retailing and wholesaling structure of Ecuador has become increasingly complex. The 'traditional' commercial institutions and establishments such as the general shop, the market stall, the warehouse, and the door-to-door pedlar, have been joined by such 'modern' institutions and embellishments as the specialist shop, the department store, the supermarket and mail ordering. Thus, a 'pluralistic' retailing and wholesaling structure has developed catering to an essentially 'pluralistic' society. To some extent, different types of institutions have different locational characteristics, cater to different sectors of the population, and serve demands for different types of merchandise. The structure of marketing chains depends upon the characteristics of the producers and consumers as much as, or even more than, the characteristics of the intermediaries. Although the relative importance of market-place trade in the total commercial structure has probably declined somewhat in the twentieth century with the development of new commercial institutions, the absolute importance of market-place trade expressed in total turnover has increased enormously in parallel with population growth and increases in consumer demand. There are signs that market-place trade in highland Ecuador is beginning to follow certain trends which have occurred in Western Europe in the nineteenth and twentieth centuries (e.g. Kirk, Ellis and Medland 1972). These include: an increase in the importance of daily markets relative to periodic markets; an increase in the proportion of market activity which takes place in covered buildings; a growing specialization of individual market-places in particular types of merchandise, and on either wholesale or retail trading; and an increasing concentration of market activity on trading in fresh foodstuffs, cheap, lightweight consumer durables, and livestock.

Periodic and daily markets have formed a major focus for circulation in the Central Highlands for at least four hundred years. Particularly since the latter part of the nineteenth century, however, the characteristics of this circulation have been changing at an increasingly rapid rate in response to major changes in transport and central place systems, and in the structure of production and consumer demand. The larger market centres have become increasingly diversified in the range of services and income opportunities that they offer, and major growth has occurred in the variety and complexity of consumer demand. As a result, trips to market centres now usually involve a series of additional objectives as well as purchasing and/or selling in the market-place. The main determinant of the periodicity of visits to market centres, however, is the timing of the periodic markets, and the spatio-temporal distribution of commercial activities outside the market-place is adapted to the corresponding distribution of market-place trade. Journeys to and from market centres have increased in frequency in recent years, and a growing proportion of these journeys are being made in motor vehicles to larger and more distant centres, rather than on foot to smaller, nearby centres. As a result the changing nature of circulation is itself a factor in the restructuring of central place systems, the increasing frequency of transport services to major centres, and the demographic growth of the principal towns in the region. Though the patterns of circulation to periodic and daily markets are changing and the relative importance of different markets and market centres are altering, it is clear that markets are functional and resilient institutions, and that they are likely to remain major foci for circulation for many years to come.

Notes

1 The term 'market' is used to indicate the trading activities which occur in, or near, a clearly defined market-place. The term 'centre' is used synonymously with 'market centre', a nucleated settlement with one or more market-places and one or more markets per week.
2 Data calculated by the author from official censuses and estimates given in DGEC (1964, 1968a, and 1968b).
3 The procedure adopted for the market-place counts and for defining and classifying 'trading units' is set out in Bromley (1974: 50-2; 1975: 40-54 and 365-73; 1976: 94-6).
4 In the few cases where the house chosen was uninhabited, where none of the occupants could be found, or where an interview was refused or considered unsatisfactory, an additional random number was drawn to select another house.

17 Town-city circulation among young Yucatec shoemakers

Guy T. Ashton

To date the great volume of urban migration research in Latin America has largely dealt with the adaptive processes which people experience as they move permanently to cities (Butterworth 1971; Germani 1961; Lewis 1952; Mangin 1967; Matos-Mar 1961; Morse 1965, 1971; Pearse 1961; Schaedel 1974). Little attention has been paid to the effects temporary urban movements (Nelson 1976) have on people when they return to their home communities or towns, largely because these movements are not as prevalent as the former and also because it is somewhat difficult to locate and question returning or circulating migrants (Feindt and Browning 1972; Simmons and Cardona 1972). This paper discusses the impact an urban experience has on adolescent Yucatec shoemakers who move from the Maya speaking town of Ticul in Mexico to Belize City, the port and largest city of Belize (formerly British Honduras). The back-and-forth movements of these shoemakers fall into the 'circulation' definition of Zelinsky (1971: 225-6). They accelerate the process of attaining adult status in Ticul and instil a stronger feeling of Mexican national identity (*mexicanidad*) in those who move. Although the time they spend in Belize City is not long enough to effect changes in their basic value structures they become aware of values quite different from those in Ticul.

African studies suggest that labour migration has served as a rite of passage, facilitating the transition from adolescence to adulthood (Gulliver 1957; Harris 1959; Mayer 1961; Skinner 1960). The fact that African males are able to successfully live and work on their own in a foreign (often urban) environment is viewed by people in the home community as a form of initiation rite, and the migrants assume adult status upon their return. Movement in and out of Ticul is too frequent for townspeople to

350

view it in this light. The Belize circulatory pattern, however, does serve to teach adolescents adult social and economic behaviour more quickly than if they remained at home.

A male is recognized as adult in Ticul when he achieves economic independence from his family and engages in such manly (*macho*) activities as drinking and experiencing sexual relations. The hastening of economic freedom through movement is more important than adult *macho* behaviour as there are few opportunities available for adolescents who remain in Ticul to become economically independent of their families. In Belize City the migrants earn at least twice as much money as they could in Ticul and can spend it as they please as they are largely free from the social control of relatives and friends. All shoemakers purchase consumption items and send money home. Most migrants desire to become small entrepreneurs and accumulate savings to invest in various businesses upon their return. At the same time they acquire greater manliness (*machismo*) through frequent attendance at the Belize City 'night clubs' where they drink heavily and demonstrate their sexual prowess.

Butterworth (1962: 256) reports that among Mixtec migrants in Mexico City there is an increase in Mexican national identity without a corresponding decrease in identification with the home community of Tilantongo. A similar result occurs among Yucatec shoemakers in Belize City. Belize City residents, the great majority of whom are Creoles (negroes and coloureds), associate the Yucatec migrants with the city's discriminated Spanish minority (Spanish and Amerindian mixture) which has its cultural affinities with Mexico. The Creoles constitute 80-90% of the Belize City population (Waddell 1961: 70-1). There is little social interaction between Creole and Spaniard, the latter often going as far as to make a point of failing to understand Creole English. The Yucatec shoemakers find it difficult to avoid hostile Creoles and interact with only a small number of Spanish-speaking Belicenos and Mexican merchants. They spend most of their leisure hours together and utilize mass communication sources of Mexican origin – movies, radio, magazines, picture novels, and comics. The increase in Mexican national identity achieved in Belize City, an important aspect of which is a greater proficiency in speaking and reading the Spanish language, allows those who circulate to serve as economic and political 'brokers' (Wolf 1965) who are now in a position of being able to introduce ideas and economic goods identified with the Mexican nation to the local community.

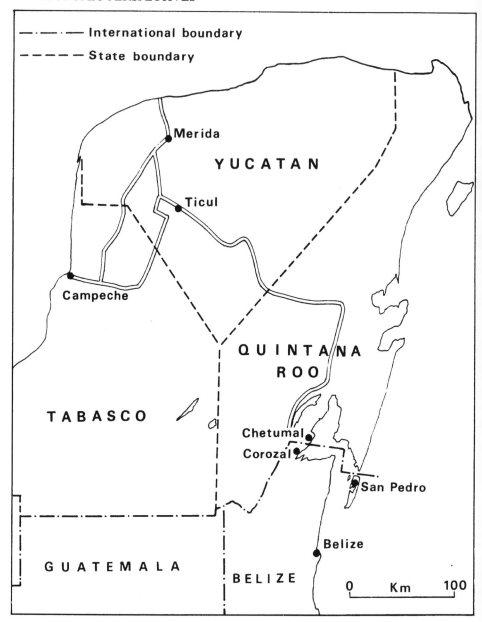

FIGURE 17.1 Yucatan peninsula

Ticul and the shoemaker circulatory pattern

Ticul is a town of 12,000 people located along a paved and extremely well-travelled highway an hour's ride from Merida (pop. 175,000), the capital of Yucatan State. It is a county seat (*cabecera*) serving two small communities and, as a unit of government, has national level social, economic, and political institutions such as schools, a health clinic, an electric plant, a bank, and a court. The town's business section includes doctor and dentist offices, an electric appliance store, small shops, bars, a restaurant, an ice cream parlour, and two movie theatres. Buying and selling takes place in the local market every day of the week.

Ticul is divided into six *barrios* (neighbourhoods) and a central commercial area. Except for a small number of more cosmopolitan and Merida-oriented wealthier merchants, professionals and property owners in the town's centre (about 5 per cent of the population), the great majority of Ticuleños live in the more traditional style of a small Yucatecan town. This traditional lifestyle entails speaking more Maya (sometimes exclusively) than Spanish, adhering to a more strictly corn diet, dressing in white, embroidered muu-muus (women) and white shirts and hats and either white or coloured trousers (men), wearing sandals or going barefoot, and living in low rock or dirt and thatch houses and sending children through the first few primary school grades. Close family ties are maintained along an extended patrilineage model, with participation in *barrio*, town, and nearby community fiestas. Employment is in agriculture, artisan trades, and/or petty commerce, which often leads to migrations to rural, small town, and/or other urban environments. Slow economic development and the physical isolation of the Yucatan Peninsula from the rest of Mexico until the early 1960s have helped to maintain the culturally distinctive Maya tradition, especially in the small towns and the countryside. The traditional Ticuleño views his community as a *medio-ciudad* (half city), justifying this description on the lack of social and economic progress.

Only superficial data were collected on the large number of agriculturalists who cultivate corn plots (*milpas*) both near and far from Ticul, using the frequent and excellent bus service. Ticul's scarce economic resources result in many artisans and merchants still clinging marginally to agriculture, especially during slack periods of the year. In fact, 64 per cent of the migrant shoemakers interviewed reported their father's occupation as farmer; 19 per cent listed his occupation as artisan, 12 per cent as small merchant, and 5 per cent other. Because of the large number of craftsmen in Ticul, outsiders label the community as a 'town of craftsmen'. Craftsmen make shoes, hats, pots and hammocks which they sell throughout the Peninsula. The shoemakers constitute the largest craft group with a total of

452 persons who work in 55 shops (*talleres*). The hat-makers rank second with about 100 persons working in 14 shops. The potters and makers of hammocks are much smaller groups and they work at home. In terms of social status, shoemakers rank second after hatmakers and they are followed by potters, largely because of their heavy agricultural background and excessive drinking activities. There are so many small shoemaker workshops that approximately one out of eight shoemakers becomes a small entrepreneur. This figure rises if shoemakers who become entrepreneurs in areas outside their craft are included.

Circular movement by Ticuleños to rural and urban places is very common. Informants still report (1976) that probably no less than one-third of townspeople move regularly at one time or another for work purposes during their lifetimes. This led to the development of a general typology (Ashton 1966) for all Ticul-based movements: (1) rural or urban commuting; (2) rural or urban circulation; and (3) rural or urban permanent migration. Commuters and circulators, rather than permanent migrants are the norm for Ticul and conservatively account for close to 75 per cent of movement out of the town. Furthermore, these two primary types of movement are quite evenly divided between rural and urban environments.

The 'rural or urban commuter' retains a home and usually a family plus a constantly renewed set of social relationships in Ticul during daily or weekly movement. Of the 'daily commuters' (Table 17.1), all 19 categories move in a rural context while 7 also move to a more urban environment than Ticul. Of the 'weekly commuters' (Table 17.2), 10 of the 13 categories move in a more urban environment and 8 of 13 in a more rural context.

The 'rural or urban circulator' is absent from Ticul long enough (2 months to 3 years) that he/she must establish a set of social relationships in the community at destination. Of the 10 rural or urban circulator categories (Table 17.3), 7 move to more rural locales and 7 to more urban places.

The 'rural or urban migrant' is someone who leaves Ticul permanently, but may return occasionally to visit. Essentially, the permanent migrant's set of social relationships is severed and a new set is acquired in the permanent destination. This migrant type is much less frequent than the 'commuter' or 'circulator', generally includes wealthy merchants who move to Merida, persons with vocational/professional skills who can benefit more in an urban place, and agriculturalists who establish small settlements (*campamentos*) in sparsely populated areas near the Yucatan-Quintana Roo state line.

TABLE 17.1

Daily commuter categories	Type of movement (R = rural, U = urban)
Agriculturalists	R
Bakers	R
Baseball players	R
Bee-keepers	R
Beggars	R and U
Butchers	R
Cattle owners	R
Corn merchants	R and U
Fruit merchants	R and U
Hatmakers	R and U
Hunters (deer)	R
Masons	R
Musicians	R
Potters	R and U
Railroad workers	R
Shoe store owners	R and U
Taxi/bus drivers	R and U
Teachers	R
Waiters	R

TABLE 17.2

Weekly commuter categories	Type of movement (R = rural, U = urban)
Agriculturalists	R
Bakers	R
Maids	U
Masons	U
Potters	R
Road workers	R and U
Sick people	U
Students	R and U
Tailors	U
Teachers	R and U
Tourists	R and U
Travel and sales agents	R and U
Water plant workers	U

TABLE 17.3

Circulating categories	Type of movement (R = rural, U = urban)
Agriculturalists (in the Yucatan Peninsula)	R
Braceros (to the USA)	R
Maids	U
Masons	R and U
Roadworkers	R
Shoemakers	U
Soldiers	R and U
Students	R and U
Teachers	R and U
Vocational/professional skills (various)	U

Circulating shoemakers

In the urban circulatory pattern of Ticul shoemakers adolescents are first apprenticed in workshops at the age of 15 or 16 where they take one-and-a-half to two years to learn the trade. Most boys are apprenticed in shops where relatives (uncles, brothers, cousins, and nephews) are shoemakers. A few are apprenticed with friends. At age 16 or 17 they have mastered the trade and it is possible to move. One-fourth of the total Ticul work force, or about 125 shoemakers, have moved in the past. Heaviest movement occurs during *la epoca buena* (the good season) which lasts from late September until early June. *La epoca mala* (slack season), lasting from June through mid-September, is when people are waiting for the harvest and possess little income. At this time many shoemakers and other Ticuleños must look to alternative forms of economic livelihood.

Approximately 70 per cent of the shoemakers who move go to Belize, while the remaining 30 per cent obtain employment in Merida, Campeche (pop. 44,000), and other nearby towns. It is not profitable to commute and work in Merida because wages are the same as those in Ticul and one has to pay room-and-board plus bus fare to come home on weekends. Thus, those going to Merida usually either become disenchanted and soon return to Ticul or become more longer-term permanent migrants to the State capital.

The first shoemakers who migrated to Belize were two men who left in 1941 to seek jobs cutting mahogany in the northern part of the then British colony. They cut mahogany for several months until offered employment as shoemakers in a town nearby. They accepted the jobs and six months later their employer moved his business to Belize City. The shoemakers accompanied him and remained there for a year. They became friends with several other shopowners, informing them that Ticul had many shoemakers who were eager to move. Late in 1943 a Belize City shopowner (*patron*) came to Ticul and recruited four workers. They returned with him and the circulatory pattern was established. Since then there have always been shoemakers from Ticul in Belize City, even when Hurricane Hattie destroyed a large part of the city in 1961. A road was completed across the sparsely populated Territory of Quintana Roo in 1957 and the number of shoemakers moving increased. Depending on bus connections and the border crossing itself, their journey from Ticul to Belize City takes about ten hours.

Three Belize *patrones* presently recruit shoemakers by coming to Ticul themselves, sending an employee, or writing letters to previous workers. One of them is from Ticul, having married a Belize City girl he is the only permanently settled migrant there. Over four years there have been no less than 18 Ticul shoemakers in Belize at any one time. During the time of the study there were 19, 16 in Belize City and 3 in the small northern town of Corozal. They remain in Belize an average of six months, are single, and between the ages of 16 and 25. Data on 59 migrants indicate that 91 per cent are 25 or younger, 59 per cent of them between the age of 16 and 20. Sixty-three per cent are single, while another 19 per cent marry during the period of their Belize movement. Shoemakers rarely circulate more than three times, this being the number of movements in more than 80 per cent of the case histories compiled.

While the excitement of the 'night-clubs' and higher wages are the most prevalent reasons given for migration, there is frequently a conflict situation which triggers the adolescent shoemakers to leave the home community. These situations of conflict (41 per cent of the sample) tend to arise with members of the immediate family but also occur with more distant relatives, girl friends and male acquaintances.

The circulatory pattern: Ticul and Belize City

Belize City (pop. 40,000) comprises two-thirds of the population of Belize and provides the majority of services to the country. Limited industrial development results in most Beliceños earning their livelihood from the sea, port activities, trade and commerce, and seasonal work on sugar plantations and at wood-cutting (mahogany) mills. The port population is predominantly

Negroid and Creole-speaking and not overly friendly to Spanish and Mayan minorities which are dispersed more inland, most notably along the Mexican and Guatemalan borders. Beliceños generally live in closely-compacted two storey wooden houses with galvanized iron roofs. The ground floor of these structures is seldom used as it is damp and receives the foul smells from open sewage canals which traverse large areas of the city.

Ticul shoemakers adapt to Belize City with the assistance of 'old hands' who are present or have been there before. The shoemakers live together, eat at the same restaurants, and participate in the same social activities. The intense group social solidarity serves many of the functions that Little (1965) describes for African migrants, but among the Yucatec shoemakers these functions are on an informal rather than formal basis. Yucatec group solidarity functions to secure living quarters for countrymen, to introduce newcomers to selected city residents, to teach shoemakers how to operate shop machinery, to instruct them in economic transactions with Beliceños, to protect group members from physical harm, and to encourage participation in recreational activities. Migrants seldom walk around the city alone because they have been told that former migrants have been beaten, robbed, and cheated in economic dealings when alone. It is also possible to encounter an unsympathetic policeman when alone who, at the very least, will rudely check your work permit.

Living arrangements are most austere. Shoemakers are divided into two groups: one sleeps in the cramped quarters of their workshop in hammocks or on top of leather materials used in making shoes and sandals, while the second occupies a small wooden shanty fronting a major sewage canal and individuals sleep in hammocks or on top of cardboard sheets. The first group pays no rent while the second pays one Belize dollar (£0.80; $1.64 US) per person weekly to their *patron* who owns the shanty (figures quoted are for 1965 when $1 Belize = $1 US = 8.5 pesos Mexican). Both living quarters have little ventilation but electricity and running water (tap) are present; both lack toilet/bath facilities and the migrants must use public facilities along the sewage canals. Clothes are washed by neighbours for a small fee. Arrangements for eating meals, often just two a day, are made with restaurants nearby and bills paid weekly by each migrant. Rice and beans with a soda is the common meal as tortillas and other Mexican foods are not served. Mexican cigarettes are obtained cheaply from a Spanish-speaking Beliceño merchant in contraband who makes daily trips to the Mexican border town of Chetumal.

Leisure time is spent going to the 'night clubs', playing and watching baseball, attending movies, walking around the business district looking at store window displays, and reading, playing cards, and listening to the radio in the crowded and inhospitable communal living quarters. More time is consumed going to movies than doing anything else. No migrants attend less than twice a week, and several go six nights a week. Mexican films are preferred, but there is attendance at American movies with Spanish subtitles. Mexican westerns are enjoyed most of all. Those shoemakers who do not attend movies on week nights read, play poker, and listen to popular music and sports programmes from a Spanish radio station transmitting from Chetumal.

On Saturday and Sunday afternoons the migrants either play baseball or are spectators at the games. Two shoemakers play for a Spanish-Creole team once a week. Saturday evening is always spent 'night-clubbing'. The migrants frequent 'night-clubs', where they drink in groups and dance and bargain with Beliceñas if it is necessary to pay for sexual favours. The aggressiveness of Belize City females in comparison with those in Ticul results in the adolescents viewing them as brazen and oversexed. On fiesta weekends of three or four days, they journey by sailboat to a Spanish-speaking island, San Pedro, where a former Ticul (shoemaker) resident lives.

The work pattern is longer and more restrictive in Belize shops than in Ticul. In Belize City shoemakers work eleven hours a day and are permitted an hour off for lunch. Otherwise they are seldom allowed to leave the *taller* during the day, and this restriction results in them viewing themselves as 'prisoners' of the workplace. Additionally, they labour six days a week and are expected to work on Sundays and holidays if needed. The Belize shops have machines which most migrants must learn to operate. In contrast, shoemakers in Ticul work no more than nine hours a day and take a three-hour siesta in the afternoon. They have complete freedom in Ticul to enter and leave the *taller* during the day, rarely work on Sundays and holidays, and are given Monday off.

Spanish-Creole hostility exists at work between the migrants and the negro workers. Migrants and Creoles separate into two groups and work on opposite sides of the shop. Both groups constantly make fun of each other and will attempt to take economic advantage of one another. On one occasion a migrant was able to sell a wrist watch to a Creole shoemaker for twice its value. Upon completion of the transaction, the Yucatec migrants all laughed and ridiculed the victim in Maya for being so easily deceived. In spite of their negative feelings for Creole shoe-makers, the migrants recognize the fact that their Belize City counterparts occupy a higher social and economic position in society there than they themselves do in the Ticul social hierarchy. Belize City shoemakers earn more money and are able to rent or own a comfortable house, buy numerous household appliances, purchase a bicycle, and become members of a Credit Union.

Belize *patrones* are impersonal and often dishonest with employees. They rarely converse or drink with their workers inside or outside the *taller*. Employees are paid their weekly earnings in cash on Saturday afternoon. Sometimes owners will cheat or hold up paying them especially with migrants. On the other hand, Ticul owners are more personable with their workers as they talk and drink with them inside and outside the shop, especially on work-free Monday which is known among shoemakers as Sunday's little Brother (*El Hermanito del Domingo*). The daily wage (*el diario*) is an economic pattern which exists in Ticul whereby employers pay workers part of their weekly earnings each day. Final earnings are disbursed on Saturday afternoon. Ticul *patrones* do not cheat or hold back paying workers and, in some cases, will lend money to trusted employees.

Surplus income sent home by these workers in Belize is used to purchase consumption items for themselves and for persons in Ticul, and saved for investment. One migrant shoemaker broke down his weekly earning of 35 Belize dollars ($1 Belize = 8.5 Mexican pesos) as shown in Table 17.4. Money sent home helps to maintain the Ticul social system, being spent by the family usually for maintenance of the household. Sums are sent every three or four weeks with returning migrants or Ticul merchants and tourists who visit Belize City at weekends. By sending money home, the shoemakers continue to contribute to household expenses as if they were present. Items purchased for themselves, relatives, and friends while in Belize include liquor, watches, rings, bracelets, earrings, transistor radios, cameras, clothing, small suitcases, shoes, toys, and talcum powder. These items are cheaper in the free port city than in either Ticul or Merida.

Money-lending between individual migrants is common. It is understood that the loan is to be repaid as soon as possible. There are no formal organizations or social relationships which function to help the migrants save money such as the group *tandas* (savings clubs) among Mexican slum dwellers (Lewis 1961) or forced partner savings among African migrants (Mayer 1961: 140). Money-lending does not occur often among shoemakers in

Ticul because rarely does anyone have any surplus income.

Return movement

After several periods in Belize and approaching the age of twenty-five, most shoemaker migrants have accumulated some savings and are tired of the hectic and unpleasant Belize lifestyle. At this stage in their life cycle they are pulled back to Ticul by a desire to enter fully the social life of the home town and to develop stronger individual and family responsibilities there. Thus, at about twenty-five, most young men return permanently, set themselves up as small entrepreneurs or secure well-paid jobs in local *talleros*, and quickly marry local girls.

Those migrants who become entrepreneurs on their return are most likely to invest savings in a shoe business. Some will do this with a partner. Market-place operations are another very common form of investment because many shoemakers are familiar with the market as they either supplement shop income or wholly support themselves from buying and selling during the slack season. During *la epoca mala* 30 per cent (115 of 452) of Ticul shoemakers are laid off work. A third area of investment is in bars. This requires a large outlay but is considered safe because there is always a heavy-drinking clientele of shoemakers. Those few migrants who already own small shoe shops usually invest savings in their businesses upon return. This involves buying more and better materials and just recently machinery. These migrant-entrepreneurs travel to Merida to purchase

TABLE 17.4 *Weekly income and expenditure in 1965 (in Belize dollars)*

Weekly income	35.00	Weekly living expenses	20.00
Weekly living	20.00	Room	1.00
Sent home	5.00	Food	9.00
Spent/saved	10.00	Night-clubs	4.00
		Cinema	1.50
		Baseball	30
		Reading	70
		Cigarettes	1.00
		Lottery tickets	1.50
		Other	1.00

machinery and serve as mediators in the introduction of new technology. In 1965 there were six machines in Ticul, five of which were bought by Belize migrants. The sixth was purchased in Merida by a migrant after four years of labour in that city. Although more machines have been purchased over the years by local owners, this has not radically changed the small-scale nature of this craft industry.

Some migrants upon return look towards marriage and spend savings to buy a piece of land, build a house, or pay the cost of a wedding and honeymoon. A number of shoemakers return with money and use it to pay past doctors' bills, or for operations and cures which they and family members require. Those who spend savings for medical purposes tend to be older and to move just once.

Items purchased in Ticul either during or following circulation include household goods, yard animals, and bicycles. Household goods are clothes closets, tables, chairs, sewing machines (foot-style), and hammocks. Clothes closets are a treasured piece of furniture where family heirlooms and money are kept. Tables, chairs and hammocks are necessities and bought when needed. Sewing machines allow women to make many of their own clothes and mend those of other family members, and they can earn extra money making *huipiles* and *ternos* (both similar to muu-muus) which are worn at Fiestas. Many migrant shoemakers purchase small animals such as turkeys, chickens, and pigs which are kept at home. These animals are their property which they may sell at any time. Bicycles are a prestige item and returning shoemakers buy second-hand or new models. They are used for transportation by people of all ages.

Circulation enhances the occupational status of shoemakers. Returning migrants are more skilled in the craft and mature in the knowledge of operating a shoe business. Those who return frequently become trusted employees of *patrones* and take over the workshops when the owners are absent. With an ability to speak quite fluent Spanish, they are often given the weekly task of taking the shoes to Merida and other cities and towns where they sell them to storeowners. Thus, they are mediators in the distribution of a local product to areas outside Ticul.

In one case a returning migrant assumed the role of political mediary. For two years a group of 30 shoemakers had informally served as waiters at local fiestas. José was a member of this group prior to moving. On his return he suggested at a meeting that they become a union and extend their services to other communities. All agreed and José was elected president of the organization. He proceeded to go to Merida and register the waiter organization as a union, filing the numerous forms. At present the union is successful and offers its services to villages and towns throughout Yucatan. A rotation system has been adopted where the 30 members are given employment if they attend meetings twice a month and perform well at fiestas. If they are guilty of missing meetings or not working hard at fiestas, they are dropped from the rotation system from one to five times depending on the seriousness of the infraction. Persons who commit infractions are given open hearings at the regular meetings where they present a defence, a group discussion of the case follows, and a binding hand vote is taken.

Shoemakers returning to Ticul from Belize often mark this by throwing drinking bouts (*borracheras*) in local bars. They buy all drinks and often bring whiskey from Belize for this special occasion. The drinking bouts serve to renew old acquaintances and the migrants tell of Belize adventures and inquire about friends and events in Ticul. By contrast shoemakers who move to Merida do not hold drinking bouts as they retain social ties in Ticul by commuting home on weekends.

Machismo is expressed in more frequent drinking activities and sexual experiences. Drinking occurs at the local pool hall, bars, the workshop, and at baseball and softball games. Returning shoemakers now attend athletic events more as spectators, drinking on the sidelines, rather than participating as players. Interest increases in local girls and the females who come to Ticul to shop in the important Sunday market and for the principal fiestas. More time is spent courting females. The shoemakers visit their girl friends at home several nights a week and meet them on Sunday morning at the movies. Young shoemakers are best able to demonstrate their knowledge of sexual matters at fiestas when many out-of-town females are present.

Circulation is a crucial step away from parental authority. A non-circulating shoemaker remains under the social and economic control of relatives for a longer period of time than one who moves. Adult social and economic behaviour learned in Belize City encourages a break with parental authority and control. Returning youths spend less time at home as they come in late at night and are usually absent on Sunday mornings and afternoons when there is family visiting.

Circulating shoemakers improve their ability to speak and read Spanish through interaction with Spanish-speaking shop-owners and other acquaintances in Belize City and their intense use of the mass media. As children the shoemakers learn Spanish at school, but rarely remain in school beyond the third or fourth grade because they are needed to contribute support to the household. Shopowners find it an asset to know Spanish well as they often enter into buying and selling where fluent knowledge of the language is required. Returning shoemakers utilize mass communications − reading newspapers and magazines, listen to the radio, and attend movies − more frequently than before moving. The ability to speak and read the national language alerts adolescent shoemakers to national and international events and increases the spread of new ideas and material innovations among Maya-speaking townspeople. Two returning shoemakers were motivated to learn English and plan to go to the United States and work. They enrolled in night classes which meet three days a week. One student wishes to become employed as a shoemaker while the other wants to become a mechanic and live in California.

Conclusion

Adolescent shoemakers who move to Belize attain adult status more quickly than if they remain in Ticul. The Belize City experiences allow them to achieve simultaneously economic independence from their extended families (and patrilineage) and become experienced in adult social behaviour accepted in the home community. The acceleration of economic independence is the major factor in becoming an adult, because economic freedom otherwise comes late due to overpopulation and limited economic resources in Ticul. The young shoemakers return with savings which allow them to become small entrepreneurs at an earlier age than those who stay at home. Clearly, the stage in the life cycle of those who move to Belize City is crucial in terms of the rapid changes achieved in economic as well as social behaviour.

Moving to Belize also develops a stronger sense of Mexican national identity (*mexicanidad*) in the shoemakers without a decrease in the attachment to Ticul and their Mayan heritage. Although no obvious change can be observed in the basic value structure of individual migrants, this does not mean that change is not occurring. Ticul has a history of being quite open to outside influences, and subtle changes that could not be detected in the short-term are undoubtedly gradually taking place in shoemakers and other townspeople.

This case of skilled (urban) labour circulation additionally shows how young men exploit a circulatory pattern to expand their class position within the confines of the home community. Older shoemakers rarely migrate to Belize, and the young ones cannot endure the negative environment there for much more than eight months at a time. The one Ticul migrant who has remained in Belize City has set up a *taller* (with the aid of his Belize wife and her shoemaker relatives), joining the Beliceño *patrones* in exploiting his own countrymen. At a young, innovative period in their lives, the adolescent migrants observe the higher status of their Beliceño counterparts (*vis-à-vis* the Belize City system) and accumulate information oriented to improving their socioeconomic position in Ticul (*vis-à-vis* the Ticul system). Thus, the socialization experience of these young men is versed primarily in terms of accommodating new ideas and behaviour to the home context.

The shoemaker circulatory pattern has and will probably continue indefinitely as long as the foreign exchange rate permits migrant shoemakers to earn higher wages than in Ticul and a scarcity of workers persists in Belize. However, it is doubtful that many individuals would migrate if the economic advantage were lost. Informants indicate that if this were to occur they would restrict their movements to rural and urban points throughout the Yucatan Peninsula in terms of their craft and other skills they possess, most notable those in agriculture and marketing. Agriculture entails opening a *milpa* within commuting distance of Ticul or circulating as a field labourer on the Peninsula and possibly to the USA. Marketing involves daily/weekly trips to rural and urban places hawking perishable and non-perishable goods. Several individuals suggest the option of bringing non-perishable contraband goods from the Belize border to a rural and urban clientele.

In order to understand the consequences of circular movement it is important to view the relationship between the 'sending' and 'receiving' areas. To what extent do boundary-maintaining mechanisms (internal) shield the home area and result in an accommodation phenomenon? To what degree do conquest/colonial/national structures (external) force the home area to integrate new values along modernization lines? And when are *both* processes in operation? Zelinsky (1971) and Mitchell (1961, 1969) view external forces (modernization, urbanization) as the primary factors in circulation, while Chapman and Prothero (1977: 5) suggest that circulation need not be necessarily associated with (external) modernizing influences but 'is a time-honoured and enduring mode of behaviour deeply-rooted in a great variety of cultures and found at *all stages of socio-economic change*' (italics mine). The Chapman/Prothero statement may be favoured because it does not lead into a theoretical strait-jacket. While circular migrants move for social but more importantly economic motives, their 'circulating strategies' may be developed for reasons internal to the home community, external to that home area, or a combination of both. This is especially relevant in this day and age when many rural and urban segments suffer inequality and/or social isolation from the larger, global society (Lewellen 1978; Lewis 1965; Liebow 1967; Miller 1970; Stack 1974). Thus, the structural factors linking the 'home' and destination communities become crucial in deciphering the 'circulating strategies' developed.

Most Ticuleños view movement in general as a way of sustaining their families and/or as an avenue for limited social mobility. Given the general poverty of the town and of the resources throughout the region, people most often view commuting and circulating as more conducive to economic survival than permanent migration elsewhere. However, although Belize City shoemaker owners pay higher salaries than local ones, they are unsuccessful in attracting older and more experienced workers because such persons have steady, well-paying jobs and refuse to relinquish them for the squalid living conditions and negative work environment of Belize. The young adventuresome individuals, who possess sufficient ego strength, are the ones who decide to circulate to obtain a good job instead of poor wages or no job in Ticul. On their part, they pose no threat to the Belize social system because they are there temporarily, working hard, and spending a large part of their wages. The young men see themselves as having no stake in the Belize social system other than earning good money, having a good social life, and returning home to possibly become a small entrepreneur and eventually to marry a local girl. And this is what most achieve.

Acknowledgment

Fieldwork was carried out from February through August 1965, with support from the Ford Foundation and the Department of Anthropology, University of Illinois, Urbana. Continued correspondence over the years has supplemented the original field investigation (Ashton, 1966, 1967).

18 Is a proletariat emerging in Nairobi?

Walter Elkan

This paper poses the question whether there are beginning to be substantial numbers in Nairobi who are wholly and permanently dependent upon wage employment and whose ties with their villages of origin have become severed. The term 'proletariat' is used in that sense, in preference to the most customary term 'working class', because the latter implies social relations and attitudes which are more properly treated by sociologists. This paper focuses more narrowly on economic status. It looks first at the statistical evidence and then at the evidence collected by sociologists and social anthropologists who have done relevant 'field' work in different parts of Nairobi. Its principal conclusion is that many people do now stay much longer in Nairobi but that, in contrast especially with Europe in the nineteenth century, links with the rural areas remain as strong as ever. If this is so, then, as Dr Grillo has persuasively argued in his book on railwaymen in Kampala, it has important implications for the pattern of urban development (Grillo 1973) but these are treated only incidentally in the present paper.

It is often said that the population of Nairobi has become much more stable in recent years and that there has emerged a work force wholly and permanently dependent upon wage employment and fully committed to urban life. Circular migration into and out of Nairobi is said to have virtually ceased. Only young school leavers still swarm into Nairobi and out again if they have not found a job within a reasonable period of time. Others come and stay. Thus Professor Henry Rempel in his comprehensive survey of recent migrants to Nairobi and seven other towns concludes that 'temporary migration still occurs, but it is a minority occurrence which does not involve a majority of the rural-urban migrants in Kenya' (Rempel 1970: 115). In the case of these newly arrived migrants, when asked if they wished to stay in the town for the rest of their lives, 59 per cent 'replied in a sense which indicates that they consider themselves as a permanent part of the urban labor force' (ibid., 84-6). From this it is inferred that Nairobi's working population is now becoming a distinct proletariat whose attitudes, ambitions, and interests are purely urban and whose ties with their rural areas of origin have become increasingly tenuous.

Statistical evidence

The statistical evidence is at first sight ambiguous. Labour turnover statistics seem to imply that people are staying much longer than a decade ago, when short-term 'circular' migration was still the common pattern. Thus, the special Labour Turnover Survey undertaken for the International Labour Office's Kenya Mission (Nigam and Singer 1974) found that in 37 manufacturing establishments in Nairobi, labour turnover from all causes was only 11.2 per cent of the 'permanent' (i.e. noncasual) labour force in the preceding twelve months, and this was thought to be 'normal'. If Manufacturing is combined with Commerce, Transport and Tourism and Hotel Services, the rate of labour turnover is still only 11.5 per cent. That turnover rate implies that on average employees at any one time have held their jobs for just under five years, which is regarded as very satisfactory. Since turnover is in fact much higher among unskilled workers than among those in higher echelons, the median period for trained operatives and above is correspondingly higher. The Carpenter report had found that in 1953 the median period of employment in the private sector in Nairobi — and the recent survey only covered the private sector — was 1.1 years, considerably shorter than now (Carpenter 1954).

Similarly, a sample survey of low-income households carried out by Nairobi University's Housing Research Unit found that 21 per cent of employees had been in employment for five to ten years and a further 18 per cent for over ten years. Both surveys therefore seem to imply considerable job stability, but there is also other statistical evidence which suggests the contrary.

One symptom of short-term circular migration has always been a marked imbalance in the population between men and women and between adults and children because it made better economic sense to leave one's family at home, where they could continue to enjoy an income from their farm. If it is true that circular migration has largely ceased then one would expect a significant reduction in the imbalance between men and women in the population, indicating that more men had brought their wives with them instead of leaving them behind in the rural areas. One would also expect to find an increase in the ratio of children to adults, indicating that people were increasingly bringing up families in the town instead of in what they had previously regarded as their permanent homes: their villages of origin.

The recent publication of some of the findings of the 1969 census, supplemented by some tables especially computed for the ILO Mission, provides an opportunity to make comparisons with the previous census of 1962 and thus to examine what has actually happened, and this evidence seems to be at variance with the implications of the Labour Turnover Study and of the Housing Survey.

Looking first at the overall sex ratio, defined as the number of males per 100 females, it appears that this has indeed declined from 187 in 1962 to 159 in 1969, which must seem to indicate support for the thesis of greater stability of residence. But it is worth examining these figures in more detail, especially in relation to the age structure of the African population (Table 18.1).

The important points to notice in Table 18.1 are, first, that part of the improved sex ratio is accounted for by those between 10 and 19 years old, which is irrelevant to the argument about stability. Second, there has been no change in the sex ratio of young adults between 20 and 24, and it is only among those 25 or over that the balance has improved. But more significant than the improvement is the fact that the disparity between men and women is still very large. It is smallest (2:1) in the case of those aged 25-9 but thereafter rises steeply, and at no age above 30 is the ratio lower than 3:1, which is hardly what one would expect to find in a stable urban population! Moreover, these figures must be regarded as *maxima*, since the census in both 1962 and 1969 was taken in August, a time of year when wives and children most frequently visit husbands in Nairobi because it is the slack agricultural season and schoolchildren are on holiday.

These figures accord closely with those found by the Nairobi Urban Study of over 1,000 low- and middle-income earners. George E. Johnson reports that only 34 per cent of employed males had wives living with them in Nairobi, while 46 per cent had wives outside Nairobi; 13 per cent were unmarried (Johnson 1971). Nor is it legitimate to infer from the relatively favourable sex ratio of those aged 25-9 that newly arrived men now bring their wives to Nairobi once they have found a job. One knows that there are rather large numbers of unmarried women under 30 in Nairobi and that their number is much greater than the

TABLE 18.1 *Percentage age distribution of Nairobi African population 1962 and 1969 by sex*

Age (years)	Males		Females		Sex ratio	
	1962 *(100)*	*1969* *(100)*	*1962* *(100)*	*1969* *(100)*	*1962* *(187.3)*	*1969* *(158.6)*
0-4	11.2	13.5	23.0	21.0	99.0	102.1
5-9	7.0	9.4	13.6	15.0	104.3	99.0
10-14	4.6	5.6	6.7	9.8	140.4	90.8
15-19	6.4	8.0	10.4	12.8	126.6	99.0
20-4	13.2	15.8	15.9	14.9	169.2	169.0
25-9	16.1	13.3	13.6	10.4	241.2	203.8
30-4	12.3	10.4	6.4	5.6	391.4	295.3
35-9	9.2	8.6	3.9	3.8	481.4	359.5
40-4	7.1	5.6	2.2	2.2	664.2	395.7
45-9	5.0	4.2	1.5	1.5	676.5	446.5
50+	8.8	5.6	2.8	3.0	. . .	. . .

Sources: 1962 *Census of the Population*, 3.27; 1969 *Census of the Population*, table specially computed for the ILO visiting team, 1972.

Note: The 1962 figures refer to the population of the Extra-Provincial District of Nairobi. Sex ratio is defined as number of males per 100 females. The overall sex ratio of 187.3 in 1962 is that given by the general census, which is somewhat lower than the 203.1 given by the sample census. Totals shown in parentheses.

numbers who have regular 'formal sector' jobs. Unmarried women under 30 have opportunities of earning a living in the 'informal sector'. In West African towns this is true for women of all ages because of the opportunities offered by trade, and this no doubt explains the more favourable sex ratio in many West African towns, though in neither East nor West Africa do women have much chance of paid employment. Only 15 per cent of the enumerated labour force of Nairobi are female, and if non-Africans were excluded the proportion would be even smaller.

To sum up: To be living in Nairobi with one's wife is still very exceptional despite the apparent improvement in the sex ratio.

Let us now look at the evidence provided by the proportion of children in Nairobi's population. In 1962, it was 32 per cent (Government Printer 1962), while the latest census gives it as 36 per cent, which is no great change. For the population of Kenya as a whole, children constituted 46 per cent in 1962 and 50 per cent in 1969, so that the increase in the proportion of children in Nairobi is probably no more than a reflection of an overall trend and lends no support to the thesis of greater stability.

The thesis of a fundamental change toward greater stability therefore receives some, but not very much support from the evidence presented by the census. More than likely, such improvements in the sex and child ratios as have taken place are accounted for largely by developments in the middle class. There has been a substantial increase in Nairobi's African middle class since Independence as Africanization has proceeded at a rapid pace in the civil service as well as in private industry and commerce and in the field of education. There can be little doubt that in these higher echelons of the social scale people regard Nairobi as their homes and live normal, settled family lives even though this by no means rules out a second home in the countryside (Southall 1966: 475).

Before proceeding further, we need to be clear what is at issue. The pattern which prevailed two decades ago, and certainly until the mid-1950s when the Mau-Mau Emergency supervened, was one of what has come to be called 'circular migration'. Employers in Nairobi found that unskilled and semi-skilled workers rarely stayed with them for more than one or two years because employment was seen not as *superseding* farm income but as a way of *supplementing* it – often in order to have savings to invest in their farms and thus enhance their potential for earning a regular cash income. Consequently people left their families behind to look after their farms, to which they returned when they had saved out of their meagre wages what they had set out to save. In this way, family income was maximized. To have moved their families to Nairobi would have meant abandoning a part of family income. They might have sold their farms and thus capitalized a future stream of income, but before land registration they had no title to land and therefore none to sell. At any rate, they could have sold their farms only at prices depressed by the lack of legal title and the absence of banks whose lending normally enhances the price of real estate above the level that would prevail if all purchases had to be made out of past savings. The conventional wisdom of the early 1950s was that the reason why people did not stay permanently in Nairobi was that wages were low and that available housing was suitable only for bachelor occupation and ruled out any possibility of bringing a family to Nairobi. But this can have been only a part of the explanation and perhaps a less important part than the fact that total family income would have been reduced by a permanent withdrawal from the countryside.

Even in the 1950s, this pattern was not universal, and the position of Luo, for example, already approximated much more that described by Grillo in his more recent study of Kampala's

371

railwaymen (Grillo 1973, chap. 3; Elkan and Fallers 1960: 251-4).

The question posed here is whether all this has changed, and, to summarize the discussion to this point, it is suggested that the evidence for major structural change so far adduced can hardly be described as overwhelming.

There is, however, evidence that things have in some ways remained curiously the same, although the much lower turnover figures may indicate a lengthening of the period people spend in Nairobi. Even that cannot be certain without much more detailed information about the nature of turnover. Labour turnover has to be seen as comprising two components; movement into and out of employment as such, and movement between employers. There is every reason to suppose that there will have been a sharp decline of the latter ever since competition for jobs increased. The harder it has become to get a job the more the people who were lucky enough to have one clung to it until they were ready to leave employment altogether, and at any rate a part of the reduction of turnover must therefore be regarded as a reduction in movement between employers ('interemployer mobility'). It is therefore not necessarily the case that a halving of labour turnover must represent a corresponding decline in movement as such.

Let us now examine the evidence for the contrary thesis, namely that the structure of circular migration has remained largely unchanged. One prominent symptom of this structure has always been a high rate of saving. This was characteristic because it indicated the major purpose of wage employment: the desire to accumulate a surplus that could be invested in the farms and which would perhaps turn a subsistence farm into one capable of producing crops for sale. Has saving declined? On the contrary: in 1957-8, an official household budget survey of people earning under 300 shillings per month found that 7.6 per cent of income was saved, given away, or remitted outside Nairobi, and by far the greater part fell into this last category (East African Statistical Dept 1959). Out of much higher wages in 1970, 20.7 per cent were reported by G.E. Johnson and W.E. Whitelaw to have been remitted outside Nairobi − a staggeringly high rate (Johnson and Whitelaw 1974). Joyce Moock has estimated that among the Abaluhya of Kakamega District migrants away from home − most of them working as domestic servants in Nairobi − remitted as much as half their wages (Moock 1973). If there was no other evidence at all, then, even allowing for the fact that these studies are not strictly speaking comparable, one would have to infer from such figures of remittances that the link between town and country dwellers, which the Carpenter

Committee of 1954 so deplored, still continues. But the *nature* of links can change.

The link between town dwellers and members of their families in the rural areas need not necessarily be of the kind described earlier in this paper. It is possible that greater numbers now have their nuclear families with them in Nairobi and that the remittances are to other members of their extended family for whose maintenance they are responsible, and no doubt in some cases this is the correct explanation. But the continued sex imbalance in Nairobi is matched by an opposite imbalance in the rural areas, and the 1969 census also shows that over one quarter of rural households were headed by women. In short, the evidence so far considered does not provide any clear-cut answer to the question posed in this paper.

The evidence of sociologists

But what we have examined has been mainly statistical evidence. Let us now turn to the more direct observations of sociologists. These do point to the emergence of a more stable urban work force, but to its divorce from what the Carpenter report of 1954 described as the 'enervating influence of the countryside'. In other words, it tends to corroborate that people stay longer in their jobs but casts great doubt on the thesis of increasing specialization between urban and rural households.

In a fascinating study of Kisa households in Nairobi, Professor Thomas S. Weisner found that households were constantly changing their membership: 'Wives visit, return home, visit again; children come . . . for holidays. Brothers come looking for jobs and stay.' He argues that it is most misleading to take a 'snapshot' census at one point of time and then to consider the results the typical residence pattern. He described his respondents as 'an urban colony [who] may live for many years in a town yet always retain their ties with the rural home of origin' (Weisner 1969: 1010). 'Every man', says Weisner, 'maintains ties with his home. . . . Jobs are gained and lost, illness may send men home for periods and so on. As men . . . pass through their working lives . . . they are continually moving back and forth between employment and [their] shambas . . .' (ibid.: 1015). Weisner also notices, interestingly, that a sample of men of similar age and education living at home in Kakamega District were similar in virtually all respects to his Nairobi group, even to the point of having spent the same number of years away from home. He therefore concludes that the most useful way to look at the families of town dwellers in Nairobi is to view them as '*one*

373

family unit, often extended in form with two or more households, one in Nairobi and one on a rural farm' (ibid.: 1016).

The median income of these men was 260 shillings and all but two (who were unemployed) appeared to have what are now described as formal (alias 'modern') sector jobs (ILO 1972: 5-6). They were therefore typical only of those in such jobs. Many people from Kakamega also work as domestic servants, living in housing provided by their employers, but there is no reason to suppose that their pattern of life differs markedly from that described by Weisner. What is more uncertain is what light it might throw on the patterns of those in the 'informal' sector whose number and proportion in the labour force have greatly increased in the past decade. Their number is almost certainly well in excess of the 30,000 or so estimated by the recent ILO report (ibid.: 343). But there is no obvious way of determining their length of stay in Nairobi or the character of any links they may have with places outside Nairobi.

In another study, this time of a predominantly Kikuyu area of Nairobi, Dr Gary Feraro found that 'the urban and rural sectors are not isolated or discrete populations, but rather are closely interrelated' (Ferara 1971: 190). The explanation he advances is, first, that some Kikuyu are 'target workers' who stay only long enough to earn money 'for specific desired items or for a sum of cash to invest in their rural farms before returning home again'. Second, for the majority of unskilled labourers as well as the numerous holders of school certificates there is little job security in the face of sickness, accidents, old age, or unemployment. 'Should a man be suddenly unemployed he always has recourse to his rural shamba or that of his kinsmen.' Third, he reiterates the point made in the report of the East African Royal Commission of 1955 that the retention of ties with the rural hinterland is 'the most economic choice' which people can make, and goes on to explain that 'only the small Kikuyu *elite* can afford the luxury of living with their families in Nairobi'. Finally, he points out that despite the creation of freehold plots in Central Province by the programme of land consolidation much land is still controlled by lineages, and inheritance of land to a large measure still takes place within the elementary polygynous family. 'If a migrant opts to sever all connections with his rural homeland, he is in effect relinquishing his rights to the inheritance of his father's land, which in the case of migrants remains his one and only retreat from the insecurities of urban unemployment' (ibid.: 190). Failure of land consolidation and continuance of farms that are not large enough to support all the inhabitants leave men with little choice but to seek supplemental cash in the form of urban wages. On the other hand, urban wages are too low and accommodation too costly to permit the urban migrant to take his family with him to Nairobi, especially as by so doing he would, of course, forego the rural component of his total family income.

Feraro in fact interviewed two groups, one (the 'Old Timers') who had been in Nairobi for five or more years and the other whom he describes as 'Newcomers'. Among the Old Timers, some of whom had lived in Nairobi all their lives, he did indeed find that ties with the rural areas had become largely severed. But most of them belonged to a minority: they were self-employed landlords and owners of small workshops rather than employees or family workers, who constitute the great majority, and their permanence does not therefore substantially affect the question posed in this paper. But of the 44 Newcomers he interviewed, only one regarded Nairobi as his home. The other 43 said that their home was either the rural area where they were raised and in which they have some claim to land, or some other rural area where they had acquired some land. 'All but two wanted to be buried on their fathers' or their own purchased plots.' Clearly, the establishment of the National Social Security Fund so far had no significant impact on this pattern of existence.

We have looked at a study of Abaluhya residents and at another of Kikuyu. A third study by Dr. David Parkin undertaken in 1968-9 in a city council housing estate concentrates on Luo households. Those who lived there were not typical of Luo in Nairobi as a whole but rather constitute a sort of 'aristocracy of labour' − all 'long-settled townsmen in secure and relatively prestigious jobs' (Parkin 1976). Their median residence in Nairobi was 17.6 years and their median income 539 shillings. A few had even spent up to 40 years in employment. Nearly all were married, and many had several wives who alternated between Nyanza Province and Nairobi so that their husband was seldom on his own. These must be the real townsmen we have been looking for, but, contrary to the expectations of most of those who write about urbanization, they have by no means severed their links with the countryside. Instead, they have been busy investing in their rural homes, buying more land, building houses (sometimes of mud and wattle but increasingly of plaster with corrugated iron roofs), and venturing into shopkeeping or running a transport service. Parkin's description resembles closely that of Grillo of Luo residents in Kampala, and there is evidence that the amount of investment into ventures outside Nairobi is greater the higher the person's socioeconomic status and the more securely he was based in Nairobi (Ross 1968: 73-4).

The phenomenon is complained of with monotonous regularity in the daily newspapers, so there is no reason to doubt that it exists.

Once this pattern is acknowledged it also becomes clear why leave entitlement plays such an important role in wage negotiations. It has often been noticed that unions negotiate for an amount of annual leave which would have seemed preposterous in Europe at a time when wages were broadly comparable with wages in Kenya, and this has sometimes been interpreted as indicating an excessive leisure preference. Typically, manual workers have three weeks paid leave a year, and this is the amount that the industrial court regards as its norm. Bank clerks get four weeks, and in addition there are ten statutory days off a year. But leave is not sought simply as a break from 'the routine of daily employment' but as the Ndegwa Commission noticed, it is something which people do their best to enjoy 'having regard to their other commitments' (Ndegwa 1971: 254). People need a relatively long leave, because it is essential to the maintenance of the links with rural homes. Anyone who has lived in Nairobi will have experienced the look of anguish which comes over the faces of those whom we wish a restful holiday as they depart on their annual leave. The holiday is more likely to be devoted to the back-breaking task of clearing land than to a rest!

When do people leave?

If people do not stay in Nairobi until the 'normal retiring age', one must pose the question whether it is possible to identify the time in their lives when they are on average most likely to leave. According to the 1969 census, only 11 per cent of Nairobi's male labour force was 45 years old or over, but this does not help us in finding an answer, since this relatively small proportion might be no more than a phenomenon of transition: there has not yet been enough time for the proportion to rise, given that most enter the labour force in their teens or twenties. One possibility is that at some point the productivity of a man's farm rises to a level where the addition of one family worker will lead to an increase in the value of output which exceeds the wage he would forgo by abandoning his urban job. One would then assume that it is at that point that he leaves town and returns home or goes to live on the farm. But this is singularly unconvincing: given the traditional division of labour in agriculture, a man's marginal product is likely to be the increased output attributable to his presence during some critical month or two when clearing or planting have to be done. Even assuming that this critical period extends to two months in the year, it must seem improbable that the resulting increase in farm output will exceed a full year's urban pay. Under all other circumstances it must pay him better, if it pays at all, to hire labour for this peak period, since the cost of two months' hired labour is unlikely to exceed a year's urban pay. Even so he will, of course, hire labour only if the value of the increase in output exceeds the wage that has to be paid.

If the 'equalization of rural and urban income hypothesis' has therefore to be abandoned, one is driven back to the old explanation of why people do not stay indefinitely in town: There comes a point when people decide that they have invested enough of urban surplus income in their farms and that it is now time to ditch the town and enjoy the fruits of that investment by living on the farm. The trouble with this explanation is that it does not provide a 'determinate' solution. In other words, there is no knowing just when people have had enough!

Can the conflicting evidence by reconciled?

We have seen that there is some apparent divergence between the findings of Rempel and of the Labour Turnover Study on the one hand, and the census as well as some of the findings of sociologists on the other. There are a number of possible explanations for this apparent divergence. First Rempel of course only reported the intentions declared by recent migrants to his interviewers. One knows from experience that what people intend – or *say* they intend – is rarely what they do, and in this particular respect it would, therefore, be mistaken to give too much weight to Rempel's otherwise very revealing findings.

Second, a median number of ten years in a job is not of course a lifetime, especially when one remembers that most people are lucky to be successful once in finding a job.

Third, all the information we have used relates to 'formal' employment. The informal sector may be much less stable, except for the petty capitalists who have established successful business or the rentiers of low-cost housing – most of them apparently Kikuyu. But there is not sufficient evidence to form a judgment.

One possibility remains: the Turnover Study was confined to private-sector employment. Is it possible that turnover is greater in the public sector? It is usually said that in the civil service and in parastate bodies turnover is minimal, but the public sector also includes numbers of unskilled workers, especially in the Ministry of Works and in Nairobi City Council. We know from the Turnover Study that turnover is much higher in unskilled work than in employment as a whole, and the public sector may have more than its 'fair' share of unskilled workers.

Conclusion

One is left, therefore, with considerable uncertainty. If one were forced to reach a conclusion, it would probably be that nothing that could conceivably be described as a permanent proletariat is emerging in Nairobi – if by proletariat one means people who no longer have a farm income and who are totally dependent upon a wage income for their livelihood. It may be, as Rempel found, that only one-third of his newly arrived migrants had land and that they had less actual or potential claim to land than the average Kenyan (Rempel 1970: 37, 39, 41). But the *Urban Household Budget Survey* of 1968-9, which covered a random sample of *all* lower and middle income earners and not just recent arrivals, found that in Nairobi the proportion who had at least 1 acre of land was 63 per cent, and in addition many others will have had expectations of inheriting or acquiring land, and this is in line with the findings of the Nairobi urban study (Johnson 1971: 6). On the other hand, the very temporary migration lasting typically no more than two or three years is also probably no longer the dominant pattern which it was in the 1950s. For the great majority the village is still home, but this does not preclude them from spending a considerable period of their lives in Nairobi, returning home during that time as often as they can. Like the Tonga of Malawi described by van Velsen, the majority in Nairobi maintain social and economic links with their villages. In that sense they remain migrants.

But the rural society to which they intend eventually to return will not be there for them to fall back upon unless they take active steps during the whole of their working lives to contribute to its continuance (van Velsen 1961). More recently Grillo, writing about Kampala, reaches a similar conclusion, but argues that this is not incompatible with being 'highly committed to industrial employment' (Grillo 1973: 61). In the 1950s when urban pay was low there was, in the longer run, more money to be made from growing cash crops. That is why most people did not stay in the towns for long unless either, like the Ganda of Kampala, they happened to have farms within commuting distance or, like the Luo, there was no way of really making their farms pay. More recently the reverse has been the case – for anyone lucky enough to have a formal sector urban job and even for some in the 'informal sector', it is likely to be a long time before there is an economic gain to be derived from voluntarily relinquishing urban employment. At the same time, the rural area still remains home in a sense in which it never did in Europe in the nineteenth century. Whether an urban labour force which continues to retain such intimate links with the countryside can be described as a proletariat, or even as being wholly and permanently dependent upon wage employment − the phrase used at the beginning of this paper − is largely a matter of definition. Nor does it really matter. What is not in dispute is that people now stay longer in Nairobi while they continue to have close ties with their rural homes. If the African townsman is a townsman − to quote Max Gluckman's aphorism − he is a townsman with a difference (Gluckman 1972).

If it proved possible, despite much wringing of hands by employers, to get goods produced and services manned within a framework of short-term migration in the 1950s, the problem now must be infinitely smaller. And who is wanting a proletariat anyhow?

Acknowledgements

Reprinted from *Economic Development and Cultural Change* 24, 4 (1976); 695-706, with the kind permission of the editor.

An earlier version of this paper was presented to the annual East African Universities Social Science Conference, December 1972. I wish to acknowledge the stimulus received from Colin Leys's article 'Politics in Kenya: the Development of Peasant Society', *British Journal of Political Science* 1972: 307-37, and from discussions with Ike Inukai and Richard Porter.

19 Differentials in repeat and return migration in Thailand, 1965–1970

Sidney Goldstein and Alice Goldstein

A growing body of research (Goldstein 1964; Morrison 1970; Long and Hansen 1977; and Miller 1977) documents that the migration process is much more complex than traditional published census-type information suggests. For many individuals, the most recent move is only the last of a long series of moves. For some, migration involves many moves in a stepping-stone process from less to more developed locations or from rural to smaller urban to larger urban places; for others, the migration history may be quite random; and for others, it might consist of a pattern of circulating moves between two or more places (Chapman and Prothero 1977). Some persons may move only once, directly to their ultimate destination, but often they are only a minority of all migrants.

Significant obstacles impede efforts to assess these various aspects of mobility, especially with respect to the existing conceptual treatment of population movement as a demographic process. All too often, when data are collected and analysed, concepts developed for use in the Western world have been employed uncritically in less developed countries. The restriction, in most instances, to measuring migration defined only as permanent moves, involving the crossing of boundaries which generally encompass large areal units insures the exclusion of most short-term moves and those which are more temporary (Goldstein 1978). Yet, research has shown that such mobility often constitutes a very high percentage of all moves and with significant implications for the mover and for the places of origin and destination (Hugo 1978). Relevant data on migration in South-east Asia strongly suggest that a considerable part of the total movement is hidden by failure to ask the right questions or to use appropriate political or geographic units of measurement

380

in overall research designs. Consistently, the limited survey data available indicate that measured levels of mobility rise as the size of the units under analysis is reduced, and as the opportunity to record or to observe short-term movements is enhanced. The extent of circulation or return migration is likely far greater than censuses reveal.

The evidence from such survey data stresses the need to give more attention to circular and repeat movement in any overall assessment of migration patterns. To do otherwise could result in misleading conclusions about the extent and character of population redistribution, of rural-urban linkages, and of the role of movement in the development process. This situation argues strongly in favour of taking advantage of whatever new data sources on population movement develop and/or of exploiting existing data sources more fully to assess the role of population movement in urban growth and in redistribution generally. Such an opportunity has arisen for Thailand with a 2 per cent sample tape from the 1970 Census which allows integrated use of information on province of birth and place of last previous residence in the five years preceding the Census, together with information on place of residence at the 1970 Census. These data make it possible to ascertain the extent of return and repeat migration and whether these types of population movement vary, depending on the rural and urban destination of the latest move and the socioeconomic status of the migrants. Before turning to these data, some indication of urbanization in Thailand is in order.

Urbanization in Thailand

Urbanization has been assuming increased importance. Analyses of the patterns of urbanization in Thailand (Goldstein 1971 and 1973) between the 1947 and 1970 Censuses indicated that Thailand's urban population (defined as persons living in municipal areas) increased from 10 to 13 per cent of the total population, and the number of urban places containing 20,000 or more persons grew from 6 to 38. The urban growth rate has been high, averaging about 5 per cent a year, just above the average of the world's less developed countries. Yet, because the rural growth, about 3 per cent during this period, was also quite high, the speed of urbanization is not as marked as elsewhere.

Particularly noteworthy has been the very rapid growth of Greater Bangkok, consisting of the twin cities of Bangkok and Thonburi, which between 1947 and 1970 grew from just over 780,000 persons to about 3 million. Its 1970 population, over half of Thailand's urban population, was 32 times that of the next largest city, making its primacy one of the most striking in the world. Yet urban development has begun to permeate all regions of Thailand and is an important factor in the complex process of national, social, and economic development. For this reason, attention to the role of migration in urban growth must take account of differences in types of movement to Bangkok and to the smaller urban places, and attempt especially to assess whether movement to particular types of locations consists disproportionately of migrants who become long-term settlers or of individuals whose in-movement was more recent and represents for some either a return move or a repeat move that could portend still another move later on.

Assessment of the relation between type of migration and urbanization is in part affected by the definition of urban. For a number of years, experts on urbanization have argued that the Thai system of classifying places as urban on the basis of their political status as municipal areas should be changed to correct for the fact that the number of such places has virtually not changed since 1947, while the number of locations actually having an urban character has increased considerably (Robinson 1975 and 1976). The use of areas designated as 'sanitary districts' to allow for greater flexibility in an urban classification system has been strongly recommended. A recent assessment of the population characteristics of such units (Goldstein and Goldstein 1978) indicates that in many respects they more closely resemble the smaller municipal areas of Thailand than they do rural places. The inclusion of all of the sanitary districts' 3.2 million population with the 4.6 million in municipal areas in 1970 would increase the total urban population to 23 per cent of the kingdom's total population. However, even with this very substantial increase in the level of urbanization, Thailand would remain a heavily rural country, with over three-fourths of its population in villages and at least half of its 'urban' population in small localities.

In this analysis of the relation between type of residence and type of migration, sanitary districts will be considered apart from the remaining rural areas, allowing comparison with both the rural population and the populations of Bangkok and the other urban places in Thailand, the two groups into which the municipal areas are categorized here. Using the four residence categories in conjunction with a refined classification of migrants provides a unique opportunity to assess the interrelations between population movement and urbanization, and may provide new insights with broader relevance for less developed countries generally.

Migration concepts and data

The first comprehensive data on migration in Thailand became available from the 1960 Census, which asked questions on both place of birth and place of residence five years prior to the census (Prachuabmoh and Tirasawat 1974). Migration in both instances was defined in terms of changes in residence between provinces. The 1970 Census retained the place of birth question in basically the same form, but the five-year question was replaced by one asking length of residence in present village or municipal area. A major improvement in 1970 was the attempt to identify, for those who had moved within the previous five years, whether the place of origin was urban or rural. The wording of the question also allowed determination of whether the move within the last five years was within or between provinces. Nonetheless, in the published data for the 1960 and 1970 Censuses, no attempts were made to use either the place of birth or the place of residence question to ascertain the extent of repeat or return migration. The availability of the 1970 Census data on tape makes such cross-tabulations and subsequent analysis possible (Arnold and Boonpratuang 1976; Goldstein 1977).

Using an expanded and somewhat modified version of the typology established by Hope Eldridge (1965), the place of birth, previous place of residence, and current place of residence information in the 1970 Census have been grouped into five migration-status categories: (1) non-migrants: individuals 5 years of age and over who were living in their province of birth in both 1965 and 1970; (2) settled migrants: those whose province of residence in 1965 was different from province of birth but who were living in the same province in 1970 as in 1965; (3) primary migrants: who moved to their 1970 province of residence since 1965 and whose previous province of residence was the same as their province of birth; (4) return migrants: who since 1965 had moved back to their province of birth from a different province; (5) repeat migrants: whose province of birth was different from their 1970 province of residence, and who had moved to their 1970 province since 1965 from a third province.

For the last three categories, unlike the Eldridge typology, the place of origin of the latest move varies within the period 1965-70, because the information is based on last change in place of residence within the five-year interval rather than on a five-year question tied specifically to residence in 1965. The typology's most serious limitation is its necessary reliance on the province as the areal unit for measuring migration: Thai place of birth data are tabulated only in terms of province, and no information is provided on the rural or urban character of the place of birth. The limitation is particularly serious for analysis concerned with the questions of migration to urban locations and return movement to rural places. With this in mind, the evaluation of the 1970 Census data must be seen as exploratory, seeking to take maximum advantage of a new set of data.

In a partial attempt to overcome the limitation imposed by use of provinces, the analysis can give special attention to those individuals who qualify as primary, repeat, or return migrants. By definition, all of them have made at least one move during the five years preceding the census, and the census did ascertain the rural/urban origin of the move. The extent to which different types of moves vary with respect to the rural-urban origin of the migrant at the time of the last move during the five-year interval can be determined. For both this limited set of data and for the broader set described earlier, comparisons are feasible by rural-urban residence in 1970. In the analysis which follows, only the population 15 years of age and over is included since most children move with parents.

Findings

Types of migration by 1970 residence

For Thailand as a whole, the vast majority of men and women 15 years of age and over (henceforth referred to in the text as adults) were classified as non-migrants; over eight out of every ten persons of either sex were reported as living in the same province at all three times for which the information was collected (Table 19.1). These indicate a high degree of residential stability. Moreover, among the migrants, the single largest category by far consists of settled migrants, individuals who changed their province of residence between birth and 1965 but not again between 1965 and 1970; just over 10 per cent of all adults, about two-thirds of all migrants, belong to this category. With the non-migrants they account for about 95 per cent of the adult population.

Of the remaining three migration categories, all of which involved some movement between 1965 and 1970, the largest by far is composed of primary migrants, who constitute only 5 per cent of the adult males and 4 per cent of the adult females. Repeat migrants are about twice as numerous as return migrants, but both are extremely small percentages of the total adult population, and together comprise only 10 per cent of all migrants. Judged by movement between provinces, therefore,

TABLE 19.1 *Distribution by type of migration by 1970 place of residence, for total population, all migrants, and recent migrants, by sex (persons aged 15 and over)*

Residence in 1970	Males						Females					
	Non-migrants	Settled migrants	Primary migrants	Return migrants	Repeat migrants	Total per cent*	Non-migrants	Settled migrants	Primary migrants	Return migrants	Repeat migrants	Total per cent*
	As per cent of total population											
Bangkok	56.3	28.0	13.6	0.5	1.6	100.0	56.0	30.1	12.0	0.6	1.3	100.0
Other urban places	66.7	19.3	8.4	1.2	4.4	100.0	70.9	17.4	7.5	1.0	3.2	100.0
Sanitary districts	77.2	13.1	6.0	0.8	2.9	100.0	81.7	10.3	4.6	0.9	2.5	100.0
Rural	86.0	9.5	3.2	0.5	0.8	100.0	88.8	7.8	2.3	0.5	0.6	100.0
Total kingdom	81.9	11.6	4.6	0.5	1.3	100.0	84.6	10.2	3.6	0.6	1.0	100.0
	As per cent of total migrants											
Bangkok	—	64.1	31.1	1.1	3.7	100.0	—	68.4	27.2	1.4	3.0	100.0
Other urban places	—	57.9	25.4	3.6	13.1	100.0	—	60.0	25.6	3.5	10.9	100.0
Sanitary districts	—	57.2	26.3	3.6	12.9	100.0	—	56.5	24.9	5.1	13.5	100.0
Rural	—	67.5	23.0	3.7	5.8	100.0	—	69.8	20.5	4.2	5.5	100.0
Total kingdom	—	64.4	25.6	2.8	7.2	100.0	—	66.2	23.4	3.9	6.5	100.0
	As per cent of recent migrants											
Bangkok	—	—	86.6	3.2	10.2	100.0	—	—	86.3	4.3	9.4	100.0
Other urban places	—	—	60.0	8.6	31.4	100.0	—	—	64.1	8.5	27.4	100.0
Sanitary districts	—	—	61.9	8.2	29.9	100.0	—	—	57.5	11.2	31.2	100.0
Rural	—	—	71.1	11.1	17.8	100.0	—	—	67.7	14.7	17.7	100.0
Total kingdom	—	—	71.9	7.8	20.3	100.0	—	—	69.2	11.5	19.3	100.0

* For population size, see Table 19.7

Source: From a 2 per cent sample tape of the 1970 Census of Thailand

and relying upon the particular definition employed here, repeat and return migration are not a significant proportion of total movement in Thailand. But the fact that this classification does not include any form of movement within provinces must be stressed. Nonetheless, about 10 per cent of all migrants either returned to province of origin or moved to a third province, and the likelihood that these types of migration would be much greater if shorter distance moves and fuller coverage of the entire migration history were included, points to the import-ance of identifying the migration experience of multiple movers rather than limiting assessment of migration to the single move determined by the answer to either a place of birth question or to the location of the last previous residence. The evidence (bottom panel of Table 19.1) that almost one-third of all recent migrants are either repeat or return migrants supports this argument.

The patterns of migration in Thailand as a whole are strongly influenced by the experience of the rural population, which is so much larger than the urban. Therefore, a more meaningful assessment of migration patterns results from a comparative analysis of the patterns for specific residence categories. These data point to sharp differences that are closely tied to where the residence category falls on the urban-rural continuum.

For both males and females, continuous residence in a single province is most characteristic of the rural population and least characteristic of the population living in Bangkok (Table 19.1). The key role of migration in urban growth, especially of the metropolis, and its much lesser role in population distribution in rural places, is also reflected in the distribution by type of migration. In Bangkok three out of every ten adult males and females were identified as settled migrants, reflecting the capital's long history as a centre of attraction. The proportion of settled migrants declines steadily, to only 10 per cent of the males living in rural locations and to just 8 per cent of rural females, and is considerably higher in other urban places than in sanitary districts. If, following the original typology by Hope Eldridge, settled migrants are considered as non-migrants, then a very high percentage of the residents in both rural locations and urban places, including Bangkok, can be considered stable.

Despite evidence of stability for a considerable portion of all persons classified as interprovincial migrants in the 1970 Census, perhaps the more significant insights relate to the primary migrants. For every residence category, the primary migrants, whose first enumerated move occurred between 1965 and 1970, constituted the second largest migrant group. However, the relative number of primary migrants in a given population varied directly with the urban level, from 14 per cent of all adult males and 12 per cent of all adult females in Bangkok to only 3 and 2 per cent respectively of those in rural places. The substantially higher proportion of primary migrants in Bangkok compared to all other residence categories testifies to its continued attractiveness. Yet the percentages of primary migrants in both other urban places and sanitary districts also indicate that these have considerable drawing power. If the comparison is restricted to the four types of migrants (middle panel of Table 19.1), that is, excluding non-migrants, the proportion of primary migrants varies much less among the residence categories: between about one-fourth and one-third of all male migrants and one-fifth and one-fourth of all female migrants. Again, proportions tend to vary directly with the urban character of the residence category. Primary migrants constitute the vast majority of all recent migrants in every residence category (third panel of Table 19.1), but particularly of those in Bangkok, again pointing to the attraction of the capital.

Return migrants constitute only a small percentage of the total adult population in Thailand. For no residence category are they much more than 1 per cent of the adult population and the pattern of variation among places is not clear. Since a considerable part of the movement to urban places in Thailand is from rural locations, the percentage of return migrants might have been expected to be higher among the rural population than among the urban. The data for the total adult population do not support this expectation.[1]

If return migrants are assessed only in relation to all migrants rather than to the total population, the rate of return remains low, especially in Bangkok. However, if return migrants are related only to those individuals who had moved between birth and 1965, those who provide the pool for return migrants − the settled migrants, repeat migrants, and return migrants combined − the lowest rate of return (not shown in Table 19.1) again characterizes Bangkok: 2 per cent among males and females; for the other three residence categories the rate of return varies minimally at about 5 per cent. Thus, regardless of the measure employed, the evidence points neither to very high rates of return migration nor to higher rates for rural than for urban locations. Whether the extent of return movement would be greater if shorter distance moves could be incorporated into the analysis must remain speculative.

When the rate of return migration is expressed as a per cent of all recent migration, it bears an inverse relation to the urban character of the current residence (bottom panel of Table 19.1). This suggests the considerable contribution of return migration to recent movement into rural areas and emphasizes the need for more attention to the composition, motivation, and impact of those involved.

For all residence categories, repeat movement is more frequent than return movement, and particularly for Bangkok, other urban places, and sanitary districts. The higher ratio of repeat to return migration for the more urban places suggests that the tendency for repeated movement is associated closely with the urbanization process. For both men and women, however, the highest percentage of repeat migrants is found not in Bangkok, but in the smaller urban places. As suggested by other research (Goldstein, Pitaktepsombati and Goldstein 1977), this pattern may reflect that certain segments of the occupational hierarchy, especially government employees and other white collar workers, tend to move from one urban place to another, often because of job transfers. Later analysis allows examination of this suggestion. Evidence of the importance of repeat movement as a component of recent migration is that among recent migrants, as many as 31 per cent of the males in other urban places are repeat migrants. The pattern in sanitary districts more closely resembles that of small municipal areas than rural places, again suggesting the more urban character of the sanitary districts. The same basic pattern characterizes the female migrants.

Again, it must be stressed that repeat migration is defined in terms of different provinces of residence at three points in time. In that additional moves may have occurred between these points, and that some movement may have been intraprovincial, a number of the individuals classified here as primary, settled, or return migrants might be more properly categorized as repeat migrants on the basis of their complete mobility experience. This means that the amount of identified repeat mobility is a minimum estimate, and thus the finding that almost one-third of all recent movement to smaller urban places is repeat movement takes on added significance.

Rural-urban origins

The 1970 Census collected information on the rural-urban character of the place of origin of persons who moved between 1965 and 1970, all of whom are 'recent migrants'. For them, the rural-urban place of origin by type of migration for the various 1970 residence categories may be ascertained. The extent of rural origins varies considerably by 1970 place of residence (Table 19.2). Migrants living in more urban places were much less likely to come from rural origins than those residing in sanitary districts or other rural places; but the capital city tended to attract relatively more of its migrants from rural areas than did smaller urban places. These differences also extended to the type of migration. For example, among primary migrants, 72 per cent of the males and slightly fewer of the females in Bangkok and only about 60 per cent of the males and females in other urban places were of rural origin, compared to 87 per cent of those who were living in sanitary districts and over 90 per cent of those in rural places in 1970. Similarly, the percentage of return migrants whose place of previous residence was rural rose from just under one-half of the males and females in Bangkok, and about four out of every ten in smaller urban places, to 73 per cent of the males and 81 per cent of the females in sanitary districts, and even higher percentages in rural places in 1970. Clearly, return migration to an urban place was more likely to involve a move from another urban place; the chance that the origin would be urban declined with the increasing rural character of the eventual destination. This same pattern characterized repeat movement. Of the repeat migrants in Bangkok, only half of the men and somewhat fewer of the women came from rural places; and this was true of about 30 per cent in other urban places. By contrast, among the repeat migrants in sanitary districts seven out of ten were of rural origin, as were about eight out of every ten of the repeat migrants to other rural places.

Overall, these data suggest that among recent migrants, regardless of destination, primary moves tend to be rural in origin, although much more so for destinations that are also rural and for sanitary districts. In contrast, a majority of the moves to Bangkok and especially to other urban places, that are either return moves or repeat moves, are from locations which are also urban. This points to a considerable interchange between urban places of individuals whose residential experience consists of several moves. To the extent, however, that both return and repeat migration is still a fairly limited phenomenon, the urban origins of these migrants do not very substantially affect the overall origins of the total migrant segments of the population in either Bangkok or other urban places. The latter is still determined largely by the origin of the primary migrants and especially of the settled migrants.

Although a very large majority of the migrants to both sanitary districts and other rural places moved there from rural places, as many as one-fourth of the return and repeat migrants to the

TABLE 19.2 *Percentage of recent migrants from rural areas by type of migration, by 1970 place of residence, and sex (for persons aged 15 and over)*

Residence in 1970	Primary migrants		Return migrants		Repeat migrants	
	Males	Females	Males	Females	Males	Females
Bangkok	71.7	66.4	47.7	45.9	51.0	44.0
Other urban places	61.5	58.1	43.0	39.7	30.6	28.8
Sanitary districts	86.9	87.0	73.3	81.0	71.2	73.2
Rural	91.8	94.1	83.8	87.2	82.1	76.1
Total kingdom	83.2	81.6	75.6	77.7	66.4	63.0

Source: as Table 19.1

sanitary districts and approximately 20 per cent of those moving to other rural places were of urban origin. This points to an important interchange involving an urban to rural move as opposed to the much more commonly researched rural to urban movement. It argues again for giving much closer attention to the character of movement into the smallest urban locations and into rural places, and of the need to explore the ways in which the urban origin of the return and repeat migrants as well as of some 10 to 15 per cent of the primary migrants affects both the migrants themselves and the demographic, social, and economic structure of these types of locations. Since some of the sanitary districts provide potential nuclei of urban centres, the role of urban to rural migration in their growth takes on added significance. Urban to rural migrants may serve as agents of social change, and their potential in the modernization and development of rural areas warrants more attention.

Age differentials

Both migration status and type of move are influenced by the characteristics of the individual; age and sex selectivity has been clearly demonstrated (Eldridge 1965; Lee 1974). In part, the marked differences by age reflect the universal pattern of higher migration rates associated with entrance into the labour force and with family formation. To a lesser degree, they also reflect that the opportunity to qualify as a repeat or return migrant depends on whether a prior move had been made; rates of return and repeat migration should tend, therefore, to be higher at older ages. Since the age patterns for males and females are quite similar, the data cited will refer largely to males; statistics for both males and females are presented in the tables.[2] Particular attention is focused on the return and repeat migrants.

In Bangkok, for all age groups except the youngest, almost half of the population were in-migrants, indicating the important role of migration in the growth of its population (Table 19.3). The lower percentage of migrants among those aged 15-24 reflects the high proportion of this cohort, especially those aged 15-19, who were born in Bangkok, many of them children of earlier immigrants. The high percentages of settled migrants among the older groups reflect the large number of persons who migrated into the city in earlier periods and at earlier stages of the life cycle. It may also reflect a higher rate of return or onward movement among earlier cohorts of in-migrants, leaving only the more settled to be enumerated. If the settled migrants are combined with the non-migrants to constitute the more stable segments of the population, a very high level of stability is indicated for all groups above age 35. Beginning at that age, over 90 per cent of the population were either born in Bangkok or had lived there since 1965, and even for those aged 25-34 as many as 88 per cent qualify as stable under this definition. Only for the 15-24 year age group, characterized by the peak levels of recent migration, was 'stability' less; the heavy concentration of recent migrants in this narrow age range poses major challenges to provide adequate employment and housing in this critical stage of the life cycle.

The differences noted earlier (Table 19.1) in the overall comparisons of levels and types of movement to other urban places, sanitary districts, and rural areas in general extend to the specific age groups, with a few interesting exceptions. Reflecting more recent development, the other urban places and sanitary districts tend to have their highest proportions of non-migrants in the youngest and the oldest age groups. The low levels of in-migration before the 1960s account for the decline, particularly noticeable in the sanitary districts, in the proportion of settled migrants among the older segments of the population. The contrast with Bangkok is especially sharp. For both other urban places and sanitary districts, however, age selectivity favouring higher mobility for those aged 15-34 is apparent among recent migrants, although at levels well below those of Bangkok; and the levels in sanitary districts are below those of the other urban places. Similar selectivity operates in rural places as well, but at levels far below those characterizing Bangkok, and even

391

TABLE 19.3 *Distribution of migrants by type of migration by age and sex, by 1970 place of residence*

Age category	Males						Females					
	Percentage in total population of		Distribution of recent migrants				Percentage in total population of		Distribution of recent migrants			
	All migrants	Recent migrants	Primary migrants	Return migrants	Repeat migrants	Total per cent	All migrants	Recent migrants	Primary migrants	Return migrants	Repeat migrants	Total per cent
Bangkok												
15-24	38.7	23.8	90.8	2.5	6.7	100.0	40.4	21.3	90.6	3.3	6.1	100.0
25-34	47.6	12.4	80.7	4.0	15.3	100.0	48.7	11.4	81.6	4.4	14.0	100.0
35-44	49.4	6.1	70.5	4.9	24.6	100.0	43.5	5.7	73.7	8.8	17.5	100.0
45-64	46.1	5.7	68.4	7.0	24.6	100.0	46.8	5.7	73.7	8.8	17.5	100.0
65 and over	51.3	7.2	70.8	7.0	22.2	100.0	41.7	5.1	84.3	—	15.7	100.0
Total	43.7	15.7	86.6	3.2	10.2	100.0	44.0	13.9	86.3	4.3	9.4	100.0
Other urban places												
15-24	28.1	16.8	69.7	7.7	22.6	100.0	27.2	15.8	73.4	7.6	19.0	100.0
25-34	39.4	17.9	57.0	8.9	34.1	100.0	33.6	14.7	57.2	9.5	33.3	100.0
35-44	37.1	11.1	49.5	9.9	40.6	100.0	30.8	7.4	48.6	12.2	39.2	100.0
45-64	30.5	6.5	43.1	7.7	49.2	100.0	25.8	5.1	54.9	9.8	35.3	100.0
65 and over	26.5	3.4	64.7	2.9	32.4	100.0	22.3	4.0	50.0	15.0	35.0	100.0
Total	33.3	14.0	60.0	8.6	31.4	100.0	29.1	11.7	64.1	8.5	27.4	100.0

Sanitary districts

15-24	20.0	11.6	69.0	6.9	24.1	100.0	17.2	9.9	63.6	11.1	25.3	100.0
25-34	25.0	13.2	59.1	9.8	31.1	100.0	22.1	10.1	56.4	10.9	32.7	100.0
35-44	24.0	7.0	57.1	8.6	34.3	100.0	17.6	6.7	43.3	17.9	38.8	100.0
45-64	28.6	7.5	49.3	8.0	42.7	100.0	17.2	5.5	60.0	7.3	32.7	100.0
65 and over	13.1	2.2	*	*	*	*	13.6	3.5	*	*	*	*
Total	22.8	9.7	61.9	8.2	29.9	100.0	18.3	8.0	57.5	11.2	31.3	100.0

Rural

15-24	10.8	5.5	76.4	11.0	12.6	100.0	9.5	4.0	72.5	12.5	15.0	100.0
25-34	15.3	5.6	71.1	11.8	17.1	100.0	11.8	4.1	63.4	17.1	19.5	100.0
35-44	16.5	3.7	61.8	12.0	26.2	100.0	11.5	3.0	66.7	10.0	23.3	100.0
45-64	14.7	2.8	64.1	10.6	25.3	100.0	12.5	2.2	68.2	13.6	18.2	100.0
65 and over	16.5	3.3	69.5	10.2	20.3	100.0	11.3	1.4	57.1	14.3	28.6	100.0
Total	14.0	4.5	71.1	11.1	17.8	100.0	11.2	3.4	67.7	14.7	17.6	100.0

Total kingdom

15-24	15.3	8.3	79.5	7.2	13.3	100.0	14.0	6.7	77.6	9.0	13.4	100.0
25-34	20.5	7.5	69.4	9.3	21.3	100.0	17.1	5.8	65.5	12.1	22.4	100.0
35-44	20.4	4.6	60.8	10.9	28.3	100.0	15.4	3.7	62.2	10.8	27.0	100.0
45-64	18.0	3.5	60.0	8.6	31.4	100.0	15.4	2.8	67.9	10.7	21.4	100.0
65 and over	17.7	3.2	68.7	9.4	21.9	100.0	15.9	2.0	55.0	15.0	30.0	100.0
Total	18.1	6.5	71.9	7.8	20.3	100.0	15.4	5.2	69.2	11.5	19.3	100.0

* No percentages are calculated if the unweighted base contains fewer than 20 cases

** In this and succeeding tables, 'non-migrants' equal 100 minus 'all migrants'; and 'settled migrants' equal 'all migrants' minus 'recent migrants'

Source: as Table 19.1

noticeably below those of sanitary districts, for all but the oldest age group.

In general, the levels of return and especially repeat migration, although very low when expressed as a percentage of the total population (data not shown here), tend to peak in the 25-34 age group, the age group which follows the one characterized by peak levels of primary migration, suggesting that migration onwards or back to place of origin occurs fairly soon after the initial move; but this relation remains to be demonstrated more definitively.

When return and recent migrants are related exclusively to recent migrants to the capital (the combination of primary, return, and repeat migrants), older return migrants constitute a higher percentage of the total than do the younger ones. Nonetheless, return migrants in Bangkok constitute no more than 7 per cent of all the recent migrants. Return migration, as measured in this analysis, therefore is not a major factor in the population dynamics of Bangkok. In fact, the proportion of repeat migrants in Bangkok's population is much greater in each age group than is the proportion of return migrants. Moreover, among older migrants, repeat migration constitutes a considerably higher percentage of all recent moves than it does among the younger ones, undoubtedly reflecting the cumulative effects through the life cycle. Migration as a 'stepping stone' process is clearly more common among older persons even while accounting, overall, for a relatively small proportion of all movement to the capital.

The percentages of return migrants among all recent migrants in other urban places and in sanitary districts are, for many age groups, above those for Bangkok. This is not surprising since a high proportion of migrants crossing provincial boundaries in Thailand move to the capital, which in turn, provides the major reservoir for return migration. For example, among the recent male migrants aged 15-24 to other urban places, about 8 per cent are return migrants, as are 10 per cent among those aged 35-44. These levels contrast with only 2 and 5 per cent respectively for the comparable age groups in Bangkok. Sanitary districts display similar levels of return migration. The highest levels of return migration among recent migrants are found in rural places where 11-12 per cent of all recent male migrants in all age groups under age 65 are return migrants. The percentages are generally as high or higher for females. Although the ideal base for computing the return migration rates would be the earlier out-migrants from the specific locations, a measure which is not feasible here, the cruder measures nonetheless suggest that among recent migrants into the smaller urban places and rural locations a not insignificant number are returning to the same province which they had left some time after their birth.

For virtually all age groups, repeat migration is much more common among recent migrants in other urban places and sanitary districts than it is in Bangkok or in rural areas. Moreover, in other urban places and sanitary districts, considerably more of the population in each age group are repeat migrants than return migrants; differences are in the same direction for rural places, but not as sharp. Repeat migrants constitute over one-third of all recent migrants in most age groups in both other urban places and sanitary districts, and closely resemble the proportion of primary migrants among some age groups in these residence categories. Selection of an urban place as the culmination of a series of moves occurs with sufficient frequency to give repeat movement considerable importance in accounting for recent migration. Together with return migration, which is also a form of repeat movement, this indication of the comparatively high proportion of recent movers who have a history of repeated movement, especially at more advanced stages of the life cycle, emphasizes the desirability of obtaining longitudinal data that allow more careful assessment both of the relation of movement to various stages of the life cycle and of the complexity of the migration process overall.

Educational differentials

Since the economic and educational considerations account for a very high proportion of the motives for movement, the proportion of migrants and their type of movement might be expected to vary by educational and occupational status. Research on the United States (Miller 1977) has demonstrated that repeat movers are a highly selective group, with educational levels and occupational status far above the average of the total population and above the average for all migrants. By contrast, return migrants seem to be much more randomly selected in terms of education and occupation. Primary movers, like repeat movers, are characterized by high educational and occupational levels.

The relation between education and occupation on the one hand and the extent of return and repeat movement on the other is complex. If 'expected' employment opportunities are not realized at the point of destination, many migrants may either return to their place of origin, to the security offered by family and alternative economic opportunities, or move to a third destination. At the same time, the extent to which return or repeat movement occurs may be considerably affected by the level of education achieved and the type of occupation for which the individual is trained. Since white collar employment generally and professional work in particular is less available in rural or smaller urban locations, a return move to such locations by a migrant qualified for such employment seems less likely than such a move by a person trained for manual employment. Yet, as Miller and others suggest, individuals with higher training and with white collar and professional employment are more likely to become repeat migrants, moving as new opportunities open. Such movement will include rural areas, as efforts to develop them require persons with appropriate white collar skills. In fact, government employees engaged in both administrative and development efforts may be shifted about fairly frequently as the need for their services and skills in particular locations changes. It is sometimes established government policy not to allow government officials to settle 'permanently' in a particular location.

The ability to use the 1970 Thai Census data to assess type of migration by educational and occupational levels presents a unique opportunity to gain insights into the extent to which the patterns observed for the United States and the relations hypothesized above characterize the situation in Thailand. Because age is a key variable affecting migration levels as well as type of migration, these data have been standardized for age differences among the various educational and occupational groups, thereby allowing clearer insights into the relation between migration on the one hand and education and occupation on the other hand.

For the total kingdom, as well as for each of the four residence categories, education is clearly and positively related to migration status (Table 19.4). For example, for the total kingdom, only 15 per cent of all males with a primary education or less are migrants, but, one-third of the males with a secondary education and almost half of those with a university education had moved at least once between provinces. Similar sharp differences characterize females. Although the levels of migrants in the population varied, the same basic pattern, with minor exceptions, characterized each of the four residence categories. Of more interest here, however, are differentials in the extent of return and repeat migration.

Measured in terms of recent migration only, return migrants constitute between 10 and 13 per cent of men and women with a primary education or less. They comprise a lower proportion of males with more education, and a much higher proportion among

396

university educated females. Repeat migration was as frequent, and usually considerably more frequent, than return migration for all educational categories, but the differences were particularly sharp for males with secondary and university educations. Females also tended to have higher proportions of repeat than return migrants in all education categories, but the differences between the two migration categories were not as sharp as for males. Higher education is associated with more frequent repeat movement.

The same general relations between educational level for the total kingdom hold for the various residence categories. The major exception is Bangkok where the relation between education and type of movement is more irregular, although the university educated have the highest percentage of repeat movers, especially for males. By contrast, the level of return migration does not vary as consistently with education among the various residence categories. Only for rural males do the data suggest that rising education is associated with lower rates of return movement.

The particularly high proportion of university educated male migrants in Bangkok and in smaller urban places who are repeat migrants as well as the generally positive association between education and per cent of repeat migrants in smaller urban places and in rural locations conforms to the association between repeat migration and higher-than-average educational levels observed for the United States by Miller (1977). It also lends support to the hypothesis that individuals with higher education would be more likely, not only to be included among migrants initially, but also to be disproportionately represented among migrants who make more than one move. The combination of skills, the nature of occupations, and the distribution of occupations are all conducive to a history of repeat movement. Evidently in a less developed country such as Thailand, direction of such repeat moves is toward the less developed or more recently developed areas, such as smaller urban places and rural locations, rather than to the big city. Although the facilities for obtaining higher education are more heavily concentrated in big cities, the opportunities for the full use of such education in large urban centres may be somewhat restricted because such places have a high percentage of highly trained individuals.

Occupational differentials

As suggested earlier, occupation, like education, could substantially affect both the overall level of migration and the type of

TABLE 19.4 Distribution of migrants aged 15 and over by type of migration by education and sex, by 1970 place of residence (standardized for age)

Education	Males						Females					
	Percentage in total population of		Distribution of recent migrants				Percentage in total population of		Distribution of recent migrants			
	All migrants	Recent migrants	Primary migrants	Return migrants	Repeat migrants	Total per cent	All migrants	Recent migrants	Primary migrants	Return migrants	Repeat migrants	Total per cent
Bangkok												
None	24.6	7.5	77.3	4.0	18.7	100.0	35.2	8.4	80.5	5.7	13.8	100.0
Primary	47.1	16.2	88.9	2.5	8.6	100.0	40.1	14.6	88.4	3.4	8.2	100.0
Secondary	42.4	11.4	78.1	6.1	15.8	100.0	32.9	8.8	78.4	8.0	13.6	100.0
University	52.7	9.5	70.5	3.2	26.3	100.0	48.3	10.5	77.1	6.7	16.2	100.0
Other urban places												
None	25.5	8.1	65.4	8.7	25.9	100.0	25.3	9.5	67.4	10.5	22.1	100.0
Primary	30.3	11.8	71.2	7.6	21.2	100.0	29.6	11.6	66.4	7.8	25.8	100.0
Secondary	39.8	16.7	45.5	9.6	44.9	100.0	32.6	13.2	49.2	7.6	43.2	100.0
University	58.1	32.3	33.7	8.7	57.6	100.0	54.4	18.7	47.6	14.4	38.0	100.0

Sanitary districts												
None	22.5	3.5	*	*	*	*	24.7	9.8	55.1	7.1	37.8	100.0
Primary	21.8	9.0	63.3	8.9	27.8	100.0	17.6	8.1	59.2	9.9	30.9	100.0
Secondary	41.8	20.5	37.1	16.6	46.3	100.0	13.5	7.1	*	*	*	*
University	45.4	23.1	*	*	*	*	*	*	*	*	*	*
Rural												
None	13.4	4.6	74.0	13.0	13.0	100.0	12.7	3.8	68.4	13.2	18.4	100.0
Primary	13.8	4.4	72.7	11.4	15.9	100.0	10.7	3.2	65.6	15.6	18.8	100.0
Secondary	22.1	10.4	59.6	9.6	30.8	100.0	14.7	6.9	59.4	13.0	27.6	100.0
University	26.8	10.8	*	*	*	*	*	*	*	*	*	*
Total kingdom												
None	14.4	4.7	74.4	12.8	12.8	100.0	14.7	4.5	67.6	12.8	19.6	100.0
Primary	16.9	5.6	72.4	10.3	17.3	100.0	15.0	4.7	70.2	10.6	19.2	100.0
Secondary	33.1	12.7	59.8	7.9	32.3	100.0	27.1	9.0	65.6	10.0	24.4	100.0
University	44.6	14.3	43.4	6.3	50.3	100.0	52.4	14.1	53.2	18.4	28.4	100.0

* No percentages are calculated if the unweighted base contains fewer than 20 cases

Source: as Table 19.1

movement. To assess the relation between migration and occupation in Thailand, the labour force has been subdivided into four major occupational groups: white collar workers, manual workers, service workers, and agricultural workers. Overall, the data show that for the total kingdom and for all residence categories except Bangkok (which still has some agricultural workers in its labour force), those engaged in agriculture have the highest levels of stability, with at least four out of every eight defined as non-migrants. Levels of migration for each of the other three occupational groups, with only minor exception, are clearly correlated with the urban character of the place of residence, for both males and females. However, within specific locations, the patterns of differentials by occupation are not as consistent. Among non-agricultural workers in Bangkok, the highest levels of migration characterize both male and female service workers, but the difference is relatively small for males. The same pattern of differentials holds for sanitary districts. In other urban places, however, the migration levels of service workers closely resemble those of the white collar workers, and are higher than those of the manual workers.

These data document, first, that for the employed population in all four residence categories at least a majority were born in the particular province in which they were working in 1970, and that the level of stability rises from the urban to the more rural end of the location continuum. Because of the definitions used here, however, a number of the 'non-migrants' may have moved from one location to another within the province. Second, in the capital, among all occupational categories, almost as many individuals moved from outside the province as were born in it, attesting to the major contribution which migration has made to all segments of the occupational structure of the primate city. Third, the lack of sharp differentials in the proportion of migrants by occupational category and the inconsistency in pattern among different types of locations suggests that migration has operated less selectively by occupation than by education; in part, however, the selectivity may be masked by the inability to identify occupation before migration. Finally, the greater differences for women than for men suggest that occupational opportunities for women are more differentially distributed, thereby possibly accounting for more of the movement of employed women than of men.

To assess the relation between type of movement and occupation, the analysis is restricted, as for the analysis of age and education differentials, to individuals moving in the five-year interval preceding the 1970 Census. The absence of information on occupation before the move precludes attention to whether type of movement is related to any particular patterns of occupational change.

The great majority of all recent migrants in each occupational category are primary movers, suggesting a high degree of stability. Yet, at least 25 per cent of males in every occupational category and as many as one-third of those in white collar occupations are either return or repeat migrants as are at least 30 per cent of the female white collar, manual, and agricultural workers, stressing the complexity of migration among the Thai labour force (Table 19.5). Moreover, data for the total kingdom suggest that return movement is less characteristic of non-agricultural workers, and that repeat movement tends to occur more frequently among non-agricultural workers, although female service workers are an exception.

The distribution of the various occupation groups by type of move varies considerably in the different residence categories. At the same time the magnitude of the differentials and, in some instances, the patterns of differentials varied within residence categories. For all occupational categories, Bangkok has by far the highest percentage of primary movers. Regardless of occupational category, movement to the capital therefore tends to consist very heavily of individuals making interprovincial moves for the first time; return migrants account for the lowest proportion of both males and females in all occupational categories. The differentials between the capital and other locations are sharp in virtually every instance, though some caution is needed in interpreting these data since the return migrants and the repeat migrants cannot be related here to the base population from which they come. Outside Bangkok, return migration contributes substantially to total recent male and female movement. Within residence categories, for both males and females, no clear relation exists between the percentage of return migration and occupation.

Repeat migration, regardless of occupation, does not account for a high proportion of the movement to the capital. It is much more characteristic of those going to other urban places and sanitary districts, and to a lesser extent this differential even holds among migrants residing in rural areas. That at least one-fourth of male manual, service, and white collar workers in other urban places and in sanitary districts are repeat migrants points to the very dynamic character of population movement and the importance of obtaining more detail on migration histories, and the extent, origins, and reasons for repeat movement. The need is reinforced when note is taken of the additional movement

TABLE 19.5 *Distribution of migrants aged 15 and over by type of migration by occupation and sex, by 1970 place of residence (standardized for age)*

Occupation	Males						Females					
	Percentage in total population of		Distribution of recent migrants				Percentage in total population of		Distribution of recent migrants			
	All migrants	Recent migrants	Primary migrants	Return migrants	Repeat migrants	Total per cent	All migrants	Recent migrants	Primary migrants	Return migrants	Repeat migrants	Total per cent
Bangkok												
White collar	45.0	15.1	83.4	2.7	13.9	100.0	40.1	7.7	80.5	6.5	13.0	100.0
Manual work	46.2	13.7	87.6	2.9	9.5	100.0	44.4	10.5	80.9	2.9	16.2	100.0
Service work	49.4	15.9	89.3	3.8	6.9	100.0	56.5	21.3	92.0	3.3	4.7	100.0
Agriculture	57.4	35.8	96.9	0.3	2.8	100.0	44.0	29.4	92.5	2.0	5.5	100.0
Other urban places												
White collar	42.1	18.4	50.0	7.6	42.4	100.0	31.1	9.6	61.5	10.4	28.1	100.0
Manual work	32.4	13.3	66.2	9.0	24.8	100.0	28.3	9.7	70.1	9.3	20.6	100.0
Service work	39.6	16.9	66.3	8.9	24.8	100.0	32.0	12.8	71.9	8.6	19.5	100.0
Agriculture	16.2	6.7	76.1	7.5	16.4	100.0	10.2	4.5	73.3	11.1	15.6	100.0

									*	*	*	*
Sanitary districts												
White collar	30.9	15.3	52.3	3.9	43.8	100.0	21.9	5.9	*	*	*	*
Manual work	35.5	19.2	63.0	7.8	29.2	100.0	22.4	13.4	44.8	14.2	41.0	100.0
Service work	37.8	15.8	43.0	10.1	46.9	100.0	29.9	9.7	58.8	15.4	25.8	100.0
Agriculture	18.7	6.2	67.7	8.1	24.2	100.0	15.4	5.4	66.7	13.0	20.3	100.0
Rural												
White collar	21.9	9.6	68.8	12.5	18.7	100.0	15.9	6.4	65.6	7.8	26.6	100.0
Manual work	19.6	8.8	62.5	11.4	26.1	100.0	11.5	4.5	60.0	8.9	31.1	100.0
Service work	24.3	15.0	75.2	7.6	17.2	100.0	22.6	7.2	62.5	15.3	22.2	100.0
Agriculture	13.2	4.0	72.5	10.0	17.5	100.0	10.5	3.0	66.6	16.7	16.7	100.0
Total kingdom												
White collar	35.2	14.7	68.7	6.1	25.2	100.0	25.8	7.2	69.4	8.4	22.2	100.0
Manual work	29.4	11.9	70.6	7.6	21.8	100.0	21.0	7.3	65.8	8.2	26.0	100.0
Service work	34.2	15.1	72.2	7.3	20.5	100.0	38.7	14.3	81.8	6.3	11.9	100.0
Agriculture	13.6	4.2	73.8	9.5	16.7	100.0	10.7	3.2	68.8	15.6	15.6	100.0

* No percentages are calculated if the unweighted base contains fewer than 20 cases

Source: as Table 19.1

accounted for by return migration which, though consistently less common than onward migration, is also a form of repeat movement. Although the differences are not nearly as sharp in most instances, the same general pattern noted for males applies to females.

Overall, repeat movement makes a much more impressive contribution to recent migration in smaller urban places and in rural locations than does return movement to the province of birth. Moreover, no strong, clear relation exists between either return or repeat movement and occupation, despite some tendency for repeat movement to be more characteristic of white collar workers among males and manual workers among females, and least characteristic of male and female agricultural workers. Because of the limitations in the census data to assess type of movement, the lack of clearer occupational patterns must not be accepted as a definitive finding. Rather, both the high levels of repeat movement and the lack of clear occupational differentials suggest the pressing need for more refined data that allow for more careful attention to the interactions among the type of movement, timing of the move, specific origins of the repeat moves, and occupations before migration. The fact that return and repeat migration permeates all educational and occupational segments of the population also suggests that much closer attention needs to be given to the impact of success or failure of the initial move in accounting for return or repeat moves.

Employment status

One indication of the extent to which movement may be influenced by livelihood can be obtained from the individual's employment status: whether self-employed, the employer of others, working for the government or in the private sector, or whether an unpaid family worker. Ownership of a business, like ownership of a home or land, may well tie an individual to a given location to a much greater extent than working for someone else. At the same time, persons working for the government may well experience different levels and types of moves, reflecting their 'national' employer needing to shift employees to meet changing demands for government services in different locations as regional developments are initiated.

Employment status is not independent of a host of other variables; to the extent that individuals move as members of family units rather than on their own, the decision to move or not may well be made by the head of the household for the entire family. Under such circumstances, the employment status of particular individuals may not fully reflect the extent of economic ties to a particular location. Assessment requires multivariate analysis of employment status, household status, and other variables affecting migration. Such analyses are planned for later. It is also essential to note that, reflecting the economic motives that account for most migration, current employment status, like current occupation, may be very different from that before migration. Ideally, therefore, assessment of the relation between migration and employment status should rely on longitudinal data which provide information on occupation and employment status both before and after the move has been made. At best, current employment status can only suggest possible relations.

For Thailand as a whole, it is, nonetheless, quite clear that employment status is a relevant variable in migration. The percentage of males and females classified as migrants under the broad definition used varies significantly by employment status. Whereas only 10 per cent of all unpaid family workers among both men and women, and only about 16 per cent of all the self-employed are classified as migrants, this proportion increases to about one-fourth of all private sector employees and to substantially higher percentages of employers and government employees (Table 19.6).

Attention here focuses primarily on the type of movement of recent migrants in relation to employment status. For the total kingdom, the relation between type of movement and employment status is generally in the expected directions. Employers have the highest proportion of primary migrants and government employees the lowest. The same pattern characterizes men and women, except that the degree of differences among categories is considerably greater for men than women. These data suggest that for recent migrants, ownership of an enterprise is associated with less frequent movement than is working for someone else, and that among employees, government employment is most conducive to frequent movement. These relations are further evidenced in the proportion of migrants classified as either return or repeat movers. For both males and females, return migration is much less common among those classified as employers or government employees than among the other three employment status categories. Judged by 1970 employment status, self-employment and unpaid family work (possibly interrelated) seem more conducive to return movement than ownership of a firm or government employment. On the other hand, the proportion of recent migrants classified as repeat movers is clearly highest for government employees, accounting for over one-fourth of the total recent migration of all males and 30 per cent of all females so employed. At the same time, the fact that every other employment status category had as many as 15 to 20 per cent of the males and 10 to 20 per cent of the females classified as repeat migrants attests to the degree to which repeated movement extends to all segments of the population.

Assessment of the relation between employment status and type of movement by residence category shows significant deviations from the patterns noted for the total kingdom. In Bangkok, the male employer group is characterized by the lowest proportion of primary movers and the highest of repeat movers; the same pattern, but sharper in level of difference, holds in other urban places, although for this residence category government employees also have a low percentage of primary migrants and a very high percentage of repeat migrants. By contrast, in rural locations employers have the highest percentage of primary migrants; and this group accounts for the similar pattern for the total kingdom.

In Bangkok, there are minimal differentials in distribution by type of movement for the various employment status categories other than the employer group. Particularly interesting is that so low a percentage of all recent male migrants who are government employees are return migrants to the capital. The proportions are higher for all other residence categories, but especially in the other urban places and sanitary districts. In Bangkok, as in other residence groups, the per cent of recent migrants classified as repeat migrants is much greater; these proportions reaching particularly high levels for the employer and government employee groups in other urban places and for the government employees in sanitary districts. In rural areas, too, government employees have the highest proportion of repeat migrants, this level being shared closely by private sector employees. In the two urban residence categories, where the numbers are sufficient for comparison, female government employees also have the highest proportion of repeat migrants, confirming, as did the data for the total kingdom, that recent migration for female government employees tends to be the last of a series of moves rather than the first move.

For females, as for males, in all employment status groups many more of those who move to Bangkok are primary migrants, whereas more of those moving to small urban places and to rural locations are concentrated in the return and repeat migrant groups. This suggests that for females, as for males, a history of repeat movement is more characteristic of those taking up residence in smaller urban locations and in rural places. It remains to be demonstrated whether these are migrants who had moved previously to the capital or represent a segment of the population which either voluntarily or by assignment has been shifted from one small urban place to another as opportunities in these develop.

The fact that Bangkok differs in this important regard from the other three residence categories undoubtedly is related to its primacy. Since the capital has served as the major single goal of migrants in Thailand, it likely is also a major source of return migration to other locations as well as of onward movement to a third location. The evidence seems clear, however, that for most migrants to Bangkok movement does not constitute the culmination of a stepping-stone process involving prior migration to smaller locations as occurs in many other less developed countries. This conclusion, based on analysis of census data, is consistent with survey data providing migration histories of persons living in the capital and in other locations in Thailand (Goldstein, Pitaktepsombati and Goldstein 1977). Whether this situation changes as the smaller urban locations develop will be a point to be observed in future years.

Discussion

Because migration is a major force in the redistribution of population in less developed countries and particularly in urban growth, and because it may both exacerbate urban problems and alleviate or compound rural problems, more attention must be given to the various types of migration and to their impact on places of origin and destination. The ability to categorize migrants in terms of recency of movement and to ascertain whether migrants have a history of repeated movement, which may include return movement, can add significantly to assessing the migration process and its impact on urban and rural development. Such analyses are particularly useful for the development of policies to control rates of urban growth, to channel migrants toward alternative growth centres, and for efforts to retain persons in their original place of settlement.

Concern with the extent and character of repeat migration in Thailand is not new. Textor (1956) in a study of some 1,200 pedicab drivers who had moved from the north-east to Bangkok confirmed that circulation was a common form of movement, affecting the composition of the migration streams and the nature of the links maintained both with fellow migrants in the capital and with places of origin. Meinkoth (1962), studying all types of in-migrants to the capital, confirmed that most saw their move as

TABLE 19.6 Distribution of migrants aged 15 and over by type of migration by employment status and sex, by 1970 place of residence (standardized for age)

Employment status	Males						Females					
	Percentage in total population of		Distribution of recent migrants				Percentage in total population of		Distribution of recent migrants			
	All migrants	Recent migrants	Primary migrants	Return migrants	Repeat migrants	Total per cent	All migrants	Recent migrants	Primary migrants	Return migrants	Repeat migrants	Total per cent
Bangkok												
Employer	31.9	5.6	73.2	—	26.8	100.0	75.2	11.0	*	*	*	*
Self-employed	37.2	12.6	88.1	4.0	7.9	100.0	39.8	8.1	87.7	3.7	8.6	100.0
Gov't employee	57.1	20.7	85.5	1.9	12.6	100.0	44.2	8.0	76.2	5.0	18.8	100.0
Private sector employee	45.6	14.5	86.9	2.8	10.3	100.0	51.4	16.2	90.7	3.7	5.6	100.0
Unpaid family worker	20.9	10.8	89.8	2.8	7.4	100.0	34.9	9.3	84.9	6.5	8.6	100.0
Other urban places												
Employer	45.3	12.8	43.7	5.5	50.8	100.0	42.4	13.9	*	*	*	*
Self-employed	26.5	9.9	72.7	8.1	19.2	100.0	27.3	8.9	67.4	10.1	22.5	100.0
Gov't employee	48.9	24.3	44.9	8.6	46.5	100.0	33.1	13.4	54.5	13.4	32.1	100.0
Private sector employee	33.9	15.0	70.0	7.3	22.7	100.0	30.5	13.3	70.7	8.3	21.0	100.0
Unpaid family worker	25.6	9.6	82.3	8.3	9.4	100.0	23.5	6.9	68.1	10.1	21.8	100.0

Sanitary districts

Occupation	(1)	(2)	(3)	(4)	(5)	Total	(1)	(2)	(3)	(4)	(5)	Total
Employer	*	*	*	*	*	*	*	*	*	*	*	*
Self-employed	25.1	8.8	65.9	6.8	27.3	100.0	20.8	9.6	44.8	27.1	28.1	100.0
Gov't employee	40.9	22.9	32.7	6.6	60.7	100.0	*	*	*	*	*	*
Private sector employee	27.7	15.7	68.8	16.6	14.6	100.0	15.4	9.0	64.5	14.4	21.1	100.0
Unpaid family worker	14.5	7.1	74.7	4.2	21.1	100.0	15.8	5.3	58.5	13.2	28.3	100.0

Rural

Occupation	(1)	(2)	(3)	(4)	(5)	Total	(1)	(2)	(3)	(4)	(5)	Total
Employer	43.5	9.9	87.9	—	12.1	100.0	*	*	*	*	*	*
Self-employed	14.4	4.3	72.0	14.0	14.0	100.0	10.6	2.8	71.4	7.2	21.4	100.0
Gov't employee	25.2	12.8	72.7	3.9	23.4	100.0	19.9	11.0	*	*	*	*
Private sector employee	22.0	11.4	69.3	8.8	21.9	100.0	16.5	6.2	69.4	21.0	9.6	100.0
Unpaid family worker	9.6	3.1	71.0	16.1	12.9	100.0	10.6	3.1	67.7	12.9	19.4	100.0

Total kingdom

Occupation	(1)	(2)	(3)	(4)	(5)	Total	(1)	(2)	(3)	(4)	(5)	Total
Employer	36.0	11.1	83.8	1.8	14.4	100.0	46.9	9.3	68.9	11.1	20.0	100.0
Self-employed	16.0	5.1	72.5	11.8	15.7	100.0	15.6	4.5	64.1	6.0	29.9	100.0
Gov't employee	41.0	19.3	67.3	4.7	28.0	100.0	31.4	9.0	*	*	*	*
Private sector employee	28.8	12.9	73.6	7.8	18.6	100.0	25.1	9.5	79.0	10.5	10.5	100.0
Unpaid family worker	10.4	3.5	74.3	11.4	14.3	100.0	11.1	3.2	68.8	12.5	18.7	100.0

* No percentages are calculated if the unweighted base contains fewer than 20 cases

Source: as Table 19.1

temporary, with permanent residence in their origin villages preferred over residence in Bangkok. Until the 1970s, these studies provided the only insights on the extent and character of return and repeat movement.

The first opportunity to assess repeat and return migration on a national scale in Thailand came from the data of the 1969-70 Longitudinal Survey of Social, Economic, and Demographic Change in Thailand, conducted by the Institute of Population Studies (Goldstein 1977: 238-64). Analysis showed that almost half of all migrants resident in Bangkok and smaller urban places had histories of residence in three or more provinces and over one-fourth had lived in at least three different urban locations. Moreover, the frequency of such repeated moves was much more characteristic of the urban-born than the rural-born. A considerable part of repeat movement involves moves to and from the same location, especially an urban one. Moreover, multiple-move migrants had higher educational levels and consisted disproportionately of government officials, especially in smaller urban places. These findings suggested that repeat migrants play a unique role in the economic, educational and government structures, especially in intended development centres.

Unfortunately, the migration analysis of the Longitudinal Survey was restricted to persons living in urban areas. Insights on circular movement in rural Thailand are even more limited than those on the urban population, although some preliminary findings of mobility in Mae Sa, a northern Thai village, have suggested that short-term, repetitive, and cyclic movements in Thailand may be more significant than permanent migration (Singhanetra-Renard 1977). The Mae Sa survey has clearly documented that a high degree of population mobility – commuting, circulation, and migration – has characterized this rural location for decades, much of which would have been masked if reliance were placed only on official statistics and definitions.

These studies in Thailand, and others conducted elsewhere, point to the existence of many different types of population movement. It is therefore essential to have data which allow much more refined assessment of movement in relation to changing social and economic conditions. In the absence of such data, the fullest exploitation of existing statistics becomes especially desirable. The present analysis was stimulated by such a belief. Integrated analysis of census data in Thailand permits exploration of the extent to which migration into urban and rural places consists of different types of moves as defined by prior migration experience and the degree to which these vary among different socioeconomic segments of the population.

The results of the analysis point to high levels of stability, reflecting in part the reliance on provinces as areal units for measuring migration. Nonetheless, migration contributed substantially to urban growth and recent migration plays an important role in population redistribution. Among recent migrants, a considerable portion are repeat or return migrants. Such movement is particularly prevalent among persons aged 25-34, and among those with more than a primary education and with white collar occupations. However, clear relations between type of migration and socioeconomic variables do not always obtain, suggesting that a multiplicity of factors affect the process. More significant perhaps is the fact that both repeat and return migration permeate all educational and occupational segments of the population, but tend to be consistently higher in smaller urban places and in rural areas than in Bangkok.

Given the high rates of urban growth noted for South-east Asia and the substantial contribution of migration to these, the extent to which 'urbanizing villagers' (Lipton 1977) have no intention of staying in the cities and the extent to which many of those who do intend to stay are driven back to the villages by the growing shortage of urban jobs takes on particular importance. It could mean that the actual movement into and out of cities is substantially greater than the data from censuses and surveys frequently indicate. Furthermore, high turnover rates could also mean that a substantial self-correcting factor operates in the migration process, such that the net results are not as injurious either to the cities as a whole or to the individual migrants who settle in them.

Not all movement from urban to rural locations necessarily represents the exodus of less successful migrants or maladjusted urban natives. Part of this consists of government officials and other white collar workers moved to rural locations; and some may consist of manual labourers and the unemployed who are seeking better opportunities for making a livelihood in rural places. Still others may be returning to rural locations as they originally planned, after achieving the goals which motivated their moves to the cities. Who are these migrants from urban to rural locations and what their impact is on rural places merits fuller study.

Population movement may very well provide much more of an adjustment factor in population dynamics than has been posited for it heretofore; the many different forms of movement, from permanent migration at one extreme to daily commuting at the

411

other, allow a maximum number of individuals to take advantage of economic and social opportunities provided by both urban and rural places. At the same time, the growing network of urban locations, including the sanitary districts, which have been shown to have many of the features of smaller urban places, provide an increasing set of destination alternatives for both the rural population and those living in urban places. The sizeable amount of return and repeat migration to Bangkok and other urban places originating in other urban locations points to the significance that such interchanges already have had and likely will have in the future as factors in urban growth and national development.

Above all, this analysis has emphasized the complexity of population movement, indicating challenges with respect both to the quality and the quantity of data and to the appropriateness of concepts. By attempting to meet these challenges, the understanding of the process will advance, as will the ability to use this understanding for more effective planning of both urban and rural development.

Notes

1 To evaluate the rates of return migration, the most realistic base would be the out-migrants from rural locations who were resident in other provinces; it is they who constitute the pool from which return migrants can be drawn. The data needed to measure the rate of return migration on this basis are not available.

2 In this discussion of age differentials and in succeeding discussions of education, occupation, and employment status differentials, the analysis is restricted to the per cent of total migrants (defined as all individuals who moved at least once across a provincial boundary during their lifetime), and the type of move made by all recent migrants (all individuals whose last interprovincial move occurred between 1965 and 1970).

Acknowledgments

Special appreciation is due to the National Statistical Office, Bangkok, Thailand, and particularly to Anuri Wanglee, for making available the 1970 Census sample tape on which this analysis is based. This research was facilitated by a Ford Foundation grant to the Population Studies and Training Center of Brown University. This paper makes use of some material previously presented at the IUSSP 'Conference on Economic and Demographic Change: Issues for the 1980s,' Helsinki, Finland, 1978.

TABLE 19.7 *Number (in '000s) of persons by selected characteristics and 1970 place of residence, by sex*

Characteristics	Males					Females				
	Bangkok	Other urban places	Sanitary districts	Rural	Total kingdom	Bangkok	Other urban places	Sanitary districts	Rural	Total kingdom
Age										
15-24	294	210	226	2,410	3,140	296	217	210	2,520	3,243
25-34	181	139	180	1,594	2,094	185	139	157	1,732	2,213
35-44	102	103	145	1,312	1,662	122	106	130	1,401	1,759
45-64	77	86	106	1,403	1,672	89	95	146	1,403	1,733
65 and over	14	17	40	334	405	30	31	44	454	559
Total	668	555	697	7,053	8,973	722	588	687	7,510	9,507
Education*										
None	33	43	89	1,265	1,430	116	124	190	2,532	2,962
Primary	331	320	503	5,349	6,503	373	335	455	4,785	5,948
Secondary	229	148	72	255	704	171	97	31	116	415
University	43	17	15	15	90	37	12	1	9	59
Occupation**										
White collar	218	137	74	200	629	125	102	52	161	440
Manual work	191	154	120	390	855	85	42	68	176	371
Service work	66	61	41	113	281	104	82	36	64	286
Agriculture	13	65	344	5,666	6,088	7	43	303	5,787	6,140
Employment status										
Employer	9	7	3	29	48	1	2	2	10	15
Self-employed	76	128	267	3,456	3,927	66	84	80	696	926
Government employee	147	103	59	310	519	50	32	7	50	139
Private sector employee	227	139	116	540	1,022	160	62	70	353	645
Unpaid family worker	26	36	124	2,119	2,305	42	86	289	5,056	5,473

* Omits persons of unknown education.   ** Omits persons of unclassified occupation.   *Source:* as Table 19.1

20 New Polynesian voyagers: visitors workers and migrants in New Zealand

Edward M.K. Douglas

Compared with their near neighbours in the South Pacific, both Australia and New Zealand are highly urbanized, 'western', wealthy, post-industrial countries. Although New Zealand has only three million people, its population is large in comparison with the South Pacific Island populations. It is, for example, five times larger than that of Fiji, larger than that of Niue, Tokelau or Tuvalu. The per capita income of New Zealand is more than five times that of Fiji and fifteen times that of Tonga. Remittances make up a substantial proportion of foreign exchange earnings in all of these countries including Fiji. If the remittances sent home by Tongans, Samoans, Cook Islanders, Niueans, Tokelauans and Tuvaluans were not included in the islands' national income, then the gaping disparity between metropolitan New Zealand and these island countries would be even wider.

All the Pacific Island countries have high rates of natural increase. In Fiji where the demographic transition has proceeded furthest, fertility is still high (mid-1970s census-based estimates are CBR 29‰ and a TFR 4001). In Tonga and Western Samoa less far in the demographic transition CBR are 39‰ and 37‰ and TFR 5500 and 5300 respectively. In the Cooks, Niue and Tokelau wholesale out-movement has depleted the 20-40 age cohorts and brought the birth rates down to around 30 per thousand. Nevertheless the ratio of dependants (under 15 and over 60) to young adult males (15-44) is very high in all these five countries, and in some of the more migrant communities the burden of dependence appears to be almost intolerable, e.g. on Palmerston Atoll (Cook Islands) there were only seven males aged 15-44 in a total population of fifty-six.

The Pacific countries are poor; their agricultural systems are basically at subsistence level with a small marketable surplus;

414

opportunities for economic development are limited; natural increase and the expectations of the population have risen rapidly. Almost everywhere the fragile island economies are unable to sustain real increases in per capita income without aid from metropolitan countries and the export of labour with the subsequent monetary support that remittances give to families left in the villages. New Zealand, from a sense of duty, regional identification, capitalist adventure, or whatever, has become in the eyes of the islanders, a source of wealth (through grants, loans, investment, work opportunities). It is an answer to the economic, political and social frustrations of the islanders through migration.

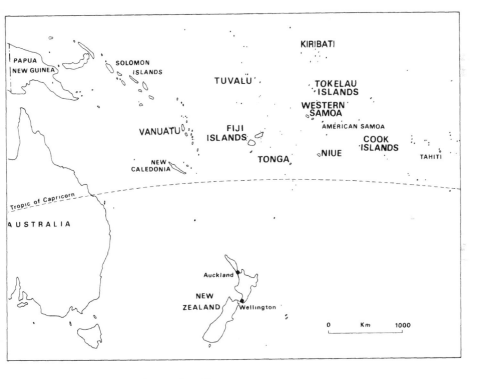

FIGURE 20.1 South-west Pacific

Economic reasons are not the only ones that cause Pacific Islanders to move to New Zealand. Reasons vary for different people at different times. The first Pacific Island arrivals in New Zealand were young, single men; in the last 12 years or so family groups have been more important. Economic reasons are significant, but other reasons need to be remembered. In Tonga and Samoa (de Bres 1974; Pitt and Macpherson 1974: 12) the

415

demand for education, particularly a western, academic education, has far outstripped the local supply, and many migrants emphasize educational goals for themselves or their children in explaining their exodus from the islands. For all migrants there is an element of prestige involved (Pitt and Macpherson 1974: 14). Leaving the village and experiencing the world beyond gives status. This status may be coupled with the desire of many men to acquire titles in their family and community. Indeed for Samoans, the importance of acquiring titles needs to be emphasized, the money earned as migrants may help to buy a title on return to Samoa. The desire to become a *matai* and to exercise the rights of the *matai* title in Samoa keep many from committing themselves to permanent New Zealand residence and citizenship.

Migration policies and responses

New Zealand is a predominantly white 'British' country on the southern boundary of Polynesia. Almost 90 per cent of its population is of European origin, overwhelmingly British. The indigenous Maori, now about 10 per cent of the population, were largely dispossessed of their land during the nineteenth century and are culturally, socially and economically marginal to the mainstream of New Zealand life. Since the establishment of colonial settlement and government in 1840, settlement from Britain and from nearby Australia has been encouraged. Until 1974, New Zealand immigration policy granted almost anyone who was a British subject and wholly of European descent (i.e. white) the right to free entry and settlement. In contrast official regulations and the immigration Minister's discretionary powers have effectively excluded non-white and non-British. Asians (mainly Cantonese Chinese and Gujerati Indians) number about 18,000 and together with Pacific Islanders comprised less than 3 per cent of the census population in 1976. During the first half of this century, New Zealand had direct colonial control over the Cook Islands, Niue and the Tokelau Islands, a UN mandate over Western Samoa, and regional influences on Tonga, Fiji, Solomon Islands, the Gilbert and Ellice Islands (later Tuvalu and Kiribati). Yet very few Pacific Islanders had ever been to New Zealand, even for short durations and few were enumerated in the 1951 Census of New Zealand.

Until mid-century only small numbers of Pacific Islanders had been educated in New Zealand, and almost all the permanent residents in New Zealand from the Pacific Islands were women

416

TABLE 20.1 *Selected statistics of Pacific Islanders in New Zealand*

Census year	Ethnic group	Total in NZ	% in Auck-land	% in Welling-ton	% born in NZ	% mixed blood	% in NZ < 5 yrs
1951	Cook	1,359[1]	. .	. .	. .	31	17
1956	Islanders	2,320	66	20	31	29	18
1961		4,499	67	18	39	32	25
1966		8,663	64	23	41	28	25
1971		13,772	53	17	47	28	14
1976		18,610	59	15	. .	. .	23
1951	Niueans	. .[1]	. .	. .	. .	. .	. .
1956		848	79	13	19	21	46
1961		1,728	82	5	28	19	29
1966		2,848	86	7	34	16	19
1971		4,264	82	8	37	17	20
1976		5,688	86	6	. .	. .	. .
1951	Samoans	2,265[2]	. .	. .	. .	67	. .
1956		3,760	73	16	31	62	40
1961		6,481	62	16	40	54	21
1966		11,842	70	19	45	43	23
1971		22,198	61	20	47	38	21
1976		22,876	62	22	. .	. .	24
1971	Tokelauans	1,195	20	64	21	25	51
1976		1,737	19	63	. .	. .	. .
1951	Other	337[3]			. .	74	. .
1956	Pacific	1,195	73	17	42	70	37
1961	Islanders	2,378	. .	. .	48	73	20
1966		2,920	62	16	47	51	44
1971		6,005	. .	. .	45	65	24
1976		7,443[4]	72	13	. .	. .	. .

Notes:
1 Cook Islanders and Niueans combined in 1951
2 Polynesians other than Cook Islanders and Niueans (mostly from Western Samoa)
3 Melanesians and Micronesians but mostly 'part Fijians'
4 Other *Polynesians* only
. . Not available

Source: New Zealand Census of Population & Dwellings 1951-1976

married to New Zealanders whom they had met in the islands, together with the offspring of these unions. Only from the early 1950s was New Zealand perceived as a possible place to live and work, firstly by Cook Islanders then later by other Island Polynesians. At each quinquennial census since 1951 the number of Pacific Islanders in New Zealand has increased. While numbers increased, the proportion of mixed European-Islanders decreased, and the proportion of New Zealand-born people of Pacific Island parentage (second and third generation residents) increased (Table 20.1). During the Western Samoan transition to independence (which occurred in 1962) several hundred families of mixed Samoan-New Zealand European descent settled in New Zealand and after independence New Zealand agreed to accept an annual quota of Samoan nationals for settlement.

Expanding, largely endogamous, Pacific Islander communities exist in Auckland, Wellington and some secondary urban centres. Membership in some of these communities is highly transitory with new arrivals from the islands and departures weekly.

Auckland, the largest urban area in New Zealand has been called 'the capital of Polynesia'. It is not a title that could be claimed in cultural, social, or political terms, but demographically, Auckland's 105,000 Polynesians (66,000 indigenous Maori and 39,000 Pacific Islanders) put it far ahead of any competing city (e.g. Papeete 40,000, Apia 32,000, Nukualofa 22,000). Even so, Polynesians comprise only one in eight, and Pacific Island Polynesians only one in twenty, of urban Auckland's population.

The actual size and composition of the circulation between New Zealand and the various island countries has always been difficult to determine. Not only do individuals leave the communities by returning to their homelands, but others sever their social links and become absorbed into the networks of their non-islander spouses. Census enumerations give an incomplete picture of the processes involved, recording little more than the net balance of arrivals and departures at five-yearly intervals, missing out all those people who may have come after one census and left again before the next. New Zealand migration statistics have long been inadequate records of arrivals and departures from Island Polynesian and other Pacific countries. Delays of two years or more in reconciling arrival records with departure records, and the difficulties of classifying visitors who intend to stay 'temporarily' and end up staying 'permanently', have meant that migration statistics have been all but useless in determining the size of Pacific Island communities in New Zealand, let alone their importance in economic and social terms (Table 20.2).

Five major policy decisions have affected the movement of Pacific people to and from New Zealand. First, there are no controls on movement of permanent residents between Australia and New Zealand – this is completely free. Secondly, until 1974

418

Year ended 31 March	Niueans, Tokelauans, Cook Islanders²				Western Samoans²				Tongans and Fijians²				All Pacific Islanders¹			
	Arrivals		Departures	Net gain or loss (−)	Arrivals		Departures	Net gain or loss (−)	Arrivals		Departures	Net gain or loss (−)	Arrivals		Departures	Net gain or loss (−)
	no.	sex ratio⁵			no.	sex ratio⁵			no.	sex ratio⁵			no.	sex ratio⁵		
1964	961	103	372	589	1,947	124	1,352	595	814	137	646	168	3,928	120	2,509	1,419
1965	1,196	116	607	589	2,046	118	1,602	444	1,120	142	994	126	4,555	123	3,293	1,262
1966	1,329	124	636	693	2,721	145	1,901	820	1,359	223	1,108	251	5,791	154	3,915	1,876
1967	1,347	110	718	629	3,374	127	2,004	1,370	3,560	419	2,929	631	8,619	190	5,875	2,744
1968	1,102	90	798	304	2,600	117	2,226	374	1,635	182	2,239	−604	5,757	125	5,578	179
1969	1,028	101	806	222	2,418	103	1,822	596	1,226	128	1,112	114	5,106	110	4,027	1,079
1970	1,732	95	1,015	712	3,996	120	2,554	1,442	1,638	151	1,438	200	8,090	117	5,518	2,572
1971³	1,896	96	—	—	4,508	115	—	—	2,997	251	—	—	9,794	138	—	—
1972	1,933	111	1,004	929	5,834	119	4,274	1,560	4,060	276	3,351	709	12,373	143	8,978	3,395
1973	2,742	99	1,017	1,725	6,194	129	4,147	2,047	4,335	287	3,000	1,335	14,035	148	9,888	4,147
1974	4,152	102	1,971	2,181	9,222	136	5,997	3,225	7,508	287	4,565	2,943	21,431	162	12,834	8,597
1975	5,071	97	3,222	1,849	8,575	148	5,940	2,635	6,777	256	7,830	−1,053	20,856	159	17,482	3,374
1976	4,008	102	3,554	454	7,084	129	5,870	1,214	5,174	168	6,054	−880	16,758	131	15,970	788
1977	3,384	97	3,422	−38	4,600	98	4,264	336	3,862	156	3,434	428	12,344	113	11,394	950
1978	4,376	104	4,520	−144	4,420	101	4,560	−140	3,520	155	3,724	−204	12,528	115	13,300	−772
Total 1962-78	36,492	101	25,345	11,147	73,172	124	53,100	20,072	50,950	227	45,789	5,161	169,303	139	127,663	41,640

Notes:

1 Exclusive of crews, through passengers, tourists on cruise ships and members of the armed forces

2 Refers to ethnic group not citizenship or birthplace. Excludes Fiji Indians and includes persons of mixed European/Pacific Islander ancestry. Includes New Zealand-born persons of Pacific Island ancestry

3 Departures by ethnic group are not available for 1971

4 Refers to arrivals from and departures to all destinations, not just movement between New Zealand and the Pacific Islands

5 Sex ratio – number of males per 100 females in arrival stream. High sex ratio indicates temporary movements

Source: New Zealand Statistics of External Migration 1977-8, Table 3.

there was effectively an open-door policy for 'white' Common-wealth citizens, particularly from the United Kingdom. Thirdly, Pacific Islanders who have New Zealand citizenship (i.e. Cook, Niue and Tokelau Islanders and any others who can verify descent from a male New Zealand citizen) also have free entry. This group totals less than 30,000. Fourthly, any other Pacific Islanders who have had the necessary passage money have been able to enter New Zealand subject to entry controls. Since 1975, restrictions on Pacific Islander movement to New Zealand have become more severe than those applied to other nationalities. Finally, controls on entry are designed to ensure that most Pacific Island movement to New Zealand is in response to short-term employment opportunities on the New Zealand labour market without this response leading to permanent settlement.

In summary, New Zealand's immigration policies have been to encourage British settlers and to place little restriction on the movement of white Britons or Australians. New Zealand citizens of Island Polynesian birth are also unrestricted. About 1,000 Western Samoans per year have been permitted to settle in New Zealand under the terms of the bilateral treaty of friendship that exists between the two countries. Other Samoans and all other Pacific Islanders require non-renewable work permits or non-working visitors' visas both of which are of limited duration. From the perspective of the Tongan, Fijian and Samoan, New Zealand is a white man's country with abundant employment opportunities but with a 'high white wall' that can only be breached for short-term visits. In the period 1970-5 movement (all durations) from Fiji, Tonga and Western Samoa accounted for 40 per cent of temporary migration to New Zealand but only 3 per cent of permanent migration (Campbell 1975: 2).

In this essay Pacific Islanders who move to New Zealand may be classified as visitors, guest-workers, sojourners, and settlers (Table 20.3). The classification is based on the following criteria − the legal status of the mover; whether a citizen or not, and the type of entry document which is issued; the intended duration and officially stated purpose and duration of stay at the time of entry; any change in intention or purpose that may have occurred since entry. Such a classification is imperfect because all parties to the movement − the mover, the employer in New Zealand, the New Zealand government, and the networks of kinfolk in New Zealand and in the islands − change their expectations and their policies as time passes. Besides, not all arrivals in New Zealand fully disclose their intention to immigration officials.

TABLE 20.3 *Mobility classification – Pacific Islands and New Zealand*

| Pacific Island country of origin | Duration of stay in New Zealand | | | |
| | Less than 3 months | Between 3 months and 1 year | More than one year | |
			Intention to return	Intention to remain
Cook Islands*, Niue*	Visitor	Visitor/sojourner	Sojourner	Settler
Tokelau*	Visitor	Visitor/sojourner	Sojourner	Settler
Western Samoa	Visitor	Guestworker	Sojourner	Settler
Tonga	Visitor	Guestworker	Sojourner	Settler
Fiji	Visitor	Guestworker	Sojourner	Settler
Tuvalu	Visitor	Guestworker	Sojourner	Settler
Others	Visitor	Guestworker	Sojourner	Settler

* As New Zealand citizens they have unrestricted entry rights

Visitors from the Pacific Islands

For any Pacific Islanders with the money for a return fare and evidence of support for the duration of stay, visitors' visas to New Zealand have been readily obtainable. They are not required for Cook, Niue and Tokelau Islanders who accounted for between one-fifth and one-quarter of all Pacific Islander arrivals between 1972 and 1977. Until 1975 visas were issued for three months though a majority of visitors overstayed the duration of their visas. This was allowed and encouraged during times of high labour demand in New Zealand by all concerned − visitors, the New Zealand government, employers, New Zealand trade union officials and the Pacific Island governments. When work was readily available, willingness to work and a job to go to were counted as evidence of support by the immigration authorities.

In 1974, the New Zealand government representative in Western Samoa reported that the average length of stay in New Zealand for visitors on three-month visas was more than seven months. In the same year it was estimated that 8,000 Tongans travelled overseas for various reasons (de Bres 1974) out of an estimated population of 88,000. The Tongan Ministry of Labour reported that as much as 25 per cent of the entire male labour force of Tonga would be overseas for part of that year (Amnesty Aroha 1976: 5), almost all of whom would be in New Zealand on short-term visitors' visas. In the eight years from 1967 to 1975 the number of Tongans visiting New Zealand had increased eighteenfold. Similarly for Western Samoa, in 1975 one-fifth of all adults were in New Zealand on temporary visits.

Incomes are so low in Samoa and Tonga that with the exception of officials, a few members of the business elite or Tongan nobility, almost no-one in either of these countries can afford to visit New Zealand as a tourist or a visitor. Almost all the fares for travel from the Pacific Islands to New Zealand are paid by family members in New Zealand. Almost all of the day to day support required by visitors is also generated in New Zealand, either by the visitors' relatives or friends who sponsor them or by the visitors working contrary to the provisions of their visas.

Since 1975, however, official attitudes towards the movement of non-citizen Pacific Islanders to New Zealand have changed. Visa regulations have been rigidly enforced, computer control of arrival and departure documents instituted and police and immigration department raids on Pacific Islanders' homes have become a regular method of detecting people who have overstayed their visitors' visas or work permits. From 1975 to

1978 the number of Tongans in New Zealand was reduced to perhaps a tenth of the 1974 figure.

Most visitors to New Zealand from the Pacific Islands come with the hope of working, for they must earn enough to repay their airfares (between US \$200 and US \$300) and cover housing, food, and clothing costs in New Zealand before showing a net return. When a visitors' visa was for three months and ample work was available, many were able to accomplish this task within the time allowed. When costs rose, when work especially with overtime became more difficult to obtain, and when net earning goals rose, there were three major effects. Living standards declined as overcrowding in accommodation and restricted diets were used to reduce daily expenses; visitors were unable to question the practices of their employers; they began to overstay their permits in order to make a more significant net gain than was possible within the legal time. Overstaying became the norm, apparently accepted by both employers and government authorities.

Because many Pacific Islander families have settled in New Zealand in the last two decades, there has been an increasing desire for interchange between the islands and New Zealand. Although most visitors are lured to New Zealand by the prospect of finding work, some visitors come more for family reasons than to earn money. Access to New Zealand has denuded many families of their young adults and as the balance of numbers in New Zealand overtakes those left behind, family re-unions are often cheaper to organize in Auckland than at home. Many parents visit New Zealand to attend the weddings of their children, the confinements of their daughters and eventually various celebrations for their grandchildren (Pitt and Macpherson 1974: 42). During times of high labour demand, visits might be augmented by working, or more often visitors release daughters from child-care responsibilities so that they may work.

Guest-workers from the Pacific Islands

Guest-workers are recruited under official or unofficial schemes for a specified job for a specified duration. The policy of recent New Zealand governments is to convert the 'visitors who work' schemes to regulated, labour contracts organized through government agencies, designed to meet the needs of New Zealand industries (de Bres and Campbell 1976a: 33), not the needs of potential migrant labourers. The first guest-worker schemes were organized by rural employers through farmer organizations, the New Zealand Labour Department and the

Labour Department in Fiji, and the first guest-workers were Fijian scrub-cutters who came to New Zealand in 1967. Since then Fijian guest-workers have come in organized groups on contracts to work in jobs such as scrub-cutting, fruit and tobacco harvesting, and tussock-grass eradication. The work bands often consist of thirty or more men from a village or church group in Fiji who have been assisted by their government to negotiate contracts with New Zealand employers (Douglas 1977: 145).

Much of the work is short-term and seasonal and the four- or six-month contract periods have fitted in well with both the agricultural rhythm and the ability of the individual farmers to pay wages and find accommodation. Not all contract work has been agricultural, but because of seasonal demand, isolation, and the unwillingness of New Zealand workers to take these jobs, farmers have had more government encouragement and assistance in finding overseas workers than have urban industrial employers. The number of guest-workers has fluctuated in response to New Zealand economic conditions, particularly New Zealand farmers' incomes, tax and fiscal incentives to invest in farm improvements, and the availability of local workers. The labour movement between the two countries follows the pattern of what has been called *konjunkturpuffer* (the import of foreign labour when it is needed during a boom and its repatriation during a recession) (Böhning 1972: 36).

Tongan guest-worker schemes began in 1971. They were slowly extended during the next four years, cancelled in late 1975, and reinstated as a prototype for the new Pacific migration policy in mid-1976. In absolute numbers, Tongan guest-workers have been insignificant − never more than 250 in New Zealand at any time, and representing less than 5 per cent of all Tongan short-term visitors. Their significance lies in the pattern of employer-response schemes that have now become government policy. Guest-worker schemes were emphasized so that the self-regulating 'visitors who work' arrangement could be eliminated by reducing the visa duration to only one month.

Guest-workers from Tonga were initially employed for six months. Fares and settling-in allowances including cold weather clothing were advanced by the New Zealand employer, who was able to recover this expenditure from their wages. Employers had also to provide accommodation of a suitable standard and had to guarantee six months' employment. Prospective employers have had to demonstrate that local labour supplies were inadequate before they could recruit from Tonga. Most employers had suffered excessive annual labour turnover; one participating industrial plant experiencing a 240 per cent turnover in 1971. The

Tongan scheme significantly reduced such turnover, and on the face of it all parties to the scheme appeared to benefit (Douglas 1977: 146-7).

Workers were selected by the Tongan Department of Labour, thus ensuring that only unemployed workers or surplus agricultural workers in the subsistence economy were chosen. Patronage is an important element in this selection and its exercise aids in maintaining social control on Tonga. New Zealand employers were happy with the scheme; it silenced criticism from employers bedevilled with labour problems especially in lower paid, onerous jobs. Presented as part of a foreign aid package to Tonga, Fiji and Western Samoa, the guest-worker schemes have silenced some criticism from citizens concerned about the maldistribution of wealth and opportunities in the South Pacific region. Employers faced with boom and bust cycles of demand for their products can adjust some of their labour supply by increasing or decreasing their recruits through the scheme. The labour is steady, amenable and willing. All outlays are fully recoverable from the guest-workers' earnings, or are written off as tax-deductible expenses. With guest-workers, employers have men willing to work long hours and erratic shifts at jobs shunned by local workers. Although unfamiliarity with modern machinery and a poor command of English are disadvantages, employers report that these guest-workers are genial, industrious and intelligent even though the jobs assigned to them are generally repetitive, simple processes (Douglas 1977: 147).

Under the *new* guest-worker policy which has been extended to Fijians, Western Samoans and Tuvalu Islanders, the workers, now eligible for eleven months' work permits, have much greater opportunities to earn and save worthwhile sums. It is now possible for a guest-worker to return to the Islands with US $2,000 net savings or remittances for his eleven-month stay. On the surface the revised scheme has many improvements, but a closer scrutiny shows its many flaws.

The Guest-worker Schemes result in metropolitan countries such as New Zealand importing and exporting man-hours from a (hopefully) placid pool of under-utilized labour. The metropolitan countries are by and large uninterested in promoting the better welfare of the workers or of their families and countries of origin. Guest-workers in New Zealand are encouraged as unencumbered, unattached, temporary, expendable, and replaceable, labour inputs into the profit-generating process. The costs of education and raising Pacific Island labour to adulthood when it can be recruited for New Zealand factories is not borne by the New Zealand economy. Guest-workers are not eligible for the medical or social benefits of other workers in the society unless special insurance cover is taken out on their behalf. When they become redundant or unemployable they are not supported, but exported. Their families are neither housed, cared for, nor educated by New Zealand society, except to the extent that the guest-worker is allowed to repatriate his net savings. Additionally the guest-worker is encouraged to demand New Zealand-made goods and services. Western-style houses, clothing, food and education are evident throughout Island Polynesia. The demand for these is exacerbated by the shift in consumption preferences that occurs while guest-workers live in New Zealand. The schemes aggravate tendencies to westernization – very much to New Zealand's benefit. New Zealand exports to Tonga and Western Samoa have annually doubled the invisible exports that Tongan and Samoan labour have earned in remittances from New Zealand. For Tongans, Tuvaluans and Fijians in particular, who still have only nominal access to New Zealand as permanent residents, the courtship with western values cannot be consummated by permanent residence in New Zealand.

The number of guest-workers is reduced to a trickle or completely stopped when it suits the New Zealand Department of Labour acting for the employers. In 1978 two years after the scheme was modified, the number of guest-workers in the country was almost zero. With official unemployment figures at 50,000 and unofficial estimates closer to 150,000, there appeared to be little or no justification for importing unskilled contract workers. With severe reductions in the number of visitors' visas and the much lower incidence of visitors seeking work or overstaying their visas, the amount of money remitted to Tonga, Western Samoa and Tuvalu has been drastically reduced. Whereas remittances were received by families in all Tongan and Samoan villages, now they are much fewer and available for a much smaller number of families. Already amongst the twenty poorest nations in the world (Shankman 1976: 22), Tonga and Western Samoa have suffered drastic cuts in their foreign exchange earnings as a result of the changing circumstances of guest-workers and visitors who work.

Sojourners from the Pacific Islands

Most Pacific Islanders now in New Zealand hope to stay there for some years, only returning home to the islands for short-term visits, or at the end of their working lives. They wish to stay until they have achieved their goals of providing a better life for their families, or when they feel that the disadvantages of life in urban society outweigh the disadvantages of a return home. Almost all long-term migrants leave home with the intention of returning. Most of the sojourners in New Zealand are from one of three groups. Cook, Niue and Tokelau Islanders who are already citizens; Western Samoans who have entered New Zealand and stayed under a quota system; former overstayers from Fiji, Tonga and Western Samoa who registered with the New Zealand government in 1976 and were eventually permitted to remain in the country.

In 1962 when Western Samoa became independent of the UN Trusteeship administered by New Zealand, a bilateral Treaty of Friendship between the two countries provided access to New Zealand for a quota of Samoan citizens on what were called six-month duration temporary permits. These permits, initially 1,000 per year, were increased progressively to 1,500 per year, until 1976 when it was decided that no new permits would be issued. These permits allowed Western Samoans, aged between 18 and 45 years and with no more than two dependents, to live and work in New Zealand. They were renewable every six months and after five years' residence the holder became a permanent resident. Permanent residents may apply for New Zealand citizenship, but fewer than 100 Western Samoans per year do so (New Zealand Parliamentary Debates 1974: 5043-4). Temporary permits had to be obtained outside New Zealand and travellers from Western Samoa on visitors' visas could not have them changed to temporary permits while still in New Zealand. To secure a six-month permit, the Western Samoan migrant had to have a suitable job or other satisfactory support guaranteed (such as a marriage offer from a New Zealand resident), and adequate accommodation.

Although some employers have advertised and recruited labour in Samoa, many intending migrants have found it more suitable or even necessary to go to New Zealand on a visitor's visa, arrange a job and accommodation through family members there, and then return home to apply and wait for the temporary permit. Samoans with permanent resident status (after five years) are eligible to sponsor other migrants and there is considerable pressure on them from their families to provide sponsorship, guarantees and airfares in advance. Permanent residence in New Zealand is dependent on continual 'good behaviour', and migrants are left in no doubt by government officials, ethnic community leaders and the host community at large, that they are on a good behaviour bond.

Before the major policy change in 1976 there were usually long queues of people in Apia waiting to get six-month permits, and the waiting time from first application to departure varied from around ten months to nearly two years. Since 1976, the Samoan permanent settler quota of 1,000-1,100 per year has been abolished and permanent settlement from Samoa, Tonga and Fiji has been dealt with under the government's new world-wide immigration quota of 5,000 per year. Now people wishing to enter New Zealand for a year or more have to take their place in the general queue with all other source areas including Britain, North America and Southern Africa. Currently, immigration selection favours migrants with badly needed skills in short supply and migrants who can satisfy specified humanitarian criteria. On both counts, selection discriminates against Samoans and other Pacific Islanders. The skills in demand are technical and educational and most likely found in urban industrial societies, and the humanitarian criteria are based on either refugee status, or reuniting families of New Zealand residents. The family reunion criteria are clearly defined as the Anglo-Saxon type nuclear family and pay no heed to the extended family structure of Polynesia and the importance attached to intergenerational support and unity in this structure.

There are other sojourners from the Pacific – former residents of Niue, the Cook Islands and the Tokelau Islands. Because they have New Zealand citizenship, they are free to enter New Zealand at will. By the beginning of the 1960s, migration to New Zealand from Niue and the Cooks had become inevitable, at least from the main islands. It was part of growing up, and almost all school leavers who had not secured permanent employment by the time they reached 18 or 19 sought jobs in New Zealand (Douglas 1965: 133). Already half of all Niueans live in Auckland and almost half of all Cook Islanders live in metropolitan New Zealand.

This migration of Cook Islanders and Niueans has been almost wholly community organized; it was organized on family-based and village-based migration chains using credit unions and co-operative savings groups to advance airfares to young migrants who were selected by family and village elders. The first Cook and Niuean migrants came as sojourners with clearly defined goals. A succession of hurricanes destroyed hundreds of houses on Niue, Rarotonga (Cook Islands) and Aitutaki (Cook Islands) and the desire to rebuild family homes in the western style drove hundreds of them to New Zealand. For others the frustration of poorly developed agriculture and inadequate transport and marketing services led them to abandon commercial agriculture and seek 'fast money' in urban New Zealand. Others sought the faster pace and the supposedly restriction-free life of the big bright city. Like most economically-motivated migration it was age and sex selective; the majority of migrants were single, male and in their 20s. Their remittances home set up migratory chains and sweethearts, brothers and sisters and later parents began to follow (Walsh and Trlin 1973: 65). More than half the Cook Islanders and Niueans in New Zealand in 1976 were born in New Zealand, and their education and urban upbringing there has helped to change their parents from sojourners to settlers.

Early in the 1970s Cook Islanders and Niueans began to purchase houses in New Zealand. For most of them this was the symbolic act of becoming a settler, for while they rented houses and looked upon their villages as home their permanency as settlers was in doubt (Douglas 1972: 3-4). When they transferred their housing goals to the city from the village, from building a family home at Alofi (Niue), Arutanga (Cook Islands) or Avatiu (Cook Islands) to buying a house in Ponsonby (Auckland) or in Porirua (Wellington), this signified to themselves, to their families back home and to their families in the city, that they were there to stay. With the improvement of air transport between New Zealand and Niue and Rarotonga, large groups of sojourners return each Christmas and New Year to the islands. In the Cook Islands these groups are called *tere paati* (lit. travelling group), and have been a feature of inter-village and inter-island social intercourse since before European contact. Aitutaki with eight distinct villages maintains a twice-yearly dance and entertainment festival which involves one of the village dance teams travelling to each of the other villages to dance, sing and celebrate the festivities. Now incorporated into the Christmas dance festival, each of the eight villages of Aitutaki takes it in turn to host a visiting *tere paati* from New Zealand. Other *tere paati* may visit during the year too from French Polynesia, other Cook Islands or further afield. An elaborate network of reciprocal visits between different islands has been built up and maintained. Often decades will elapse before a *tere paati* visit is reciprocated.

The *tere paati* from New Zealand perhaps 120-150 strong comprises village sojourners, families and their friends who return to Aitutaki often after 10 or 15 years absence. These reunions are joyous occasions which reaffirm family ties, arrange marriages, patch up quarrels, attend to the succession of estates, adopt children and celebrate clan and tribal membership. Many sojourners bring back their New Zealand-born children into the bosom of the family and leave them with relatives when they return to New Zealand. Hosting a visiting *tere paati* of such a size is a great drain on village resources, for the host village may have a population scarcely double that of the visiting party. In return for this hospitality the *tere paati* members bring individual and group gifts for their hosts − money, food, roofing iron or electricity generators for the village hall or school, motors for boats, sports clothing and equipment for the village cricket, rugby or netball teams. During the two or three weeks of the visit, houses are repaired, fishing nets renewed, crops planted and other tasks requiring a lot of labour. For Niue the *tere paati* has been reversed. The village comes to Auckland where the more affluent urban-dwellers can fete and fuss over their parents, grandparents and country cousins.

The same pattern of return visits to their island homes has developed for Samoans and Tongans. Once their status as permanent residents in New Zealand has been confirmed, they are able to return home for Christmas and other holidays as employment and finances allow. Often reunions have been arranged to coincide with the consecration of a new church building or of some other village project to which sojourners in New Zealand have been major contributors.

Many sojourners are unable to return regularly to their villages. The Tokelau sojourners are least able to return home to their isolated atolls because there is no regular shipping service. Visits require long-term planning and waiting until shipping is available. Although there is return movement to Tokelau it is small in comparison with the exodus. Most Tokelauans in New Zealand have come on a resettlement scheme, for since 1966 it has been New Zealand Government policy to reduce the population of Tokelau and resettle all those who desire it in metropolitan New Zealand. Their fares were paid by the New Zealand Government and their accommodation and employment specially arranged. Initially resettlement was to rural forestry camps but after two or three years the majority moved to Wellington where a small Tokelauan community was already established. Although willing to participate in the resettlement scheme, most Tokelauan movers want to maintain Tokelauan identity and culture and to keep close contact with their kinsfolk who remain in Tokelau. Tokelau is still home to them and despite the distance, the isolation and the lack of transport they still see themselves as sojourners with both rights and obligations to return there. Already there are more Tokelauans in New Zealand than on the three Tokelau atolls and the urban population, because of its youthfulness and because of continued movement from the islands, is likely to grow larger still. As the centre of Tokelauan life gravitates more and more towards

Wellington and away from the atolls, so might expectations of permanent resettlement in Wellington also grow.

Settlers from the Pacific Islands

During the past decades, some visitors have become guest-workers, some guest-workers have become sojourners, and some sojourners have become settlers. Besides the temporary movers who become permanent, the other groups of settlers from the Pacific Islands are the Island women married to New Zealanders and their descendants and Pacific Island residents who feel unable to achieve their goal aspirations in their country of origin. These latter people include the part-Europeans of the Pacific Islands, increasingly the urban Indians from Fiji, and many Tongans, Samoans, Niueans and Cook Islanders.

In 1977, the New Zealand Ministry of Immigration granted permanent residence to nearly 4,000 overstayers who had registered and expressed their wish to remain in New Zealand permanently. Amnesty Aroha, a Wellington-based organization had unsuccessfully petitioned government for a full amnesty for all Pacific Islanders who had overstayed the limits of their visas. The Minister's response was that overstayers must leave the country or register with his department and have their cases considered individually. It was very difficult to determine how many overstayers there were in 1976, or what proportion of them registered, but about three-quarters of those who registered were eventually granted residence. Many of these overstayers (perhaps half of them) were married to New Zealand citizens and permanent residents, but the rest were not. Altogether 1,600 Tongans, 1,800 Western Samoans and 200 Fijians were granted the right to stay (New Zealand Demographic Society 1977, Section 3). These people having fought so hard to remain in New Zealand have become a new group of permanent settlers rather than sojourners.

The part-Europeans and the Tongan, Samoan or Fijian wives of New Zealanders are unlikely to be significant cultural forces in New Zealand life; their numbers are very small (probably less than 2,000) and they are widely dispersed throughout the country, and their cultural backgrounds are the least distinguishable from New Zealand culture. Other settlers are much more likely to make a cultural impact on New Zealand society. The majority of Tongans have left their government 'in no doubt that given the opportunity they would prefer to live overseas at least temporarily and possibly for the duration of their working lives' (de Bres 1974). Their goals are economic and educational, but they do not see this outside the context of Tongan culture and as sojourners or settlers in New Zealand they seek to remain culturally Tongan. The same can be said of Western Samoa. It has been suggested that migration and settlement in New Zealand can be seen as a normal *rite de passage*. Auckland provides the opportunities for Samoan settlers to earn high wages, maintain contact with the extended family and the village in Samoa, come to an understanding about western civilization (*fa'apalagi*) and yet still live in an identifiably Samoan style (*fa'asamoa*) (Pitt 1975: 181).

The importance of remittances

Pacific Islanders in New Zealand are largely instrumental in maintaining the economic and cultural viability of Tongan, Samoan, and Cook Island society. Without their monetary support and their strongly expressed desire to have a 'traditional' society maintained at home, the viability of village and national life in Island Polynesia would be in question.

In 1964 remittances by money order from the Cook Islanders in Tokoroa, New Zealand to the Cook Islands was equivalent to $50 per person per annum (Douglas 1965: 50). It was estimated that an equivalent sum was sent in banknotes enclosed in ordinary mail, or carried back to the islands by returning sojourners. Many of the more recently arrived migrants were remitting half of their net weekly earnings. Amuri village between 1960 and 1964 received remittances that surpassed in value all the income earned from agricultural exports over that period. Similar patterns of remittances have been reported for Niue (Pollard 1978) and Tokelau (Hooper and Huntsman 1973). In Western Samoa, Shankman reports that in 1973 remittances from New Zealand and the United States of America accounted for half the national income (Shankman 1976: 38) going on to detail the effects of exporting labour and earning remittances on the *aiga* (extended family) in a small village on Upolu.

> Wage labour, usually acquired through kin-ties was especially attractive to the young adults of the village . . . [it provided] . . . a chance for security apart from the *aiga*, a means of meeting *aiga* obligations without the pressure of being in the village, the excitement of town and the encouragement of relatives both in town and inside of the village.

In 1975 Samoans remitted $6.9 million, while in the same year, the Western Samoan Government approved a total budget of $16.6 million (de Bres and Campbell 1976b: 30).

Within the kinship structure, young men and women are often encouraged to migrate by the head of the family who is not only a title-holder but the family's entrepreneur, planner and overseer. If the *matai* (titled family head in Samoa) or *mataiapo* (the equivalent in Cook Islands) needs money for a family project, such as a major contribution to a village scheme, or to plant new crops, or to buy an outboard motor, he may arrange for one of his daughters, sons or young relatives to go to work in New Zealand to provide the money required. Title-holders arrange these opportunities hoping that movement will ease the tension at home and supply the money required to compensate for the loss of labour and services. As time goes by and movement becomes more widespread it becomes institutionalized. Young adults expect to get the opportunity to migrate and those left behind in the village expect to receive the monetary benefits that accrue. In addition to sending or bringing remittances back to the village, sojourners have been expected to help to finance the movement of other family members, often providing airfares, housing, food, pocket money and job connections. Relatives who go to New Zealand as guest-workers are then able to remit more because the bulk of their expenses are underwritten by permanent migrants (Shankman 1976: 59). Other research reports that some families in Samoa depend entirely on the regular airmail envelope from Auckland (Pitt and Macpherson 1974: 13).

Samoan village studies in 1964 indicated that because migration, either temporary or long-term, takes place within the context of a rigid social structure, the potentially damaging effects on Samoan customs tend to be negligible and do not undermine the basis of village life (Pitt 1970: 185). Both Pitt and Shankman cite the positive features of the Samoan mobility pattern. Receiving families have higher incomes than would be possible under agriculture alone, manpower losses are negligible, migration can be used to bolster prestige and skills are acquired abroad (Shankman 1976: 88). While there are these positive features there are a number of negative effects too. Shankman argues that migration and remittances adversely modify Samoan custom, lead to further migration, to greater dependence on remittances, and to the deterioration of village economic enterprises. The same has been reported for Niue (Walsh and Trlin 1973; and Pollock 1976). A number of changes occurring recently in Tokelau have been detailed, particularly the developing independence of the nuclear family at the expense of the *kaiga* (clan), the undermining of the status and authority of the elders, the decline in living standards brought about by higher dependency loads and inequalities in subsistence production

(Hooper and Huntsman 1973: 405-6). The dysfunctional aspects of a labour-exporting economy have been stressed for Tonga. Besides creating an acute labour shortage there in 1974, and then an acute oversupply by 1976, migration has had the effect of changing consumption patterns, creating balance of payments difficulties, engendering disenchantment and feeding the desire for renewed emigration (de Bres and Campbell 1976a: 26-8).

The future

The foregoing seems to point clearly to a need for regulation; but regulating the flow of labour and/or settlers between the Pacific Island countries and New Zealand needs to be for the benefit of all parties concerned, not solely for the benefit of the strongest. Tonga, Samoa, and the other island states need to have a greater say in determining overall mobility levels and the extent of temporal fluctuations. Given the uneven nature of the power positions of New Zealand and the other countries involved, any sharing in decision-making about South-Pacific emigration to New Zealand will have to be initiated by the latter − an initiative she has been unwilling so far to take.

The dependency of labour-exporting societies and the instability of their incomes as the demand for labour fluctuates is clearly seen in the Pacific. In the short-term remitted income and the extent of population mobility between Island Polynesia and New Zealand depends on the political response in New Zealand to the difficulties she faces in buffering her own externally-propelled and vulnerable economy. As the current (1978) situation makes clear, when employment conditions are in a parlous state none of the Pacific Island governments can expect much relief from New Zealand. Like many of the countries of north-west Europe New Zealand intends to continue to use the Pacific Island labour pool as a convenient recession buffer (Paine 1974: 60-5). Until she and other richer countries of the world do more than talk about a new economic order, fairer trade practices and a more equable distribution of wealth, the fragile Pacific Island economies and their increasingly heavy dependence on metropolitan countries will continue.

In the longer-term there appears to be some grounds for optimism. Tongans and Samoans have established viable communities in New Zealand; they are able to sponsor others for residence in these. Links between New Zealand and the other Pacific countries will increase through marriage, kin, culture and common interest. As Anglo-Saxon New Zealanders edge towards realizing the benefits of a multi-cultural society these linkages with their near neighbours will be more highly valued.

Many small organizations have argued strongly with the New Zealand Government for a future commitment to the peoples of the Pacific which will allow some continuing permanent settlement from the islands (Amnesty Aroha 1976; New Zealand Demographic Society 1976). Amnesty Aroha has argued that New Zealand should provide for a specified minimum number of guest-workers every year no matter how internal labour demands fluctuate. This would provide Samoa, Tonga, Tuvalu and Fiji with the security of remittance income that they lack at present, and a basis on which to plan their futures. Similar views have been put by the New Zealand Inter-Church Commission on Migration, and by the New Zealand Overseas Aid Organization CORSO.

Contrary to the fears of many New Zealanders, not all Pacific Islanders want to come to New Zealand. As the Cook Islanders have demonstrated, steady jobs at home are usually more desirable than migration and the possibility of unemployment in Auckland. All Pacific Island governments look beyond migration for solutions to their long-term development dilemmas. Fertility is declining in all these countries, and while replacement level fertility is still a long way off, even in Fiji, in the longer term much more modest rates of natural increase, the better exploitation of agricultural, industrial and fishing resources, tourism and the remitted earnings of guest-workers and sojourners will each have a part to play in balancing the fragile economies of the Pacific Islands. Of course the solutions, like the problems, are not merely economic. Whether New Zealand chooses to emphasize a 'guest-workers' or a 'settlers' relationship with its neighbours there are cultural and social issues that will need to be recognized, confronted and resolved.

The future of New Zealand and the other South Pacific countries is inextricably bound together. At present Maoris and other Polynesians in New Zealand society are disproportionately concentrated in low status and low prestige positions in the class structure. Within New Zealand a perpetuation of the current ethnic and class structure will not serve the best interests of the country as a whole and will do little to promote the mutual respect and understanding on which a closely-tied future must depend.

Conclusion

In the introductory essay to this volume we defined and outlined our ideas and views on circulation, which derive from our respective experience in two very dissimilar, but at the same time comparable, parts of the Third World. The essays which followed have demonstrated that these views and ideas relate to the experience of other researchers drawn from a variety of disciplines and working elsewhere in the Third World in a variety of differing physical environmental and cultural, social and economic circumstances.

Many of the essays identify circulation as having existed in the past, to be ongoing at the present and some cite evidence to suggest that it may continue in the future. Reciprocal flows of people, goods and ideas have persisted over time; links are maintained between places of origin and of destination and traditional modes of circulation are manifest in contemporary mobility behaviour. At the same time changes have occurred in the nature of these flows and these links. The growth of more efficient inexpensive transport permits villagers to commute to wage employment in towns or in other local communities rather than be absent for long periods (Hugo, Bromley, this volume). Cross flows of remittances, investments, and gifts may substitute for the physical transfer of people.

Circulation responds to changes in the wider political and socio-economic contexts in which it occurs. These contexts are themselves influenced by circulatory movements in ways which are different from those when there is a permanent transfer of population through migration. A specific example is provided by the changing nature of circulation as a factor in the restructuring of central place systems (Bromley, this volume). More generally and more widely applicable, circulatory movements which were

436

formerly based on rural villages, from where there was out-movement to towns and other centres of wage employment, are now based on towns from which there is circulation to other towns and to the rural areas (Hugo, Skeldon, Swindell, this volume). The implications of such changes for the planning of administrative services and for social provision in spheres such as housing, education and health are considerable. Yet most political and social infrastructures are undoubtedly based largely on the premise that they are catering for populations which are relatively fixed and not ones in which there are considerable elements of continuing mobility through circulation.

We maintain the need to face up to realities in studies of circulation and mobility in general, concurring with the views expressed by Janet Abu-Lughod (1975) that we are, and certainly that we should be 'at the end of the age of innocence' in the study of the movements of people. For too long there has been an implicit, if not explicit, acceptance of a uniform phenomenon, 'migration', and a uniform participant 'migrant'. This acceptance is naive and misleading; 'the monolithic category called "migrant" has had to be broken down into a complex army of subtypes' (Abu-Lughod 1975).

Attempts at integrated explanation of mobility in its various forms are inevitably tentative, but promise to be distinguishing features in the foreseeable future. Based upon Indonesian experience, especially in Sulawesi, Forbes (1981) argues for a more 'comprehensive theory of mobility' in which differences between 'scalar levels of analysis' are avoided by viewing individuals and society as being in a 'two-way dialectical relationship'.

> We need to ensure that we approach . . . the individual not from the point of view of the way time, space, and society (in its broadest sense) *constrain* the behaviour of the individual, but from the way in which time, space and society selectively *influence* the individual, and, just as importantly, the way the individual *feeds back* into (and, ultimately, *reproduces*) the society and transforms it. Similarly, when we approach the analysis from the political economy standpoint we are not talking about a simple process of *determination*, but a process which individuals and classes can and do *transform, opt out of,* or *avoid*. In other words, we are talking about a complete socioeconomic process which, like society as a whole, depends upon people to reproduce it and which, in turn, is shaped and reproduced by it (Forbes 1981: 76, italics in original).

Parallel thinking has prompted Mortimore (1982) to take a

systems approach to population movement, set within the context of associated flows (money, ideas, information), and articulated through the structuring and maximization of opportunities both at home and elsewhere. Based upon the response of Nigerian farmers in north Kano State to drought in the first half of the 1970s, he argues that the basic goals for any person are to accumulate wealth, survive in the face of risk, and achieve social or self-ascribed status. Given a fairly constant setting composed of interlocking parts − natural resources, economy, social structure, communications, administration/legislation − the ability of the individual to address such goals is influenced by factors like prices, access to land and labour, extreme natural or social events, diffusion of technology, and government policies, which in themselves 'are spatially, temporally, and socially variable'. Mortimore concludes: 'The spatial fragmentation of this opportunity structure, and the nature of the risks involved, lies at the root of the bilocal life-style which is becoming common among African populations.'

Prognosis

The conceptual stances advocated by Forbes and Mortimore are symptomatic of the greater sophistication in research on circulation undertaken during the 1970s. They point to the much greater integration of different scales of enquiry, to the various contexts within which mobility behaviour occurs, and to the common ground which is gradually emerging from diverse philosophical positions. As with previous investigations in the Third World, the conduct of field enquiries in depth during the next decade will permit more than one plausible explanation to be tested at any one time and for alternative themes to be pursued as they emerge from primary data during the progress of research.

To comprehend its complex nature more adequately, circulation needs to be investigated and analysed at a variety of different scales. These range from the micro (individual, family), through meso (community, settlement system, region), to macro (country, continent, world). Integration of these different scales of enquiry will be achieved through the better understanding of each and of the ways in which they relate to one another.

The importance of investigating indigenous concepts, beliefs and terms related to the movements of people needs to be much more emphasized. We have described these as comprising 'the language of the people who move'; the limited and fragmentary evidence available points to its richness. Only through this may unique meanings of mobility be captured. They are not accommodated by the western concepts and terms which are most frequently used in Third World studies of mobility. The indigenous material frequently reveals ambiguities which do not fit the discrete criteria of time and place associated with western concepts and terms (cf. Olofson, this volume). There is simply no point in selecting terms which are commonly used in western mobility studies, then attempting to translate them into an indigenous language for a questionnaire survey in which they will not be understood by those to whom the questions are addressed. Certainly misunderstanding occurs, particularly in large-scale studies where even the enumerators being used may not fully understand the questions they are asking in the ways intended by those who designed the questionnaire. It is vital to establish clearly what we are investigating rather than what we believe we are investigating on the basis of western experience. Only in this way can we establish more accurately what people are actually doing and from this develop policy-making which is realistic. Initially work on indigenous concepts of mobility can be undertaken only at micro scale from intensive field investigation. Extending this work to meso and macro scales will present formidable difficulties because of the levels of generalization involved.

The strong field tradition which has been established in previous investigation of circulation in the Third World must be continued. This tradition is explicit in the majority of studies in this volume and it underpins them all. Field investigation is essential since by its very nature circulation is excluded from most census and other conventional forms of data collection on the movements of population. The forms of data collection presently employed in the Third World are based very largely on the experience of data collection in the developed world; within the times, terms and techniques which are used circulatory forms of movement cannot be accommodated.

Techniques for studying circulation must be both cross-sectional and longitudinal. The former have been mostly employed, the latter have been sorely neglected. Yet recognition of the ongoing, often-changing, adapting and modifying nature of mobility is a major key to the better understanding of the processes involved. Static concepts and techniques are inadequate for the study of phenomena which are so dynamic.

In general in studies of circulation which have some longitudinal component the emphasis has been on *retrospective* data collection, for example in movement histories, there is a need to experiment more widely in longitudinal studies with concepts and related methodologies and techniques which are *ongoing* and *prospective*. It has been established in meteorology and

439

climatology that the interpretation and explanations of physical processes which are being attempted, and the forecasts which can be made on the basis of these, are possible only if there are past long-term and present data available from ongoing observations. Why, at least on a sample basis, should there not be ongoing monitoring of circulation to provide the better means for understanding the processes associated with it? And why for that matter should there not be similar monitoring of many other aspects of human conditions for which there are limited explanations and powers of prediction?

There is a broader contribution to be made by Third World studies of circulation through the transfer of concepts and methods to societies and populations very different from those for which they were developed initially and in which they were first tested (cf. Marshall and Mukherji, this volume). Such transfers would be the reverse of that normally found in scholarship; the flow of concepts and techniques would be from Third to First World realities. In the opinion of some observers this process already has begun (Ward 1980: 132; Goldstein, in press), and its roots go far deeper. It may be identified as part of the intellectual history of African studies. On the basis of reviews of nineteen areas of knowledge to assess the status of social research in Africa in the 1960s it was concluded:

> The feeling is strong that the distortion of concrete African social realities is too great, the omission of relevant, even crucial, data too likely when the data are injected into categories predefined on the basis of non-African materials and from 'Western' models. Writers in nearly all disciplines have encountered these conceptual difficulties on the level at which raw data are minimally organized and at the next highest levels on which relationships among minimum categories are being determined. At the same time, the need to define new (or to modify 'Western') categories has the salutary effect of forcing a discipline's non-Africanists to review and revise those categories that fail adequately to comprehend African data. This, more than perhaps any other, is the principal service African . . . studies can provide to theoreticians in any discipline working towards general models and theories (Lystad 1965: 2).

With reference to studies of circulation in particular and of population mobility in general, we hope that the growing involvement of scholars from the Third World will continue on similar lines, with heightened vigour and resulting in ever increasing understanding and explanation.

Bibliography

Abir, M. (1968), *Ethiopia: The Era of the Princes*, London: Longman.

Acosta-Solis, Misael (1969), 'Glumifloras del Ecuador', *Flora* (Quito) 13: 1-216.

Ahlers, Theodore H. (1978), 'Haitian Rural-Urban Migration: A Case Study in Four Small Towns', mimeo, paper presented to the Annual Conference of the Caribbean Studies Association, Santiago, Dominican Republic.

Al-Nagar, Umar (1972), *The Pilgrimage Tradition in West Africa*, Khartoum University Press.

Amenumey, D.K. (1964), 'The Ewe People and the Coming of European Rule 1914-1950', unpublished MA thesis, University of London.

Amin, S. (1974), 'Introduction', in S. Amin (ed.), *Modern Migrations in Western Africa*, London: Oxford University Press for the International African Institute, 65-124.

Amnesty Aroha (1976), Submission to Government, November 1976. Amnesty Aroha, Wellington.

Anderson, J. (1970), *The Struggle for the School*, London: Longman.

Armstrong, W.R. and McGee, T.G. (1968), 'Revolutionary change and the third world city: a theory of urban involution', *Civilizations* 18: 353-78.

Arnold, Fred and Supani Boonpratuang (1976), 1970 *Population and Housing Census: Migration*, Subject Report no. 2, Bangkok: National Statistical Office.

Arrighi, G. (1967), International corporations, labour aristocracies and economic development in tropical Africa, in D. Horowitz (ed.), 'The Corporation and the Cold War', unpublished papers, Tanzania: University College, Dar es Salaam.

Asad, T. (1970), *The Kababish Arabs*, London: C. Hurst.

Ashton, Guy T. (1966), 'The Zapateros: A Case of Circulatory Migration', unpublished manuscript.

Ashton, Guy T. (1967), 'Consecuencias de la Migración de Zapateros Adolescentes a Belice', *América Indígena* 27, 2: 301-16.

BIBLIOGRAPHY

Australian Council for Overseas Aid (1978), in Gay Woods (ed.), *South Pacific Dossier*, Canberra: Australian Council for Overseas Aid.

Balán, J., Browning, H.L., Jelin, E., and Litzler, L. (1969), 'A computerized approach to the processing and analysis of life histories obtained in sample surveys', *Behavioral Science* 14: 105-20.

Balán, J., Browning, H.L. and Jelin, E. (1973), *Men in a Developing Society: Geographic and Social Mobility in Monterrey, Mexico*, Austin: University of Texas Press.

Bamisaiye, A. (1974), 'Begging in Ibadan, Southern Nigeria', *Human Organization* 33: 197-202.

Bardhan, P.K. and Srinivasan, T.N. (eds) (1974), *Poverty and Income Distribution in India*, Calcutta: Statistical Publishing Society.

Bargery, G.P. (1934), *A Hausa-English Dictionary and English-Hausa Vocabulary*, London: Oxford University Press.

Bedford, R.D. (1973a), *New Hebridean Mobility: A Study of Circular Migration*, Department of Human Geography Publication HG/9, Canberra: Australian National University.

Bedford, R.D. (1973b), 'A transition in circular mobility: population in the New Hebrides, 1800-1970', in H. Brookfield (ed.), *The Pacific in Transition: Geographical Perspectives on Adaptation and Change*, London: Edward Arnold: 187-227.

Belote, Jim and Belote, Linda (1977a), 'The limitation of obligation in Saraguro kinship', in Ralph Bolton and Enrique Mayer (eds), *Andean Kinship and Marriage*, Washington DC: American Anthropological Association Special Publication, no. 7: 106-16.

Belote, Jim and Belote, Linda (1977b), 'El sistima de cargos de fiesta en Saraguro', in Marcel F. Narango, Jose L. Pereira and Norman E. Whitten, Jr (eds), *Temas sobre la Continuidad y Adaptacion Cultural Ecuatoriama*, Quito: Pontifica Universidad Catolica del Ecuador: 47-73.

Belote, Linda (1978), 'Prejudice and Price: Indian-White Relations in Saraguro, Ecuador', unpublished PhD dissertation, University of Illinois, Urbana, Ann Arbor: University Microfilms.

Berg, E.J. (1965), 'The economics of the migrant labor system', in *Urbanization and Migration in West Africa*, H. Kuper (ed.), Los Angeles: University of California Press: 160-81.

Berry, B.J.L. (1966), *Essays on Commodity Flows and the Spatial Structure of the Indian Economy*, research paper no. 111, Department of Geography, University of Chicago.

Bharati, Agehananda (1970), 'Pilgrimage sites and Indian civilization' in Joseph Elder (ed.), *Chapters in Indian Civilization*, Dubuque: Kendall/Hunt.

Bhardwaj, Surinder M. (1973), *Hindu Places of Pilgrimage in India: A Study in Cultural Geography*, Berkeley: University of California Press.

Birks, J.S. (1978), 'Development or decline of pastoralists: the Bani Qitab of the Sultanate of Oman', *Arabian Studies* 4: 7-19.

Birks, J.S. and Letts, S.E. (1977a), 'Diqal and Mugayah: dying oases in Arabia', *Tijdschrift voor Economische en Sociale Geografie* 68, 3: 145-51.

Birks, J.S. and Letts, S.E. (1977b), 'Women in rural Arab society: old roles and new in the Sultanate of Oman', *Journal of Gulf and Arabian Peninsula Studies* 3: 10 (Arabic).

Birks, J.S. and Sinclair, C.A. (1977), *Movements of Migrant Labour from the North of the Sultanate of Oman*, International Migration Project Working Paper, Department of Economics, Durham University.

Blau, Peter M. (1960), 'Structural effects', *American Sociological Review* 25: 178-93.

Bohning, W.R. (1972), *The Migration of Workers in the United Kingdom and the European Community*, London: Oxford University Press.

Bondestam, L. (1972), 'The population situation in Ethiopia', in *On Family Planning in Ethiopia*, 1: 4-14, Addis Ababa: Ethiopian Nutrition Institute.

Bose, Ashish (1967), 'The process of urbanization in India: some emerging issues', in R.G. Fox (ed.), *Urban India: Society, Space and Image*, Providence: Brown University: 1-22.

Bose, Ashish (1975), 'Basic data needed for the study of migration: a case study of the Indian Census', in Sidney Goldstein and David Sly (eds), *Basic Data Needed for the Study of Urbanization*, Liege: IUSSP: 71-100.

Boute, P. (1975), 'Conditions et effets de l'implantation d'industries minières en milieu pastoral: l'exemple de la Mauritanie', in T. Monod (ed.), *Pastoralism in Tropical Africa*, London: Oxford University Press for the International African Institute: 245-62.

Bowman, I. (1916), *The Andes of Southern Peru*, New York: American Geographical Society.

Breman, J. (1978-79), 'Seasonal migration and cooperative capitalism: the crushing of cane and of labour by the sugar factories of Bardoli, South Gujarat', *Journal of Peasant Studies*, 6 (1): 41-70, (2): 168-209.

de Bres, Joris (1974), *How Tonga Aids New Zealand*, Wellington: South Pacific Action Network.

de Bres, J. *et al.* (1974), *Migrant Labour in the Pacific*, CORSO, Auckland Resource Centre for World Development.

de Bres, J. and Campbell, R. (1976a), *Worth Their Weight in Gold*, Auckland Resource Centre for World Development.

de Bres, J. and Campbell, R. (1976b), *The Overstayers*, Auckland Resource Centre for World Development.

Bromley, R.J. (1974), 'The organization of Quito's urban markers: towards a reinterpretation of periodic central places', Institute of British Geographers, *Transactions*, 62: 45-70.

Bromley, R.J. (1975), 'Periodic and Daily Markets in Highland Ecuador', unpublished PhD thesis, Cambridge University (U.M. order no. 76-21,058).

Bromley, R.J. (1976), 'Contemporary market periodicity in highland Ecuador', in C.A. Smith (ed.), *Regional Analysis, Volume I: Economic Systems*, New York: Academic Press: 91-122.

Bromley, R.J. (1978), 'Traditional and modern change in the growth of systems of market centres in highland Ecuador', in R.H.T. Smith (ed.), *Market-place Trade: Periodic Markets, Hawkers and Traders in Africa, Asia, and Latin America*, Vancouver: University of British Columbia, Centre for Transportation Studies: 31-47.

Bronitsky, Gordan J. (1977), 'An ecological model of trade: prehistoric economic change in the Northern Rio Grande Region of New Mexico', *Dissertation Abstracts International*, 38.

Brookfield, Harold C. (1970), 'Dualism, and the geography of developing countries', Presidential address delivered to Section 21 (Geographical Sciences), Australian and New Zealand Association for the Advancement of Science, Port Moresby, Papua New Guinea, August.

Brookfield, Harold C. (1973), 'Explaining or understanding? the study of adaptation and change' in H.C. Brookfield (ed.), *The Pacific in Transition: Geographical Perspectives on Adaptation and Change*, London: Edward Arnold.

Brooks, G.E. (1975), 'Peanuts and colonialism: consequences of the commercialisation of peanuts in West Africa 1830-70', *Journal of African History* 16 (1): 52-4.

Browne, G.St.J. Orde (1933), *The African Labourer*, London: Oxford University Press.

Brunhes, J. and Vallaux, C. (1921), *La Géographie de l'histoire*, Paris: Felix Alcan.

Brush, Stephen (1977), *Mountain, Field and Family: the Economy and Human Ecology of an Andean Valley*, Philadelphia: University of Pennsylvania Press.

Brydon, L. (1976), 'Status Ambiguity in Amedzofe-Avatime: Women and Men in a Changing Patrilineal Society', unpublished PhD thesis, University of Cambridge.

Buell, Raymond Leslie (1928), *The Native Problem in Africa* (2 vols), New York: Macmillan.

Burawoy, Michael (1976), 'The functions and reproduction of migrant labor: comparative material from Southern Africa and the United States', *American Journal of Sociology* 81: 1051-87.

Burgos, Hugo (1970), *Relaciones Interethnicas en Riobamba*, Ediciones especiale, no. 55, Mexico: Instituto Indigenista Interamericano.

Butterworth, Douglas (1962), 'A study of the urbanization process among Mixtec migrants from Tilantongo in Mexico City', *América Indígena* 22: 257-74.

Butterworth, Douglas (1971), 'Migracion rural-urbana en America Latina: el estado de nuestro conocimiento', *América Indígena* 31: 85-105.

Buttimer, Anne (1971), *Society and Milieu in the French Geographic Tradition*, Chicago: Association of American Geographers.

Byerlee, D. and Eicher, C.K. (1972), *Rural Employment and Economic Development*, African Rural Employment Papers no. 1, East Lansing: Michigan State University.

Byres, T.J. (1979), 'Of neo-populist pipe dreams: Daedalus in the Third World and the myth of urban bias', *Journal of Peasant Studies*, 6:210-44.

Caldwell, J.C. (1969), *African Rural-Urban Migration*, Canberra: Australian National University Press.

Caldwell, J.C. (1976), 'Toward a restatement of demographic transition theory', *Population and Development Review*, 2:321-66.

Campbell, R. (1975), *Tongan Newsletter* no. 2, August 6, Auckland Resource Centre for World Development.

Cancian, F. (1965), *Economics and Prestige in a Maya Community: the Religious Cargo in Zinacantan*, Stanford University Press.

Capot-Rey, R. (1946), *Géographie de la circulation sur les continents*, Paris: Gallimard.

Carpenter, F.W. (1954), *Report of the Committee on African Wages*, Nairobi: Government Printer.

Casagrande, Joseph B. (1974), 'Strategies for survival: the Indians of Highland Ecuador', in Dwight B. Heath (ed.), *Contemporary Cultures and Societies of Latin America*, New York: Random House: 93-107.

Castles, L. (1967), *Religion, Politics and Economic Behaviour in Java: The Kudus Cigarette Industry*, New Haven: Yale University.

Castles, S. and Kosack, G. (1972), *Immigrant Workers and Class Structure in Western Europe*, London: Oxford University Press for the Institute for Race Relations.

Cavalli-Sforza, L. (1963), 'The distribution of migration distances: models, and applications to genetics', in J. Sutter (ed.), *Human Displacements: Measurement, Methodological Aspects*, Monaco: Centre International d'Etude des Problèmes Humaines: 139-58.

Chapman, M., (1969), 'A population policy in south Guadalcanal: some results and implications', *Oceania* 40:119-47.

Chapman, M. (1970), 'Population movement in tribal society: the case of Duidui and Pichahila, British Solomon Islands', PhD dissertation, University of Washington, Seattle.

Chapman, M. (1975), 'Mobility in a non-literate society: method and analysis for two Guadalcanal communities', in L.A. Kosinski and R.M. Prothero (eds), *People on the Move: Studies on Internal Migration*, London: Methuen: 129-45.

Chapman, M. (1976), 'Tribal mobility as circulation: a Solomon Islands example of micro/macro linkages', in L.A. Kosinski and J.W. Webb (eds), *Population at Microscale*, Christchurch: New Zealand Geographical Society and Commission on Population Geography: 127-42.

Chapman, M. (1978), 'On the cross-cultural study of circulation', *International Migration Review* 12: 559-69.

Chapman, M. (1979), 'The cross-cultural study of circulation', *Current Anthropology* 20:111-14.

Chapman, M. (1981), 'Policy implications of circulation: some answers from the grassroots', in G.W. Jones and H.V. Richter (eds), *Population Mobility and Development: Southeast Asia and the Pacific*, Development Studies Centre Monograph No. 27, Canberra: Australian National University: 71-87.

Chapman, Murray and Prothero, R. Mansell (1977), 'Circulation between home places and towns: a village approach to urbanization', paper for the Working Session on Urbanization, Pacific Association for Social Anthropology in Oceania: Monterey, California.

Cieze de Leon, P. de (1945), *La Crónica del Perú*, Madrid: Espasa-Calpe.

Cohen, A. (1969), *Custom and Politics in Urban Africa*, London: Routledge & Kegan Paul.

Cole, D. (1973), 'The enmeshment of nomads in Saudi Arabian society', in C. Nelson (ed.), *The Desert and the Sown*: 113-28.

Cole, D. (1975), *The Nomads of the Nomads*, Chicago: Aldine Press.

Collier, W.L. (1978), 'Food problems, unemployment and the Green Revolution in rural Java', *Prisma* 9: 38-52.

Collier, W.L., Wiradi, G., and Soentoro (1973), 'Recent changes in rice harvesting methods', *Bulletin of Indonesian Economic Studies* 9, 2: 36-45.

Collins, E.J. (1976), 'Migrant labour in British agriculture in the Nineteenth Century', *Economic History Review* 29, 1: 38-59.

Conaway, M.E. (1977), *Circular Migration: A Summary and Bibliography*, Exchange Bibliography no. 1250, Monticello, Illinois: Council of Planning Librarians.

Conroy, J.D. (1976), *Education, employment and migration in Papua New Guinea*, Development Studies Centre, Monograph no. 3, Canberra: Australian National University.

Corno, R.B. (1979), 'Migrant Adjustment in Bogota, Columbia: Occupation and Health Care', unpublished PhD thesis, Brown University, Providence.

CORSO (1974), *The New Tonga Migrant Worker Scheme*, Report of a Trade Union Seminar, Auckland. CORSO, Auckland Resource Centre for World Development.

Cotler, J. (1969), 'Actuales pautas de cambio en la sociedad rural del Peru', in J. Matos Mar *et al.* (eds), *Dominacion ye Cambios en el Peru Rural*, Lima: Instituto de Estudios Peruanos.

Critchfield, R. (1970), *Hello Mister, Where Are you Going?*, New York: Alicia Patterson Fund.

Cunnison, I. (1966), *Baggara Arabs*, Oxford: Clarendon Press.

Daroesman, R. (1972), 'An economic survey of West Java', *Bulletin of Indonesian Economic Studies* 8, 2: 29-54.

Davis, James A., Spaeth, J.L. and Huson, Carolyn (1961), 'A technique for analysing the effects of group composition', *American Sociological Review* 26: 215-25.

Davis, J. Merle (1933), *Modern Industry and the African*, London: Macmillan.

de Gonzalez, N.L.S. (1961), 'Family organization in five types of migratory wage labor', *American Anthropologist*, 63:126 4-80.

de la Blache, P. Vidal (1926), *Principles of Human Geography*, New York: Holt.

Devons, Ely, and Gluckman, Max (1964), 'Conclusions: modes and consequences of limiting a field of study', in Max Gluckman (ed.), *Closed Systems and Open Minds: The Limits of Naivety in Social*

Anthropology, London: Oliver & Boyd: 158-261.

DGEC (Direccion General de Estadística y Censos) (1964), *Segundo Censo de Población y Primer Censo de Vivienda, 1962*, Quito.

DGEC (1968a), *Proyección de la Población del Ecuador, 1960-1980*, Quito.

DGEC (1968b), *Cartografía Estadística Demográfica a 1962*, Quito.

Diallo, I. (1971), 'La migration en Afrique de l'Ouest: les migrations frontiales entre Le Sénégal et La Gambie', seminar, *Institut Africain de Développement Economique et de Planification*, Dakar: 1-22.

Dias, Hiren D. (1977), 'Dispersal of human settlements: a study of the Sri Lanka experience', paper prepared for ESCAP Expert Group Meeting on Migration and Human Settlements, Bangkok.

Dietz, H. (1976), 'Who, how, and why: rural migration to Lima', Migration and Development Study group, Centre for International Studies, Massachusetts Institute of Technology, Document C/76-4: 26-37.

Dillehay, Tom D. (1979), 'Pre-Hispanic resource sharing in the Central Andes', *Science* 204: 24-31.

Dore, R. (1976), *The Diploma Disease: Education, Qualification and Development*, London: George Allen & Unwin.

Douglas, E.M.K. (1965), 'A Migration Study of Cook Islanders', unpublished MSc thesis, Victoria University of Wellington.

Doughty, P.L. (1969), 'La cultura de regionalismo en la vida urbana de Lima, Peru', *America Indigena*, 29: 949-81.

Doughty, P.L. (1970), 'Behind the back of the city: provincial life in Lima, Peru', in W. Mangin (ed.), *Peasants in Cities*, Boston: Houghton Mifflin: 30-46.

Dry, E. (1956), 'The social development of the Hausa child', in *Proceedings of the International African Conference 1949*: 164-70.

Dubbeldam, L.F.B. (1970), *The Primary School and the Community in Mwanza District, Tanzania*, Groningen: Wolters-Noordhoff.

Dutt, J.S. (1976), 'Population movement and gene flow', in P.T. Baker and M.A. Little (eds), *Man in the Andes: a Multidisciplinary Study of High Altitude Quechua*, Stroudsburg, Pennsylvania: Dowden, Hutchinson and Ross: 115-27.

East African Statistical Department (1959), *Patterns of Income Expenditure and Consumption of Africans in Nairobi, 1957/58*, Nairobi: Kenya Unit.

East-West Population Institute, 1978, 'Summary report: International Seminar on the Cross-Cultural Study of Circulation, 3-7 April', Honolulu: East-West Center.

Echols, J.M. and Shaddily, H. (1970), *An Indonesia-English Dictionary*, Ithaca: Cornell University Press.

Ekstrom, J. Peter (1975), 'Responding to a new ecology: adaptations of colonists in Eastern Ecuador', *Papers in Anthropology* 16: 25-38.

Eldridge, Hope T. (1965), 'Primary, secondary, and return migration in the United States, 1955-1960', *Demography* 2: 445-55.

Elizaga, Juan C. (1972), 'Internal migration: an overview', *International Migration Review* 6: 121-46.

Elkan, W. (1959), 'Migrant labour in Africa: an economist's approach', *American Economic Review* 49: 188-97.

Elkan, W. (1960), *Migrants and Proletarians: Urban labour in the Economic Development of Uganda*, London: Oxford University Press for the East African Institute of Social Research.

Elkan, W. (1967), 'Circular migration and the growth of towns in East Africa', *International Labour Review* 96: 581-9.

Elkan, W. (1976), 'Is a proletariat emerging in Nairobi?', *Economic Development and Cultural Change* 24 (4), 695-706.

Elkan, W. and Fallers, L.A. (1960), 'Mobility of labour', in W.E. Moore and A.S. Geldman (eds), *Labour Commitment and Social Change in Developing Areas*, New York: Social Science Research Council: 251-4.

Ethiopian Government (1975), *A Proclamation to Provide for the Nationalisation of Rural Land*, Addis Ababa: Provisional Military Administration.

Fallers, M. (1960), *The Eastern Lacustrine Bantu* (Ganda, Soga), Ethnographic Survey of Africa, part XI, London: International African Institute.

Fan, Y-K. and Stretton, A. (1980), *Circular Migration in Southeast Asia: Some Theoretical Explanations*, Research Papers in Economics No. 8002, Department of Economics, Los Angeles: University of Southern California.

Feindt, W. and Browning, H.L. (1972), 'Return migration: its significance in an industrial metropolis and an agricultural town in Mexico', *International Migration Review* 6, 2: 158-65.

Feraro, G.P. (1971), 'Kikuyu Kinship Interaction: a Rural-urban Comparison', unpublished PhD thesis, Syracuse University.

Finau, Patelisio (Bishop of Tonga) (1976), *Some Theological Reflections on Migration*, Auckland Resource Centre for World Development.

Findley, S. (1977), *Planning for Internal Migration: a Review of Policies in Developing Countries*, Washington, DC: US Department of Commerce, Bureau of the Census.

First, Ruth (1979), 'Migrant Labour in Southern Africa', in R. Synge (ed.), *New African Yearbook 1979*, London: I.C. Magazines: 63-8.

Forbes, D.K. (1977), 'On urban-rural interdependence', paper presented to Section 21 Australian and New Zealand Association for the Advancement of Science, Melbourne.

Fortes, M. (1971), 'Some aspects of migration and mobility in Ghana', *Journal of Asian and African Studies* 6: 1-20.

Fouquet, J. (1958), 'La traité des arachides dans le Pays de Kalok', *Études Sénégalaises*, IFAN, no. 8: 68.

Franks, R. (1972), 'The Green Revolution in a Javanese Village', unpublished PhD thesis, Harvard University, Cambridge.

Friedmann, J. and Wulff, R. (1975), *The Urban Transition: Comparative Studies of Newly Industrializing Societies*, London: Edward Arnold.

Fuchs, R.J. and Demko, G.J. (1978), 'The post-war mobility transition in Eastern Europe', *Geographical Review* 68: 171-82.

Fuenzalida, F. (1970), 'La estructura de la comunidad de indigenas tradicional', in R.G. Keith *et al.* (eds), *El Campesino en al Peru*, Peru Problems 3, Lima: Instituto de Estudios Peruanos.

Furley, D.W. and Watson, T. (1978), *A History of Education in East Africa*, New York: NOK Publishers.

Gade, D.W. (1975), *Plants, Man and the Land in the Vilcanota Valley of Peru*, The Hague: Dr.W. Junk B.V.

Gamble, D.P. (1957), *The Wolof of Senegambia*, London: 49.

Garbett, G.K. (1975), 'Circulatory migration in Rhodesia: towards a decision model', in D. Parkin (ed.), *Town and Country in Central and Eastern Africa*, London: Oxford University Press for the International African Institute: 113-25.

Garbett, G. Kingsley and Kapferer, Bruce (1970), 'Theoretical orientations in the study of labour migration', *The New Atlantis* 2: 179-97.

Gayot, Francois (1971), 'La Pastorale Face a L'Evolution de La Vie Rurale en Haiti: Etude Socio-Religieuse de Diocese de Port-de-Paix', unpublished doctoral thesis, Faculté de Théologie Catholique, University of Strasbourg.

Geertz, C. (1963a), *Agricultural Involution. The Processes of Ecological Change in Indonesia*, Berkeley: University of California Press.

Geertz, C. (1963b), *Peddlers and Princes: Social Change and Economic Modernization in Two Indonesian Towns*, University of Chicago Press.

Germani, Gino (1961), 'Inquiry into the social effects of urbanization in a working class sector of Greater Buenos Aires', in P.M. Hauser (ed.), *Urbanization in Latin America*, New York: Columbia University Press.

Gerold-Scheepers, T.J.F.A. and W.M.J. van Binsbergen (1978), 'Marxist and non-Marxist approaches to migration in Tropical Africa', in W.M.J. van Binsbergen and H.A. Meilink (eds), *Migration and the Transformation of Modern African Society: African Perspectives 1978/1*, Leiden: Afrika-Studiecentrum: 21-35.

Gilbert, A. (1974), *Latin American Development: a Geographical Perspective*, Harmondsworth: Penguin Books.

Gluckman, Max (1947), 'Malinowski's "functional" analysis of social change', *Africa* 17: 103-21.

Goddard, A.D. (1974), 'Population movement and land shortages in the Sokoto close-settled zone, Nigeria', in S. Amin (ed.), *Modern Migrations in Western Africa*, London: Oxford University Press for the International African Institute: 258-80.

Goldstein, Sidney (1964), 'The extent of repeated migration: an analysis based on the Danish Population Register', *Journal of the American Statistical Association* 59: 1121-31.

Goldstein, Sidney (1971), 'Urbanization in Thailand, 1947-1967', *Demography* 8: 205-23.

Goldstein, Sidney (1973), 'Urbanization and Migration in Southeast Asia, with illustrations from Thailand', paper presented to SEADAG Population Panel Seminar, San Francisco, CA.

Goldstein, Sidney (1975), *The Measurement of Urbanization and*

Projection of Urban Population, International Union for the Scientific Study of Population, Liège.

Goldstein, Sidney (1976), 'Facets of redistribution: research challenges and opportunities', *Demography* 13, 423-34.

Goldstein, Sidney (1977), 'Urbanization, migration, and fertility in Thailand', Report prepared for Center for Population Research, National Institutes of Child Health and Human Development, Washington, DC.

Goldstein, Sidney (1978), *Circulation in the Context of Total Mobility in South-east Asia*, paper no. 53, East-West Population Institute, East-West Center, Honolulu.

Goldstein, S. and Goldstein, Alice (1978), 'Thailand's urban population re-considered', *Demography* 15: 239-58.

Goldstein, S. and Goldstein, A. (1979), 'Types of migration in Thailand in relation to urban-rural residence', in *Economic and Demographic Change: Issues for the 1980s*, proceedings of the conference, Helsinki, 1978, vol. 2, Liège: International Union for the Scientific Study of Population: 351-75.

Goldstein, S. and Goldstein, A, (1981), *Surveys of Migration in Developing Countries: a Methodological Review*, papers of the East-West Population Institute no. 71, Honolulu: East-West Center.

Goldstein, Sidney, Prachuabmoh, Visid and Goldstein, Alice (1974), *Urban-Rural Migration Differentials in Thailand*, Research Report no. 12, Institute of Population Studies, Bangkok: Chulalongkorn University.

Goldstein, Sidney and Sly, David F. (eds) (1975), *Basic Data Needed for the Study of Urbanization*, Liège: International Union for the Scientific Study of Population.

de Gonzalez, N.L.S. (1961), 'Family organization in five types of migratory wage labour', *American Anthropologist* 63: 1264-80.

Goode, W.J. (1963), *World Revolutions and Family Patterns*, Glencoe, IL: The Free Press.

Gould, Harold A. (1974), 'Lucknow rickshawallas: the social organization of an occupational category', in M.S.A. Rao (ed.), *Urban Sociology in India*, New Delhi: Orient Longman: 90-100.

Gould, W.T.S. (1973a), 'Secondary school provisions in African towns: The case of Addis Ababa', *Town Planning Review* 44: 391-403.

Gould, W.T.S. (1973b), *Planning the location of schools: 3. Ankole, Uganda*, Paris: International Institute for Educational Planning.

Gould, W.T.S. (1974), 'Secondary school admissions policies in Eastern Africa: some regional issues', *Comparative Education Review*, 18: 374-87.

Gould, W.T.S. (1975), 'Movements of school children and provision of secondary schools in Uganda', in D. Parkin (ed.), *Town and Country in Central and Eastern Africa*, London: Oxford University Press for International African Institute: 250-62.

Gould, W.T.S. (1978), *Guidelines for School Location Planning*, Washington, DC: The World Bank, Staff Working Paper no. 308.

Gould, W.T.S. (1982), 'Provision of primary schools and population redistribution in Africa', in J.I. Clarke and L.A. Kosinski (eds), *Redistribution of Population in Africa*, London: Heinemann: 44-9.

Gould, W.T.S. and Prothero, R.M. (1975), 'Space and time in African population mobility', in L.A. Kosinski and R.M. Prothero (eds), *People on the Move: Studies on Internal Migration*, London: Methuen: 39-49.

Government Printer (1962), *Kenya Population Census*, Nairobi.

Graves, Nancy B. and Graves, Theodore D. (1974), 'Adaptive Strategies in Urban Migration', in A.R. Beals and S.A. Tyler (eds), *Annual Review of Anthropology*, vol. 3 Annual Reviews Inc., Palo Alto: 117-51.

Gregory, J.W. and Piché, V. (1978), 'African migration and peripheral capitalism', in W.M.J. van Binsbergen and H.A. Meilink (eds), *Migration and the Transformation of Modern African Society*, African Perspectives 1978/1, Leiden: Afrika-Studiecentrum: 37-50.

Grillo, R.D. (1973), *African Railwaymen*, Cambridge University Press.

Gugler, Josef (1969), 'On the theory of rural-urban migration: the case of Subsaharan Africa', in J.A. Jackson (ed.), *Migration: Sociological Studies* 2, Cambridge University Press: 134-55.

Guillet, D. (1976), 'Migration, agrarian reform and structural change in rural Peru', *Human Organization* 35: 295-302.

Gulliver, Philip M. (1957), 'Nyakusa labour migration', *Rhodes-Livingstone Journal* 21: 32-63.

Gulliver, P.H. (1975), 'Nomadic movements: causes and implications', in T. Monod (ed.), *Pastoralism in Tropical Africa*, London: Oxford University Press for International African Institute: 369-86.

Haan, F. de (1910-1912), *Priangan*, Batavia: Bataviaasch Genootschap Van Kunsten En Wetenschappen.

Haas, A. (1977), *New Zealand and the South Pacific*, Wellington: Asia and Pacific Research Unit.

Haeringer, P. (1972), 'Méthodes de recherche sur les migrations africaines: un modèle d'interview biographique et sa transcription synoptique', *Cahiers de l'ORSTOM*, Série Sciences Humaines, 9: 439-53.

Hägerstrand, T. (1957), 'Migration and area: survey of a sample of Swedish migration fields and hypothetic considerations on their genesis', in D. Hannerberg *et al.* (eds), *Lund Studies in Geography*, Lund University.

Hailey, Lord (1938), *An African Survey: a Study of the Problems arising in Africa South of the Sahara*, London: Oxford University Press.

Harner, Michael J. (1972), *The Jivaro: People of the Sacred Waterfalls*, Garden City: Doubleday/Natural History.

Harpending, Henry and Davis, Herbert (1977), 'Some implications for hunter-gatherer ecology derived from the spatial structure of resources', *World Archaeology* 8: 275-86.

Harries-Jones, Peter (1969), ' "Home-boy" ties and political organization in a Copperbelt Township', in J.C. Mitchell (ed.), *Social Networks in Social Situations*, Manchester University Press: 297-347.

Harries-Jones, Peter (1975), *Freedom and Labour: Mobilization and*

Political Control on the Zambian Copperbelt, Oxford: Basil Blackwell.

Harris, Marvin (1959), 'Labour emigration among the Mocambique Thonga: cultural and political factors', *Africa* 29: 50-65.

Headland, Thomas N. and Headland, Janet D. (1974), *A Dumagat (Casiguran)-English Dictionary*, Pacific Linguistics Series C, no. 28, Department of Linguistics, Research School of Pacific Studies, Canberra: Australian National University.

Headland, Thomas N. and Wolfenden, Elmer P. (1967), 'The Vowels of Casiguran Dumagat', in Mario D. Zamora (ed.), *Studies in Philippine Anthropology*, Manila: Alemar: 592-7.

Hellman, Ellen (1948), *Rooiyard: a Sociological Survey of an Urban Slum Yard*, Rhodes-Livingstone Paper 13, Manchester University Press for Rhodes-Livingstone Institute.

Hill, Polly (1963), *Migrant Cocoa Farmers of Southern Ghana*, Cambridge University Press.

Hoben, A. (1973), *Land Tenure among the Amhara of Ethiopia*, University of Chicago Press.

Hogendorn, J.S. (1976), 'The vent for surplus model and African agriculture to 1914', *Savanna* 5: 26-8.

Hooper, A. and Huntsman, J. (1973), 'A demographic history of the Tokelau Islands', *Journal of the Polynesian Society* 82: 366-411.

Hopkins, A.G. (1973), *An Economic History of West Africa*, London: Longman, 231-6.

Hugo, G.J. (1975), 'Population Mobility in West Java, Indonesia', unpublished PhD thesis, Canberra: Australian National University.

Hugo, G.J. (1977), 'Commuting, circulation and migration in West Java; policy implication', paper prepared for Workshop on Circular Mobility and Policy, East-West Population Institute, East-West Center, Honolulu: 32-5.

Hugo, G.J. (1978a), *Population mobility in West Java*, Yogyakarta: Gadjah Mada University Press.

Hugo, G.J. (1978b), 'Indonesia: the impact of migration on villages in Java', in R.J. Pryor (ed.), *Migration and Development in Southeast Asia*, Kuala Lumpur: Oxford University Press: chapter 16.

Hugo, G.J. (1981), 'Population mobility and wealth transfers in Third World societies with particular reference to Indonesia', Paper presented at Seminar on Interrelationships between Demographic Factors and Income Distribution: Individuals and Families in Income Distribution, Organized by the Committee on Interactions between Demographic Variables and Income Distribution of the International Union for the Scientific Study of Population, April 6-9, Honolulu, Hawaii.

Hugo, G.J. (1982), 'Circular migration in Indonesia', *Population and Development Review* 8:59-83.

Hugo, G.J. (1983), 'New conceptual approaches to migration in the context of urbanization: a discussion based on Indonesian experience', in P. Morrison (ed.), *Population Movements: Their Forms and Functions in Urbanization and Development*, Liège:

International Union for the Scientific Study of Population: 69-113.

Hugo, G.J. and Mantra, I.B. (forthcoming), *Population Mobility in Indonesia: Proceedings of a Workshop*, Yogyakarta: Population Institute, Gadjah Mada University.

Hune, S. (1977), *Pacific Migration to the United States: Trends and Themes in Historical and Sociological Literature*, Bibliographical Studies no. 2, Research Institute on Immigration and Ethnic Studies, Washington, DC: Smithsonian Institution.

Hunter, Monica (1936), *Reaction to Conquest: Effects of Contact with Europeans on the Pondo of South Africa*, London: Oxford University Press for International African Institute.

Hymer, S. and Resnick, R. (1969), 'A model of an agrarian economy with non-agricultural activities', *American Economic Review*, 59.

ILO (1972), *Employment, Incomes and Equality*, 5-6, Geneva: International Labour Office.

INE (Instituto Nacional de Eastadística) (1973), *Annuario de Estadística de Transportes, 1971-1972*, Quito.

INEC (Instituto Nacional de Estadística y Censos) (1976-7), *III Censo de Población 1974: Resultados Definitives*, Quito.

Indonesia, Biro Pusat Statistik (1974), *1971 Population Census Series E*, Jakarta: Biro Pusat Statistik.

Indonesia, Departemen Pekerdjaan Umum Dan Tenaga Listrik (1970), *Rencana Kotamadya Bandung-Kompilasi Data*, Jakarta: Direktorat Djenderal Tjipta Karya.

Institute of Rural and Regional Studies (1977), *Seasonal Migrants and Commuters in Yogyakarta*, Yogyakarta: Institute of Rural and Regional Studies, Gadjah Mada University.

Irons, W. and Dyson-Hudson, N. (eds) (1973), 'The study of nomads', *Journal of Asian and African Studies*, 7.

Jackson, K.D. (1978), 'Urbanization and the rise of patron-client relations: the changing quality of interpersonal communications in the neighbourhoods of Bandung and the villages of West Java', in K.D. Jackson and L.W. Pye (eds), *Political Power and Communications in Indonesia*, Berkeley: University of California Press: 343-94.

Jarrett, H.R. (1948), 'The Strange Farmers of the Gambia', *Geographical Review* 39: 649-57.

Jellinek, L. (1978), 'Circular migration and the Pondok dwelling system', in P.J. Rimmer *et al.* (eds), *Food Shelter and Transport in Southeast Asia and the Pacific*, Canberra: Australian National University, Department of Human Geography: 135-54.

Johnson, G.E. (1971), 'Notes on wages, employment and income distribution in Kenya', paper presented to a Conference at the University of Nairobi.

Johnson, G.E. and Whitelaw, W.E. (1974), 'Urban-rural income tranfers: an estimated remittances function', *Economic Development and Cultural Change* 22: 473-9.

Jongkind, C.J. (1974), 'A reappraisal of the role of regional associations in Lima, Peru', *Comparative Studies in Society and History* 14: 471-82.

BIBLIOGRAPHY

Kamal, Ahmad (1964), *The Sacred Journey: being the Pilgrimage to Makkah*, London: George Allen & Unwin.

Karsten, Rafael (1935), *The Head-hunters of Western Amazonas*, Helsinki: Societas Scientiarum Fennica.

Kenyatta, J. (1938), *Facing Mount Kenya*, London: Secker & Warburg.

King, K. (1974), 'Primary schools in Kenya: some critical constraints on their effectiveness', in D. Court and D.P. Ghai (eds), *Education, Society and Development: New Perspectives from Kenya*, Nairobi: Open University Press.

Kinsley, David R. (1975), *The Sword and the Flute*, Berkeley, Los Angeles, London: University of California Press.

Kirk, J.H., Ellis, P.G. and Medland, J.R. (1972), *Retail Stall Markets in Great Britain*, Wye College, Marketing Series no. 8, Wye College.

Krishna, Raj (1975), 'Unemployment in India with special reference to agriculture', in A.V. Bhuleshkar (ed.), *Growth of Indian Economy in Socialism*, Calcutta: Oxford and IBH Publishing Company: 234-59.

Kroeber, Alfred L. (1928), *Peoples of the Philippines*, Washington, DC: American Museum Press.

Kuhanga, N. (1978), 'Education and self-reliance in Tanzania: a national perspective', *Development Dialogue* 2: 37-50.

Labouret, H. (1941), *Les Paysans d'Afrique Occidentale*, Paris: 222-6.

Lacombe, B. (1969), 'Mobilité et migration: quelques résultats de l'enquête du Siné-Saloum, Sénégal', *Cahiers de l'ORSTOM*, Série Sciences Humaines, 6: 11-42.

Lacombe, B. (1972), 'Etude démographique des migrations et des migrants relevés de 1963 à 1965 dans l'enquête du Siné-Saloum (Sénégal)', *Cahiers de l'ORSTOM*, Série Sciences Humaines, 9: 393-412.

Lambert, Bernd (1977), 'Bilaterality in the Andes', in R. Bolton and E. Mayer (eds), *Andean Kinship and Marriage*, American Anthropological Association Special Publication number 7, Washington DC: 28-42.

Last, G.C. (1969), *Report on a Survey for Educational Development in Illubabor Province*, Addis Ababa: Ministry of Education.

Lauro, D.J. (1979a), 'The Demography of a Thai Village: Methodological Considerations and Substantive Conclusions from Field Study in a Central Plains Community', PhD thesis, Canberra: Australian National University.

Lauro, D.J. (1979b), 'Life history matrix analysis: a progress report', in R.J. Pryor (ed.), *Residence History Analysis*, Studies in Migration and Urbanization no. 3, Department of Demography, Canberra: Australian National University: 135-54.

Lee, Anne S. (1974), 'Return migration in the United States', *International Migration Review* 8: 283-300.

Lee, E.S. (1966), 'A theory of migration', *Demography* 3: 47-57.

Lee, Richard B. (1969), 'Kung Bushman subsistence: an input-output analysis', in Andrew P. Vayda (ed.), *Environment and Cultural Behavior: Ecological Studies in Cultural Anthropology*, Garden City, NY: Natural History Press: 47-9.

Lee, Richard B. (1972), 'Kung spatial organization: an ecological and historical perspective', *Human Ecology* 1: 125-48.

Legassick, Martin (1974a), 'Capital accumulation and violence', *Economy and Society*, 3.

Legassick, Martin (1974b), 'Legislation, ideology and economy in post-1948 South Africa', *Journal of Southern African Studies*, 1.

Leinbach, T.R. (1981), 'Travel characteristics and mobility behavior: aspects of rural transport impact in Indonesia', *Geografiska Annaler*, 63B: 119-29.

Levine, D.N. (1965), *Wax and Gold: Tradition and Innovation in Ethiopian Culture*, University of Chicago Press.

Lewellen, Ted (1978), *Peasants in Transition: The Changing Economy of the Peruvian Aymara*, Boulder, Colorado: Westview Press.

Lewin, K. (1952), *Field Theory in Social Science*, London: Tavistock Publications.

Lewis, Oscar (1952), 'Urbanization without breakdown: a case study', *Scientific Monthly* 75: 31-41.

Lewis, Oscar (1961), *The Children of Sánchez*, New York: Random House.

Lewis, Oscar (1965), *La Vida: A Puerto Rican Family in the Culture of Poverty − San Juan and New York*, New York: Random House.

Liebow, Elliot (1967), *Tally's Corner: A Study of Negro Street-Corner Men*, Boston: Little, Brown.

Lipton, Michael (1977), *Why Poor People Stay Poor*, Cambridge: Harvard University Press.

Lipton, Michael (1980), 'Migration from rural areas of poor countries: the impact on rural productivity and income distribution', *World Development*, 8: 1-24.

Listowel, J. (1965), *The Making of Tanganyika*, London: Chatto & Windus.

Little, Kenneth (1965), *West African Urbanization: A Study of Voluntary Associations in Social Change*, Cambridge University Press.

Long, Larry and Hansen, Kristin A. (1977), 'Interdivisional primary return, and repeat migration', *Public Data Use* 5: 3-10.

Lopez Cordovez, Luis A. (1961), *Zonas Agricolas del Ecuador*, Quito: Junta Nacional de Planificacion.

McGee, T.G. (1971), *The Urbanization Process in the Third World: Exploration in Search of a Theory*, London: Bell.

McGee, T.G. (1973), 'Peasants in cities: a paradox, a paradox, a most ingenious paradox', *Human Organization* 32, 2: 135-42.

McGee, T.G. (1979), 'Rural-urban mobility in south and southeast Asia. Different formulations, different answers', in W.H. McNeill and Ruth S. Adams (eds), *Human Migration Patterns and Policies*, Bloomington and London: Indiana University Press: 199-224.

McGregor, G.P. (1967), *Kings College, Budo: the First Sixty Years*, Nairobi: Oxford University Press.

Macisco, John J. Jr (1975), *Migrants to Metropolitan Lima*, Santiago: CELADE.

Macmillan, W.M. (1930), *Complex South Africa: An Economic Footnote to History*, London: Faber & Faber.

McNicoll, G. (1968), 'Internal migration in Indonesia: descriptive notes', *Indonesia* 5: 29-92.

Magubane, B. and O'Brien, J. (1972), 'The political economy of migrant labour: a critique of conventional wisdom, or a case study in the functions of functionalism', *Current Anthropology* 11: 88-103.

Mair, L.P. (1934), *An African People in the Twentieth Century*, London: Routledge & Kegan Paul.

Mandelbaum, David G. (1970), *Society in India: Change and Continuity*, Berkeley: University of California Press.

Mangin, W. (1959), 'The role of regional associations in the adaptation of rural population in Peru', *Sociologus* 9: 23-35.

Mangin, W. (1967), 'Latin American squatter settlements: a problem and a solution', *Latin American Research Review* 2: 65-98.

Mantra, I.B. (1978), 'Population Movement in Wet Rice Communities: a Case Study of two Dukuh in Yogyakarta Special Region', unpublished PhD thesis, Department of Geography, University of Hawaii.

Mantra, I.B. (1981), *Population Movement in Wet Rice Communities: a Case Study of Two Dukuh in Yogyakarta Special Region*, Yogyakarta: Gadjah Mada University Press.

Martinez, H., Prado, W. and Quintanilla, J. (1973), 'El éxodo rural en el Perú', Working paper of the Centro de Estudios de Población y Desarrollo, Lima.

Marvin, R. (1977), *Determining the Feasibility of Government-Aided Day Secondary Schools in Rural Uganda*, Research Report 26, Paris: International Institute for Educational Planning.

Masser, I. and Gould, W.T.S. (1975), *Inter-Regional Migration in Tropical Africa*, special publication no. 8, London: Institute of British Geographers.

Masson, Peter (1977), ' "Cholo" y "China". Contenidos situacionales de dos términos interetnicos en Saraguro (Ecuador)', *Journal de la Société des Américanistes* 64: 107-14.

Matos-Mar, Jose (1961), 'Migration and urbanization – the barriadas of Lima: an example of integrating into urban life', in P.M. Hauser (ed.), *Urbanization in Latin America*, New York: Columbia Press.

Maude, A. (1981), 'Population mobility and rural households in north Kelantan, Malaysia', in G.W. Jones and H.V. Richter (eds), *Population Mobility and Development: Southeast Asia and the Pacific*, Development Studies Centre Monograph no. 27, Canberra: Australian National University: 93-116.

May, R.J. and Skeldon, R. (1977), 'Internal migration in Papua New Guinea: an introduction to its description and analysis', in R.J. May (ed.), *Change and Movement: Readings on Internal Migration in Papua New Guinea*, Canberra: Australian National University Press: 1-26.

Mayer, P. (1961), *Tribesmen or Townsmen: Conservatism and the Process of Urbanization in a South African City*, Cape Town: Oxford University Press.

Mayer, P. (1962), 'Migrancy and the study of Africans in towns', *American Anthropologist* 64: 576-92.

Mayer, P. (1964), 'Labour migrancy and the social network', in J.F. Holleman (ed.), *Problems of Transition: Proceedings of the Social Sciences Research Conference held in the University of Natal, Durban, July 1962*, Pietermaritzburg: Natal University Press: 21-34.

Maynard, Eileen (1965), *Colta: Indians in Misery*, Ithaca: Cornell University Press.

Mazumdar, D. (1976), 'The urban informal sector', *World Development* 4: 655-79.

Meillassoux, C. (1972), 'From reproduction to production: a Marxist approach to economic anthropology', *Economy and Society*, 1: 93-105.

Meillassoux, C. (1975), *Femmes, greniers et capitaux*, Paris: Maspero.

Meinkoth, Marian Richards (1962), 'Migration in Thailand with particular reference to the Northeast', *Economics and Business Bulletin* 14: 2-45.

Migration and Health in New Zealand and the Pacific (1975), Proceedings of a seminar, July 1975, Epidemiology Unit, Wellington Hospital.

Miller, Ann R. (1977), 'Interstate migrants in the United States: some social and economic differences by type of move', *Demography* 14: 117.

Millor, Soloman (1970), 'Hacienda to plantation in northern Peru: the processes of proletarianization of a tenant farmer society', in J.H. Steward (ed.), *Contemporary Change in Traditional Societies: Mexican and Peruvian Communities*, vol. 3, Urbana: University of Illinois Press.

Missen, G.J. (1972), *Viewpoint on Indonesia: a Geographical Study*, Melbourne: Nelson.

Mitchell, J. Clyde (1959), 'The causes of labour migration', *Bulletin of the Inter-African Labour Institute* 6: 12-46. Reprinted in J. Middleton (ed.) (1970), *Black Africa: its Peoples and Culture Today*, New York: Macmillan: 257-69.

Mitchell, J. Clyde (1961a), 'The causes of labour migration', in *Migrant Labour in Africa South of the Sahara*, Commission for Technical Cooperation in Africa South of the Sahara, Abidjan: 259-80.

Mitchell, J. Clyde (1961b), 'Wage labour and African population movements in Central Africa', in K.M. Barbour and R.M. Prothero (eds), *Essays on African Population*, London: Routledge & Kegan Paul: 193-248.

Mitchell, J. Clyde (1964), 'Opening discussion to Mayer's labour migrancy and the social network', in J.F. Hollemann, Joan Knox, J.W. Mann and K.A. Heard (eds), *Problems of Transition: Proceedings of the Social Sciences Research Conference 1962*, Pietermaritzburg: Natal University Press for Institute for Social Research: 35-41.

Mitchell, J. Clyde (1969a), 'The concept and use of social networks', in J. Clyde Mitchell (ed.), *Social Networks in Social Situations*,

Manchester University Press: 1-50.

Mitchell, J. Clyde (1969b), 'Structural plurality, urbanization and labour circulation in Southern Rhodesia', in J.A. Jackson (ed.), *Migration*, Cambridge University Press: 156-80.

Mitchell, J. Clyde (1970), 'Tribe and social change in South Central Africa: a situational approach', *Journal of Asian and African Studies* 5: 83-101.

Mitchell, J. Clyde (in preparation), *Cities, Society and Social Perception*, London: Longman.

Mitra, Asok (1967), *Internal Migration and Urbanization in India*, Bangkok: ESCAP Expert Group on Problems of Internal Migration and Urbanization.

Moock, J.W. (1973), 'Pragmatism and the primary school: the case of a non-rural village', *Africa* 43, 3: 302-15.

Mookerji, Radha Kumud (1960), *The Fundamental Unity of India*, Bombay: Bharatiya Vidya Bhavan.

Morris, Brian (1977), 'Tappers, trappers and the Hill Pandaran (South India)', *Anthropos* 72: 225-41.

Morrison, D.R. (1976), *Education and Politics in Africa: the Tanzanian Case*, London: Heinemann.

Morrison, Peter (1970), 'Implications of migration histories for model design', 4342, Santa Monica, Calif: The Rand Corporation.

Morse, Richard M. (1965), 'Recent research on Latin American urbanization: a selective survey with commentary', *Latin American Research Review* 1, 1: 35-74.

Morse, Richard M. (1971), 'Trends and issues in Latin American research, 1965-70 (Part I and II)', *Latin American Research Review* 6, 1: 3-52; 6, 4: 19-76.

Mudjiman, H. (1978), 'Consequences of recurrent movement on the family at place of origin: a comparative study of two villages around Surakarta', mimeographed research proposal, University of Surakarta.

Muijzenberg, O.D. van den (1975), 'Involution or evolution in Central Luzon?' in H.J.M. Classen and P.Kloos (eds), *Current Anthropology in the Netherlands*, The Hague: NSAV Staatsdrukkerj: 141-55.

Mukherji, Shekhar (1975a), 'The Mobility Field Theory of Human Spatial Behavior: a Behavioral Approach to the Study of Migration and Circulation in the Indian Situation', unpublished PhD dissertation, Department of Geography, University of Hawaii, Honolulu (Xerox University Microfilms, Ann Arbor).

Mukherji, Shekhar (1975b), 'A spatio-temporal model of the mobility patterns in a multiethnic population, Hawaii', in L.A. Kosinski and R.M. Prothero (eds), *People on the Move: Studies on Internal Migration*, London: Methuen: 324-46.

Mukherji, Shekhar (1977), 'Spatial disorganization and internal migration in India: alternative strategies for restructuring the space economy and development', Presented to the ESCAP Expert Group Meeting on Population Growth and Economic Development in Subnational Areas, Bangkok: 8-14.

Mukherji, Shekhar (1978), *Spatial Disorganization, Labour Migration and Planning Strategies in India*, New Delhi: Allied Publishers.

Mukherji, Shekar (1981), *Mechanisms of Underdevelopment, Labour Migration and Planning Strategies in India*, Calcutta: Prajna.

Murra, John V. (1968), 'An Aymara Kingdom in 1567', *Ethnohistory* 15: 115-51.

Murra, John V. (1970), 'Current research and prospects in Andean ethnohistory', *Latin American Research Review* 5: 3-36.

Murra, John V. (1972), 'El "Control Vertical" de un maximo de pisos ecológicos en la economiá de las sociedades Andinas', in J.V. Murra (ed.), *Vista de la Provincia de Léon de Huánuco (1562)*, Iñigo Ortiz de Zuñiga, II. Huanuco: Universidad Hermilio Valdizán: 429-76.

Murra, John V. (1975), 'El control vertical de un maximo de pisos ecológicos en la economiá de las sociedades andinas', in J.V. Murra (ed.), *Formaciones Economicas y Politicas del Mundo Andino*, Lima: Instituto de Estudios Peruanos: 59-116.

Murray, C.G. (1976), 'Keeping House in Lesotho: a Study of Oscillating Migration', unpublished PhD thesis, University of Cambridge.

Murray, C.G. (1978), 'Migration, differentiation and the developmental cycle in Lesotho', in W.M.J. van Binsbergen and H.A. Meilink (eds), *Migration and the Transformation of Modern African Society: African Perspectives 1978/1*, Leiden: Afrika-Studiecentrum: 127-43.

Murray, C.G. (1980), 'Migrant labour and changing family structure in the rural periphery of southern Africa', *Journal of Southern African Studies*, 6: 139-56.

Murray, C.G. (1981), *Families Divided: The Impact of Migrant Labour in Lesotho*, Cambridge University Press.

Nagata, J.A. (1974), 'Urban interlude: some aspects of internal Malay migration in West Malaysia', *International Migration Review* 8: 301-24.

National Sample Survey (1961), *Report on Labour Force and Unemployment. Sixth Round (May-August, 1953)*, Calcutta: Indian Statistical Institute.

National Sample Survey (1969a), *Tables with Notes on Employment and Unemployment, Rural, Seventeenth Round (1961-62)*, Calcutta: Indian Statistical Institute.

National Sample Survey (1969b), *Tables with Notes on Urban Labour Force. Seventeenth Round (1961-62)*, Calcutta: Indian Statistical Institute.

Ndegwa Commission (1971), *Report on the Commission of Enquiry*, 254, Public Service Structure and Remuneration Commission, Chairman D.N. Ndegwa. Nairobi: Government Printer.

Nelson, J.M. (1976), 'Sojourners versus new urbanites: causes and consequences of temporary versus permanent cityward migration in developing countries', *Economic Development and Cultural Change* 24: 721-57.

Nelson, J.M. (1978), 'Population redistribution and migrants' choices', Paper presented to Seminar on New Conceptual Approaches to Migration in the Context of Urbanization, organized by the

International Union for the Scientific Study of Population Committee on Urbanization and Population Redistribution, Bellagio, Italy.

New Zealand Demographic Society (1976), *Proceedings, Second Annual Conference (July) 1976*, Section 1, Towards a Population policy for New Zealand. Wellington: New Zealand Demographic Society.

New Zealand Demographic Society (1977), *Proceedings, Third Annual Conference (July) 1977*, Section 3, New Zealand and the South Pacific: Issues and Policies. Wellington: New Zealand Demographic Society.

New Zealand Department of Statistics (various years), *Census of Population and Dwellings*, Wellington: New Zealand Department of Statistics.

Ningam, S.L.B. and Singer, H.W. (1974), 'Labour employment and turnover: some evidence from Kenya', *International Labour Review* 110: 479-93.

Northern Rhodesian Government (1935), *Report of the Commission appointed to Enquire into the Disturbances in the Copperbelt, Northern Rhodesia* (Russell Commission), Lusaka: Government Printer.

Nyasaland Government (1935), *Report of the Committee appointed by His Excellency the Governor to Enquire into Migrant Labour*, Zomba: Government Printer.

OECD (1975), *The OECD and International Migration*, Paris: Organization for Economic Co-operation and Development.

Ojo, G.J.A. (1970), 'Some observations on journey to agricultural work in Yorubaland, southwestern Nigeria', *Economic Geography* 46, 3: 459-71.

Ojo, G.J.A. (1973), 'Journey to agricultural work in Yorubaland', *Annals Association of American Geographers* 63, 1: 85-96.

Olofson, H. (1976), 'Yawon Dandi: a Hausa category of migration', *Africa* 46: 66-79.

Oostingh, R.Z. (1970), 'The Pegawai Negri of Bandung: Structure and Process in Indonesia', unpublished PhD thesis, University of Virginia.

Orlove, Benjamin, S. (1977), 'Integration through production: the use of zonation in Espinar', *American Ethnologist* 4: 84-101.

Paine, Suzanne (1974), *Exporting Workers: the Turkish Case*, Cambridge University Press.

Parkin, D. (ed.) (1975), *Town and Country in Central and Eastern Africa*, London: Oxford University Press for International African Institute.

Parkin, D. (1975), 'Migration, settlement, and the politics of unemployment: a Nairobi case study', in David Parkin (ed.), *Town and Country in Central and Eastern Africa*, London: Oxford University Press for International African Institute.

Pearse, Andrew (1961), 'Some characteristics of urbanization in the city of Rio de Janeiro', in P.M. Hauser (ed.), *Urbanization in Latin America*, New York: Columbia University Press.

Peil, M. (1975), 'Female roles in West African towns', in J.R. Goody (ed.), *Changing Social Structure in Ghana*, London: International

African Institute.

Pendleton, Wade C. (1975), 'Introduction', in Clive Kileff and Wade C. Pendleton (eds), *Urban Man in Southern Africa*, Gwelo, Rhodesia: Mambo Press: 9-17.

Perlman, J.E. (1976), *The Myth of Marginality: Urban Poverty and Politics in Rio de Janeiro*, Berkeley: University of California Press.

Perrings, Charles (1979), *Black Mineworkers in Central Africa: Industrial Strategies and the Evolution of an African Proletariat in the Copperbelt 1911-1941*, London: Heinemann.

Petersen, W. (1958), 'A general typology of migration', *American Sociological Review* 23: 256-66.

Peterson, Jean Treloggon (1977), 'The merits of margins', in William Wood (ed.), *Cultural Ecological Perspectives on Southeast Asia*. Papers in International Studies, Southeast Asia Series, no. 41, Athens, Ohio: Ohio University Center for International Studies, Southeast Asia Program.

Peterson, Jean Treloggon (1978a), *The Ecology of Social Boundaries: Agta Foragers of the Philippines*, Illinois Studies in Anthropology 11. Urbana: University of Illinois Press.

Peterson, Jean Treloggon (1978b), 'Hunter-gatherer/farmer exchange', *American Anthropologist* 80: 335-54.

Peterson, Jean T. and Peterson, Warren (1977), 'Implications of contemporary and prehistoric exchange systems' in Jim Allen, Jack Golson and Rhys Jones (eds), *Sunda and Sahul*, London: Academic Press: 533-64.

Pitt, David C. (1975), 'Social boundaries and migration in New Zealand', in Yunshik Chang and Peter J. Donaldson (eds), *Population Change in the Pacific Region*, 13th Pacific Science Congress, Vancouver.

Pitt, D.C. and Macpherson, C. (1974), *Emerging Pluralism: the Samoan Community in New Zealand*, Auckland: Longman Paul.

Pitt-Rivers, J. (1967), 'Race, color and class in Central America and the Andes', *Daedalus* 96: 542-59.

Planning Commission (1967), *Industrial Planning and Licensing Policy*, New Delhi: Government of India, Planning Commission.

Planning Commission (1972), *Draft Five Year Plan, 1978-83*, vol. 1, New Delhi: Government of India, Planning Commission.

Pollard, Brian (1978), 'The problem of an aid-dependent economy: the case of Niue', in *South Pacific Dossier*, Canberra: Australian Council for Overseas Aid.

Pollet, E. and Winter, G. (1969), *La Société Soniké (Dyamu, Mali)*, Brussels.

Pollock, Nancy J. (1976), 'Niue resources and their use − work patterns on Niue', Preliminary Report (mimeographed). Wellington: Department of Anthropology, Victoria University of Wellington.

Prabhu, P.N. (1956), 'A study of the social effects of urbanization', in *The Social Implications of Industrialization and Urbanization*, Calcutta: UNESCO.

Prachuabmoh, Visid and Tirasawat, Penport (1974), 'Internal Migration in Thailand, 1947-1972', Working Paper no. 7, Bangkok: Institute of Population Studies, Chulalongkorn University.

Premi, Mahendra K. (1978), 'Migration to cities: its socio-economic correlates', unpublished manuscript, New Delhi: Jawaharlal Nehru University.

Prothero, R.M. (1957), 'Migratory labour from north-western Nigeria', *Africa* 27: 251-61.

Prothero, R.M. (1959), *Migrant labour from Sokoto Province, Northern Nigeria*, Kaduna: Government Printer.

Prothero, R.M. (1977), 'Disease and mobility: a neglected factor in epidemiology', *International Journal of Epidemiology* 6: 259-67.

Ranneft, J. Meyer (1916), 'Volksverplaatsing op Java', *Tijdschrift voor het Binnelandsch Bestuur* 49: 59-87 and 165-84.

Rempel, H. (1970), 'Labor migration into urban centers and urban unemployment in Kenya', unpublished PhD thesis, University of Wisconsin.

Rempel, H. and R.A. Lobdell (1978), 'The role of urban-to-rural remittances in rural development', *Journal of Development Studies*, 14: 324-41.

Reserve Bank of India (1972), *All-India Debt and Investment Survey, 1971-72*, New Delhi: Reserve Bank of India.

Rey, P-P. (1973), *Les Alliances de Classes*, Paris: Maspero.

Rhoades, Robert E. and Thompson, Stephen (1975), 'Adaptive strategies in Alpine environments: beyond ecological particularism', *American Ethnologist* 2: 535-51.

Rocheteau, G. (1975), 'Société Wolof et mobilité', *Cah. ORSTOM*, Ser. Sci. Humaine, 12: 3-18.

Roberts, B.R. (1976), 'The provincial urban system and the process of dependency', in A. Portes and H.L. Browning (eds), *Current Perspectives in Latin American Urban Research*, Institute of Latin American Studies, University of Texas at Austin: 99-131.

Roberts, K.D. (1982), 'Agrarian structure and labor mobility in rural Mexico', *Population and Development Review*, 8: 299-322.

Roberts, K.D. with G.T. Elizondo (1980), *Agrarian Structure and Labor Migration in Rural Mexico: The Case of Circular Migration of Undocumented Workers to the U.S.*, Austin: University of Texas, Institute of Latin American Studies and Mexico City: Centro Nacional de Investigaciones Agrarias.

Robinson, Warren C. (1975), 'A note on the definition and measurement of the urban population of Thailand for planning purposes', Bangkok: Population and Manpower Planning Division, National Economic and Social Development Board (mimeographed).

Robinson, Warren C. (1976), 'A new look at urbanization in Thailand', unpublished paper, Pennsylvania State University, University Park, PA.

Roseman, C.C. (1971), 'Migration as a spatial and temporal process', *Annals of the Association of American Geographers* 61: 589-98.

Ross, M.H. (1968), 'Politics and urbanization: two communities in Nairobi', unpublished PhD thesis, Northwestern University,

Evanston: 73-4.

Ross, M.H. and Weisner, T.S. (1977), 'The rural-urban migrant network in Kenya: some general implications', *American Ethnologist* 4: 359-75.

Rowe, J.H. (1957), 'The Incas under Spanish colonial institutions', *Hispanic American Historical Review* 37: 155-99.

Ryan, D. (1970) 'Rural and urban villages: a bi-local social system in Papua', PhD thesis, University of Hawaii, Honolulu.

Sahlins, Marshall D. (1969), 'Land use and the extended family in Moala, Fiji', in Andrew Vayder (ed.), *Environment and Cultural Behavior*, Garden City, NY: Natural History Press: 395-415.

Saint-Vil, J. (1975), 'L'immigration scolaire et ses conséquences sur la démographie urbaine en Afrique Noire: l'exemple de Gagnoa (Côte d'Ivoire)', *Cahiers d'Outre-Mer* 28: 376-8.

Salamone, F. (1973), 'An example of urban ethnicity in Nigeria', *Afrika und Ubersee* 57: 115-23.

Schaedel, Richard P. (1974), 'The anthropological study of Latin American cities in intra- and interdisciplinary perspective', *Urban Anthropology* 3: 139-70.

Schapera, Isaac (ed.) (1934), *Western Civilization and the Natives of South Africa: Studies in Culture Contact*, London: Routledge & Kegan Paul.

Schapera, Isaac (ed.) (1947), *Migrant Labour and Tribal Life*, London: Oxford University Press.

Scheltema, A.M.P.A. (1926), 'De groi van Java's bevolking', *Koloniale Studien* 10: 849-83.

Schildkrout, E. (1973), 'The fostering of children in urban Ghana', *Urban Anthropology* 2: 48-73.

Schmitz, H. Walter (1977), 'Interethnic relations in Saraguro (Ecuador) from the point of view of an anthropology of communication', *Sociologus* 27: 64-84.

Schoeps, Hans-Joachim (1968), *The Religions of Mankind*, New York: Doubleday.

Scott, C.D. (1976), 'Peasants, proletarianization and the articulation of modes of production: the Case of sugar cane cutters in northern Peru, 1940-68', *Journal of Peasant Studies* 3: 321-41.

Scott, James C. (1976), *The Moral Economy of the Peasant: Rebellion and Subsistence in Southeast Asia*, New Haven: Yale University Press.

Shankman, Paul (1976), *Migration and underdevelopment: the Case of Western Samoa*, Boulder, Colorado: Westview Press.

Shryock, H.S. and Nam, C.B. (1965), 'Educational selectivity of interregional migration', *Social Forces* 40: 299-310.

Simmons, A.B. and Cardona, R. (1972), 'Rural-urban migration: who comes, who stays, who returns?: the case of Bogota, Colombia, 1929-1968', *International Migration Review* 6: 166-81.

Simmons, Alan, Diaz-Briquets, Sergio, and Laquian, Aprodicio A. (1977), *Social Change and Internal Migration*, IDRC-TS6e, Ottawa: International Development Research Centre.

Singhanetra-Renard, Anchalee (1977), 'Circular Mobility of the

Northern Thai Village', mimeographed report, Honolulu: East-West
Population Institute, East-West Center.

Singhanetra-Renard, Anchalee (1981), 'Mobility in north Thailand: a
view from within', in G.W. Jones and H.V. Richter (eds), *Population
Mobility and Development: Southeast Asia and the Pacific*,
Development Studies Centre Monograph no. 27, Canberra:
Australian National University: 125-53.

Sircar, D.C. (1948), 'The Sakta Pithas', *Journal of the Royal Asiatic
Society of Bengal* 1: 1-108.

Siu, P.C.P. (1952), 'The Sojourner', *American Journal of Sociology* 58:
34-44.

Skeldon, R. (1976), 'Regional associations and population migration in
Peru: an interpretation', *Urban Anthropology* 5: 233-52.

Skeldon, R. (1977), 'The evolution of migration patterns during
urbanization in Peru', *Geographical Review* 67: 394-411.

Skeldon, R. (1978), 'Evolving patterns of population movement in
Papua New Guinea with reference to policy implications', Papua New
Guinea Institute of Applied Social and Economic Research,
Discussion Paper No. 17.

Skinner, G.W. (1976), 'Mobility strategies in late Imperial China: a
regional systems analysis', in C.A. Smith (ed.), *Regional Analysis,
Volume 2: Social Systems*, New York: Academic Press: 327-64.

Skinner, N. (1971), 'Realism and fantasy in Hausa literature', *Review of
National Literatures*, Spring: 167-87.

Smith, E.R. (1977), *Short-Term Circulation Movements at a Micro-Scale:
Nimba, Liberia*, Working Paper no. 32, African Population Mobility
Project, Liverpool: Department of Geography, University of
Liverpool.

Smith, M.G. (1955), *The Economy of Hausa Communities of Zaria*,
London: Her Majesty's Stationery Office.

Smith, M.L. (1971), 'Institutionalized Servitude: the Female Domestic
Servant in Lima, Peru', unpublished PhD thesis, Indiana University:
Department of Anthropology.

Somerset, H.C.A. (1974), 'Educational aspirations of fourth-form pupils
in Kenya', in D. Court and D.P. Ghai (eds), *Education, Society and
Development: New Perspectives from Kenya*, Nairobi: Oxford
University Press.

Sopher, David E. (1968), 'Pilgrim circulation in Gujarat', *Geographical
Review* 58: 392-425.

Sorre, M. (1961), 'La vie de l'Oekumene et la circulation', in *L'homme
sur la terre: Traité de géographie humaine*: Part 4, Paris: Hachette.

Sorre, M. (1963), 'The concept of genre de vie', in P.O. Wagner and
M.W. Mikesell (eds), *Readings in Cultural Geography*, University of
Chicago Press.

Southall, A.W. (1966), 'Growth of urban society', in S. Diamond and
F.G. Burke (eds), *Transformation in East Africa*, New York: Basic
Books.

Southall, A.W. and Gutkind, P.C.W. (1957), *Townsmen in the Making,
Kampala and its Suburbs*, East African Institute of Social Research,

464

East African Studies, no. 9.

South African Government (1932), *Report of the Native Economic Commission*, Pretoria: Government Printer.

Speare, Alden, Jr (1973), 'The determinants of migration to a major city in a developing country: Taichung, Taiwan', in *Essays on the Population of Taiwan*, Taipei: Institute of Economics, Academia Sinica, 167-88.

Spencer, Joseph E. and Wernstedt, Frederick L. (1967), *The Philippine Island World*, Berkeley: University of California Press.

Stack, Carol (1974), *All our Kin: Strategies for Survival in a Black Community*, New York: Harper & Row.

Stark, O. (1978), *Economic-Demographic Interactions in Agricultural Development: The Case of Rural-to-Urban Migration*, Rome: Food and Agriculture Organization, United Nations.

Stark, O. (1980), 'On the role of rural-to-rural remittances in rural development', *Journal of Development Studies*, 16: 369-74.

Stein, Burton (1973), 'Devi shrines and folk Hinduism in medieval Tamilnad', in Edwin Gerow and M.D. Land (eds), *Studies in Language and Culture of South Asia*, Seattle: University of Washington Press.

Stein, Burton (1977), 'Circulation and the historical geography of Tamil country', *Journal of Asian Studies* 37: 7-26.

Sternstein, L. (1974), 'Migration to and from Bangkok', *Annals of the Association of American Geographers* 64: 138-47.

Stewart, Norman R., Belote, Jim and Belote, Linda (1976), 'Transhumance in the Central Andes', *Annals of the Association of American Geographers* 66: 377-97.

Stirling, Matthew W. (1938), 'Historical and ethnographical material on the Uivaro Indians', *Bureau of American Ethnology Bulletin* 117, Washington DC: Smithsonian Institution.

Strauch, J. (1980), 'Circulation in Malaysia and Hong Kong: linkages between town and villages', Paper presented at Intermediate Cities in Asia Meeting, East-West Population Institute, East-West Center, Honolulu, July.

Strauch, J. (1984), 'Women in rural-urban circulation networks: implications for social structural change', in J.T. Fawcett, S.-E. Khoo and P.C. Smith (eds), *Women in the Cities of Asia: Migration and Urban Adaptation*, Boulder, Colorado: Westview Press. 60-77.

Stretton, A.W. (1981), 'The building industry and urbanization in the Third World: a Philippine case study', *Economic Development and Cultural Change* 29: 325-39.

Strickon, Arnold (1965), 'The Euro-American ranching complex', in Anthony Leeds and Andrew Vayda (eds), *Man, Culture and Animals*, Washington DC: American Association for the Advancement of Science Publication no. 78: 229-58.

Suharto, S. and Abdulmajid, M. (1973), *The 1971 Population Census of Indonesia*, Jakarta: Biro Pusat Statistik.

Sumption, Jonathan (1975), *Pilgrimage: an Image of Medieval Religion*, London: Faber & Faber.

Swindell, K. (1970), 'The provision of secondary education and migration to school in Sierra Leone', *Sierra Leone Geographical Journal* 14: 10-19.

Swindell, K. (1978), 'Family farms and migrant labour: the Strange Farmers of the Gambia', *Canadian Journal of African Studies* 12: 3-17.

Swindell, K. (1979), 'Labour migration in underdeveloped countries: the case of subSaharan Africa', *Progress in Human Geography* 3: 241-59.

Swindell, K. (1980), 'Serawoollies, Tillibunkas and Strange Farmers: the development of migrant groundnut farming along the Gambia river, 1848-95', *Journal of African History* 21: 93-104.

Swindell, K. (1984), 'Dry season migration from northwest Nigeria, 1900-33', *Africa* 54: 3-19.

Symanski, R. and Bromley, R.J. (1974), 'Market development and the ecological complex', *Professional Geographer* 26: 382-8.

Textor, R.B. (1956), 'The northeast samlor driver in Bangkok', in *Social Implications of Industrialization and Urbanization*, Calcutta: UNESCO.

Todaro, M.P. (1969), 'A model of labour migration and urban unemployment in less developed countries', *American Economic Review*, 59: 138-48.

Todaro, M.P. (1976), *Internal Migration in Developing Countries: A Review of Theory, Evidence, Methodology and Research Priorities*, Geneva: International Labour Office.

Townsend, D. (1980), 'Articulation, dissolution and migration: the partial integration of Hube area, Papua New Guinea', *Tijdschrift voor Economische en Sociale Geografie*, 71: 285-94.

Trapido, Stanley (1971), 'South Africa as a comparative study of industrialization', *Journal of Development Studies*, 7.

Turner, V. (1969), *The Ritual Process*, Chicago: Aldine Press.

Turner, V. (1973), 'The center out there: pilgrim's goal', *History of Religions* 12: 191-230.

Turner, V. (1977), 'Process, system and symbol: a new anthropological synthesis', *Daedalus*, Summer: 61-80.

Turner, Victor and Turner, Edith (1978), *Image and Pilgrimage in Christian Culture*, New York: Columbia University Press.

Twisleton-Wykeham-Fiennes, R. (1970), 'Sweet water for the hottest land', *Geographical Magazine* 42: 888-93.

United Nations (1975), 'Trends and prospects in urban and rural population 1950-2000 as assessed in 1973-1974', prepared by the Population Division of the Department of Economic and Social Affairs of the United Nations Secretariat, Document ESA/P/WP54.

van Amersfoort, J.M.M. (1978), 'Migrant workers, circular migration and development', *Tijschrift voor Economische en Sociale Geografie*, 69: 17-26.

Van Buitenen, J.A.B. (1975), *The Mahabharata*, volume 2, University of Chicago Press.

Van der Horst, Sheila (1942), *Native Labour in South Africa*, Cape Town: Oxford University Press.

Van Haeverbeke, A. (1970), *Rémuneration de Travail et Commerce Extérieur*, Louvain.

Van Onselen, Charles (1975), 'Black workers in Central African industry: a critical essay on the historiography and sociology of Rhodesia', *Journal of Southern African Studies* 1.

Van Velsen, Jaap (1963), 'Some methodological problems of the study of labour migration', in Kenneth Little (ed.), *Urbanization in African Social Change: Proceedings of the Inaugural Seminar of the Centre of African Studies*, University of Edinburgh: 34-42.

Verdon, M. (1975), 'A Study of Residence amongst the Abutia Ewe of South Eastern Ghana', unpublished PhD thesis, University of Cambridge.

Vidal de la Blache, P. (1926), *Principles of Human Geography*, New York: Holt.

Volkstelling (Population Census) (1933-36), *Definitieve Uitkomsten van de Volkstelling 1930*, Batavia: Department van Landbouw, Nijverheid en Handel.

Waddell, David (1961), *British Honduras: a Historical and Contemporary Survey*, London: Royal Institute of International Affairs, Oxford University Press.

Wallace, T. (1974), 'Educational opportunities and the role of family background factors in rural Buganda', *Rural Africana* 25: 29-46.

Walsh, A.C. and Trlin, A.D. (1973), 'Niuean migration', *Journal of the Polynesian Society* 82: 47-85.

Ward, B.E. (1950), 'Some notes on migration from Togoland', *African Affairs* 49: 129-35.

Ward, B.E. (1955), 'An analysis of the distribution of population in a town in British Togoland', *Man* 55: 35-9.

Ward, R.G. (1980), 'Migration, myth and magic in Papua New Guinea', *Australian Geographical Studies* 18: 119-34.

Watson, T. (1969), 'A History of Church Missionary Society High Schools in Uganda, 1900-24: the Education of a Protestant Elite', unpublished PhD thesis, University of East Africa, Nairobi.

Weeks, S.G. (1967), 'Are hostels necessary? a study of senior secondary pupils in Greater Kampala', *Journal of Developing Areas* 1: 357-74.

Weisner, T.S. (1969), 'One family two households: a rural-urban model of urbanism', Mimeographed paper in the Proceedings of the 5th Annual Conference, University of East Africa, Social Science Research Council, 1010, Nairobi.

Weisner, Thomas S. (1976), 'The structure of sociability: urban migration and urban-rural ties in Kenya', *Urban Anthropology* 5: 199-223.

Westermann, D.H. and Bryan, M.A. (1952), *The Languages of West Africa*, London: Oxford University Press for International African Institute.

Western Samoan Department of Statistics (1977a), *Migration Report, 1976*, Apia, Western Samoa.

Western Samoan Department of Statistics (1977b), *Pre Release Information of the 1976 Western Samoan National Census of*

Population and Housing (mimeographed), Apia, Western Samoa.

Wharton, Clifton R., Jr (1971), 'Risk, uncertainty and the subsistence farmer: technological innovation and resistance to change in the context of survival', in George Dalton (ed.), *Studies in Economic Anthropology*, Washington DC: American Anthropological Association: 151-78.

White, B. (1979), 'Political aspects of poverty, income distribution and their measurement: some examples from rural Java', *Development and Change* 10: 91-114.

Wilkinson, J.C. (1974), *The Organization of the Falaj Irrigation System in the Sultanate of Oman*, School of Geography, University of Oxford, Research Paper no. 10.

Williams, B.J. (1974), 'A model of Band society', *American Antiquity* 39, Memoir 29, Society for American Archaeology.

Wilmsen, Edwin N. (1973), 'Interaction, spacing behavior and the organization of hunting bands', *Journal of Anthropological Research* 29: 1-31.

Wilson, F. (1972a), *Labour in the South African Gold Mines: 1911-1969*, Cambridge University Press.

Wilson, F. (1972b), *Migrant Labour in South Africa*, Johannesburg: South African Council of Churches and SPRO-CAS.

Wilson, Godfrey (1941-2), *An Essay on the Economics of Detribalization in Northern Rhodesia*, Parts I and II, Rhodes-Livingstone Papers, nos. 5 and 6. Livingstone: Rhodes-Livingstone Institute.

Wilson, M. and Mafeje, A. (1963), *Langa: a Study of Social Groups in an African Township*, Cape Town: Oxford University Press.

Wilson, Monica (1964), 'The coherence of groups', in J.H. Hollemann, Joan Knox, J.W. Mann and K.A. Heard (eds), *Problems of Transition: Proceedings of the Social Sciences Research Conference 1962*, Natal University Press for Institute of Social Research: 1-12.

Wobst, H. Martin (1978), 'The archaeo-ethnology of hunter-gatherers or the tyranny of the ethnographic record in archaeology', *American Antiquity* 43: 303-9.

Wolf, E.R. (1957), 'Closed corporate peasant communities in Mesoamerica and central Java', *Southwestern Journal of Anthropology* 13: 1-14.

Wolf, E.R. (1965), 'Aspects of group relations in a complex society: Mexico', in R.N. Adams and D.B. Heath (eds), *Contemporary Cultures and Societies of Latin America*, New York: Random House.

Wolf, E.R. (1966), 'Kinship, friendship and patron-client relations in complex societies', in M. Banton (ed.), *The Social Anthropology of Complex Societies*, London: Tavistock Publications.

Wolpe, Harold (1972), 'Capitalism and cheap labour-power in South Africa: from segregation to apartheid', *Economy and Society* 1: 425-56.

World Bank (1978), *World Development Report, 1978*, Washington DC.

Yellen, John E. (1977a), *Archaeological Approaches to the Present: Models for Reconstructing the Past*, New York: Academic Press.

Yellen, John E. (1977b), 'Long-term hunter-gatherer adaptation to desert environments: a biogeographical perspective', *World Archaeology* 8: 262-74.

Yellen, John and Harpending, Henry (1972), 'Hunter-gatherer populations and archaeological inference', *World Archaeology* 4: 244-53.

Yusuf, A.B. (1977), 'Capital formation and management among the Muslim Hausa traders of Kano, Nigeria', *Africa* 45: 167-82.

Zachariah, K.C. (1968), *Migrants in Greater Bombay*, Bombay: Asia Publishing House.

Zachariah, K.C. and Ambannavar, J.P. (1967), 'Population redistribution in India: inter-state and rural-urban', in Ashish Bose (ed.), *Patterns of Population Change in India*, New Delhi: Hind Publishers: 95-100.

Zelinsky, W. (1971), 'The hypothesis of the mobility transition', *Geographical Review* 61: 219-49.

Zelinsky, W. (1979), 'The demographic transition: changing patterns of migration', in *Population Science in the Service of Mankind*, Liège: International Union for the Scientific Study of Population: 165-89.

Index

Terms which occur frequently (e.g. 'circulation', 'origins', 'destinations', 'causes and consequences of movement') have not been indexed.